BEHIND THE MEXICAN MOUNTAINS

BEHIND
THE MEXICAN
MOUNTAINS

R O B E R T   Z I N G G

▲ ▲ ▲ ▲ ▲ ▲ ▲ ▲ ▲ ▲ ▲ ▲ ▲ ▲ ▲ ▲ ▲ ▲ ▲ ▲

Edited by Howard Campbell, John Peterson & David Carmichael

Introduction by Howard Campbell

University of Texas Press
Austin

First edition, 2001

Requests for permission to reproduce material from this work should be sent to
Permissions, University of Texas Press, P.O. Box 7819, Austin, TX 78713-7819.

♾ The paper used in this book meets the minimum requirements of ANSI/NISO Z39.48-1992
(R1997) (Permanence of Paper).

Library of Congress Cataloging-in-Publication Data

Zingg, Robert M. (Robert Mowry), 1900–1957.
    Behind the Mexican mountains / Robert Zingg ; edited by Howard Campbell, John
Peterson, and David Carmichael.—1st ed.
        p.   cm.
    Includes bibliographical references and index.
    ISBN 0-292-79808-3 (alk. paper)—ISBN 0-292-79809-1 (pbk. : alk. paper)
        1. Tarahumara Indians. 2. Chihuahua (Mexico)—Description and travel. 3. Zingg,
Robert M. (Robert Mowry), 1900–1957. I. Campbell, Howard, 1957– II. Peterson,
John Allen, 1950– III. Carmichael, David L. IV. Title.
    F1221.T25 Z56 2001
    972'.16—dc21   2001023084

▸ *Contents*

▸

▸

▸

▸

▸

▸

▸

▶ *Introduction*

▶

▶ HOWARD CAMPBELL

▶

▶

▶

▶

▶

▶ This book is based on the University of Chicago Expedition
▶ of Tarahumara Ethnography to Chihuahua, Mexico, in
▶ 1930.[1] The author, Robert Zingg, was trained at
Chicago's famous anthropology department, where he completed his
dissertation (1933) and worked with prominent professors such as
Robert Redfield, Edward Sapir, and Fay Cooper-Cole. The University
of Chicago also published his classic ethnography with Wendell Bennett, *The Tarahumara: An Indian Tribe of Northern Mexico* (1935). The
current book, written in the 1930's and early 1940's, is Zingg's personal
account of the Tarahumara[2] fieldwork he engaged in with Bennett.

Robert Zingg was an ethnographer of the old school who relished
meticulous data collection and the rustic life of the field. His passion for
rural Mexican culture began during his childhood in the U.S. Southwest. Zingg was born in Colorado in 1900 and grew up in northern
New Mexico speaking Spanish and English. His first exposure to living
in Latin America occurred at the age of twenty-two when he taught
English in Cárdenas, Cuba. This year abroad increased Zingg's appetite
for travel and improved his Spanish (although it left a bit to be desired,
as several errors in the text illustrate). From Cuba, he traveled to the
Philippines, where Zingg lived for five years and worked as an English
teacher and later as a salesman for the Goodyear Tire Company.

Except for a period between 1936 and 1937 in which he did
research in German universities and museums, Zingg's major anthropological travels took him to Mexico, where he studied the Tarahumara and Huichol Indians. Zingg conducted about eighteen months of
fieldwork among the Huichols between 1933 and 1935, the results of

which were published in his 1938 book *The Huichols: Primitive Artists.* In addition to the previously mentioned books, his major publications were *Report on the Archaeology of Southern Chihuahua* (1940) and *Wolf Children and Feral Man* (Singh and Zingg 1942).

Zingg's first love, however, was his Tarahumara research. Indeed, Zingg was very fond of the Tarahumara people. In 1947 he brought a group of about ten Tarahumara runners to El Paso, Texas (where he lived), to perform at halftime of the annual Sun Bowl football game. The Tarahumara group then stayed for another week at the Zingg household in southeast El Paso. Emma Zingg, widow of the deceased anthropologist, told me in an interview in 1993 that she cooked break- fast and supper for the Tarahumaras, whom she described as "good houseguests." Dr. Zingg gave them clothing and other gifts before they returned to their homes in the Chihuahua canyon lands, Mrs. Zingg noted.

Zingg's original Tarahumara fieldwork required arduous travel by mule in remote areas of the Sierra Madre and challenging encounters with relatively unassimilated Indians. His publications about the Tarahumara are studded with "realistic" photographs, indigenous vocabulary, trait lists, informative appendices, and chapter titles such as "Natural Environment," "Agriculture and Food," "Government," "Birth," and "Death." In short, all the trappings of "scientific" anthro- pology of the period (Stocking 1992). Moreover, Zingg's work was done at a time in American anthropology when it was still possible to talk about "primitive," unstudied tribes and the salvaging of anthropo- logical data before unsullied cultures were contaminated by civilization.

Behind the Mexican Mountains is a free-flowing description of nine months of travel and residence in Tarahumara country. It is a swash- buckling account of perilous treks through rugged terrain and delicate interactions with inscrutable "natives." The text is colorful and unvar- nished. In spite of Zingg's avowed love for the Tarahumaras, it is replete with often negative comments about "half-castes," "wooden Indians," "*Tarahumaritos,*" and "our man Friday." Additionally, Zingg's references to women are almost invariably derogatory, emphasizing their supposed ugliness and crabby characters. Indeed, *Behind the Mex- ican Mountains* is reminiscent of Bronislaw Malinowski's controversial diary (1967) in its letting-one's-hair-down candidness, nonprofessional soul-baring, and crude criticism of "the natives."

Zingg's travel narrative emerged from an anthropology that was new and enthralled with the native peoples of the American West and northern Mexico. In the 1880's Adolf Bandelier recorded his travels through the region as a diary filled with the raw and unedited material from his daily studies (1966–1976). He translated Spanish archives, searched for the last of the Manso Indians, drew native pottery in watercolors, and recorded archaeological sites. In his multidisciplinary and multi-sited anthropology in the nineteenth century, he grasped the region and its people like no one before. He set a standard for observation and documentation that prevailed well into the twentieth century. Others, like Carl Lumholtz, emphasized the natural land-scape, day-by-day descriptions, and outback adventure in northern Mexico (1973 [1902]). The diary or travelogue genre of many of these books provokes a sense of adventure and immediacy, which makes them invaluable documents of their time, as well as appealing discovery narratives. *Behind the Mexican Mountains* is a fine addition to the travel literature of the U.S. Southwest and northern Mexico.

Dr. Zingg submitted the manuscript to Alfred A. Knopf, the University of Oklahoma Press, and other prominent publishers in the early 1940's. These presses expressed some interest, but ultimately the project languished because of the economic hardships of the Second World War. The manuscript may also have received less than complete acceptance by reviewers because it was written in a nonscientific, travelogue style rather than the standard ethnographic format of the time. It was an adventure tale, not an anthropological monograph.

Today's anthropological fascination with literary forms and constructions, and the reappraisal of earlier ethnography and travel writing, increase the relevance of Zingg's Tarahumara trips (Clifford 1992). Ironically, Zingg's work is also of interest because of ways in which it illustrates styles of anthropological writing and commentary (e.g., Zingg's marked sexism and seemingly crude ethnocentrism) now deemed verboten. The Zingg travelogue, then, is an ideal venue for examining U.S. anthropology in a formative period and exploring the embeddedness of colonial and misogynist discourses and relationships in ethnographic fieldwork.

Writing and the Future of Ethnography

The publication of Malinowski's diary[3] in 1967 and the expanding interpretive and literary turn in American anthropology in the 1970's culminated in 1986 with the publication of *Writing Culture: The Poetics and Politics of Ethnography*, edited by Clifford and Marcus (1986). *Writ-*

ing Culture celebrated anthropologists' role as writers and heralded a new focus on the ethnographic text. In the words of James Clifford:

> No longer a marginal, or occulted, dimension, writing has emerged as central to what anthropologists do both in the field and thereafter. The fact that it has not until recently been portrayed or seriously discussed reflects the persistence of an ideology claiming transparency of representation and immediacy of experience. . . . The essays in this volume do not claim ethnography is "only literature." They do insist it is always writing. (Clifford 1986: 2, 26)

Anthropologists began to view their work as texts, and a flurry of books emerged that evaluated the literary bases of earlier ethnographies, while others encouraged or engaged in literary experiments (Marcus and Fischer 1986; Clifford 1988; Crapanzano 1985; Clifford and Marcus 1986; Tedlock 1991; Behar and Gordon 1995). The buzzwords of literary theory became commonplace in anthropological discourse, and a new postmodern era was saluted (or bitterly lamented). One of the most useful interventions in these discussions was Clifford Geertz's *Works and Lives: The Anthropologist as Author* (1988). According to Geertz, an ethnographer's success with the reading (mainly anthropological) public is based not so much on the weightiness or sophistication of his or her theoretical arsenal or collection of "facts" as on his or her ability to convince us that she or he has "been there." The condition of "being there" (i.e., that the ethnographer has spent an extended period in the place under study and will guide the reader through the terrain) is evoked through sheer literary talent and the skillful wielding of standard anthropological gambits such as the "arrival scene." In the process, the anthropologist puts his or her "signature" or identity on the work and creates an indelible style that has ranged from the powerfully "realistic" descriptions of Edward Evan Evans-Pritchard to Claude Lévi-Strauss's highly abstract and literary structuralism.

At its best, the focus on the "anthropologist as author" has made us more aware of the hidden assumptions (and possibilities) of the language and texts of anthropology. It has caused us yet again to question our ancestors in the field, deconstruct our methodologies and theories, and search our souls for a political justification for doing anthropology at all. At its worst, however, the new textual emphasis has degenerated into word games, political-correctness one-upmanship contests, and a nihilistic outlook that denies ethnography any relevance while exalting the navel-gazing author (Polier and Roseberry 1989). Ironically, at the same time that imperialistic wars have continued, indigenous peoples' lands have been destroyed, and human rights abuses have been committed, stylish anthropologists have gathered in posh hotels to debate—not the politics of human rights or cultural survival—but the "politics of representations" of "the Other" (Moore, ed. 1996). But here I concur with John Watanabe (1995: 28), who argues that

> post-modern poetics fares no better than artless positivism in resolving the inherent political asymmetries in ethnography's problematic —indeed, inescapable—appropriation of its subjects' lives for purposes beyond the living of those lives. Like all anthropologists, whatever their rhetoric, post-modernists pursue an agenda distinct from that of their subjects: the more they imagine others (or themselves) into their texts, the more they reveal their overriding concern with how ethnography gets read by a largely Western (or Westernised) audience, not with how ethnography might actually empower the "real people" it represents. Contending with the crisis of representation in Western intellectual circles may make "writing culture" more deliberate, but this changes neither the status nor the power of those so represented—even vis-à-vis anthropologists.[4]

Nowadays the focus is on the writing and the representing (Domínguez 1994). This, above all, appears to be the issue for many anthropologists. Not whether the Lacandóns or Garifuna are in danger of extinction. Not how to fight the Guatemalan government's genocidal war against Mayan people. Not questions of fact or data, but issues of interpretation and style, of how to represent cultures textually or how to deconstruct such textual representations (Sacks 1995). One unfortunate consequence of this in many ways healthy and necessary turn in recent American anthropology is a downgrading or even retreat from ethnographic fieldwork (Manganaro 1990). For many anthropologists, today, it is more comfortable and safe, as well as in vogue, to study mass media representations or written texts than to do fieldwork (e.g., Marcus 1998: 21–25). While this trend may reflect a broadening and enriching of anthropological subject matter and theory, it may also indicate a weakening of anthropologists' claim to uniqueness and relevance. And it may take anthropologists away from what is our primary source of strength and originality: ethnography (cf. Ortner 1999).

Ethnography remains the main area that distinguishes anthropology from other disciplines, and the retreat from fieldwork in recent years is highly problematic. With the rise of Foucauldian, antipositivist, postmodern, and deconstructive approaches has also emerged a problematic smugness and ironic attitude (Ahmed and Shore, eds. 1995). According to this new style, previous ethnographic works must be picked apart—in a predictable fashion—to reveal that, in fact, the author was a racist, sexist colonialist (Sacks 1995: 104).[5] In the meantime, the contemporary anthropologist shields him- or herself from the messy contradictions of fieldwork by holing up in the archives or engaging in a kind of ivory tower literary criticism that leaves no room for refutation, comparison with "data" (an outmoded term that if mentioned with seriousness provokes scorn), or actual contact or dialogue with living people who might force political engagement rather than literary distancing (Ahmed and Shore, eds. 1995).

I still believe that anthropological fieldwork can produce something resembling reliable information about a group of people in a particular time and place rather than merely sophisticated postmodern critiques of representations (Sahlins 1999). In this regard I agree with Virginia Domínguez and others "who refuse to believe that in this post-Said, post-Foucault, post-Clifford era, the only valid anthropological work is the textual critique of canonized scholarship produced by privileged European and North American scholars" (Domínguez 1994: 1280).[6] I say this, not with the intention of returning to an antebellum anthropological status quo, but because I feel that a progressive anthropological agenda (Marxist, feminist, and/or poststructuralist) can also and should include empirically driven fieldwork. Indeed, the escape from fieldwork into expectable critiques of representations, rather than transcending the tremendous power of racial, sexual, and class hierarchies and discourses, may have the counterproductive effect of rendering anthropology irrelevant and unread by other than a cult of esoteric sophisticates (cf. Knauft 1994: 129).

Watanabe has nicely summarized the continued value of anthropological writing and fieldwork:

> Given the inescapable hubris of authorship, the anthropologist's need to write about otherness,[7] and the inadequacies of a Cliffordian poetics in dealing with either—let alone with the emerging agendas of anthropologised peoples—anthropologists can perhaps best serve their varied constituencies by writing as forthrightly as possible

about what they think might be going on "elsewhere" and why. By this, I do not mean reverting to some unreflective, imperious empiricism—or imitating the encyclopedias or chronicles other people might write about themselves. Instead, I mean attempting to widen anthropology's readership beyond the privileged scientific or literary few by writing as if one's subjects might some day read what one has written with anthropological concerns of their own—as pan-Mayanists have already begun to do. While by no means guaranteeing anthropology's relevance—or even acceptability—to these others, such a "reimagining" of colleagues might at least make it more accessible. (Watanabe 1995: 40–41)

Moreover, fieldwork is precisely the means by which anthropologists can expose their vulnerability and shed their burden of intellectual "authority" through contact with those who promote or resist hegemonic processes and discourses. In other words, the personal experience of, or contact with, sexual, racial, and class hierarchies and an empirically informed anthropological practice must be emphasized in order for the contemporary fascination with representations, irony, and text to remain relevant to the lives of the people we profess to care so much about (Ortner 1999).

In fact, the postmodern focus on deconstruction of past ethnographies and on the ethnographer's own experience gets the anthropologist off the hook of the spiny dilemma of writing about modern culture and addressing the dilemmas (poverty, repression, racism, sexism) of contemporary people while living among them (Hubinger, ed. 1996). Instead of doing something really radical and risky,[8] such as working with the people of South-Central L.A., researching the killing fields of Guatemala, or doing fieldwork in the *favelas* of Rio, the postmodernists take their risks on the battle front of the word processor—put a word in quotes here, a hyphen and parenthesis there.

Granted, it is important to deconstruct the anthropological corpus, to expose the hidden assumptions of colonialist Victorian anthropology. But if anthropology is to have any claim to originality or relevance, the next step must also be taken: we must continue to do fieldwork and write ethnographies. Cute, wordy language games and sophisticated dissections of the old masters will not resolve the challenge of ethnography. Nor will efforts to share authorship, authority, and voice, although these initiatives are surely welcome and vital. We (i.e., the writers of monographs, dialogical texts, or autoethnographies) still must attempt to present, evoke, or represent cultural worlds in original ways—based on fieldwork, "being there"—or else anthropology may as well become a minor branch of English departments or Cultural Studies programs. We have to be cognizant and reflexive about the ethnographer's role in the construction of knowledge, but an obsession with this issue will not resolve the dilemma. Like it or not, ethnography is our primary contribution to modern intellectual life and our best hope for contributing to the very vital public debates about culture today. It is with these ideas in mind that I read Zingg's writings, and it is with these concepts that I feel that we can salvage something of value from Zingg's fieldwork.

Zingg and the Tarahumaras

Robert Zingg's arrival in the Tarahumara country is characteristically colorful. Riding on the Porfirian train that will bring "progress" and "civilization" to rural Mexico, he ponders tales of the Mexican Revolution and the "bandit" Pancho Villa, and the creative engineering feats of Mexican railroad men. At the end of the first chapter Zingg says good-bye to the last vestiges of "civilization," such as the Chihuahuan schoolteachers and their cosmetics, and heads down the Continental Divide to the town of Creel on the edge of Tarahumara territory. As the rickety train lumbers through rugged sierras and gorges, Zingg's mind peruses the state of postrevolutionary Mexico while he prepares to explore the rugged, untamed land of the Sierra Madre.

Zingg and his anthropological colleague, Wendell Bennett, quickly leave behind the non-Indian town of Creel, "with nothing to interest us," in search of "native" settlements. The anthropologists hire servants from the local population, including their "man Friday" (note the colonialist reference to Robinson Crusoe's devoted servant) and a muleteer Zingg nicknames "Pancho Villa." This picturesque, but lightly equipped, crew sets off into the mountains and canyons of the Sierra Madre. Lest Zingg be branded as an unregenerate colonialist, it should be noted that he praises the abilities of his muleteers, as he does the skills of various Mexican teachers and working people throughout the book. He also goes out of his way to compliment the Mexican people for their grace and dignity. Although, as we will see, he is also quite quick to criticize what he views as major flaws in Tarahumara culture.

True to his training as an all-around anthropologist, Zingg carefully describes the physical landscape and flora of his ethnographic area. At this point Zingg confidently assumes the role of the field-worker recording his daily observations and entries into his field notebook, although the flowing travelogue of his prose continues. Along the way he describes the various American entrepreneurs who ventured into the Chihuahua backcountry. His comments are somewhat negative, although he does point out that the capital the North Americans infused was much needed and he lauds the hanging bridge built by a U.S. engineer named Shepherd.

First encounter scene: Zingg meets two Tarahumara men and one woman trying to saddle a donkey. But the Tarahumaras were unsuccessful: "Their efforts to master even so lethargic a beast as the Mexican burro were ludicrous, bespeaking the slight use of domestic animals among the tribe." Yet "they moved with that unconscious grace and dignity that contribute so much to the impression of nobility noted by all observers." They were, says Zingg, "Indians in a state of nature." This mixture of admiration and scorn colors Zingg's depictions of Tarahumara culture throughout the book (although he is equally critical of other groups, as well as his own culture). Elated by this first meeting with Tarahumara people and his subsequent arrival at the Indian town of Samachique, Zingg, à la Malinowski, exclaims: "At last we had the elusive Tarahumara right under our noses for observation."

Chapter 3, with the embarrassing title of "Personalities Emerge from Wooden Indians," heralds Zingg's penetration into "the field," his entree into Tarahumara society and homes. Not surprisingly, Zingg used trade goods to encourage the reticent Tarahumaras to provide him with cultural information and submit to the gaze of his motion-picture camera. Eventually, Zingg states that he and Bennett "were so popular in this community and were asked to so many feasts that we had to leave." Obviously Zingg participated with great gusto in the Tarahumara drinking parties, which gave him "a feeling of contentment and oneness with the Indians."[9] He even became the server of *tesgüino* (corn beer) at one of the events and eventually passed out from excessive consumption of the beverage.

Mutual misunderstandings between anthropologists and Indians occurred, however, as when the Tarahumaras thought that Zingg was killing and skinning local birds in order to take them back to the United States where he would bring them back to life (instead of using them as zoological samples as was his intention). These confusions were ultimately overcome, says Zingg, and the anthropologists established tight bonds with the Indians, including key informants like

Lorenzo. What follows are rich ethnographic descriptions of Tarahumara life in 1930 and 1931. Zingg's field observations are interspersed with comments on Mexican politics and society, descriptions of the lives of Catholic missionaries stationed in the Sierra, and musings about similarities between Tarahumara lifeways and cultural practices in other anthropologically studied places such as the Philippines. Additionally, very much in the mode of the four-field anthropologist, he conducted extensive archaeological excavations of Tarahumara caves and burials, during which he collected mummies and artifacts.

Zingg pays special attention to the Tarahumara beer parties *(tesgüi-nadas)* and exults that the Indians' willingness to let him attend the parties was a high point of his fieldwork. At one of these drinking bouts, Lorenzo announced to the group of Tarahumaras gathered there that the anthropologist had been granted permission to study them by *Don* Porfirio Díaz himself (who was by 1930 quite dead). At another, Zingg's sore neck was cured by a shaman. As his relationships with the Tarahumaras deepened, Zingg became a doctor to Patricio, who was beset with a spiritually based illness. Although Patricio finally died, his willingness to take on Zingg as his physician indicates the trust the anthropologist had gained among many local people. This trust allowed him to sketch out the main features of a Tarahumara culture that in the 1930's retained a considerable degree of separateness and independence from life in urban Mexico. Zingg even went so far as to say that "The Tarahumaras . . . have fared admirably well on the whole, and still rule almost the entirety of the great mountainous chain of southern Chihuahua, a region embracing one-third of this largest state of the Mexican union."

Zingg is at his best in straightforward descriptions of Tarahumara social practices and the natural environment of the Sierra Madre. For example, in this passage he portrays a cactus plant of great importance to the Tarahumaras:

> The *maguey* has several leaves five or six feet long and as tough as rhinoceros hide. The tip of each leaf is armed with a stiff, thornlike point as sharp as a needle. Only so grim and arid a country as Mexico can produce such a plant. It is not surprising, furthermore, that the *maguey* should die from the final effort of bursting into flower. It sends out a flower spine from twenty to thirty feet long, which is held upright on a strong skeletal structure. This spine is covered with thousands of small yellow-white flowers, the fragrance of which

attracts dozens of hummingbirds. To suck the honey out of flowers these graceful little birds hover in the air by beating their wings so fast that all one sees is a blur on either side of them.

The skeleton of the enormous flower spine of these century plants sustains a fresh and succulent flesh. The Indians utilize this for food, as they do other plants of the sierra. It is roasted in the ashes of a large fire. The result, when eaten with sugar, is a delicious food, as I myself can attest.

Reading Zingg we get a good feel for the basic lifestyle and adaptation to the environment of specific Tarahumara groups in the 1930's. His descriptions of Tarahumara farming methods, technology, dwellings, social organization, and fiestas are compelling. He also has a knack for chronicling his fieldwork in exuberant lyrical tones, as in this paragraph:

But in other adventures the wilds of Mexico are singularly replete. I shall never forget nights spent before blazing campfires, the fellow travelers met along the way, the toil of long hot days and the cool freshness of evenings climaxed by sunsets that blazoned.

In other passages, such as this description of a Tarahumara race, Zingg displays a gift for vivid evocations of local life:

It is at night that the scene is the most spectacular of any other in Tarahumaraland. Torches of pitch pine, which burns like oil, are lighted all along the course. Hundreds of these blaze across the sierra, and flicker in the distance like a myriad of fireflies. And through this weird illumination, watched over by the dim outlines of the towering pines, dart the glistening figures of the runners followed by the frenzied, encouraging shouts of the half-naked spectators.

Excitement mounts as the race progresses. The runners begin to show signs of fatigue; for sometimes these trying competitions have lasted as long as seventy-two hours, continuing on into the following days. The wives or female relatives of the runners prepare *pinole*, and the runners stop and hastily gulp this down for strength, and then catch up with their teammates a little farther on. Despite these aids the runners one by one begin to fall out of the race exhausted, until finally only the strongest are left.

The human side of Zingg's writing is one of his major strengths, as University of Texas student Suzan Kern (pers. comm.) noted when she helped edit the manuscript:

> Zingg is arrogant and paternalistic when reporting about the Tarahumaras' lives and customs to an implicitly elite in-the-know audience. Yet, when he records his own feelings and reactions to particular individuals and incidents, Zingg's writing takes on the quality of a personal journal. His loneliness, his grudging respect for many of the Tarahumaras' skills, his growing friendship with several native informants, his joy at being able to carouse with his subjects during *tesgüinadas*, his humor at their (and his own) human weakness, his nostalgia on taking leave of the Tarahumaras and their valley: all these emotions reveal the man behind the anthropologist and keep the modern reader interested.

Zingg is at his worst when he defines "the primitive" and philosophizes about the differences between "primitive" Tarahumara culture and civilization. Indeed, at times Zingg's use of expressions like "personalities emerge from wooden Indians," "the philistine spirit of Tarahumara culture," "cigar-store Indians," and "the little savages" almost seems like a bizarre parody of anthropology. Consider these passages: "Primitive man is always an uncertain creature when he is nonplussed and afraid." "This unquestioning adherence to traditional patterns is the essence of the primitive." "Life is simple for the Tarahumaras, and from the day of birth is practically one glorified camping trip." "Lorenzo had a curious monkeylike face, and was dressed in tatterdemalion overalls and a shirt. Some scamp of a culturally bastardized Indian." The apotheosis of his arrogance comes in Chapters 16 and 17, where Zingg identifies what he considers the "spurious" aspects of Tarahumara culture and its "philistine spirit."

These chapters soar off into new heights of ethnocentrism, essentialism, and just plain wacky logic. As if imitating Ed Wood's cinematic technique, the two chapters are such bad anthropology they almost become classics of a genre—in this case, a genre of mediocre, kitschy, Indiana Jones–style adventures among non-Western primitives. For example, in Chapter 16 Zingg lists those elements of Tarahumara culture that are spurious in the sense that "they thwart and defeat the individuals who participate in them." Hence the Tarahumaras' need to migrate from the mountains to the canyons is a "cultural defect."

Another supposed failure of the Tarahumaras is their aesthetic culture, which "is greatly inhibited." A further area of "cultural paucity" is that related to character because "very meager are the organizations, devices, and methods set up in Tarahumara culture for the adjustment of its individuals to one another and for their conditioning into secure and well-rounded personalities." Tarahumara social organization is also weak (according to Zingg), and sheep-herding is problematic because the "constant association with animals in the isolation of rocks and forest seems to be the most important factor underlying the wooden personalities and manners of the tribe." The result is a "lack of normal personality."

Zingg continues the parade of perceived Tarahumara cultural errors, which include the absence of literature and plastic arts as well as the existence of "pagan ceremonies" which "utterly lack color, romance, drama, and pageantry." According to Zingg, the Tarahumaras' only escape from this extremely spurious culture is drinking. And the anthropologist concludes his frenzy of essentialist, self-righteous moralizing with this rhetorical flourish:

> The case for the "spurious" quality of the Tarahumara articulation of their culture around drunkenness lies in the bleak, drab tone of Tarahumara life with its starkness of cultural simplicity utterly primitive in all its features. It is a vicious cycle: the drabness encourages the escape through drunkenness; the drunkenness encourages the drabness.

At this point, the reader might wonder if, with friends like Robert Zingg, the Tarahumara needed enemies. And the diatribe continues in Chapter 17, where Zingg discusses the Tarahumaras' supposed philistinism. This chapter is not good anthropology. Yet there are still many redeeming features of the book, some of which will be discussed below. But first, a few words about the "philistine spirit" of the Tarahumaras epitomized by their philosophy (according to Zingg) of "work hard and get drunk."

Like the U.S. middle class of Matthew Arnold, the Tarahumaras, per Zingg, are "realistic" and "materialistic." They have no aesthetic appreciation of flowers, sunsets, and other natural beauty, and "the animal world is productive of no mystical meanings and connotations." These Indians are obsessed with thriftiness and wealth, and men are judged by the number of cattle they possess. Not only are the

Tarahumara collectively philistine in their tawdry beer-drinking ceremonies, but on an individual and family level as well, their lives are
(supposedly) strictly utilitarian and materialistic. Even Tarahumara
religion is inauthentic and spurious: "Its mysticism is so crude as to be
scarcely rationalized into simple intelligibility." Art, soul, and spiritu-
ality are all lacking, and the void is filled by drinking. Or at least that is
Zingg's interpretation.

Zingg's depiction of women is equally bleak and prone to the worst
kind of essentialism and misogyny. Some examples: "Lorenzo's woman
was a paragon—of ugliness and surliness, a termagant of the strongest
vintage"; "Lorenzo's hag of a wife"; "One [Mexican woman] was about
twenty-five and already spinsterish, the good wine having turned
slightly to vinegar in that dismal isolation"; and "their [Tarahumara
women's] nagging and general surliness." The Tarahumara women,
invariably unnamed, who appear in these pages are uniformly drab,
unpleasant, and hostile. Zingg seems to revel in the most blatant sexism. And, unlike most contemporary male anthropologists, he is not
shy about revealing his sexual desire for certain women he encountered during his fieldwork: "The younger girl was about sixteen, so
that with her the wine had not yet begun to turn. What we two anthropologists wouldn't have given to take the younger girl along with us to
grind our *tortillas!*"

What is perhaps even more alarming than the content of these
comments is the ease with which they were made and inserted into a
text that Zingg hoped would gain him greater renown as an anthropologist. Yet in spite of the Archie Bunker–level sexism that colors sections of the text, there are moments in which Zingg tries to come to
grips with women's lives in a less demeaning fashion. For example, in
Chapter 4 he notes that "the woman is no chattel among the Tarahumaras" and goes on to describe women's important productive activities, such as weaving, pottery-making, child-rearing, animal-herding,
and food preparation. Zingg observes that women have control of
what they weave, veto power over commercial transactions, and the
high esteem of their families. Indeed, he states that the Tarahumara
women enjoyed "high status" in their society and that each sex was
wholly dependent on the other. And Zingg concludes that Indian
women have more freedom than do mestizo women in Mexico. As he
put it: "The patriarchal system of Catholic Spain does not exist among
the Tarahumaras; and among them the women may be as surly and as
independent as they please, thus gaining a relatively high status."

Surprisingly also, in the last chapter, Zingg criticizes the negative impact of religious conservatism on Mennonite and Mexican women, which he said forced them "to be servants of men" and caused the efforts of "half the human race [to be] wasted in ministering to the other half"! He questions what "all their saintly virtue gained these Mennonite women" and defends the more liberated modern Mexican women ("the Jezebels"), who were "cocky" and "ostentatiously enjoyed their new freedom." However groping and embarrassing some of this may seem today, it was, at least, Zingg's attempt at a kind of cultural understanding and relativism that permeates the text.

Zingg's relationships with his informants, servants, and helpers are, likewise, tinged with a mixture of sympathy, paternalism, and ethnocentrism. For instance, Zingg repeatedly refers to "our *mozo*," "my muleteer," "our man Friday," etc., indicating a possessive, master-servant attitude about the people who helped him do his fieldwork. Moreover, in patronizing fashion Zingg named "his" muleteer "Pancho Villa," a label he uses throughout the book instead of the man's real name. Yet, in fairness to Zingg, he does express considerable respect for the backwoods abilities of his helpers, and he praises the intelligence of his key informant, Lorenzo. And, like many fieldworkers, Zingg recounts that "Generally I was most kindly treated."

Also familiar is Zingg's use of tobacco, money, old clothing, and other trade goods to obtain artifacts, plant and animal samples, and cultural information from the Tarahumaras. Eventually, Zingg claims, "we were so popular in this community [Samachique] and were asked to so many feasts that we had to leave." At the same time, he also mentions several individuals, such as Lorenzo's wife and Patricio, who were openly hostile to the anthropologists.

What can one say about the ethics of Zingg trading boxes of matches for lizards, toads, and snakes? Perhaps no harm was done by this (except to the reptilian and amphibian population of the sierra), and Zingg notes that the skinned carcasses of animal skeletons were returned to the Indians for food. Of more concern is Zingg's extensive harvesting of Tarahumara graves and burial sites, although he claims the local people were not particularly interested in them and he did have the permission of the Mexican government. Also highly questionable is Bennett's taking advantage of the Tarahumaras' poverty and lack of food to purchase some of their best blankets at dirt cheap prices.

Another point worth mentioning is Zingg's less than perfect Spanish. In spite of his comment that "Spanish . . . is so much mine that when I am speaking it, I am almost blood-brother to the Spaniard," a number of obvious errors appear in his use of the language. Some examples: "*Que bueno que papá mató un venado por* [should be *para]* el *Americano*," "*Fue un viaje espantosa* [should be *espantoso]*," "Tarahumara women are very *bronco [bronca]*; but drunk they are *manso [mansa]*," and "*mucho gente [mucha].*" It also bears mentioning that Zingg makes many deprecatory remarks about the poverty of Tarahumara religion, beliefs, and mentalities even though he did not himself speak or understand much of the Tarahumara language. One wonders, then, how much he really knew about these matters.

Historical mistakes enter the picture as well, such as a joke about the Villa assassination which actually referred to the Obregón killing, according to Mexican political scientist Samuel Schmidt (pers. comm.). Also, Lázaro Cárdenas was not Plutarco Elías Calles's successor, and President "Rubio" should be called "Ortíz Rubio" per Mexican usage.

Conclusions

Clearly, Robert Zingg's research was not flawless. Worse yet, his work is tinged with ethnocentrism and sexism not acceptable today. Why, then, read Zingg? There are two main reasons. The most important reason for reading Zingg's travelogue is for what his work tells us about the lives of Tarahumara people in the 1930's. In spite of Zingg's unfortunate biases, he was a solid fieldworker when it came to most basic cultural descriptions, and his writing gives us a good feel for community life in the Sierra Madre at the time. He also provides a wealth of anecdotes about various others, priests, soldiers, politicians, and mestizos, whose actions greatly affected the Tarahumara. The book, then, provides valuable information about Chihuahua history and especially about one of the largest groups of still relatively unassimilated indigenous people in Mexico.

The second reason for reading Zingg is to evaluate anthropology's own complicity in the construction of colonial discourses and political structures that have impinged on the lives of non-Western people. While Zingg is not responsible for the systems of power that have kept Tarahumara people poor and excluded from most of the economic, political, and social benefits available in Mexican society, he is responsible for painting a picture of them as "philistine" primitives. But we must also recognize the fact that Zingg was not alone in this regard and that the sexist and essentialist ethnic discourses he wielded were commonplace in the anthropology of the times and U.S. society at large.

For me, at least, the lesson of Zingg's work is not to "throw the baby out with the bathwater." Like it or not, Zingg is one of our "primitive ancestors" in anthropology. This is our history as anthropologists, and we must come to grips with it. Politically correct critiques of such writings and a retreat into arcane literary approaches will not do away with the dilemma of studying and writing about cultural processes in a world of structures of vastly unequal power and privilege. Contemporary Tarahumara people face dire threats from drought, famine, environmental degradation, violent drug traffickers, and corrupt politicians.[10] Anthropologists could play a major role in supporting this beleaguered people, but not if they retreat further into the confines of the ivory tower.

If anthropology is to have any relevance to contemporary world problems, we must continue to do fieldwork and write about it (Grimshaw and Hart 1994: 258–259). Postmodernism, poststructuralism, cultural studies, and literary theory—all can be mobilized as weapons in struggles over meaning, representation, discourse, and power. They can be used to make our work sharper, more aware of its limitations and possibilities, and more politically sophisticated—but they cannot become a replacement for fieldwork. Anthropology's strength has always been our ability to interact closely in relatively small groups of people in order to portray the richness and textures of cultural life.

Today fieldwork may occur in multiple, transnational venues in a cyberspace, postmodern world (Clifford 1992). But I would argue that the fieldworker's task remains much the same. In this respect Zingg's work, in addition to providing information about Tarahumara life historically, can help us understand where anthropology has come from as we continue to carry on the only task which we can claim to perform in a unique and relevant way: fieldwork.[11]

Notes

1. Permission to publish this book was granted by Zingg's widow, Emma, to the Centennial Museum of the University of Texas at El Paso. Florence Schwein, director of the museum, kindly allowed the editors to prepare the book for publication. The editors gratefully acknowledge the careful and insightful assistance of David Kisela in the preparation of the manuscript.

2. *Rarámuri* is the term the "Tarahumara" use to refer to themselves. Zingg used the word "Tarahumara," as do most non-Rarámuri. In order to avoid confusion, I will conform to Zingg's usage.

3. Bronislaw Malinowski is often considered the "father" of the fieldwork method of research in anthropology. Malinowski, a British-educated scholar, and Franz Boas, one of the founders of American anthropology, promoted an empirically based, positivistic approach that attempted to rescue the study of culture from "armchair" theorists and nonscientific, unsystematic researchers. The Malinowski/Boas fieldwork paradigm was, and still is, immensely influential in American anthropology.

After Malinowski's death, his widow authorized the publication of his fieldwork diary (1967). The candid revelations—including vulgar, racist, and sexist opinions about informants—contained in Malinowski's diary were shocking and contributed to a reevaluation of the empirical, positivistic ethnographic method. The Malinowski diary had a profound impact on anthropology because it showed that, not only was one of our greatest fieldworkers far from objective and unbiased, but the whole notion of value-free, scientific ethnography must be revised. By the 1980's, the "textual" or literary dimension of ethnography took center stage in debates as scholars began to investigate how anthropological studies were permeated with personal and political biases and how ethnographers created "their people" and field sites through literary tropes and evocative writing.

4. My personal impression, and I mean this quite literally, is that anthropologists could do much more for indigenous people and marginalized groups if they would simply donate the royalties of their books to such peoples rather than endlessly fulminating about the paradoxes of representation. Although the revenues from any given monograph may be small, the collected royalties from tens of thousands of anthropological books could really make a difference in the lives of the people described in those books.

5. An example of this kind of limiting literary critique is contained in the conclusion of the much-acclaimed book *Imperial Eyes* by Mary Louise Pratt (not herself an anthropologist, although her writings are very influential in anthropological circles). In the last few pages of the book Pratt (1992: 225–227) criticizes Joan Didion's *Salvador.* According to Pratt, Didion should be reproached for presenting a picture of El Salvador that emphasized confusion, murkiness, and lack of clarity. I must point out that this view of Didion's book is not uncommon among researchers who work in El Salvador, as Leigh Binford (pers. comm.) has informed me. Like Binford I also feel that the El Salvadoran right and the U.S. administration were responsible for the vast majority of killing and suffering of the Salvadoran people at the time. In this respect, I agree with critics who point to Didion's failure to direct more blame onto the U.S. government and Salvadoran regime. What I am concerned about, however, is the constraining uniformity of Pratt's critique of travel writing: i.e., Western travel writers are inherently colonialist and racist, and usually also sexist. End of story.

This critique of "Orientalism" has now been applied with some success to a wide range of travel-writing genres and ethnographies (Said 1978; Thomas 1994; Suleri 1992; Behdad 1994; Starn 1991; Castañeda 1995; Spurr 1993; Bhabha 1994). The strength of such work is the way it upends and deconstructs the epistemological applecart of the Western "seeing man's" dominant role in the representation of non-Western others. However, if taken to extremes—in which the possibility of writing about anyone other than one's self is denied—this critique would lead to the demise of anthropology.

This might please many poststructuralist critics such as Pedro Bustos-Aguilar (1995: 150), who deplores "the anthropological imperial industry." Yet I, for one, still see value in the ethnographic fieldwork enterprise, in spite of its intellectual roots in colonial power. Even Bustos-Aguilar (1995: 164) concludes that "There are no panaceas to ethnography, in literature or elsewhere." Our best hope is to learn from the mistakes of the anthropological and travel-writing past so astutely identified by Pratt, not give up in despair.

According to Pratt, Didion's worst mistake in *Salvador* was to describe the Salvadoran situation of the time as a *"noche obscura,"* which Pratt argues is a decidedly Western analysis, hence flawed. In Pratt's analysis (Pratt, a Westerner), Joan Didion (a Westerner) should be rebuked for using Western concepts to understand El Salvador (a Western country). It seems to me that this kind of criticism, bordering on "Occidentalism," may lead to theoretical dead ends. It is emblematic of a kind of facile critique—which is becoming increasingly popular in anthropology—in which there is little room for the ambiguous details of fieldwork or first-person experience (unless that experience comes from particular authorized voices). Today, rather than criticize the observations of an ethnographer with other observations, it is enough to pick apart the words used by the ethnographer to reveal his or her hidden sexism, racism, classism, etc.

But Didion's comments precisely illustrate the value of empirical observation that reveals the messiness and contradictoriness of social life as opposed to the neat abstractions of theory. Latin American revolutions may seem to be clear-cut, unambiguous phenomena at solidarity meetings in Madison, Ann Arbor, and Berkeley. But on the ground in San Salvador, Managua, Juchitán, or Port-au-Prince, things may seem a bit more confusing—perhaps the left not so pure, the government's actions not always purely evil (although probably most of the time), and the general populace a bit confused about what to do. More like a *"noche obscura"* than an Instamatic snapshot (cf. Stoll 1998).

6. The lack of originality in recent studies of "colonial discourse" has also been lamented by Karen Sacks (1995: 104): "What attracted me to anthropology long ago was its vision of social alternatives, its insistence that the way things were wasn't the only way humans had done it. I was inspired by Benedict's great arc of human possibilities; I still am. But I don't see that same vision in progressive anthropology today. Instead, I see critique: of early ethnographies for being colonialist, cultural critiques of bourgeois culture, of each other, of our own thoughts (this is called being reflexive). It never seems to stop; it fills the journals, classrooms and conferences. The work isn't all bad or ill-intentioned, but we've been knowing that for at least 25 years; it's not *new*."

7. While I presume that Watanabe is referring to members of other cultures, I would prefer to state it as the anthropologist's "need" to study people other than him- or herself. The "Other" could just as well be a member of one's "own" culture as a member of a "foreign" culture. That is, I see no particular reason why the study of foreign cultures should be privileged over autoethnography.

8. I am reminded of William Burroughs's desire to write in a way that would put him in "real danger" (Harris 1994: xxxvii). Burroughs's relentless rebellion against literary canons and constant challenging of social and political norms—as well as the boldly iconoclastic lifestyle he led—make the anthropological postmodernists' textual experimentation seem rather insipid by comparison.

For this reason, I feel that anthropological forays into the postmodern that do maintain their roots in the fieldwork experience are likely to be more fruitful than those that do not. "Being there," as Geertz puts it, may be overrated, but it remains a necessary evil for anthropologists.

9. This statement could be tempered by the fact that Zingg confides that he carried a loaded automatic pistol on his belt during his fieldwork.

10. According to a report in the *El Paso Herald-Post* (October 18, 1994, p. A-4), at least forty-five Tarahumara children died of malnutrition during a two-month period and at least sixty others were confined to a hospital in Chihuahua. These deaths and illnesses were a result of famine and the spread of tuberculosis and other serious diseases in the Sierra Madre.

11. Portions of this introduction originally appeared in *Sociological Imagination* 35, issue 2/3 (1998). I am grateful to the editors of that journal for granting permission to publish this material here.

Bibliography

Ahmed, Akbar, and Cris Shore, eds. 1995. *The Future of Anthropology: Its Relevance to the Contemporary World.* London: Athlone Press.

Bandelier, Adolf. 1966–1976. *The Southwestern Journals of Adolf F. Bandelier.* Charles H. Lange and Carroll L. Riley, with Elizabeth M. Lange, eds. 4 vols. Albuquerque: University of New Mexico Press; Santa Fe: School of American Research / Museum of New Mexico Press.

Behar, Ruth, and Deborah Gordon, eds. 1995. *Women Writing Culture.* Berkeley: University of California Press.

Behdad, Ali. 1994. *Belated Travelers: Orientalism in the Age of Colonial Dissolution.* Durham, N.C.: Duke University Press.

Bennett, Wendell, and Robert Zingg. 1935. *The Tarahumara: An Indian Tribe of Northern Mexico.* Chicago: University of Chicago Press.

Bhabha, Homi. 1994. *The Location of Culture.* New York: Routledge.

Bustos-Aguilar, Pedro. 1995. "Mister Don't Touch the Banana: Notes on the Popularity of the Ethnosexed Body South of the Border." *Critique of Anthropology* 15 (2): 149–170.

Castañeda, Quetzil. 1995. "The Progress That Chose a Village: Measuring Zero-degree Culture and the 'Impact' of Anthropology." *Critique of Anthropology* 15 (2): 115–147.

Clifford, James. 1986. "Introduction: Partial Truths." In *Writing Culture: The Poetics and Politics of Ethnography,* ed. James Clifford and George Marcus, pp. 1–26. Berkeley: University of California Press.

———. 1988. *The Predicament of Culture: Twentieth-Century Ethnography, Literature, and Art.* Cambridge, Mass.: Harvard University Press.

———. 1992. "Traveling Cultures." In *Cultural Studies,* ed. Lawrence Grossberg et al., pp. 96–116. New York: Routledge.

————, and George Marcus, eds. 1986. *Writing Culture: The Poetics and Politics of Ethnography*. Berkeley: University of California Press.

Crapanzano, Vincent. 1985. *Waiting: The Whites of South Africa*. New York: Random House.

Didion, Joan. 1983. *Salvador.* New York: Washington Square Press.

Domínguez, Virginia. 1994. "Differentiating Women/Bodies of Knowledge." *American Anthropologist* 96 (1): 127–130.

Geertz, Clifford. 1988. *Works and Lives: The Anthropologist as Author.* Stanford, Calif.: Stanford University Press.

Grimshaw, Anna, and Keith Hart. 1994. "Anthropology and the Crisis of the Intellectuals." *Critique of Anthropology* 14 (3): 227–261.

Harris, Oliver, ed. 1994. *The Letters of William S. Burroughs: 1945–1959*. New York: Penguin Books.

Hubinger, Vaclav, ed. 1996. *Grasping the Changing World: Anthropological Concepts in the Postmodern Era*. New York: Routledge Press.

Knauft, Bruce. 1994. "Pushing Anthropology Past the Posts: Critical Notes on Cultural Anthropology and Cultural Studies as Influenced by Postmodernism and Existentialism." *Critique of Anthropology* 14 (2): 117–152.

Lumholtz, Carl. 1973 [1902]. *Unknown Mexico*. 2 vols. Glorieta, N.Mex.: Rio Grande Press.

Malinowski, Bronislaw. 1967. *A Diary in the Strict Sense of the Term*. New York: Harcourt, Brace, and World.

Manganaro, Marc, ed. 1990. *Modernist Anthropology: From Fieldwork to Text*. Princeton, N.J.: Princeton University Press.

Marcus, George. 1998. *Ethnography through Thick and Thin*. Princeton, N.J.: Princeton University Press.

————, and Michael Fischer. 1986. *Anthropology as Cultural Critique: An Experimental Moment in the Human Sciences*. Chicago: University of Chicago Press.

Moore, Henrietta, ed. 1996. *The Future of Anthropological Knowledge*. New York: Routledge Press.

Ortner, Sherry. 1999. "Some Futures of Anthropology." *American Ethnologist* 26 (4): 984–991.

Polier, Nicole, and William Roseberry. 1989. "Tristes Tropes." *Economy and Society* 18 (2): 245–264.

Pratt, Mary Louise. 1992. *Imperial Eyes: Travel Writing and Transculturation*. New York: Routledge.

Sacks, Karen Brodkin. 1995. "Response to Anna Grimshaw and Keith Hart's 'Anthropology and the Crisis of the Intellectuals.'" *Critique of Anthropology* 15 (1): 103–105.

Sahlins, Marshall. 1999. "Anthropological Enlightenment? Some Lessons of the Twentieth Century." *Annual Review of Anthropology* 28: i–xxiii.

Said, Edward. 1978. *Orientalism*. New York: Pantheon Books.

Singh, J. A. L., and Robert Zingg. 1942. *Wolf Children and Feral Man*. New York: Harper and Row.

Spurr, David. 1993. *The Rhetoric of Empire: Colonial Discourse in Journalism, Travel Writing, and Imperial Administration*. Durham, N.C.: Duke University Press.

Starn, Orin. 1991. "Missing the Revolution: Anthropologists and the War in Peru." *Cultural Anthropology* 6 (1): 63–92.

Stocking, George. 1992. *The Ethnographer's Magic and Other Essays in the History of Anthropology*. Madison: University of Wisconsin Press.

Stoll, David. 1998. *Rigoberta Menchú and the Story of All Poor Guatemalans*. Boulder, Colo.: Westview Press.

Suleri, Sara. 1992. *The Rhetoric of English India*. Chicago: University of Chicago Press.

Tedlock, Barbara. 1991. "From Participant Observation to the Observation of Participation: The Emergence of Narrative Ethnography." *Journal of Anthropological Research* 47 (1): 69–94.

Thomas, Nicholas. 1994. *Colonialism's Culture: Anthropology, Travel and Government*. Princeton, N.J.: Princeton University Press.

Watanabe, John. 1995. "Unimagining the Maya: Anthropologists, Others, and the Inescapable Hubris of Authorship." *Bulletin of Latin American Research* 14 (1): 25–45.

Zingg, Robert. 1938. *The Huichols: Primitive Artists*. New York: G. E. Stechert and Co.

———. 1940. *Report on the Archaeology of Southern Chihuahua*. Contributions III. Denver: University of Denver.

Behind the Mexican Mountains

▸
▸
▸ *Railroads, Revolutions,*
▸ *and Schoolteachers*
▸
▸
▸
▸
▸
▸
▸
▸

B ehind the Mexican mountains, in almost impenetrable sierras and gorges, the Tarahumara Indians still preserve a native life virtually untouched by modern civilization. Few people have ever heard of them, yet they are the largest and most primitive tribe of all the North American Indians. They inhabit about a third of the largest Mexican state, Chihuahua, less than two hundred miles from the United States border. In the company of Dr. W. C. Bennett, of Yale University and the American Museum of Natural History, I spent nine months with this tribe, seeking as much as possible to live their life and to describe the experience from their point of view. Only thus could we hope to learn about another and more primitive life, a way of life considered the only fit and proper one by some forty thousand members of the Tarahumara tribe.

The difficulties of reaching the Tarahumaras were exaggerated. In point of fact, a railroad provided access. That a primitive tribe could have remained uninfluenced by this most efficacious carrier of civilization was puzzling. But the explanation was simple. The railroad was as primitive as the Tarahumaras.

This railroad luxuriated under the formidable moniker "Kansas City, Mexico and Orient Railroad."[1] It was far from Kansas City, far from the Orient, and, jutting into the least penetrable sierra of the hinterland of Chihuahua, seemed even to be far from Mexico itself. The grandiose name, the only touch of splendor the road possessed, was due to the inspiration of the founder, Mr. Stillwell of Kansas City, who had dreamed of the "Kansas City, Mexico and Orient Railroad" as a keystone to his rail system.

No American with childhood experiences in the midwestern United States can help but be intrigued by trains. We can still recall the pre-automobile days when trains brought the romance and pageantry of the great world to every jerkwater town in America. To rural America of that era, trains were like the tramp ships that dock in the Thames, bringing to England the world's cargoes from the tropical belt to the poles. Today a locomotive still spells glamor to an American, with its general din, the whir of the dynamo, the churning of the air compressor, and the shrill escape of steam from the safety valve. Breathes there an American with a soul so dead as never to have had an inhibited childhood desire to be a locomotive engineer? Certainly locomotives have always held a peculiar fascination for me.

We started on the Mexico Northwest train from Chihuahua. This means of conveyance seemed bad enough at the time, but later we recalled it as the apotheosis of railroad construction. It swung up steep escarpments and over extremely high steel bridges which had survived the Mexican Revolution only because Villa had needed a railroad to exploit some of the rich gold and silver mines in the sierra beyond. The great horseshoe curves taken by the road in climbing the sierra are so wide and the gradient so steep that in one place I dropped off the train at the beginning of a curve and walked the intervening distance. I caught the train on its way back, with time enough to light a cigarette. We had gained about fifty feet in altitude perhaps, but were virtually no nearer our destination.

We left the Mexico Northwest long before it wandered off through the desert of northern Mexico back to El Paso and continued our voyage on the Kansas City, Mexico and Orient Railroad. There was but one passenger car on the second train and by paying twice the second-class fare, as we had naively done, we were permitted to ride in the rear half of the car. Here some rat-eaten apologies for cushions distinguished the classes. The combination second- and first-class coach was unquestionably a museum piece.

There were half a dozen passengers in the rear end of the single passenger car: three Mexicans, an American mining engineer from the American mine at Cusihuíriachi, a rich mine famous in the annals of Villa history under the abbreviated name of Cusi, and two Mexican women schoolteachers.

We began chatting with the two teachers, almost as if they were two American girls; and soon we were sitting in their seat—to the disapproving amazement of the more conservative men on the train.

These two girls were to spend a year in the wilds of the last Mexican outpost at the edge of the Indian country. So here I shall begin a paean of praise that will echo throughout these pages; and while its beginning may be scarcely audible, it should be clear and distinct before this book is finished. Advance, modernity, progress, and separation from the old hidebound conservatism of the past—all these are embodied in a thousand ways in this new and most significant class created by the Revolution. For three hundred years men as priests have molded the spirit of Mexico. Now has fairly dawned the day of women as teachers. These women teachers have consigned to the limbo of things passed and dead the ancient conservatism of the Spanish *dueña* and the false modesty which is represented in the injustices to and debasement of Mexican women. The change is electric in its possibilities. Now years later these potentialities are being realized.

It is a truism of sociology that any newly emancipated group with real solidarity must have some collective representation to display in proof of its freedom. As the postwar emancipation of American women was expressed in bobbed hair, so in Mexico at this time the new freedom was expressed in short skirts, silk stockings and cosmetics.

We were amazed when one of the girls took from under her seat a large, paper flour sack containing nothing but cosmetics. That an American should have been thunderstruck by a woman's powdering her face is as anomalous as that the Tarahumaras should have been reached by a railroad in the first place. To understand either fully would be to understand the enigma of Mexico. This was an epochal face-powdering, done on a scale truly epic, in that wheezing little train as the last vestiges of civilization were slowly being left behind us. It was a ritual, a ceremony. But first my colleague and I were asked to get up to provide space for the ceremonial paraphernalia.

As the train penetrated farther and farther into the wilds, leaving behind the last features of civilization, this face-powdering took on precisely the significance of Kipling's tale of the young British colonial official who had dressed in his black dinner clothes every sweltering night at his African station; a sacrifice of comfort worthwhile only because it was his sole participation with home and civilization. After the face-powdering incident on the train, our conversation with the teachers lagged. Perhaps their ritual had so consecrated them to their educational mission that such secular activity as conversing with a pair of travel-stained gringo scientists could no longer interest them. No longer able to interest the good-looking teachers, at the next stop I got out and walked the length of our remarkable train to look at the engine.

As I recall now, it was at the station of Santa Isabel that the American mining engineer had got on the train. He pointed out the spot where fourteen of his colleagues had been taken off the train by one of Villa's killers. All were shot and left for dead, although one man, I believe, lived through the horror and escaped. This was Villa's answer to President Wilson for thinking better of his original folly in considering Villa as an American-made candidate for the Mexican presidency. The mining engineer's remark opened a long discussion on Villa, about whom I will speak again at the end of this chapter.

While the engineer was oiling the engine, I walked up and down, mentally cursing myself for not having brought a thermos bottle in which to keep my coffee warm. Then I noticed the train hands had their bottles of coffee snugly ensconced on the top of the boiler. I asked permission to warm my coffee thus. By virtue of the unfailing courtesy of Mexicans to a stranger, this request could not be refused, especially since we had left behind every official of the railroad company, as well as civilization itself.

So I clambered into the teakettle that passes for a locomotive on the "Kansas," hoping that the lid would not be blown off while I was inside. Since I was not ordered out, I continued to ride in the cab, which was much warmer than the coach. Soon night came down over the sierra, and the beam from the headlight illumined the great trees of the virgin forest through which we were slowly climbing. The grade got steeper, and the curves sharper. As we went around the curves, the headlight cut a silver swath through the darkness, creating the illusion that the forest was being mowed down. This effect was not caused by our speed, however, because I could easily have dropped off anywhere and still caught my car behind.

I remained in the cab for several hours, as we climbed farther and farther into the sierra. Finally, a white-painted post came into view ahead on a straight bit of track. Slowly and painfully the train panted up the last stretch. As we neared the post, I could see in English the words "Continental Divide, Altitude 8,067 feet."

When we drew level with the post, the engineer stopped the train and turned on the injector. As the water hissed into the boiler, an extraordinary thing happened: the engineer and the fireman crossed themselves. I asked them if they thanked God because they were so glad to get up the grade. "*Sí, señor,*" they replied.

And with good reason did they thank God! For they explained to me that in order to get up the last grade with the heavy load of freight the train was pulling, they had exhausted practically all the water in the boiler in order to keep up a higher pressure of purely superheated steam. (This is so perilous a practice that it would cost an American engineer his job.) If they hadn't stopped exactly at the post, the engine would have been on the down grade beyond. Then the little water remaining in the boiler would have flowed from the crown-sheet, in the rear, to the front of the boiler, which was red hot. The exhaustion of water must be calculated with the greatest precision, or the steam itself could become exhausted and the boiler would overheat. Should the latter result, the blast of cold water into the red-hot boiler would blow the engine all over the pine-clad landscape. When they told me this, I crossed myself; and they laughed at me in turn.

I asked if they were going up any more grades like the last. But they answered that the remaining hour's journey was "*pura cuesta pa' bajo*," "a pure hill for down." I have often heard this expression from mule-teers calculating the strength of their animals against the cargo and the trail. Its usage by a locomotive engineer seems to show the holdover of the phraseology of mule transportation into the iron age of Mexico.

It was four o'clock in the morning when our train slid down the Continental Divide to Creel, the metropolis at the end of the "Kansas" railroad. To keep warm in his first-class quarters, Dr. Bennett had pulled blankets from our baggage. Hours before we arrived, he had wrapped himself in one of them in true serape fashion. Thus he had gone Mexican, while I had remained beside the warm boiler of the locomotive.

Our teacher friends, the American mining engineer, and my col-league got off the first-class end of the coach. I followed the others to the hotel and general store of the little place. It was run by a Chinese, who proved himself a vital member of our expedition, and who served intelligently and loyally as our banker and agent. Although an Oriental in a far-off corner in Mexico, he could read and write both Spanish and English. He was indeed the only one in the village with such abilities, and one of the few who wrote even Spanish. Like a true son of Canton he ran a hotel, and possessing a certain realism in practical affairs, which is a part of the Chinese genius, was able to keep accounts. And with a camaraderie common to almost everyone in real frontier life, he served us ably and gratuitously, keeping scrupulous accounts of all the cash expended by our illiterate *mozo* in this center.

Having turned our backs on railroad travel for nine long months, we ate a four A.M. supper and breakfast with our traveling companions. Then we bade them good-bye, but not for nine months, for we were at least to see the schoolteachers again. Our good-bye to the mining engineer, however, turned out to be for some time. When "the hurly-burly was done and the battle lost and won," we were to meet him again on the train that took us away, chance bringing him again to this train and place nine months later.

After our supper/breakfast we piled our own blankets on the thin cover provided by our Chinese host. He had fallen into that quaint Mexican custom of expecting each guest to furnish his own blankets. Two hours later at dawn we were awakened by the whistle of the "Kansas" train starting its return trip.

That whistle was our last token of civilization for nine months to come. But it aroused in us no nostalgia for what we had departed. Rather was there the thrilling intimation that we were at the edge of the primitive life which we had come to investigate. After describing this experience with the "Kansas City, Mexico, and Orient Railroad" in particular I may justly discuss here the Mexican railroads in general.

The Mexicans love their railroads, and as in various small towns of the United States, there is always a crowd at the station to see the train go through. In Mexico railroads are even more important because they are fewer and because there are fewer highways for motor transportation. Indeed, Mexico as anything but a feudal country can be dated from the Díaz reign, when the railroads were first built. This was an epochal event in Mexican history since it consolidated the country and forced upon it the consciousness of itself as a nation and not merely a jumble of localities. Had Díaz seen these effects in other than a material light, he would not have made the fatal mistake of leaving his country with only the scientific and educational facilities of medieval times. Under Díaz the hiatus between the material advance of Mexico in its railroads, mines, and factories and its intellectual and spiritual stagnation could find a balance only in destruction. The products of the material advance were destroyed, thus removing the vacuum. The slate was wiped off, and a new beginning was made from the ruin.

The material reconstruction of post-Revolutionary Mexico has not been so rapid, but the intellectual and spiritual reconstruction under the educational policies of the government has, for once in Mexican history, more than kept pace. In the present regime, consequently, there is an infinitely better balance than Mexico has ever seen. Is this balance sufficient so that Mexico can succeed in avoiding a revolution like the last one, evidences of which still remain after intervening years?

Railroads played the romantic role in the Mexican Revolution. It was such thrilling fun at first for the peons, tied to the land for generations, to follow a leader, steal locomotives and freight cars, put their stolen horses in the cars, and then with their women and children, sit on top of the cars and travel. These *trenes militares* were put into the songs they always sang around their campfires, into the memories the Mexicans still recall, and into the pictures of the Revolution they like to remember. Two recollections of the Revolution stand out in everyone's mind: the women beside their pajama-clad men with belts of cartridges crossed over their shoulders; and the *trenes*, with the animals inside and the people on top.

Such memories are preserved in the great Villista song "Adelita." This is still sung all over the country north of Mexico City, and is one of the most popular heritages of the Revolution. I have heard this song sung many times. It contains no hint of political or economic philosophy, but is merely the romantic tale of a Mexican Joan of Arc, ending in the refrain—

> *Adelita, si fueras con otro,*
> *La seguiría por tierra o por mar,*
> *Si por mar en un buque de guerra,*
> *Si por tierra en un tren militar.*
> (Adelita, should you go with another,
> I would follow you by land or by sea,
> If by sea it would be in a warship,
> If by land in a military train.)

I shall have more to say about this song later, as it was the "Marseillaise" of the Villa Revolution. Here it helps to show the romantic place of the railroad in the Mexican mind.

Railroads are the best operated concerns in the country, and in Mexico, as in the United States, railroad work is the aristocrat of all laboring activities. Mexicans are good railroaders. As is shown by the American customs and nomenclature, they were trained by the Americans who operated the railroads for years after they were built in the Díaz regime—and the Mexicans were apt pupils. When starting a train, the "conductor" calls out in Spanish the English words, "All aboard," then gives the characteristic American "high sign," instead of blowing the whistle as is done in Spain and most other Latin countries. A study of American influences on the nomenclature of Mexican railroads would indeed be interesting.

That Mexicans work well I had particular occasion to note on the trip from Mexico City to Chihuahua. As a Mexican joke, or as a holdover trick from old Revolutionary ways, someone had taken a rail out of the track, and a few hours before our express came along a local passenger train had been wrecked. The engine had rolled halfway down the embankment, a distance of forty feet. Baggage cars lay on their sides, and the first coach teetered over the brink. By the time our express arrived, at least a hundred section and road gang workers were busy getting the line open. There was no confusion, no idle babbling and no working at cross purposes. The men worked willingly and with excellent teamwork. In three or four hours the wreck was cleared sufficiently for us to pass.

In Mexico train-wrecking is a more highly developed art than in the United States. On trains out of Chihuahua they say that Villa's idea of an afternoon's diversion was to run locomotives full speed at each other. To make the event more exciting, a box of dynamite was tied to the front of each engine. One of Villa's greatest railroad atrocities happened on the Mexican Northwest Railroad. Villa's chief, Castillo, ran a burning lumber train into the Cumbre tunnel, caving the tunnel in. An oncoming passenger train plunged into the tunnel and collided with the debris. Some twenty Americans, including women and children, were killed. It was about this time that President Wilson began to doubt that Villa was such a white hope for the Mexican Revolution.

Villa was one of the few men to ever successfully defy the armed might of the United States and get away with it. During his time we all thought, "Funston got Aguinaldo. He will also get Villa." But we reckoned without Villa's cunning and the sympathy the people of Chihuahua had for him. Chihuahuenses not only would not betray him, but were willing to throw the gringo off his trail with all sorts of stories. The anti-American spirit in Chihuahua at that time is still vividly remembered, and I have often talked with muleteers about it. Invariably, their eyes flash, and they say that if the gringos hadn't gone back they would have sniped at them from every rock and tree in the sierra. Thus a cruel, needless war would have been fought over a worthless bandit who harmed Mexico infinitely more than he did Columbus, New Mexico.

Since we had passed through Santa Isabel on the Mexico Northwest Railroad I will add a little story as it was told to me by Mexicans. Santa Isabel is the rail station for Guerrero and after Villa's Columbus raid he passed through here on March 27, 1916.[2] He attacked a small Carranza force and was shot in the leg, by one of his own men, who apparently feared the revenge of the pursuing Americans for the Columbus raid. His plan was to kill Villa and join the Carranzistas [sic]. One of Villa's men has since testified that "just at the time Villa was shot, the Carranzistas gave way and ran, leaving us with no possible way of escape, so we again assumed the pretense of loyalty and declared that if he had been shot by any of us it was purely accidental."

Villa's wound was dressed by a surgeon in Guerrero and he was carried south in a wagon. His flesh turned black for twelve inches along his leg and he suffered agonies. Later, travel by wagon became too painful, and the wagon was abandoned to be found a few days later by American troops. Villa was then carried in a litter, along with one of his generals, Pedrosa, who had been shot in the foot during the Guerrero fight.

Reduced to the worst possible conditions, suffering torments from a serious wound, and deserted by all but a handful of his men, Villa nevertheless eluded capture. Aided by his cunning and his intimate knowledge of the sierra, the wolf of the Chihuahua desert succeeded in hiding with his few followers in a cave. The story, as told to me by the Mexicans in the sierra, is that Villa and his men watched from the cave and scoffed at the passage of American troops below them.

The pursuit of Villa did not succeed because President Wilson with real statesmanship considered us "too proud to fight" bantam-cocky little Mexico. This course was wisest, as further pursuit would surely have drawn us into a second shameful war with our neighbor to the south.

But I came to Mexico to study neither the history of Villa nor their railroads. It seems just as laborious to begin my discussion of the Tarahumara Indians as it was to get to their country on the "Kansas City, Mexico and Orient Railroad."

CHAPTER 2

> > > # Mexicans, Mines, and
> > > # American Capitalists
> >
> >
> >
> >
> >
> >
> >
> >

Dawn revealed Creel to be a nondescript town with nothing to interest us. We were looking for Indians, but were to have a hard time finding them. San Ignacio, a Tarahumara village, was a few kilometers away, however, so we hiked there expecting to see at least a few of the forty thousand Indians we had been sent to study. But San Ignacio turned out to be merely a church without a priest, and a new public school—nothing more.

The school was in the charge of a peon who was drawing a Federal salary as a teacher, even though he was not keeping school. When we asked where the Indians were to be found, he replied that they lived *muy retirado*, very retired.[1] This was a surprisingly true remark. The Tarahumaras proved to be a very "retired" tribe. In fact, they were the most retiring people I ever hope to see. It took us four days by mule to get to the heart of their country. Even then we didn't see an Indian for a week, and we began to think of the expression "vanishing redskin" as being singularly appropriate. But the Tarahumaras were not vanishing in the sense that we apply the term to the Indians of the United States, that is, sinking into disintegration and extinction. They were hard to find simply because they preferred to live in isolated *rancherías*, miles away from even their nearest Indian neighbor.

We hired horses and rode to the Jesuit mission village of Sisoguichi[2] to ask help of the padres in choosing living quarters for a long winter of studying the Tarahumara. I shall have much to relate about these padres farther on, but for the present suffice it to say that they entertained us most hospitably. They directed us to a church four days away and gave us permission to live as long as we might wish in the *con-*

vento, the living quarters of a Mexican church provided for the priest. They also recommended one of their neophytes to serve us as a guide and interpreter.

We returned to Creel, taking with us our new "man Friday." Here we prepared for a sojourn of several months in the heart of the Tarahumara country. Procuring equipment and supplies for a nine months' expedition may sound like a formidable task, but it wasn't. We needed no tents, no folding cots, no camping equipment, and no gadgets. Only a few pots and pans, blankets, tarps for bedrolls, medical supplies for first aid, and food for a couple of weeks until more could be sent from Chihuahua. All this was packed on one mule. On a second mule went writing supplies, cameras and film. The third pack mule carried supplies for preparing bird and mammal skins, and preserving reptiles and amphibians that were to be collected for the Field Museum of Natural History in Chicago. All told, it was a light and mobile expedition, for although mobility was not especially a desideratum, it may be recalled that 1930 was not the best of years for financing field parties. Horses and mules had been hired for a four-day trip.

Following the advice of the padres, we picked a muleteer, who later proved to be the best, most intelligent, and most loyal of his calling I was to know in my two years in Mexico. I have forgotten his real name, but he used to be complimented in answering to the name I gave him, Pancho Villa. He rode a horse with the slouching grace of a Mexican *vaquero* or American cowboy, reminding me of a newsstrip of Pancho Villa riding a splendid animal by the side of the motley crew that comprised his famed "Army of the North."

Pancho's horse, however, was not so splendid a mount. In fact, it was little better than a walking skeleton. This was a famine year in the Sierra Tarahumara, and there wasn't even enough corn for the people. I later rode this remarkable beast all over the sierra, looking for archaeological remains, and I called it by the name "Rocinante," after the famed steed of that ill-starred knight, Don Quixote, which in truth it resembled.

Late in the morning of October 13, 1930, the animals were packed, and the University of Chicago Expedition of Tarahumara Ethnography got under way with two ethnographers, three pack mules, and two horses. At this stage the most vital members of the team were the muleteer, Pancho, and his *mozo*, for our activities at this point depended upon the skill with which our Mexicans diamond-hitched the cargo to the backs of the mules.

There is no Mexican in the hinterland who does not know how to throw a diamond-hitch.[3] But in this, as in almost everything else, abilities differ and the gamut runs from the average peasant, who uses a burro for transporting wood, to the real virtuosos, like our muleteer, Pancho, and his *mozo*. By some legerdemain an ill-assorted lot of bundles and boxes were spread over a mule's back like trimmings on a Christmas tree. Then this miraculous hitch was thrown so that the load, instead of loosening during the day's trek, snuggled down more compactly.

The inventor of this hitch aided considerably the advance of civilization in Mexico. Until the arrival of the Spaniards, the North American Indians had no domestic animals. All transportation was by human muscle. Many Indians in Mexico do not use animals even yet. The *indio*, with his *acaste*, or cratelike box, packed on his back, is still one of the characteristic features of the Mexican scene. The Tarahumaras transport most of their goods in this aboriginal way; mules, horses, or burros are mostly too modern for them. And the railroad is so far removed from their ken that they walk as far as Chihuahua City to sell medicinal herbs, which are highly prized in the capital.

Our first day's trip was along the Continental Divide, the roof of America. We were close to the headwaters of the important Río Conchos, largest Mexican tributary of the Río Bravo del Norte, "the raging river of the north," which we in the United States call the Río Grande. We looked forward to crossing, two days hence, the upper waters of the Río Fuerte, which drains into the Pacific.

The great Sierra Madre dwindles to a mere crest in Mexico's *mesa central*, that extraordinary, enormous tableland which rises gradually in altitude as it swings out as far south as Mexico City. By this rise in altitude it compensates almost exactly for latitude, giving the greater part of Mexico a temperate climate, although most of the Republic lies within the tropics.

The Tarahumaras live in the mountainous region which includes all of the southern third of the state of Chihuahua. The landscape is a high open plateau, broken frequently by deep gorges. None of the peaks rises as much as a thousand feet above the plateau; they are merely a series of buttes and mesas where the soft volcanic tufa has been protected by a horizontal layer of harder volcanic rock. Prolonged wind erosion has cut the highly friable tufa into weird escarpment and pinnacle formations similar to much of the scenery in northern New Mexico.

Though the terrain is essentially a plateau, it is very rough and broken. Even the smallest arroyos cut sharp canyons in the soft tufa. The larger rivers have gouged out formidable *barrancas*, or gorges, as deep as 8,000 feet below the surface of the plateau. In depth and grandeur they may aptly be compared to the Grand Canyon of the Colorado. At river level hard rock formations are encountered, many of which bear rich mineral veins. These deposits have stimulated the development of some of the most important silver mines in northern Mexico, including the famous mines of Batopilas.

The high altitude of 8,000 feet gives this country a cold, bracing, salubrious climate, which, though not severe, makes it the coldest part of Mexico. Mexicans from the capital, who know their country, speak of this rough portion of Chihuahua as Canadians speak of the sub-Arctic barrens. As is common all over northern Mexico, the climate is conditioned by elevation. One does not go south for warmth, but deep down into the *barrancas*. In Chihuahua this climate variation is quite marked. One may descend from snowy, pine-clad heights, through a gamut of climates, down to a tropical level filled with parrots. Thus do the Tarahumaras escape the winter cold of the highlands. They are the only troglodytes in North America. Further, much historical data and the evidence of their ancient houses in caves show indirect, past relationships with the Cliff-Dwellers of the Southwestern United States.

The highlands are well-forested with pine and oak, with many of the oaks bearing mistletoe and other parasitic growths. In some places the stands of timber are nothing less than magnificent. During the first hours of our trip we saw considerable evidence of lumbering activities among the pines. The felled trees are cut into railroad ties by both Mexicans and Indians. In 1930, when mining was at a standstill, ties were the only product of the sierra to reach civilization.

The highlands are also filled with other trees familiar to North Americans (as the Mexican neatly distinguishes the Saxon Americans and Canadians from the Latins, who live to the south as far as Patagonia). The trees we passed included the familiar quaking aspen, ash, and alder. Yucca, from which the Indians make soap, and prickly pear cacti were also common. Very small century plants likewise survive in the cold of the sierra.

Down in the gorges we later encountered an unfamiliar tropical flora. There the century plants have gigantic leaves from five to six feet long, similar to the *pulque* plants to be seen around Mexico City. The explanation of the English name, century plants, is that at the climax of its long life it produces a long flower spike measuring from twenty to thirty feet. The stalk is covered with hundreds of little flowers which attract scores of hummingbirds. After this procreative achievement the plant dies.

In the gorge grow other xerophilous plants which Americans commonly include with the century plant under the erroneous term cactus. The *Nolina* (bear grass), the Dasylirion, and yucca ("Spanish bayonet") furnish the Tarahumaras with the fibers for their basketry. These belong to the lily family, although indeed they seem to have less in common with the lily than with the cactus, with which they are classed by the laity. And although they toil not and neither do they spin, the Indians get all their vegetable fibers for spinning and weaving from these plants [sic].

Certain tropical trees, unfamiliar to us in the north, are commonplace at the bottoms of the deep gorges. One of the largest is the *chilicote*. This has a light, corklike wood that is used all over the lowland of Mexico to make rafts for crossing flooded rivers. The cotton tree is common too, and the Mexicans use its cotton for stuffing pillows. This is the kapok of commerce. It is used for life preservers, because of its buoyancy and resistance to water. The laurel is used for its leaves, which the Tarahumaras take as far as Chihuahua to sell as a fragrant tea.

The valued logwood, or brazilwood of commerce, occurs here, but in trees too small to make logging worthwhile. The large tamarind tree produces its characteristic pods, the seeds of which are surrounded by a savory aril. The Tarahumaras harvest the pods with long sticks, just as is done along the west coast of Mexico and in the Philippines, where it was introduced from this region. The universal tropical American fruit, the *guayaba*, now of worldwide distribution, is also found in the gorges of Chihuahua, as is the tree producing the medicinal "physic nut." Native cotton and a strong, coarse tobacco are wild in the *barrancas*. The indigo shrub grows well, and furnishes both the Mexicans and the Tarahumaras with the native blue dye used in Mexico in pre-Hispanic times.

However, I didn't learn all this the first day as we hiked along the Continental Divide. On the first day's trip I began my collection of birds by knocking down a duck and a turkey buzzard. In New Mexico, where I lived as a boy, there was a joke about an American and his Mexican guide. They had killed a turkey and a turkey buzzard. The American offered to divide the spoils with his Mexican assistant, saying, "Now, shall I take the turkey and you the buzzard, or will you take the buzzard and let me have the turkey?" My Pancho took this buzzard in a most original way. We had just reached the summit of a hill when the bird swept down low over the top from the other side. Although Pancho was but a little distance in front of me, I shot directly over his head, stopping the buzzard in full career. Alarmed at a shot so close to his back, Pancho whirled halfway around. His movement was timed perfectly so that he got the impact of the buzzard full force on the chest, as it fell like a plummet from over his head. Pancho confessed later that he thought another revolution had broken out and was popping all around him. The natives in this part of Chihuahua are still a little nervous on this account.

By night we reached the school of the Tarahumara community of Cusárare, where my field taxidermy greatly interested the students. The pupils of the school, about half Mexican and half Indian, sat in double seats, Indians on one side of the room, and Mexicans on the other. The little Indians in their breech-clouts, blankets, and long, tangled hair contrasted with the neatness of the Mexican children.

No prejudice was obvious on the school grounds. Unlike Americans, Mexicans even at an early age are tolerant of other races. And adult Mexicans are as free of prejudice as their children. They view the Indians with a slightly patronizing affection, expressing this in the diminutive -ito, calling them the *Tarahumaritos*. The mestizo character of the Mexican race is itself proof of a lack of deep-seated prejudice. For their part, the little Indians are more affectionate than patronizing. As for the Mexican attitude toward the Negro, I have never had occasion to observe it. But the Mexicans have absorbed racially about sixty thousand Negro slaves, who have left only a few survivors and a few traces of themselves in southwest Mexico, good evidence in itself for a lack of racial prejudice.[4]

The teacher at the community school was a worthy young Mexican. He had had his position for only four years, but in this time had tamed the Indians and persuaded both them and the Mexicans to build an excellent school building. Here he had lived, all alone and with the most meager of comforts. The ideals of freedom, tolerance, learning, and service, all of which emerged from a decade of revolution, inspire in the teachers of Mexico a spirit of self-sacrifice and devotion that cannot be questioned. A few peasant clods or revolutionary guerrillas are to be noted in the schools, it is true, although many of the obvious misfits are gradually being eliminated. But the expansion of the Mexican educational program has been so sudden and widespread that some of the weaklings are tolerated rather than leave the work untouched.

The very existence of this school so far into the Tarahumara country and beyond even the hinterland of Mexico indicates the magnitude of the efforts of the Mexican government to educate its masses. No government I know of has devoted more effort or revenue to such a task. It may well be compared to the educational program in the Philippines at the beginning of the American regime. And from my experience there, I think the Mexican government is getting comparable results with the same type of inadequately trained teachers as the Americans had to use at first.

The equipment in these new Mexican schools on the frontier is bad enough in all conscience, but it is at least as good as that of the Philippine schools under early American direction. Both systems show a Spanish influence in the double seats of rough boards of almost identical construction. Besides these, classrooms contain a blackboard, some chalk and a few books.

Much propaganda against the schools has recently swept through Mexico and from there has been introduced to the United States. This propaganda takes the form of fantastically garbled myths about "socialistic education." I met with it particularly during my second expedition. Yet my experiences with Mexican teachers on both trips indicated that Mexican pupils are not generally indoctrinated with socialistic principles. We did meet one rabid socialist who was a supervising teacher, but he was somewhat of an exception—at least from my point of view after a two-year stay in Mexico. Most of the teachers are young women, quiet and refined, and rather timid and conservative.[5]

Three years after these early experiences, I was to encounter all over Mexico a firmly knit, conservative clerical party, quite vociferous if not actually powerful. This group opposes education because the majority of teachers are nonsectarian and guide their teaching by as purely a scientific spirit as one might expect in primary teachers with inadequate training. This counterpropaganda was strong enough to have caused the assassination of a teacher in Colotlán, my base for the Huichol expedition.

Some of the Tarahumara children in Cusárare walk more than ten miles to school every morning. But this distance is a mere detail for a Tarahumara. Indeed, the name and the fame of the Tarahumaras are derived from their great feats in running, one of which is the killing of deer by running the animals to exhaustion. These Indians of Cusárare show a genuine interest in learning Spanish, arithmetic, reading, and writing.

The next day's travel was uneventful. We had not yet seen an adult Tarahumara, even though we were drawing near the very heart of their wide country. At evening we came to a little fertile valley. Its inhabitants were all Mexicans, the sons-in-law of the Mexican patriarch whose daughters were populating this tiny Mexican island in the midst of Tarahumara land. The old Mexican had miscalculated the available area of good land, and still had two daughters whom he could not dower with small farms. One was about twenty-five and already spinsterish, the good wine having turned slightly to vinegar in that dismal isolation. The younger girl was about sixteen, so that with her the wine had not yet begun to turn. What we two anthropologists wouldn't have given to take the younger girl along with us to grind our *tortillas!* We were restrained from making such a proposal, however, by the fear that the patriarch, with his excessive morality, might misunderstand our intentions, or that he might force upon us the elder of his daughters.

The family lived in a *rancho* of the best Mexican type. The house was of stone and contained three or four rooms. The entire establishment was surrounded by a high wall, acting as both a fortification and a corral. The stables were built into one of the side walls, and in them, available for our animals, was abundant fodder from the previous year's corn crop.

Our muleteer was a *compadre* of the patriarch, so we were guaranteed a special welcome. The women prepared us fresh *tortillas*, which, eaten warm, are delicious after a hard day's ride. This was our last indulgence in warm, fresh *tortillas* for many weeks. The fried eggs, meat, and *chile* sauce also made this evening's repast memorable, despite the years that have elapsed since then. That night, our second in Tarahumara country, we slept in the courtyard of that typical Mexican habitation.

In the morning, the *rancho* proved to be at the edge of the great gorge called the Barranca del Cobre. After an inexcusably late start, a result of our not yet having learned to "put the heat on" the muleteer, we began the descent that was to end late that night at the water's edge. The trail was precipitous, but impressive. A misstep could easily have sent us and our equipment tumbling a thousand feet to the bottom of the gorge. This trip provided the best scenery by far. But a very exciting day's work it was, going down the tortuous hairpin twists of this "path of nature ruined by use," which the Mexicans appreciatively call the "Royal Road." The road had once been improved considerably by the American mining company operating Batopilas. Though years had passed, evidence still remained of the balmy days of "*Don* Porfirio," as the Mexicans spoke of it. In those days it was a common sight to see trains of a hundred mule loads of silver zigzagging down the face of this steep "gorge of copper." Each train was heavily guarded by a mounted escort who was instructed to shoot at the first suspicious move of anyone they encountered.

The excellent structure of the *rancho* where we had spent the night was an artifact of the mining era, and not the result of the industry of the patriarch, whose efforts had been directed largely toward populating the valley and in reaping a living from its fertile soil. His *rancho* utilized the buildings of the way station on the "Royal Road," where the great mule trains had spent the night, safer behind the fortlike walls of the corral than in the open, exposed to attack.

The river winding through the gorge at this point is called Río Urique, following the general custom of naming rivers after the towns through or near which they pass. Thus a river may have as many names as there are towns clustered on its brink. We have here an instance of the narrow realm of the old Mexican folk. Shut off from contact with the outside world, the Mexicans of each locality thought of the river as existing only for them. Actually the so-called Río Urique is the upper stream of the important Río Fuerte, so named below its junction with the Río Chinipas.[6]

Another contribution of the mine at Batopilas is an excellent suspension bridge, supported by heavy, two-inch steel cables. On our second night in the Tarahumara country, after the mules were unpacked and food and coffee consumed, our muleteer gave us quite a lecture about the bridge.

It appeared that Pancho was somewhat of a conservative, despite the name I had given him. Poor as the proverbial church mouse, he had always been an able and thrifty representative of his profession. I say profession, because in rural Mexico *arrieros*, or muleteers, form a class that may well be called a profession; and their skill and knowledge of animals set them apart from those Mexicans who can merely throw a diamond-hitch. By his industry and skill Pancho had acquired a train of mules that found profitable employment in packing the silver from the mines and returning with the canned goods, pianos, billiard tables and the like, which the *Americanos* found necessary for successful mining operations. It should come as no great surprise that pianos and billiard tables are moved by mule in this country. Good Mexican *arrieros* can take anything to pieces and transport it by mule, as should be obvious from the large mining machines that are still standing in some of the deserted mining camps.

The Revolution came and the *Americanos* all left. The mines filled with water and Villa's troops commandeered Pancho's mules, and even his services as a guide. During the two years I lived in Villa country, I could never get any of the dozens of Mexicans I questioned to admit that they were in the Revolution of their own free will. Most of them, like Pancho, expostulated that they were impressed into service; but none of them would acknowledge having been a *sin vergüenza político* ("shameless politician"), as they call a revolutionary soldier.

Yet Pancho was sincere in his narration. Not only did he lose his animals, but several times he almost lost his life in guiding marauding bands of Villistas through the sierra. Indignantly, he told of seeing these war-maddened soldiers engaging in deliberate and purposeless destruction. He related that once at the station where we had spent the night, the Villa soldiers pillaged dozens of five-gallon cans of lard from the stores of the family that lived there, and scattered the contents on the ground to be trod into filth by the horses. Once my muleteer was able to complain to Villa himself for this abuse of the poor. With careful recognition of the alleged nobility of Villa, Pancho did admit that Villa had indeed ordered a stop to such depredations on the poor. But the orders were honored in the breach.

The Revolution was anathema to Pancho, and he pined for the prosperity of the days of Díaz, or "*Don* Porfirio." As he concluded his speech, in a dramatic gesture he pointed to the hanging bridge and said, "In those days every month saw hundreds of mules pass over that bridge, laden with pure silver. Now no one passes, except perhaps a Tarahumara with a crate of apples on his back."

When I replied that the days of "*Don* Porfirio" were also days of prosperity for the *Americanos*, he answered, "*Qué le hace.* Then at least we got the crumbs; now there is not even that. *Muerto, todo muerto.* You can't take silver out of the rocks with bare fingers. Only the *Americanos* have capital for the machinery." I suggested that these natural resources might be left for future generations. He replied, "How can there be future generations when this one is starving to death?"

This statement was actually true. It was a famine year in the sierra, and the keenest hunger prevailed everywhere among both Mexicans and Indians. There was so little corn that we had to carry it for expedition use. Finally, the government sent in corn to mitigate the severity of the famine.

But apropos of the muleteer's argument, it was just about this time in 1930 that the central government reversed its policy against foreign capital. A few months later our muleteer and I met some American capitalists from Los Angeles who were bringing some machinery into the sierra for reopening a gold mine. Indeed, the Mexicans had not been able, with bare fingers, to extract the gold and the silver from the rich mines of the Chihuahua *barrancas*.

We met these *Americanos* just after I had finished my part of the ethnographic work and was returning to the sierra to record some interesting archaeological remains I had unearthed. We rode suddenly into their camp at nightfall, looking like bandits from our long sojourn in the wilds. All the equipment for an archaeological field trip was packed on one mule, so ours was a small expedition.

Never did I appreciate my Pancho's sterling qualities more than on that night, for he, with one mule load of equipment, could make me as comfortable as they were in their camp, which looked to me like Cleopatra's barge on the Nile. Every man had a tent and all sorts of camp equipment. Cases of food, washpans, dishpans, folding bathtubs, and the like were strewn all over the place. But we got a hearty welcome and a good meal.

One of the Americans was an old hand in Mexico. The others were capitalists who were soon to return to the States. The experienced man, however, was worse than the greenhorns, because he was nervous and irritable from too long a residence in foreign climes. He abused his men over everything, and as a result they were angry and uncooperative. He immediately noticed the better spirit of my muleteer. But by this time Pancho and I had been companions at so many evening campfires that we were friends.

The American told me that he had been through the Revolution and had weathered the antiforeign policy of the government. He had important holdings in Pachuca, and could be believed when he said that the national government had temporarily decided that it could not get along without foreign capital. Thus, entry was being granted to foreigners who would obey the laws and would not appeal to their ambassadors in an effort to evade taxation.

The mining project was obviously a small-scale enterprise, but more had been invested in tents, food, and camp equipment than in machinery. There were a small gasoline engine, a mining-bucket and cable, and some tools—in all perhaps five thousand dollars' worth. In addition, they had a concession on a famous gold mine which had been worked by Villa's army during the Revolution, and which had a long record of rich yieldings. Thus, near the end of my stay in the sierra the beat of hooves resumed on the hanging bridge of the Barranca del Cobre, representing a considerable increase in traffic relative to that of the Tarahumara, with his little crate of apples.

Mining in the Sierra Tarahumara still bears the imprint of a remarkable American, recalled by older Mexicans of the sierra as *Señor* Shepherd. Shepherd went to Chihuahua and made a great fortune from the famous mines of Batopilas, which had been discovered by the Spanish in the seventeenth century. Much of the profit taken from the rich mine of Batopilas was returned to the community in the form of developments. These consisted not only of machinery and equipment. Shepherd was a builder, and in this hot, tropical gorge he built a little modern city. By 1930 it was a ghost city, which I didn't visit. He also built the hanging bridge beside which we were camped; the road, the ruins of which we descended; and the station where we had spent the night. Yet all this was nothing, for this extraordinary person, famous all over Chihuahua, was also the man who built Washington, D.C.

After the Civil War, Shepherd, then an important official of the city of Washington, was accused of graft in the building mania which changed the antebellum mudhole into one of the most beautiful of the world's great capitals. However, the federal court investigating the rampant graft of this post–Civil War government never proved that Shepherd profited by the enormous expenditures. But he did resign, and left the country under a cloud. One thing is certain: he spent so much, and got the government committed to so many improvements, that in order to retrieve the first expenditures Congress followed Shepherd's work and made Washington a great and beautiful city.

We were already far into the Tarahumara country, but here under the hanging bridge built by Boss Shepherd, we spent the first of many nights that we were to sleep in the open. As our conversation died down, new excitement came with the arrival of a burro train of Mexicans and their wives. I still recall being amazed that middle-aged Mexican women could ride a burro all day in the characteristic sidesaddle that Mexican women use. But these mestizo Mexicans of the sierra are the hardy descendants of virile ancestors, both Indian and Spanish, and they and their wives ride these ruined trails on burros with little more fatigue than an American woman would suffer riding all day in an automobile.

The newcomers camped at a short distance from us. They prepared their supper, which they ate only after asking us to join them. We sent over a pot of coffee to repay them for their hot *tortillas*, which we had been glad to accept. Later the men came over to our camp, and for me there began an experience that has since been repeated scores of times: I was mistaken for an American mining engineer, one of those wonder workers who provide jobs for Mexicans.

There is something at once noble and pathetic in the eagerness with which I have been asked if I have come to hire men. An industrious people, the Mexicans are avid for work. Yet because of an absence of initiative and capital for effective work, conditions have been at a standstill ever since the dimly remembered days of *Don* Porfirio, at least until recently. This, I believe, is the tragedy of Mexican socialism: much to do, many willing to do it, but no one to direct it.

Here, in this faraway frontier of Chihuahua, Mexicans received all the advantages of development with none of the serfdom and injustice that characterized the reign of Díaz in some parts of Mexico. Ruthlessly suppressing those who opposed him, Díaz rose to power in 1874 after a decade of aimless chaos which followed the Reform Wars of 1855–65. Under Díaz there was peace for the longest time in Mexican history.

By giving fantastic concessions to foreigners, Díaz began to draw Mexico away from its feudal economy. Overlooked in the process were the ideals of Juárez' ten-year battle for the liberation of the Mexicans from the medieval prerogatives of the Church. Foreigners and the large landholders still controlled all the wealth of the country. Education was practically nonexistent. Thus the constitution, which emerged in 1917 after a decade of revolution and is still recognized, was a logical outgrowth of the ideals of Benito Juárez, the *"Benemérito,"* not Díaz the opportunist and reactionary.

A civilized Mexico, however, could not have emerged without modern transportation. Díaz realized this, and also that silver and gold could not forever be taken out of Mexican mines by human labor unaided by machinery. Until Mexico's modern era, which began with the Díaz regime, machines were virtually unknown. Ore was mined by hand and carried by serfs up ladders for the enormous distance to which the shafts had been sunk during centuries of working by the Spaniards.

But enough of Díaz and the Revolution. The memory of Mexico that will linger longest with me is that of the camaraderie of travelers, Indian or Mexican, who meet at night around campfires where *tortillas* are heated and, if one is lucky, coffee is boiled. Then cigarettes are rolled in corn husks and conversation begins in that noble language of the *hidalgo*. The dialect is preserved in surprising purity and distinguished formality, even in these little corners of Mexico. Americans often justify their general failure at Spanish by alleging that Mexicans speak a barbarous corruption of Castilian. Nothing could be further from the truth. Certainly, Mexicans do not garble their Spanish as our southern mountaineers do their Elizabethan English. And those mountaineers are blood descendants of the English, while the Mexicans of whom I speak are mestizos. Even Mexican Indians speak better Spanish than our mountaineers do English.

In the Mexican mountains certain linguistic anachronisms of the Golden Age of Spain are still preserved. The same cannot be said about the unintelligible jargon in which Elizabethan English is represented in the mountains of the southern United States. Leagues apart, too, are Mexican customs, even in the relatively isolated regions. It is as if there is some relationship between language and custom, resulting in a deep-seated courtesy and gentleness among the Mexicans, a trait as distinguished as the formal phrases of classical Spanish, in which their thoughts are framed. This is true despite the fact that the Spanish were not gentle in their conquest, and that everywhere in Mexico there is evidence of the savage destruction that swept over the land during the Revolution, from 1910 to 1927.

There is in the Latin American, I believe, a gentler, sweeter spirit than in the Saxon. Certainly it seems to be a more resilient spirit, one that has never degenerated to the depths exhibited by some isolated peoples in the United States. For two years I associated with Mexicans representing the poorest and most isolated groups at the fringes of tribal lands. Generally, I was treated most kindly. Even on those rare occasions when I was cheated or gulled, it was with a disarmingly formal courtesy. The exigencies of making a living may sometimes call for close dealing, but unlike ourselves, the Mexicans find this no excuse for being impolite or ungracious.

The climb out of the *barranca* was much more arduous and tedious than the descent. But our pace matched that of the sun, so we reached the cool uplands while the lowlands from which we had departed early in the morning sweltered in a tropical, midday heat. At last we could bid good-bye to Mexico, for we were in the Tarahumara country, where the Indian lives his own life almost as though still separated from civilization by the wide Atlantic.

The first Indians we saw were two brothers and the elder brother's wife. The men were trying to saddle a burro to carry a supply of corn on to another house. Their efforts to master even so lethargic a beast as the Mexican burro were ludicrous, bespeaking the slight use of domestic animals among this tribe. We interrupted their labors by offering them some of that Indian ceremonial weed that has gone around the world with celebrity, furthering the amenities of friendship and social intercourse—*Nicotiana tabacum*, commonly known as tobacco.

The men were naked except for their clouts, girdles, sandals and folded head-cloths, which keep their long hair from their eyes. Like all the men of the Tarahumaras, they were tall and well-muscled. They moved with that unconscious grace and dignity that contribute so much to the impression of nobility noted by all those who have observed Indians living in a state of nature. The woman was clothed completely in several skirts of cheap cotton muslin and a crudely fashioned waist-length blouse. The latter garment is always cut short so that children carried in the arms can be fed without much difficulty. Both sexes wear beautiful girdles woven from the homespun wool of their sheep. This is almost the only decorative article worn by the Tarahumaras. In material, design, and certain other details these girdles correspond almost exactly with those of the Huichols to the south, and the Pima and even the Hopi to the north. They seem to represent a post-Hispanic diffusion over a wide area, made possible by the introduction of sheep to furnish the wool of which they are made.

We continued our journey, passing through an Indian settlement which was a dependency of Samachique, toward which we were going. A few scattered cornfields constituted the only evidence of this settlement. The fields were enclosed by the characteristic log fences that the Tarahumaras make. Two or three hours later we arrived at our destination, the deserted mission of Samachique. The church was situated near the best water hole we had seen on the trip, in the center of a small valley with steep sides. Perched on the slopes of the valley were more than fifty Tarahumara houses. At last we had the elusive Tarahumaras right under our noses for observation. I doubt if Balboa got a greater thrill out of first seeing the Pacific than we did from our arrival at Samachique. But poor Balboa was beheaded for his thrill, and ours did not last very long, although it did not end so disastrously.

After waiting a day or two for some activity around the village, we learned that this collection of houses was merely a monument to some Catholic padre who had once been sufficiently influential to induce the Indians to live under the bells during the Christmas and Easter seasons. Years had passed, and the Indians had departed for their little hilltop fields, miles removed from even their nearest neighbors. It turned out that four hundred Indians lived in the community of Samachique, but the distances between *rancherías* were so great that the "town" had an area as large as that of the city of Chicago.

The church was one of twenty or so established in the Indian country by Jesuit missionaries. It had become the center of a Tarahumara community, and all the Indians within a walking distance of fifteen miles characteristically considered themselves a part of it. Every Sunday the Indians gather at this church for prayers given by an Indian who has spent enough time with the padres to know the *Pater Noster* in Spanish. This serves the simple *Tarahumaritos* as well as the Latin mass might serve them.

After prayers, the people stand in front of the church while their *gobernador* gives them a sermon on right conduct and good morals. Then trials or complaints are heard and settled by the officials sitting *en cathedra* on their official bench with their canes in their belts. After the day has passed thus and in informal conversation, the Indians vanish to their respective *rancherías*.

I should describe this church and its *convento*, or priestly dwelling, which was to be our home for the next four months. My reason is partly sentimental, for the whole place was quite ramshackle. Both church and convent were surrounded by a high wall, and both were roofed with *canoas*. *Canoas* are long grooved planks cut, with excellent axemanship, by the Indians. They extend the length of the roof, and their grooves interlock like a line of Spanish tiles, which no doubt furnished the pattern for this imitation roofing in wood. They well serve their purpose of shedding water. Both buildings were constructed of adobe. The church had a small belfry, but the Indians had hung the bells from the porch, which made them easier to ring.

The *convento* was L-shaped and joined the rear of the church. The part we used consisted of three rooms, which provided safe storage for food and botanical and zoological specimens. The front room had a built-in fireplace, a luxury that could be used for both cooking and heating. The window to the room, however, was nothing but an opening in the wall. We made a shutter for it from the top of a packing box, which helped keep out the cold night breeze of the sierra. Three years later among the Huichols I had occasion to long for this snug little *convento*, with its built-in fireplace and watertight roof.

The fleas in the place were memorable; but every American in Mexico carries Flit for them. It is very effective. To soften life a little we filled our bedroll with pine needles. At night we slept on the floor between the fireplace and the table of hewn boards, which served science as a writing desk as it had once served religion. Soon our pots and pans were covered with soot, and we were comfortably settled in for a long and most interesting winter. But a couple more days' work was needed before these arrangements were complete.

We sent Pancho and his *mozo* back to Creel to bring the supply of tinned food we had ordered from Chihuahua because our prospects of living off the country seemed remote. The staple food of the Tarahumaras is parched cornmeal, in Mexico called *pinole*. A handful of this is mixed with water, and the mixture constitutes a Tarahumara meal. It is on such food alone that the Indians sustain their great feats of running and the hard work of wresting a living from the inhospitable heights of the sierra. But to us, *pinole* did not appear to offer even sufficient nutrition for the less arduous labor of recording the customs of this little-known tribe. We had brought food enough to last until our supply orders could be filled in Chihuahua, and shipped via the weekly train to Creel, and then packed four days back to us by mule. All our contacts with civilization in the immediate future were to be in this roundabout fashion. At last, we knew we were in the field.

CHAPTER 3

▸ *Personalities Emerge from*
▸ *Wooden Indians*

I t was with great interest and anticipation that we awaited our first Sunday in the field. Today the Tarahumaras were to come together at the church after a long hike from their distant *rancherías*. Soon the men began to approach, wrapped in their blankets like Roman senators cloaked in togas.

News of our presence in the church and its *convento* had already swept the community. At first, only a few Indians were in evidence, and they dared not enter the churchyard, so bashful and timid are these people. Reinforced by the arrival of others, however, they finally came in. Still wrapped in their blankets against the autumnal cold of the sierra, they squatted somberly on the ground or sat on rocks like carved statues. We learned later that the tribe is so bashful that even members who have known each other all their lives sit close together for hours without exchanging a dozen words.[1]

As newcomers joined the circle, they passed completely around it, touching the outstretched hands of each of those seated, saying "*Dios cuida*" ("God take care of you!"),[2] and giving a poorly assimilated imitation of the Mexican handshake. This is probably the only Spanish most of them know—if, indeed, they know it is Spanish. We didn't recognize it as such for months, because they slur the words together so.

At first we remained in the house in order not to disturb and frighten the Indians. We attributed their silence and wooden behavior to embarrassment on our account, for we knew this tribe's reputation for timidity. Their behavior on this occasion, however, was in our favor somewhat, for they always act in this manner except when they are drunk. But they were afraid, and watched us like hawks when we did not come out. I was sure of this, because the *gobernador* seemed to tremble when I was led quietly up to him by our Tarahumara interpreter. Our interpreter addressed them first, and informed them that we had come to collect various animals and plants of the sierra, and that if they brought us good specimens, we would pay them well. He also told them that we had with us a quantity of trade goods which we would sell them more cheaply than the stuff could be bought in Creel, and that we were curers, like Jesuit priests. This was true, and they were pleased, though no change in their features indicated it. The tale about our visiting their country to collect animals and plants was especially helpful, because this mission the Indians could understand. They would probably not have appreciated our real purpose.

We still remained within the building, even though we knew the Tarahumaras are considered the most pacific tribe in Mexico. Primitive man is always an uncertain creature when he is nonplussed and afraid. A sudden and unexpected move on our parts might have frightened these people off like deer and seriously crippled our work among them.

When the interpreter had learned who the officials were and, in the best Tarahumara fashion, had given them a long harangue about us, we then issued forth like the star performers in a melodrama. We told them that we were disposed to buy a steer to slaughter in order to give the whole community a feast. As a matter of fact, we tried for a couple of months to do just this, but no one would sell us any of his valuable cattle. Later on the gesture became unnecessary, for in a few months we were so popular in this community and were asked to so many feasts that we had to leave. Our work and our stomachs began to suffer from the corn beer which plays so prominent a part in a Tarahumara feast.

Bennett had brought along a five-year collection of old worn-out shirts to be sacrificed gladly in the cause of science; for we knew that though the Tarahumaras have no use for trousers, they do value shirts. We offered these to the officials on condition that they would line up for the presentation while Bennett took the first motion pictures of the expedition. The presentation of a dozen old shirts was done with as much grave ceremony as the conferring of Ph.D. degrees, except that we didn't put the shirts on the Indians as the dean had put the hoods on us.

Soon a Tarahumara began frantically to ring the church bells, which were mellow, even though they were ancient and small in size.

The bells hung over the door of the church and a leather thong depended from each clapper. The bells were tolled vigorously, thus calling the Indians to prepare for church. The women had been watching the presentation of shirts from outside the wall surrounding the compound. Reassured by our manifestations of friendship toward their men, and called by the bells, they too entered the churchyard. There they remained by themselves, off to one side. We learned later that this was their invariable custom.

The Tarahumaras then filed into the small building, a few at a time. Once inside, the women stood on one side, the men on the other. Some knelt, but all maintained a respectful silence. We entered last and remained near the door—for obvious reasons: we didn't know how to act, and didn't wish to attract attention or strain the good relations we had just established.[3]

One of the Indians, an official called a *maestro* (lay reader), approached the altar and knelt. He recited a line or two of the Lord's Prayer in Spanish, repeating these lines over and over, so slight was his knowledge of both Spanish and the Catholic religion. Even this fragment was unintelligible, not only to us but to the Indians as well. Then all knelt and chanted in unison, but in Catholic fashion rather than Indian. Finally they crossed themselves, arose, and filed out, the men first.

We were less surprised at this tangential imitation of the Catholic service than we were that it should exist at all. But the impression left by a few Jesuit missionaries had been so strong that the church had been built and kept in repair by these half-naked Indians, who gathered in it every Sunday without fail. And this in spite of the fact that a priest had not lived here for forty years, or visited the place any more frequently than from year to year.

After the prayer led by the *maestro*, the people gathered outside the church. The *gobernador* gave a sermon, and briefly told them not to fight, steal, or make trouble among themselves. This sermon is considered a very necessary part of the tribal exercises every Sunday, and is given in all churches. The chief was not a good speaker and appeared as bashful and tremulous as when I first approached him. However, this official was taller and looked more distinguished than most of the men. He impressed both Bennett and me with his dignity and his manner of thinking over a matter and then giving an opinion with a decisive nod of his head. He was a leader, and the people had chosen well. The Tarahumaras appoint their *gobernador* in an election at the first of the year by a show of hands. The native name, *selígame*, indicates a pre-Hispanic origin for this office.

Later in the afternoon the *gobernador* came into the *convento* to ask me how many Sundays would pass before the day of the Virgin of Guadalupe, the great feast day all over Indian Mexico, which is observed even in this remote corner. To attend this great ceremony here at the church, the Tarahumaras brave the cold of the sierra uplands until December 12. After that they seek the warm caves of the *barrancas*. This season marks the completion of the Tarahumara calendar round, as we shall see.

Before the day was over, I skinned a bird which I had shot the day before, to gain the interest and attention of the Indians. But they were less interested in the skinning than when I stuffed the skin. Later I learned that the Indians had decided that I was taking the skins to my country in this extraordinary way in order to bring them to life again. Had we told the Indians that we had come to study them, they would probably have been incredulous, and might well have been afraid of some fancied secret mission. But since most primitive peoples are interested in plants and animals, it was perfectly intelligible to them that we were too. During the stuffing operation they stood by with the fixed attention of medical students in an operating amphitheater.

That same day we worked out a scale of payments for certain specimens brought to us. For example, we offered one box of matches for all snakes, lizards, frogs, toads, and the like; and double that, or five *centavos*, for small birds and mammals. This was a very good move, because it gave the Indians both a reason for and an interest in visiting us. Since they lived so far away, it was much to our advantage to have them come to us, especially at first. Trading also brought them in numbers.

During the following days many Indians called on us. One brought in seven live lizards with their tails cut off. It turned out that among the Tarahumaras lizard tails are considered a most efficacious medicine. Another's contribution was the tiny but deadly sierra rattlesnake, alive and buzzing, but tied neatly on the end of a stick. Toads were also brought to us in the same careful way, because the Indians think the hapless toad is poisonous. Certain animals, too, were brought in. I shall never forget one Tarahumara who stood around the house all afternoon, wrapped in his blanket. Suddenly from under it he dragged forth a rabbit in a manner not unlike that of Houdini. Forty years ago Lumholtz observed the same trait. The Tarahumaras carry their game under their blankets so that they won't have to divide it with anyone they meet. Thus the strong native pattern of tribal hospitality is circumvented somewhat.

After skinning the game we always gave the carcasses back to the Indians to eat. This made the transactions clear profit for them. The Indians themselves do not use the skins despite the cold climate and the limited resources of their environment. In skinning the animals and preparing the skins I used an alum compound rather than an arsenic for a preservative, as the latter would have been dangerous around the camp.

As the afternoon advanced, many of the Indians overcame their timidity and entered the house, where Bennett was keeping shop. They examined our possessions with great curiosity. We had some fun with a convex shaving mirror that magnified the face. This brought the rarity of a laugh from everyone who looked into it, showing us that the Tarahumaras were human after all, and not cigar-store Indians.

We made a greater impression with this mirror later on. Our Mexican *mozo* discovered that the curved surface would focus the rays of the sun. Gathering a ring of Indian spectators about him, he lit a cigarette with it. This was indeed strong magic, because the Tarahumaras identify the Sun Father with the Christian God as their chief deity. I should never have had enough nerve to try this trick, but the *mozo* did it to the admiration of the Indians. Later on we repeated it.

By midafternoon the Tarahumara families began to file away. Their departure was timed so they would reach their *rancherías* while it was still light. Long before dusk we were alone again in our church compound, but we had met the elusive members of our new community, and had begun many friendships which, during the next nine months, would develop to an extent that I still recall with pleasure.

The next day our first Indian customer turned out to be a real neighbor who was living in one of the deserted houses that surrounded the church. But he was staying there temporarily only in order to harvest one of his several small fields of corn. His other fields were scattered all over the sierra, in typical Tarahumara fashion. Comparatively few places in the sierra will grow corn. Thus, these small parcels of inherited land account for the surprising distribution of the homesteads.

This Indian, Agustín, was the father of a six-year-old child, one of whose feet was badly infected from a stone-bruise. The little foot had been neglected and was painfully swollen to twice its normal size. The first elements of antisepsis are not known to this tribe. But the Jesuit padres had dispensed drugs and treated diseases, and the Indians expected the same of us, perhaps because we lived in the *convento.* So I treated the child for a week, by soaking the foot in warm, soapy water, massaging, and then bandaging it. The child was quite brave, despite a general tribal timidity which had made grown men tremble before us. A few days later the wound was sufficiently softened to be opened without undue pain. But in cleaning out the pus with bits of cotton, I did something which, I learned later, might have ruined not only my cure but probably the child's foot as well: I burned the contaminated cotton while some of the Indians looked on! According to their interpretation of this sacrilege, the foot, by some form of sympathetic magic, participated in the fate of the soiled cotton. I soon learned my lesson, and in subsequent operations I always burned the soiled materials after my patients had gone.

We noticed fields of stunted corn around the church compound. We knew that the Tarahumaras raised corn, beans, and squash like practically all the other tribes of Mexico, which was the center of aboriginal American civilization. But the Tarahumaras live far from the center of Mexico and their high sierra, with its cold and stony soil, is a distinctly marginal locale for corn agriculture. They produce crops only after the most careful husbandry, and this occupies most of their time. Yet, even in this inhospitable terrain, the Tarahumaras maintain themselves independently of the Mexicans as the largest Indian tribe in North America. Indeed they manage better than the few Mexicans who have cast their lots in the sierra, but they do it only by the closest of adjustments to the natural environment. This was the particular problem I was to study. The results of my observations have been published, together with those of Dr. Bennett, who studied the social and religious life of the tribe, in *The Tarahumara.*

The rough terrain affords only sporadic pockets of land suitable for corn, causing the Tarahumaras to live scattered all over the sierra. The land is so shallow and stony that it is doubtful whether it supported even one-tenth of the present population before the Spaniards introduced domestic animals. This estimate is based on the number and distribution of archaeological remains, which I investigated thoroughly.

Domestic animals brought great economic and social changes in Tarahumara life. The first Spanish priests recorded that the Tarahumaras were fierce and warlike, like their cousins the Yaqui. Indeed, during early colonial history, they successfully revolted against the

Spaniards and left a wide swath of massacre and destruction. Now they are so timid as to make the foregoing history almost incredible. The change, I think, is related to domestic animals. Domestic animals now contribute the most important element in the adjustment of Tarahumara culture to the natural environment. The animals are prized principally for their manure, which is used to fertilize the poor and stony soil. Otherwise they have little value. At night cattle are penned up in corrals on the fields, and their droppings are utilized directly. Goats are much more common than cattle, and are herded by the women and children. At night the goats are penned up in caves and the accumulation of manure is always carried away to the fields, sometimes a distance of ten miles.

The consistent isolation of the Tarahumaras during the impressionable years of childhood, when they herd the animals, is probably responsible for their wildness and timidity as adults. Quite frequently, I saw the little children alone or in pairs playing with stones, plants, or rocks in lieu of human playmates. From what we know of the importance of early childhood conditioning, it seems likely that this isolation robs them of many qualities of human personality, making them ill at ease even when they are together. Unaccustomed to human society, they are more at home with the sky, the rocks, and the trees which were the companions of their youth.

As we shall see, it is only when they are drinking their native beer that they lose their timidity and become happy human beings, deriving pleasure from association with others. It does not seem too much to say that even the sexual function of marriage is inhibited by this excessive timidity, and that the race would die out were it not for the drunken feasts, which are common enough. Marriage otherwise appears to be little more than the economic interdependence of the sexes.[4]

The deleterious effect of herding upon children evidenced itself in the family of Agustín, who had brought in his child for treatment. Just at this time Agustín's family created the scandal of the century in the little community. While we were moping about in our *convento*, a little grave had been dug in the *camposanto*, or Catholic graveyard, on a hill a short distance from the church. In this grave was buried a newborn baby killed at birth—a clear case of infanticide. The scandal itself, however, had broken some time before.

The Tarahumaras believe the fetus is connected by an invisible thread to the Sun Father or the sky. Thus pregnancy is a condition of special danger to the mother and even the people around her; for this thread is supposed to attract the lightning, which may blast the mother and unborn child to bits, and kill anyone else who happens to be nearby. Before childbirth, a ceremony must be given. A shaman, or medicine man, is called in who passes over the woman's head with a glowing corn cob. This action is supposed to sever the unborn child's dangerous connection with the sky. The shaman must know in advance who the father is, even if the mother is unmarried (which in itself is no great scandal). Otherwise, the ceremony cannot be performed.

For a long time, however, Agustín's daughter maintained a stubborn silence and refused to identify the father of her child. Finally, fearing to be blown to bits by a blast from heaven, she revealed that the father was her brother, and that conception had taken place while they were alone herding cattle. This rare case of incest among the Tarahumaras seems to have resulted from the unnatural society of these adolescent children. Incest is, of course, the greatest breach of social behavior, punished among all tribes in the world. In this instance its effect was terrific scandal. The community was hardly less horrified than the sanctimonious old shaman, who we grew to know later as the very embodiment of social propriety among the Tarahumaras.

The boy-culprit was brought before the shaman and his own relatives, the only ones who could attend this ceremony of pregnancy. The shaman said, "You are an animal, a dog, a burro, a bull calf, because you have no more consideration for your sister than an animal would have. We will throw you down and tie your hands and feet together as we do to cattle that are sacrificed in our ceremonies. We will truss you down and kill you at the next ceremony." These words so frightened the boy that a short time later he fled the community to seek residence and safety in some faraway place.

When the girl approached her time of labor, she went out alone to have her child, seeking some tree by means of which to support herself, as is the Tarahumara custom. But, departing from custom, she did not build a thick nest of grass to stop the baby's fall as it was born. On the contrary, she chose a stony place, and the skull of the infant was crushed. These were the circumstances that led to the sad burial in the *camposanto*. But it was done so discreetly that no one knew of it. We ourselves did not learn of it for some time. The shaman, as the pillar of good custom, had been the one to set the community on fire with the story.

The end of the drama shows a common human touch. A bad situation had arisen, the offender had been punished by horrible threats that drove him from home, and the community had exercised its repulsion in the exchange of considerable gossip. But memory still lingered and the group had to compose itself in order to reach a new equilibrium. In short, the mess had to be cleared up completely.

Since the girl could not be turned out into the inhospitable sierra with winter approaching, her case was turned over to one of the other officials of the community, the *mayor*. The padres had established this office in their concern for marriage and the family. The *mayor* is in special charge of the marital aspects of Tarahumara life, although the influence of Catholic ideas has waned. As symbols of his office he carries both the little cane of all the officials and a business-like Mexican quirt. During the old days of Church domination in Mexican affairs, the *mayor* used this quirt to mete out penalties against offenders of the Catholic ideal of marriage. The Mexican government no longer allows this punishment, however, so the incestuous youths were spared being tied up and given a sound beating on their bare backs. Although this official never uses the lash, he always carries it gravely with him, whether in pursuit of his duties or in simple social activities.

In this case there was nothing for the poor *mayor* to do save scurry all over the sierra looking for a youth in some remote community who could be prevailed upon to marry this erring daughter of Samachique. This was finally accomplished and life resumed its former even tenor. The remaining members of the family, including Agustín himself, were spared from the lash of group opinion.

But several months had to pass before such intimate concerns were revealed to us. For the first two months we occupied ourselves almost wholly in noting the externals of Tarahumara life. Let us turn to an examination of the houses, fields, crops, and the ordinary flow of existence among the Tarahumaras as they first appeared to us.

The corn in the fields near the church was stunted, with stalks only four or five feet high. Each stalk carried one or two ears that were never more than five or six inches in length. Since the latter part of October is the time of the Tarahumaras' harvest, the owners had already begun to reap their fields, some of them coming from many miles away. These Indians assumed an almost civilized role in their reaping activities, although they looked rather incongruous as they moved about clad only in clouts. The corn was put to dry in open box-like structures of hewn boards. After it was dry, it was carried to the distant storehouses.

Among the reapers was a family of two brothers, one of whom was married and had two children. The man had blue eyes, which made us suspect that he was a by-product of some previous ethnographic expedition among the Tarahumaras. His children, too, exhibited a Nordic strain, though this was well overlaid with Indian. Our suspicions turned out to be false, however, for these people proved to be the descendants of a Mexican woman who, almost a century before, had lived for years in the sierra with a Tarahumara man.[5]

The marital vagaries of this Mexican woman proved to be of great importance to our expedition, because one of her descendants was our best informant. The Mexicans had many romantic stories about her. One version was that she had been kidnapped by a brigand who had escaped with her to the sierra, where he soon met a richly deserved and violent death. It was said that she was so shamed by her involuntary association with the brigand that she would never return to civilization but chose to live with an Indian instead. However, her grandson—the middle-aged man who became my informant on Tarahumara culture—had a different story. According to him she was a poor Mexican girl who fell in love with a handsome Tarahumara. The Tarahumara wooed her with the beautiful music of his violin, tempting her away from her own kind to a home and life among this primitive tribe. This story is nearer the truth perhaps, although it involves incredible compliment to the quavering tunes that the Tarahumaras draw out of their homemade violins.

In Mexico there is little prejudice against intermarriage between mestizos and Indians, and the occurrence is, therefore, much more common and less difficult than it would be in the United States.[6] Further, although a Mexican woman might surrender a good deal in choosing to live in a dirty cave, the cultural gap between mestizos and Indians is not so vast. For one thing, the loss is somewhat compensated by the higher position that Tarahumara women enjoy in their freer, though more primitive, culture. The patriarchal system of Catholic Spain does not exist among the Tarahumaras, and the women may be as surly and independent as they please, thus gaining a relatively high status. Even so, not many Mexican women care to make the change. The Mexican patriarch at the station on the Royal Road where we spent our second night was endeavoring to adjust his household concerns by marrying his younger and prettier daughter to a rich Tarahumara whom we came to know very well. Months later, when I was leaving this station in search of archaeological remains, I learned of the old man's plans. The girl was far from enthusiastic about them. I still remember her looking wistfully out of her little shut-in valley, and telling me I was a great traveler, because before nightfall I would be twenty miles away. Jokingly I offered her the benefits of wide travel if she would accompany me. But either she caught my humor or remembered her stern father. Or maybe I wasn't joking. *¿Quién sabe?* Since then I have always wondered if she did marry the rich old Indian with his hundred head of cattle, which comprised his wealth.

It was almost two weeks after our arrival when we entered a Tarahumara home. After two weeks of careful work we had become sufficiently acquainted with the Indians that the "blond" family permitted us to enter their dwelling. Like all the other houses around the church which gave us our first thrill of discovery, this house was in disrepair and was used three or four times a year only during church ceremonies. The many chinks in the walls were filled temporarily to keep out the keen night air of the sierra.

The one-room house was oblong, with walls of laminated stone held with adobe mud. So elaborate a construction as this was the result of two hundred years' teaching by the Jesuit padres; the typical house of the tribe was much simpler. The roof was flat and made of *canoas.* At one end of the room was a fireplace, over which was a chimney supported by joists. This was the most sophisticated detail in the house and, like the *canoas,* could be traced back to Old Spain. The joists of this chimney were so constructed as to allow a shelf on each side. On these shelves were baskets, pots, balls of wool, and other appurtenances of Tarahumara housekeeping.

On the floor in front of the fireplace were some goatskins, sufficing the family for seats and beds. The other end of the room was devoted to storage of the recently harvested corn. Here also was the *metate,* that prehistoric household accessory common all over Mexico. On this slab the corn, after being boiled in lye, is ground by means of a small stone called the *mano,* or "hand." Several jars and bowls completed the household equipment. These held water and *nixtamal,* the grains of corn softened for grinding by having been boiled in the lye of oak ash. The woman knelt before the *metate,* while the men sat before the fireplace, resting from their day of harvesting corn.

Encouraged by our excellent reception in the first Tarahumara dwelling we had entered, we decided the next day to explore the little river valley in which the church was located. Around a sharp bend in the river we came upon a typical *ranchería*, buzzing with the daily round of Tarahumara life at harvest time.

The women were harvesting the ripe and dried beans from the upland clearings, where planting had been carried on in the spring. The beans were carried in small blankets to the house. There younger women and children placed them on a large rock and beat them out of their dried pods with long switches. The beans were stored in large baskets, along with corn, for winter use in the typical Indian diet. The men were harvesting corn. Squash had ripened among the dried corn husks. These the women also harvested. They were pared, cut into long strips, and stretched out on the flat roofs and rocks to dry in the sun, which, even at this time of the year and despite the high sierra, was quite strong. The dried squash was then stored for winter cooking. Sweet and savory, squash is a Tarahumara delicacy.

One young married man was building a house that was to have a corral, a chicken house, and "all the fixings." Of all Tarahumara structures, the chicken house is perhaps the most extraordinary. It is box shaped, a miniature reproduction of the Tarahumara corn-drying structures. Like them it stands on four posts to protect the chickens from foxes. Every night a small pole is laid up to the little square door and chickens scramble up, like amateur tightrope walkers.

Late that afternoon, after our return to the *convento*, we were pleasantly surprised to receive a visit from an Indian who spoke Spanish. He was later revealed as the grandson of the Mexican woman mentioned above. He proved to be the only one in the community blessed with a fluent command of this tongue. He offered to sell us some potatoes and apples. We lost no time in coming to terms since—God spare the man!—for two weeks we had been living on nothing but tribal food augmented by canned goods. Potatoes are a native American plant, cultivated in Mexico before the advent of the Spaniards. But although they are a staple food in Peru, in Mexico they have never been highly prized, especially since they seldom grow larger than marbles. It was unusual, then, to find them grown by such an out of the way tribe as the Tarahumaras. Yet the Indians had learned this culture from the Mexicans.

For some reason potatoes grow well and attain a respectable size in the cold climate of the sierra. As a staple food for the Tarahumaras, they would be much better than corn. But corn is the preferred food in Mexico, as the tuber is in South America. In Mexico the potato nowhere displaces corn, even though it is much easier to raise. So the Tarahumaras devote their energies to a product for which their mountainous country is distinctly marginal.

Such is the blind, unreasoning conservatism of primitive culture, they will even make tremendous sacrifices to raise corn, even to the extent of defeating the proper functions of their society, as indicated by the scandal described above. This unquestioning adherence to traditional patterns is the essence of the primitive. Among many primitive tribes an added difficulty arises, because much of this blind acceptance is backed by the mysticism of ceremony and myth. Many tribes, such as the Huichols, have a great preoccupation with mystical thought, making rational improvement impossible at those points where mysticism and reason clash. The Tarahumaras, however, are so concerned with livelihood activities that they have little time or leisure to participate in elaborate ceremony and ritual at the mystical level. It is rather their lack of rational experiment and willingness to learn from experience that keep them millennia behind the rest of the world in utilizing their own natural resources.[7]

New as I was to their culture, I could soon think of as many technical improvements within the possibilities of their milieu as a Connecticut Yankee in King Arthur's court. One of the greatest possibilities for improvement of Tarahumara culture lies in the cultivation of potatoes. The crop might increase the population sufficiently and provide leisure enough to show an extraordinary development in all aspects of Tarahumara life. When a new food finds a culture predisposed toward its acceptance by existing patterns, important results often follow. In the Philippines in pre-Hispanic times, for instance, the natives supplemented their rice with the Polynesian plants, yams and taro. When the Spaniards came and brought the similar American sweet potato, the new crop spread so fast among the people as to outstrip even the Spanish conquest, which followed along after. The first Spaniards to arrive among tribes of Luzon found them using the new plant. Today all over the archipelago, sweet potatoes, invariably known by their Aztec name, *camote*, furnish the largest fraction of the native diet. Although rice is still the only esteemed food, the bulk of the population lives on the new crop.

Thus our Spanish-speaking Indian's offer to sell us potatoes threw a significant light on human culture, as well as on our immediate culinary requirements. His desire to sell us apples shows another important aspect of the spread of foreign techniques among primitive peoples. All the Tarahumaras of the highlands raise apples and apricots and those of the gorges raise oranges. These crops were introduced to America by the Spaniards. The fruit trees spread very rapidly from Mexico, and large peach orchards already existed when the French reached Louisiana. This later caused considerable controversy as to the Old World origin of these plants.

Unfortunately, history tells us nothing about the spread of these fruits among the Tarahumaras other than that they were introduced by the missionaries. There is nothing to indicate that their incorporation into Tarahumara culture was rapid. Even today these fruits are not highly esteemed as food by the Indians. They are raised principally for sale to the Mexicans. The Indian slings a crate of fruit on his back, takes it into town to sell, and with the proceeds buys cloth for his wife's clothes. Indeed, dressing a wife is as serious a problem to the naked Tarahumara as it is to the average American husband.

The conservatism of Tarahumara culture is indicated in the slow spread of other practical things, simple and of obvious value though they may be. For instance, the Tarahumaras like honey, the only native sweet in their diet. To obtain it they put themselves in danger by robbing the hives of wild bees. Not only is the hunter always badly stung, despite using a smoky torch to stupefy the bees, but he is also in danger of falling from the precipitous cliffs or high trees where the hives are found.[8]

One of the Jesuit padres had the excellent idea of introducing bee culture to the Indians in order to make use of one of the few ecological resources of the sparse environment—the wild flowers, which are profuse in the spring. He went to Mexico City, took a short course in apiculture and returned, bringing with him a good colony of domesticated bees. But the Tarahumaras, except for the mission neophytes, would not accept the bees even as a gift. Their use is being introduced but slowly among the Tarahumaras, through the converts, whom the missionaries instruct in all departments of culture and establish on farms near the missions. In another century or two other ethnographers may find, perhaps, that domesticated bees are quite common.

This slow diffusion of foreign traits shows that Tarahumara culture must be a fairly satisfactory thing to the individual, for he holds on to it tenaciously. Such a culture is hard to change, and such facts as I have presented show the great difficulty in civilizing so large and isolated a tribe.[9]

I shall have more to say about the efforts of both priests and public school teachers in civilizing the Tarahumaras. Our interpreter, Leandro, was a product of such efforts. When he was a child, he was taken to the mission in Sisoguichi. There in that well-rounded institution, he was trained in a program of secular, vocational, and religious education. He learned to speak, read and write Spanish, breed domesticated bees, milk cattle, make cheese, and how to plow his land. Further, he lived in a community, so his wife and children were not alone herding goats.

Leandro had married a girl trained in Mexican household practices at a convent school near the Jesuit mission. Their house was of the Mexican type, and a little more comfortable than the Tarahumara shacks and caves. They lived fairly close to the church, so they were able to attend all necessary Catholic exercises. And they did not seem to need the usual Tarahumara recourse to drunkenness in order to fulfill the functions of both society and marriage.

Leandro seemed to like the priests and their ideas of civilization. Certainly, he was not held in Sisoguichi by force. But he was far from being completely rational, and was still susceptible to his Tarahumara background. His greatest lapse from a civilized philosophy occurred when he became very anxious to return home because he had dreamed his wife was ill. His use to us diminished on this account, though he was even more honest than the other Tarahumaras (who are surprisingly honest), and much more dependable, in that he was able to understand our purposes and needs. But he was either so civilized that he had forgotten the rationale of Tarahumara culture, or else he was ashamed of it. My impression is the former was perhaps the more predominant in his case, for in general, there is little evidence of an inferiority complex among the Tarahumaras in their relations to one another or to the Mexicans.

For all the foregoing reasons we were delighted when the first local Tarahumara came to us and in his fluent Spanish offered us potatoes and apples. We recognized immediately that he had possibilities as an informant. His appearance was not such as to impress me at first. In contrast to the tall, graceful Tarahumaras with Roman noses and large frames, clad only in clout and blanket, Lorenzo had a curious, monkeylike face, and was dressed in tatterdemalion overalls and a shirt. Some scamp of a culturally bastardized Indian I thought.

Before others came, I took a notebook and asked him about himself. He said he was a brother of the family harvesting corn by the church, and a grandson of the famous Mexican woman who had lived here long ago. He was the only one of the family who could speak Spanish, having been reared by his grandmother in a cave which we later visited. His grandmother's talks about her people, the Mexicans, had aroused in Lorenzo the desire to learn all that they knew. As a small lad, he had gone to Creel and indentured himself to a Mexican as a peon. He spent many years with the Mexicans and learned how to tan leather and castrate animals. On his visits to the padre at Creel he had picked up the *Pater Noster* and a few other prayers. And, of course, he learned Spanish and certain Mexican customs such as wearing trousers.

When he considered his education complete and had saved a few pesos to buy a cow and start his own herd, he returned to his people, already on the way to substance and an important position among his tribesmen. By virtue of his mixed blood and culture, he could function in either Mexican or Indian life, although he was more Indian than Mexican.

There was no evidence of conflict in Lorenzo. He liked Mexicans, and met them on their own ground when they were in the sierra. Because of their timidity none of the Tarahumaras live near the Royal Road, where Mexican mule trains pass. But Lorenzo's grandmother had a ranch near the road for contact with her countrymen and Lorenzo lived on it, although no one else in the family would. As another example of his bravery, he had once accosted an armed Mexican who, he thought, had stolen corn from a relative of his. I was with him at the time, and armed, and this may have fortified him, but he showed greater courage than I might have under the circumstances, because the Mexican was a well-known drunken maniac who almost killed our *mozo* right in our own house.

Lorenzo was very broadminded about Mexicans, admitting frankly that some of their customs were superior to those of the Tarahumara. These customs he borrowed freely. But, on the whole, he thought that most of the Indian customs were better, and so he practiced them.[10] His familiarity with both cultures and his reflective nature made him indeed a valuable informant. Most of us are so unreflective about our own cultures, which surround us completely, that we are as little conscious of them as a goldfish is of the water in which it lives.

Lorenzo's knowledge of Catholic prayers merited him the relatively high position of *maestro* in his community and made him the absolute director of all important Catholic ceremonies. He was not aggressive about his Catholicism, however, and freely acknowledged the higher status of the pagan shaman of the community. Indeed, from his father who had been a shaman he had learned enough of the simple details to serve as assistant to the present shaman, and was even proud of his ancillary role. He was also one of the few in the community who knew anything about peyote, the curious narcotic cactus of such great importance among the Huichols to the south. Peyote has lately been introduced to the Indians of the United States, where it has made a great impression and has had a very wide and rapid diffusion.

Within the limits of the possibilities of his own environment Lorenzo was thoroughly civilized. He had a keen and logical mentality that showed an untiring interest in the outside world. He loved pictures and books. Indeed, he had read enough to be able to pronounce phonetically and intelligibly, albeit laboriously, the saints' days in the almanac. This was of value to him in his office as a lay reader. On one of the many occasions we were drunk together at a ceremony, he took from me a typed letter, written in English, and awkwardly pronounced the words according to Spanish phonetics. His mind was keenly logical and his fund of information amazing. Start him at the beginning of Tarahumara agriculture, and he would talk for hours. In all the phases of the material culture of the Tarahumaras, the arrangement of his data was so logical that my report was written directly from my notes with only minor changes. Yet he seemed to believe thoroughly in the crudities of Tarahumara religion. Not being a full shaman with a knowledge of the simple artifices used in curing, he really thought the shaman spit out maggots which he had sucked from the body of his patient. Had he been more civilized, he would have investigated and discovered the trick.

Lorenzo's personal qualities endeared him to me after I got used to the incongruity of his clothes. He was humorous, friendly and kind. He was living with a terrible hag whom he kept solely because she was the most industrious woman in the community. They had no offspring, and this seemed to give him a peculiar interest in children. He never begged, whined, or abused favors or privileges. Sometimes I still shake inwardly with laughter, remembering certain fragments of my conversation with him.

One day, when I was talking with him about a trip I had planned to take to the Catholic mission, he said, "Tell the padre to come this year and baptize all the new babies; we have quite a lot of little pagans around here." And then, somewhat in the wistful voice of the unregenerate sinner, he continued, "But the padre is surely going to be mad at me again." I thought to myself, no doubt he will be mad at your usurpation of the sacred sacerdotal office. I found out later, however, that the priests do not object to this, since all over the sierra assistance from Indians helps to keep Catholicism alive in communities that the priests cannot visit very frequently. At any rate, I asked him why the padre would be mad. He replied naively, "The padre is always trying to get me to marry my wife. But she is so *brava* [mean] that if I ever married her she would run me out of the place. She is mean and ugly, but she is the best blanket weaver in the sierra. As long as I can kick her out, I can get along with her. But it makes the padre mad. What do you think, *Don* Roberto?"

I knew Lorenzo well because I spent many days with him on the trail and lived in his cave dwelling for weeks at a time. Later I spent two months living in his grain house writing my report where I could use him to fill any gaps in my information. But gaps were surprisingly few. Lorenzo was such a keen informant that several times when I described certain complex things I had seen when alone (in one instance a curiously constructed scarecrow), he would identify them and delineate their use most vividly.

He had no shame about anything in his culture. Though he himself did not eat rats, mice or insect grubs, he didn't hesitate to admit it of others. Modest and decent, he still was frank and lusty in accounting for the few formal obscenities in Tarahumara culture, such as the curious relationship that exists between certain relatives, permitting the crudest sort of humor.

Persons of mixed blood and culture, intermediate between two contacting cultures, are of considerable sociological importance. Professor Robert Park, of the University of Chicago, has shown this in his concept of the marginal man. The importance of this concept is proved in my own experiences with the Eurasian, who in Java is vital to Dutch administration, or in China may become a commercial intermediary or *comprador,* characteristic of European-Chinese business. In the Philippines mixed bloods produce all the politicians. Even among primitive peoples the concept appears to be true, for marginal types are distinctly functional at either end of the tribal norm, and never among the average. They are either superior beings and leaders of the lower group, or else maladjusted to both cultures and grossly inferior—thieves, sneaks, and rogues. The Tarahumaras even produced individuals of this type.

Early in our stay at the *convento* a young Tarahumara visited us. He was clad in typical Tarahumara costume and had with him the bow and arrows which the ordinary Tarahumara always carries, which he subsequently sold us.[11] But he conformed to the marginal type not only in that he spoke Spanish, but that he brought with him a pot of milk that he had carried for fifteen miles in hopes of a sale. No other Tarahumara in the community milked cows, which is a Mexican custom. His mother was Mexican, and later I came to know the two very well, partly because I had to use the boy as a guide to some archaeological ruins, even though I knew the deservedly bad reputation this family had.

The mother had been caught robbing a neighbor's storehouse. This is one of the most serious offenses that may be committed in the tribe, because storehouses are exposed and unprotected, and the theft of its contents may cause its owners to starve. Indeed, if the offender is caught *in flagrante delicto*, he may be killed on the spot with impunity. This had not happened, but the mother and son were taken into the Mexican town to be turned over to the authorities. Lorenzo, who related the story to me, told me with much satisfaction that the self-important *gobernador* had not taken him along to interpret for the Indians. As a result, the culprits, by their fluent use of Spanish, talked themselves out of punishment and were permitted to return to their *ranchería*. But from then on they were *personae non gratae* among the Tarahumaras.[12]

Both of them were sneaks, whiners, and petty thieves, and the only Tarahumaras to ever steal anything from me (in particular, a belt with a silver buckle), though heaven knows what the lad intended to do with it, for he wore only a clout and a girdle. They wouldn't pay their debts, and were the only ones who did not pay us in full before we left for the trade goods we sold them on credit.

The boy was even nasty and abusive to other Tarahumaras. In a very important ceremony, that of "curing" the fields and the animals, he slipped in under my protection. I didn't object, because I had no other informant. But he got drunk, and began to speak disparagingly in Spanish about his hosts and of the beautiful and interesting ritual we were witnessing. Later he began to abuse the Tarahumaras in their own language. I became afraid that there might be trouble, because when the Tarahumaras are drunk they lose their innate timidity and will tolerate no insults. In the drunken brawls that arise from such sources people are often killed. Worse still, the loose and abusive talk that is flung around on such occasions gives the offender the reputation of working black magic against the others. Recognizing that I was placed in a serious situation, and knowing the Indians well by this time, I took the boy by the neck and flung him out on his face. Further identification with him would have crippled my archaeological and ethnological work all over the sierra, due to the grapevine telegraph system.

CHAPTER 4

▶ *Tarahumara Men and Women*
▶ *at Home and at Work*
▶
▶
▶
▶
▶
▶
▶
▶

Early the next morning Lorenzo, our new discovery as a possible informant, came to the *convento* bringing a pet squirrel to sell us. We accepted it and paid him a meter of cloth, not because we wished such a mischievous little pet, which turned out to be a great nuisance, but to encourage his visits. After we had offered him a peso a day for his services, he took us out for a tour of the valley. From the start he was an extremely good informant. He collected fifteen different plants and gave us information on their use, which was mainly medicinal, because of the fragrance, pungency, or terrible taste of their decoction.

We went first to one of his several houses. Actually, however, this house with its adjoining field belonged to his wife. Among the Tarahumaras, women (as well as men) inherit property, which belongs to them quite independently of their husbands, who work the fields and keep them up. This is a sort of life insurance, because if her husband should die, the wife would have something with which to attract another mate. The product of the fields is technically hers, although all wealth produced in common is shared by both. A Tarahumara husband never sells corn, animals, or anything without first having his wife's permission.

Lorenzo's woman was a paragon of ugliness and surliness, a termagant of the strongest vintage. While she was spinning, we took pictures of her, both movies and stills, and the day after she kicked up an unconscionable row. It seems that a German expedition, passing slowly through the sierra, had given the women the idea that the movie camera was a diabolical device for looking through their dresses.

Tarahumara women are so chary of their favors, even to their husbands, unless they are drunk, that it can well be imagined what a disturbance this occasioned. Lorenzo must have put in a bad night, for when he came back the next day or so, he was quite angry with us, though still anxious to keep on the payroll. We should surely have lost him had we not promised to refrain from photographing his wife. Yet she was not alone in her protestations. All the Tarahumara women objected to our taking movies of them. We finally had to procure the services of certain half-civilized women of the *barrancas* in order to obtain shots of the women engaged in their activities.

The woman is no chattel among the Tarahumaras. The man works her fields as well as his own for their mutual benefit. Yet if the woman weaves a blanket, girdle, or ribbon for the man, it is considered as a distinct gift. Until she gives it, it is hers; or if it is to be sold, she must be consulted first.[1] Most of the fruit the man raises and laboriously carries to the distant Mexican town is sold to buy cloth for her clothes. On the other hand, the woman works hard in preparing food and watching the animals. Either sex is really almost helpless without the other.

Both sexes are quite bashful, the women, however, more so than the men. Unless she is drunk, no woman ever speaks to any man other than her husband. You soon notice this in making a visit to a Tarahumara ranch. You wait outside about a hundred yards away, perhaps for as long as half an hour. If no one comes out in that time, you can be pretty certain that only the woman is at home. A Tarahumara would never think of entering under these circumstances. He might even be passing close to a house, with only the woman in sight, and still would make no sign of recognition. Nor would the woman acknowledge him. This behavior is as true today as it was forty years ago, when Lumholtz first reported it.

This bashfulness of the Tarahumaras results in the men's conducting all business transactions, whatever their nature. The women, however, are always asked for their advice and can veto any transaction. But we found one exception to this in the family of a man who was as deaf as a post. His wife, consequently, had to take over his role in social affairs. Since we were trading with the Indians, we ran across her. By that time we had become so used to woman's passive position in our trading adventures that she seemed amazingly forward. Having assumed this part so long, however, she played it with ease and naturalness.

Woman's high status among the Tarahumaras is shown in many other ways besides her being deferred to in commercial transactions.

She is esteemed as the mother of children; and the average Tarahumara male loves children to excess. I recall Lorenzo's real sympathy and sincere commiseration for women in the pangs of labor. His childlessness, incidentally, was the result of a venereal disease he had acquired as part of his Mexican education. He didn't know this. But he had tried so many women before his present spouse that he didn't blame her. Had he felt it her fault, however, so fond was he of children that he would have put her out, despite the fact that she wove the best blankets in the community.

The old virago didn't treat us badly the first day. She welcomed, or at least allowed, us into her house, of the wooden type, and typical of the temporary Tarahumara dwellings of the sierra. She even permitted her husband to give us some freshly boiled squash and some apples which were particularly tasty after our long hike. The squash was boiled without sugar in a small pot.

Yet she never liked us, even though we paid her husband in cloth enough to keep her the best-dressed woman in the community for the rest of her life. Months later, after constant association with her husband, and after living in their grain-house nearby, I met her while she was herding goats. She didn't even look at me. But this mattered little, because she was no "phantom of delight."

This is not the usual Tarahumara pattern of behavior; although, when the women are encountered pasturing their flocks, unless they recognize you as a friend, they will scramble up the hillsides. It is said that this is because they are afraid they will be ridden down and violated. This may have happened during the Revolution, when Villa's cutthroat troops were frequently passing through the country that lies between Chihuahua City and Parral, Villa's two main centers, or when other parties were busy operating the gold and silver mines in the *barrancas*. Most of this timidity on the part of the women, however, is nothing but groundless fear.

The *ranchería* belonging to Lorenzo's wife was not elaborate; it was simply an ordinary upland dwelling. The three- or four-acre field of corn was enclaved by a typical Tarahumara log fence to protect the crop from animals belonging to the neighbors. Near the entrance to the field was a pile of saplings and uprights. These were to be used for a corral to pen in the animals on the field as soon as the crop was harvested.

The house, made of old, hand-sewn boards that rattled loosely within their framework, was cold; and the crisp sierra breeze of autumn entered through a hundred cracks. In the center of the house was a fire of oak logs, over which some squash was boiling. Although it would have been impossible to live in such a house the year round, during this season at least the fire kept the place fairly warm. Beside the fire was a "shelf" (as the Tarahumara calls his bed), made of a few planks raised a few inches from the floor by split logs at the head and foot. On this the couple slept, and on this during the day the woman sat, utilizing it to keep her skirts from the dust of the floor. The domestic utensils included a few pots of water, "dipper" gourds, and baskets used for the washing of corn after it had been boiled in lye.

The Tarahumaras show a greater simplicity than most Mexican tribes in that for them lime especially prepared for the purpose of softening corn is too great a sophistication. The natural lye contained in oak ashes suffices. Part of the ashes from the hearth is saved for this purpose. The balance is thrown on the fields to act as fertilizer.

The cuisine of the Tarahumara wife is far from elaborate. *Tortillas* and *tamales*, typical Indian foods found everywhere in Mexico, are too good for everyday use. They are eaten only during ceremonies, at which one's social status finds acknowledgement in the number one is given.

The staple food is parched corn, ground dry to make *pinole*, or wet to make *esquiate*. The damp mass of corn from the latter preparation is placed, with about four times its volume of water, in a large pot. Such is Tarahumara hospitality that one never enters a house without being offered a bowl of this mixture together with a little stick to stir up the corn that lies at the bottom like a sediment. Generally a little pot of greens boils on the fire, and these are very savory. After one has hiked a long way to reach a Tarahumara homestead, and is hungry, nothing is more pleasant than to squat by the fire mixing one's bowl of *esquiate* with the little stick, and chewing the mixture together with a pinch of greens taken in one's fingers from the nearby pot.

The dry form of the parched corn prepared merely by grinding parched corn without water is stored in a large buckskin bag. It is ready for use on the trail or when herding, and is merely mixed with water from some convenient water hole. Thus it is simple to prepare, and, as I can attest from considerable experience, it is quite tasty on the trail when one's appetite is goaded to frenzy by the laborious climbs up and down the interminable *barrancas*. But as a steady diet I cannot say very much for it. It is said to cause constipation among the Mexicans when they are forced to subsist on it for any length of time.

The preparation of these simple foods merely begins the tasks of the Tarahumara women. The girls and young wives are often occupied with herding the animals, sometimes for periods of several consecutive days at a time. On these occasions they carry bags of *pinole* with them.[2] Most wives have children, however, thus precluding their engaging in this activity. In this event children or dependents or relatives care for the animals and the married woman remains near the house or dwelling cave.

The women are excellent weavers, and almost every one of them has a blanket on her loom. But this weaving requires that considerable time be spent in spinning, and this in turn necessitates the washing and the carding of wool. Prior to this there is the care and shearing of the sheep. All these tasks are fulfilled by the Tarahumara women. The sheep are pastured near the house, and at all times are under the watchful eyes of the women. They are the "animals of the women"; while cattle are the "animals of the men." The goats, which are far more numerous than either, are cared for by the children and younger people.

Besides blankets, woven by the Tarahumara woman to protect every member of her family from the keen cold of the sierra, decorative girdles are turned out on the looms. With these the men hold up their clouts. It is a disgrace for one to use rope or some other makeshift, although occasionally a Tarahumara has to utilize such substitutes. The women also wear girdles to hold up their skirts. They are sewn around the waistband, and the loose ends are tied.

Delicate little ribbons of yarn or cotton thread are also turned out on the looms. These are given to the men as gifts of affection from their sweethearts or wives. It is a rare touch of marital felicity for the Tarahumara to have his long hair combed by his spouse. This is done with the skeleton of a pinecone, and such are always seen around Tarahumara houses filled with loose hair that has come generally from the self-service of the woman. After his hair is combed, the new ribbon, which she is presenting him, is braided into it.

The women also make all the pottery that is used in the household. They are good potters, and turn out a solid, neat vessel. After the clay is coiled into the form desired, it is sun-dried for several days. It is then fired with great care, and in a dry place, or the vessel will crack and the entire process can be ruined. Sand temper is used, and the coils are crimped on to the vessel somewhat as an American housewife crimps the crust of a pie. The coils are then smoothed with little stones, polished from long usage, as well as with pieces of broken gourd-vessels.

Baskets are likewise prominent in Tarahumara households. They are made by pleating, are of all sizes, though mostly of the same type, and are used principally for storing the various odds and ends of Tarahumara femininity. Thus they compare somewhat with the average American woman's work-basket.

The Tarahumara women do not excel at sewing, which is an unfamiliar technique of civilization.[3] The simple shirts worn by both sexes tax their limited skill to the utmost. Only lately have the men affected shirts, say within the last forty years since the tribe was first visited by an ethnographer. Within the same interval women's styles have made a similar epochal shift from wool skirts, recorded as typical by Lumholtz, to skirts of cheap, cotton muslin now bought in Mexican stores. Regarding cloth, incidentally, my Tarahumara mentor and guide, Lorenzo, once said to me, "*Don* Roberto, you are so stupid. You don't know even the first thing about some of the simple things we have. How is it that in your country you make such wonderfully fine cloth which is so much better than our women weave?"

It is interesting to see the women toiling over a piece of cheap cloth with an awkward darning needle, and to note the contrasting nimbleness with which they weave from memory the complicated designs of their beautiful girdles. Even more skillfully and delicately nimble are they when they weave ribbons. And when they are making baskets, their fingers fairly fly, even if they are drunk. On such occasions, except for the drunkenness, the unconcern with which they worked always reminded me of a tatting party at a ladies' missionary society. In all three instances the conversation is at the same level of gossip.

Having consumed our bowls of *esquiate*, along with the savory greens, and some freshly boiled squash, which we ate for dessert, we followed our guide up the river to the *ranchería* of a rich old Tarahumara named Anastacio. Anastacio was the richest man in the Tarahumara community; and since the Tarahumaras are quite realistic about wealth, this alone sufficed to give him considerable prestige. But he was also an *ex-gobernador*, and therefore a dignitary of no small importance. His *ranchería*, where he lived with his two grown sons, had larger fields than any other in the community. Further, all his landholdings were in one place, which is quite unusual among the Tarahumaras. Part of the land, however, belonged to another family.

Anastacio's house was of the ordinary board type. Thus when winter came, he and his family moved most of their corn and effects to caves in the *barrancas*. But these were not far off, and dropped away almost immediately from the side of his *ranchería*.

He owned several storehouses to hold the rich harvests of his excellent land. Some were at the farm; others were located in the caves below. As is usual among the Tarahumaras, these were the best-made structures of the *ranchería* because of their vital function of storing food. To consider one in particular, its walls were of hand-hewn boards so carefully made that they kept out moisture and vermin. No cracks were visible. The floor and the ceiling were of similar careful construction. A superstructure of interlocking *canoas* sloped above the ceiling, and projected out far enough on all sides to protect the walls from slanting rain and snow.

Tarahumara corn houses have two types of entrances. One is something like a Japanese puzzle in which the boards are fitted intricately together and are held down by the weight of the roof. Entrance can be gained only by knowing how these boards come apart. Even then, the combined efforts of several men are necessary to hold up the heavy superstructure of *canoas*. While this is being done, one who knows the construction of the building takes certain boards out of the ceiling, thus exposing the wall boards. These are lifted out. Inside, a ladder of notched logs lets one down onto the floor. The interior is roughly ten or twelve feet square and eight or ten feet high.

The other type of entrance is through a small door. This, too, is complicated; for the Tarahumaras are sufficiently skilled in woodworking to make a wooden lock. The lock consists of plungers which hold the latch to the door until they are lifted up by a large, wooden key, notched to correspond to the plungers. The plungers are concealed in a cavity inside the door frame. Nearer civilization commercial padlocks are to be seen on grain houses. But where we were, this wooden lock was the usual means of security.

Such clever constructions in wood show how important the steel axe has become in Tarahumara life. Except for domestic animals, this was perhaps the greatest Spanish contribution to Tarahumara technology; for it is clear, from archaeology, that the substitution of the steel for the stone axe made available to Tarahumara culture the vast resources of the pine woods.

Before the introduction of the steel axe, Tarahumara constructions were all of stone and mud, and of extremely crude workmanship. With the axe, these people were able to move away from the gorges and build dwellings of wood. From wood they could make corrals, so necessary for penning in their animals on the fields, storehouses, corn-drying structures, chicken houses, and the like. Notched log ladders, too, were easier to make with a steel axe, although such ladders are to be found in the archaeology of Chihuahua, even as in our own Southwest. And the axe could be used to advantage in hollowing out logs to be utilized as feeding troughs in which to put *esquiate* for the dogs' food.

Thus, over a period of several generations, the Tarahumaras have become skilled axe men, and are not excelled even by the lumberjacks of our own country and of Canada. And they are ostentatiously proud of their ability. They never lop down a tree without squaring the end of the fallen log. Except for the inevitable, shallow axe-marks, the butt of every log cut by a Tarahumara is as square and even as if the work had been done with a saw.

The cutting down of a huge pine, as large as three feet in diameter, is a mere detail for a Tarahumara. Indeed, incredible though it may sound, a commonplace of Tarahumara custom, and quite at one with that of running deer to death, is to hunt squirrels by knocking down the trees in which these little animals have taken refuge.[4] I once saw where seven pines, the largest almost a yard in diameter, had been cut down to capture one squirrel. If a Tarahumara sees a squirrel escape the first time, the man continues his efforts. The dog is rewarded with the entrails. Squirrels roasted to a turn on a spit are esteemed far above rats and mice, which are commonly eaten.[5]

I have said that most Tarahumara structures are made of hand-hewn boards. After a Tarahumara has felled and trimmed a tree, he cuts the trunk into logs the length of the boards he desires. Then he begins to split the log, using his axe as a wedge, and, as a maul, a section of oak with a limb for a handle. As the boards are split off, they are leaned on end to dry. Weeks later, the Indian carries them home on his back, held lengthwise by his carrying strap. Here they are shaped, and with such accuracy that when they are fitted onto whatever is being built, they leave cracks scarcely wide enough to admit light. Old boards, which no longer serve for storehouses, or boards cut with less care, are used for less important structures.

Fences and corrals are made from saplings or small logs. These are dragged to the *ranchería* by ropes looped around a circular notch at the butt, a typically Mexican technique. For corrals, the saplings are held in upright notched trunks; for gates, holes are cut into heavy boards to let small cross poles through. These are also Mexican techniques. The small logs for fences are supported by short cross logs of considerable diameter. Three or four courses of logs determine the height of the resulting fence.

The Tarahumara also utilizes his axe when he goes out to gather firewood. Oak is burned. The wood is cut to a length of three feet and piled so that it is free of the ground. When he has cut a load that would literally stagger a burro, he is ready to use his *mecapl*. This is simply a glorified shawl strap. Two straps are put around each end of the pile of wood. The "handle" connects these two, and is of sufficient length that the man can work his body through it until it crosses his chest. Then, with a strong heave, or the help of someone else, he raises the load from the ground. The "shawl strap" is so tied that the weight rests directly on his back. His back is protected from the rough wood by a folded blanket.

The *mecapl* carrying strap may also be used as a tumpline across the head. In this capacity the Tarahumaras use it when they are employed in the mines carrying boards. They can carry about half a burro load. Further, they move faster and more directly than burros, and this makes them cheaper, especially since they load and unload themselves. The long-distance carrying efficiency of the Tarahumaras is not inferior to that of other Mexican Indians among whom human muscle still provides the motive power of transportation, and is but one of the many muscular feats for which they are famous.

But I was speaking of Anastacio. We had an interesting and profitable visit with this old dignitary. He was a man of property, a Tarahumara of the Forsytean genre. His influence was quite extensive, and he was, therefore, in a position either to help or harm us a great deal. We took a few pictures of his family and his possessions. On our return to his *ranchería* a week or so later we were nonplussed to learn that he wasn't at all pleased about the pictures. He believed that with them we had captured a part of his spiritual essence, and I might say, parenthetically, that this is a common belief among primitive people. But he was the only Tarahumara man to object; and we finally convinced him otherwise through the good offices of our inestimable guide, Lorenzo.[6]

Late in the afternoon, as we were returning to our *convento*, we stopped at another unusually good Tarahumara *ranchería*. This belonged to Patricio, the *teniente*, or second in command of the Tarahumara community. He owned a log house of Mexican pattern, a rarity in the sierra, built so securely that he and his family did not have to retreat to the gorges for the winter months. He was the only one in Samachique who wintered in the uplands.

The pompous Tarahumara, wealthy, respected, and a high official, did not like us. He would not accept our story, and later proved to be a source of agitation against us. Lorenzo twice explained our mission, pointing out that save for Patricio the leading people in the community were our friends. But he remained stubbornly suspicious. Some time after he became ill. The pagan shaman failed to cure him, and I was called. But my efforts were unavailing, and he died. His demise, however, provided us with some firsthand data on Tarahumara death and burial ceremonies. Several seasons later, when I was among the Huichols, death struck the family of four that formed an opposition against me. Since I did not desire a reputation as a sorcerer, you may be certain that I kept this previous death a dark secret.

Anastacio and Patricio were considered wealthy Tarahumaras because they had many cattle. A certain prestige is attached to the ownership of such beasts that does not accrue from the possession of goats and sheep. Cattle are not milked, nor are they killed for meat, except in the more important ceremonies. Some of them, it is true, are used as draught-animals; but virtually their only economic value lies in their manure, which, it will be remembered, is used for fertilizer.

This value is manifested in the production of food. The wife and children of the Tarahumara whose livestock consists of cattle rather than goats are released from constant herding. Thus their time is free for other economic activities. Since cattle do not roam as do nimble-footed goats, they are pastured near the house; and often their owner does not bother with them from one month to the next, and then only when he needs them for fertilizing his fields. It is his duty, of course, to pasture them; but this entails no more work than building fences to keep them away from the cliffs, and filling all dangerous holes with logs so that they will not break their legs.

The cattle killed for ceremonial purposes produce the rawhide used by Indians for straps, sandals, and the like. The Tarahumaras, however, do not practice the Mexican folk technique of tanning leather with oak bark, although this art is being slowly diffused through the padres and through contact with Mexicans near the towns and missions.

In the appearance or the effects of a rich Tarahumara there is but little to distinguish him from the poorest of his fellows. He goes around with the same lack of clothes as the other men; and his wife and children are no whit differentiated from the other Tarahumara women and . . . [Part of original text missing.—Eds.]

Hunting is an important though minor occupation of the Tarahumaras. Besides running down deer and felling trees for squirrels, they obtain a good deal of game in less arduous ways. All the men carry bows and arrows, and with these they bring down any bird or animal that draws within range. Most game, however, is caught in a string fig-ure-four trap. Sticks and string are used to uphold a leaning rock. The disturbance of the bait brings down the rock, crushing the prey beneath. The rocks are of all sizes to crush anything from a mouse to a mountain lion, though the latter is rare. On the trail we often passed such traps set for small game. And around the houses we frequently saw the pelts of common animals that had been caught in this manner. Surprisingly, these pelts are not used for clothing or anything else.

After Lorenzo had taken his leave at night, we spent the long evenings working up our notes, writing letters, or poring over lan-guages. Bennett studied Tarahumara; I studied German. I might just as well have studied Tarahumara.

One of our first and most valued customers was the Tarahumara Sebastian, who was a relative of the *teniente*, Patricio. Uninfluenced by the prejudices of his father-in-law, he supplied us with eggs and spent much of his time around the *convento*. The eggs were a *centavo* each. But he didn't wish to be paid on the spot. Rather he preferred an account in his favor until he had built up a substantial balance. Eggs are one of the few edible products native to this country, so our con-sumption was large, too large, in fact, to leave me with any taste for them to this day. On one occasion when I was crediting him with ten *centavos*, I said, "Sebastian, you just keep on bringing us eggs and leav-ing the amounts to your credit, and before we leave, you will have enough money to buy a cow." This remark drew from Sebastian, who could speak a little Spanish, one of the few laughs I ever elicited from a Tarahumara.

When Sebastian had accumulated an appreciable balance, he asked us to order him from Chihuahua the luxury of a new overall-jumper. It arrived finally, and he was pleased as Puck. I was with him when he put it on for the first time. It was a Sunday, and there were many Indians about. But though his eyes gleamed like a child's at a new toy, he very sternly repressed any other evidence of emotion when he donned the new garment that was to make him a veritable Beau Brummell in the Indian community.

Although the Tarahumaras dislike trousers, they do clothe their trunks. Through clothing, Bennett and I ingratiated ourselves with our guide, Lorenzo. For a fine old serape which a padre had given him, I traded him my sheepskin coat. Bennett was more generous, and gave him an old pair of hiking boots. As we shall see, Lorenzo loved these habiliments, particularly the boots, which were waterproof. He used to carry them all day, whithersoever he went, in order to wear them when crossing rivers. They should last him the remainder of his natural life.

While we were at Samachique, we were visited several times by Mexicans. Although the Indians object, it is the custom of Mexican traders passing through the sierra to camp at night in the *conventos* of the churches; and for firewood these thoughtless muleteers often chop up the boards and *canoas* of these communal buildings put up by the Indians. The temptation to do this is strong, admittedly, especially when one has arrived, just at nightfall, cold and tired from a long trip across the wintry sierra. Even as I did once, as we shall see.

For these Mexican traders we left vacant the large room at the back of the *convento*, which connected with the rear of the church. After all, we had to get along with both parties, despite the rather delicate and unhappy relations existing in the sierra at this time. And out of courtesy to such guests and customers we had to stock provisions of coffee and sugar, the two commodities of civilization that the poorest Mexican will buy if he is so fortunate as to have a peseta about him.

At this time many Mexican traders were scouring the sierra for corn, because it was a famine year and their provisions were almost exhausted. They traded cloth to the Indians for cash, food, or other minor items. But their prices were about double for similar goods that we traded to the Indians. Yet at that they were not robbing their simple clients. Our studies revealed that the Indians for a given price will sell only half as much corn to a Mexican as they will to a fellow tribesman.

Among the Tarahumaras themselves trading is no sordid commercial affair. When one Indian trades with another, he establishes a permanent, friendly, social relationship, and the other party becomes his *norahua*. This relationship is explained by the Indians as similar to that existing between Mexican *compadres*. It is one of mutual help, preferment, and favor. If your *norahua* is at your feast, he must be given a special pot of beer *(tesgüino)*. If he comes to your house, he must be tendered the best seat by the fire and always treated with marked courtesy. Failure to observe this courtesy is especially reprehensible, and the offender risks the possibility of having black magic worked against him. He may even be deprived of his sense of smell, as happened to our friend Lorenzo, though for a different reason.

This rapprochement exists only between Indians, and is especially binding if cattle are exchanged. Mexican traders pretend that it exists for them in their dealings with Indian customers, and use the term *mi* (my) *norahua*. But their vociferations only bore the Tarahumaras, who, however, are too timid to object. But during communal drinking parties, or *tesgüinadas*, the Tarahumaras are by no means so timid. Then they recall any real or fancied insults, slights, or deceits they have suffered. Because of this Mexican traders are never in evidence when drinking bouts are in progress; for a drunken Indian, in contrast to his behavior when sober, is capable of violent, aggressive action.

For their part the Mexicans share a common spirit of affectionate patronage which they feel for the Indians, and this they express by calling them *compadres*. Yet while I was in the Huichol country, I heard an Indian quite pointedly correct a Mexican trader, saying, "I am not your *compadre*." When they are away from the sierra and their own fellows, however, the Indians forget their objections; because the friendly Mexicans acknowledge their goodwill toward their primitive "neighbors" with gifts of money, food, and free shelter, things that the Indians are accustomed to accept.

Bennett and I enjoyed the visits of the Mexican muleteers who passed our way. From them we were able to get some idea of the variations in Indian customs and of the extensiveness of the sierra, which was too vast for us to explore thoroughly in the limited time at our disposal. We also welcomed them because they could cut hair. Indeed, I have never known a lower-class Mexican who was not an excellent barber. Early in our stay in Samachique I had attempted a tonsorial improvement of the erudite pate of my colleague, but with outlandish results. Thereafter we both utilized the services of passing Mexicans.

One day there appeared at our *convento* a Mexican of extraordinary aspect. He will frequently return in the pages to come. *Señor* Córdoba proved to be our nearest Mexican neighbor. He lived some twenty miles away at a ruined "station" on the "Royal Road" on the way to the Jesuit mission of Norogáchic. He was about middle age, and had a long, wild beard; and his clothes, though neatly stitched, were the oddest that I had ever seen, for they were virtually a mass of patches held together by thread. He looked so wild and unkempt that at first neither Bennett nor I knew whether we were confronted by a bandit or a Robinson Crusoe.

It turned out that he was wild as the Tarahumaras are wild, that is, as deer, with a gentle, timorous shyness that had come from a lack of association with other than Indians. In our *convento* he seemed like a recently awakened and still bewildered Rip Van Winkle reclaimed by a world which had almost lost its familiarity for him. He was much bedazzled by the few concomitants of civilization with which our expedition was supplied. And here his interest was in marked contrast to the attitude of the Indians. To them our equipment was so strange and exotic that they gave it only a passing flicker of attention. But he, hungering for any contact with civilization, had to have everything explained to him. Our guns, camera, scientific equipment, and supplies for preserving plants and animal skins all keenly interested him.

He wanted sugar and coffee, and suggested an exchange of these luxuries for *tortillas* that he would have sent from his ranch twenty miles away. We gave him what he desired, never expecting to taste any *tortillas* from his wife's *metate*. A few days later, however, a half-grown lad came to us, and with him was a week's supply of this Mexican bread. After having lived a month on the thick, coarse *tortillas* of the Indians, we were delighted with those of the Mexican woman, which were finer-ground and more expertly made.

The boy, even more so than the father, was as wistful and half-startled as a fawn around us. But he, too, succumbed to his curiosity and we were soon friends.

On his first visit Córdoba told us that he had passed our way a few days before, guiding the Jesuit Father, José Lara, to an unfamiliar corner of the vast sierra which was the priest's extensive parish. Unfortunately, they had not been able to stop on the down trip, and the padre planned to return by a different route.

Córdoba, however, had stopped to give us the priest's kind invitation to visit him at the mission of Norogáchic, some thirty miles away. It was suggested that the visit would be of the greatest ethnographic interest to us, provided we got there for the Tarahumara celebration of the Mexican Catholic ceremony of Epiphany. This is called *Los Tres Reyes* (The Three Magi), and is celebrated on January 6.

The Jesuit mission of Norogáchic is located in the center of the Tarahumara region of greatest population. Five thousand Tarahumaras live within a walking distance of fifteen miles from the mission. The festivities of the several communities of this region all center in Norogáchic at Epiphany, and are, therefore, more elaborate than those given elsewhere. I went to Norogáchic, but did not arrive in time. But that is another story, to be told later.

CHAPTER 5

▶ *Tarahumara Children and Adults*
▶ *at Play*

▶

▶

▶

▶

▶

▶

▶

▶

D uring our first month in the sierra, before the advancing cold made travel impossible, we spent considerable time visiting the individual *rancherías* of our large community. Those were happy days for us as we followed our guide in Indian fashion through the interminable avenues of great pines. Ever alert, he would often stop to pick for us some plant which the Tarahumaras especially prize. At other times his keen eyes would note faint signs left by a passing animal. To aid him in his trapping of zoological specimens for us, we had a line of traps set up; and his craft in placing these was astonishing, as he had never used steel traps before.

Lorenzo justified every encomium that has been written about primitive man's ability in following spoors. To him nature was truly an open book. A dislodged stone, a broken stem, told him a story, or enabled him to reenact in imagination some drama that had taken place uninterruptedly in the silence of the woods.

The Tarahumara's life is one of continual struggle against inhospitable environment. Not only insect pests, but foxes, coyotes, gophers, and numerous other wild animals seek to destroy his crops, for they seem to like corn as well as the Indians do. So from tracks and other signs the Tarahumara studies the animals that are his competitors and learns a great deal about them, whether he hunts them for his pot, or merely to protect his cornfield. In the sierra no excuses are accepted for failure, and the penalty of laziness, stupidity, or carelessness is an empty storehouse and subsequent starvation. The Tarahumara who knows his animal adversaries well respects their cunning, for he is very often taken in by it.

Besides knowing the habits and characteristics of wild animals, each man is familiar with the tracks and dispositions of his own domestic animals, and even many of those of his neighbors. Thus the track of a cow, for example, is frequently the autograph of its owner. The Tarahumara's greatest protection against cattle theft is his ability to trail a stolen cow to the thief's house.

One cold, wet day as we were making the rounds, so to speak, we came across a lone Tarahumara who was standing by a river with his sandals in his hands. Lorenzo asked him in Tarahumara what he was doing. He replied that he was running down a deer. That he had taken off his sandals was not surprising, because these always became as limp as cloth when they are wet;[1] but his seeming inactivity struck me as a strange method of running a deer to death. Knowing the fame of this tribe for hunting deer in this way, I naturally supposed that they took after the animal in much the same way as a cowboy, though mounted, takes after a steer.

But nothing is farther from the truth. The feat is a combination of both endurance and skill. Endurance is necessary because the animal has to be kept constantly on the move until it falls from exhaustion. The skill involved is that of following the animal for a day or two days without even seeing it, so accurately does the adult Tarahumara read the trail of his invisible quarry. When he finally overtakes the deer, often with its hooves worn to the quick, he throttles it. I have seen deerskins unmarked save for the cuts left by skinning.

The Tarahumara is as at home on the wide stretches of his sierra as we are on some of our city streets. No mystery to him is his own country, which is so baffling and confusing to a stranger. During babyhood he is carried all day on his mother's back as she follows the goats. Through childhood he roams the hills, herding the animals and exploring the ever widening horizons that unfold before his awakening intelligence, living constantly out-of-doors, and wandering over the countryside in search of coyotes, which frequently carry off the younger animals. At times we would catch them wrapped in their little blankets and sitting on . . . [Part of original text missing.—Eds.]

The toys of Tarahumara children reflect the patterns of tribal culture. In their games and pastimes the children re-create the industries and occupation of their elders. At this point I can do no better than to paraphrase my section of the monograph on Tarahumara culture.

The little Tarahumara girls are to be seen playing with a smooth stone for a *metate* and a smaller one for its *mano*. With these miniature, imitative utensils they make mud *tortillas*, as our children make mud-pies. Very solemnly they grind dirt and water to a muddy consistency, until the mixture falls from the end of the *metate* into a piece of oak bark which represents the *batea*, to be seen in every home in Indian Mexico. When a sufficient quantity of mud-dough is ground, they pat it into *tortillas*. These they pretend to cook, using a large potsherd for a *comal*, the clay griddle used all over Mexico.

Similarly do the boys ape the activities of their sires. They endeavor to emulate them in cutting down trees, and woe to the young scamp who dulls the keen edge of his father's axe! Thus at an early age they begin to practice the art of axemanship in which all the men excel. And by creating a make-believe world of toy animals and corrals and the like, they set up a semblance of adult culture.[2]

One of the most common toys is a stick, one end of which is carved in the shape of the hoof of a goat, sheep, or burro. The boy holds the other end in his hand, and using the stick as a crutch, skips along making tracks in the soft earth. This is considered great fun. In one house we saw the hoof of a cow carved to natural size in soft but thick pine bark. This toy was shaped like a sandal, and the straps were attached to it so that it could be worn on the foot. Near another house we observed crude representations of the heads of cattle. These had been cut from large branches, and twigs were used to serve as horns. They were used by the boys to imitate angry bulls locking horns in fierce, bellowing dispute or were roped to a stick with yucca fiber to represent toiling oxen.

Toy plows and other things of a similar nature are not uncommon. At the house of one family that had once lived near the railroad where ties were brought in by wagon, some enterprising lad had imitated a wagon. This no doubt greatly impressed his more isolated playmates. He had carved wheels from the thick, soft bark of pine, and for axles used small sticks. He had made a horse from similar material. After I had been a month or so among the wild Tarahumaras, this toy looked surprisingly sophisticated, because so few of the Indians had ever seen a wagon.[3]

Though in the absence of the husband, the wife may have to do his chores, or contrariwise, the man himself cook *pinole*, the division of labor between the sexes is more clearly drawn in the play of the children than it is in actuality. In play is achieved the pure ideal limited by neither time and space nor the "thousand natural shocks that flesh is heir to." Under a sloping rock which represents in miniature a cave in which the children live in the world of their elders, the little girls place their dolls. They play contentedly with whatever is available, the glowing imagination of childhood supplying that which may be lacking. In a Tarahumara child's fancy the wide flowering stem of a weed may well serve as the wide-flaring skirt of a woman. Green leaves are wrapped around short stems to represent the small blanket which the women wear. The much more simply attired Tarahumara man is sufficiently well represented merely by a pine twig a couple of inches long.

With the stage set thus, what do the children play? They are too young, of course, to participate in the common recreations of the grown-ups, which are the drunken parties, or *tesgüinadas*; they imitate these, however, in their games. Using the cup-shaped bases of acorns for the beer *(tesgüino)* pots, they pretend to get their dolls gloriously drunk, and put them through the antics that they have observed in their elders on such occasions of festivity.

In one instance I saw an even more elaborate setup. The children had erected a tiny stone house on the trail, complete even to the fireplace. Small stones had been arranged on end to represent people about the fireplace. The number of them indicated that the dolls, like proper Tarahumaras, were having a *tesgüinada* or a combination beer party and working "bee" to build and to celebrate the building of the house. Adjoining the house was a sheep and goat corral, such as the Tarahumaras often build. Little stones to represent the animals had been placed inside. The entire reproduction was not more than a foot square; yet, so well was it done, and so closely had it followed the pattern, that we had no difficulty whatsoever in recognizing the model and in reconstructing the game.

Often the boys would stage foot races similar to those run by their fathers. Such sport is encouraged as excellent training for later years. For these races the boys paint their legs with white earth, and even use the decorative though utilitarian runner's belt with deer hoof rattles hung between sections of the reed. The sound of these not only enables them to "run like deer," but also keeps them from "falling asleep," that is, dropping from exhaustion in the course of the cruel grind.

Thursday, November 27, was Thanksgiving Day! One of our neighbors living some five miles away decided to remove an accumulation of goat manure from a cave to his field several miles distant. But since manure is transported in a blanket rolled up and pinned with long skewers, such a task would easily have taken him a week. However, here was a good opportunity for a *tesgüinada*, or "bee," as an

American or Canadian farmer might call it. He ordered his wife to prepare a quantity of corn for the homebrew to which the tribe is addicted.

A bushel or so of corn had first been soaked in an *olla* of water for a day. Then to permit it to sprout, it was placed in a dark, damp hole. These holes are lined with pine needles, which also cover the cereal. After three or four days the corn is sufficiently sprouted to be ground thoroughly on the *metate*. Then, covered with plenty of water, it is boiled all day in a large *olla*. At this stage it has a sweetish taste.

From this point on the process becomes complicated. From the storehouse the man had taken his "boiling pots." These pots, which are never washed or heated, are always used for the mother ferment; and they are called "boiling pots" because the liquid, while fermenting, appears to boil. In the storehouse they are placed close together, for the Indians think that the pots "learn from each other" how to make the beer ferment.

To vary the flavor of the beer, wild bromegrass, which resembles oats, various lichens, roots, etc., are put into the pots. The Tarahumaras are connoisseurs of *tesgüino* beer. Indeed, their beer, though similar, is more complicated than that of the Huichols, who otherwise have a much richer culture.

With good reason are the Tarahumaras particular about their beer. It is vitally important in almost every aspect of their culture. All livelihood tasks more formidable than mere chores are accomplished by cooperative labor rewarded by this beer and nothing else. No social gathering larger than the family ever assembles at the church, except on Sunday, without *tesgüino* beer. And finally, any religious ceremony of importance would be unthinkable without the drunken effects of this beer.

By the time we arrived at the *ranchería* the manure had been hauled. The work, apparently, had been carefully organized. Our contribution to the festivity was tobacco. Of this the Tarahumaras are inordinately fond when in their cups; and they are always short, despite the fact that a crude variety grows wild in the gorges. Consequently we felt certain that our gift would ensure us welcome.

It had marked somewhat of a high point in our expedition when we felt that we were on sufficiently friendly terms with the Indians to attend their drunken parties; and it presented a real test of our success in handling primitive people, since during these bouts, as I have pointed out, the Indians emerge from their stolidity, as it were, and losing their fear and timidity rake up scandal and disputes from the times of their grandfathers, and fights and even murders occur so often that Mexicans are afraid to go to these brawls.[4]

We, who were the last to come, got there just as the workers were shaking the remains of their loads of dried goat dung from their blankets. There had been no great damage done to the blankets.

The men were gathering expectantly around the beer pots, or *ollas*. This was to be a two-*olla* fiesta only, but for the group this much would well serve. The Indian who had turned up first for work was given the honor of ladling out the beer in gourd dippers. Yet this was more than a nominal honor, for the Tarahumara etiquette forced him to take a dipper of beer himself for every one he gave out. Needless to say, he was soon drunk as a fool, and a substitute had to take his place. By the end of the bout I was "pinch-hitting" for the last substitute.

But in order to remain moderately sober and to end the festivities in this way, restraint was necessary. On the first round, when it was my turn to drink, I gulped down only one of the huge gourds of the stuff. Lorenzo and the others each took four gourds full.

Tesgüino is a rather good drink, although it reminded me of buttermilk. Four gourds of it fill the drinker as tight as a tick, as I found out on another occasion. After this first allotment, all the drinker has to do to fill up any displacement is tipple a little. Sometimes the displacement is sudden and rapid, and a reveller breaks from the group and regurgitates. One can watch the visible effect of the *tesgüino* on the Indians as the fumes begin to rise to their heads. Their eyes get glassy and their movements uncertain, but their faces and behavior become increasingly merry.

While the men were hauling manure for their host, the women had been working for their hostess, carding and spinning wool. When the men began to drink, they timidly remained together at one side of the yard. But as soon as the men were served, someone took the dipper and started around the circle of women.

Just before I drank, my guide lectured me a little on the etiquette of a Tarahumara drinking bout. Good old Lorenzo, he never failed to give me the same advice before every one of the many shindigs we attended. Gravely he would say, "*Don* Roberto, the reason that the Mexicans do not come to our *tesgüinada* is that the Tarahumaras get mad if they become familiar" (I have translated this phrase in mild terms) "with the women."

Hardly had I consumed my gourd of beer than the four guzzled down by Lorenzo began to work on him. He waxed more and more lively and talkative. The party itself began to brighten up, even for me on my moderate intake. Then Lorenzo made the Tarahumaras a long harangue on my account. I understood him to say that no less a personage than the revered *Don* Porfirio had given me permission to visit them. (The Tarahumaras have not yet learned that Díaz is dead, for he had been a sort of habit with them which the Revolution had failed to shake off. This shows how vague and nebulous Mexican government is to them.) He also told them emphatically several times that I was not a "gringo"; and perhaps it was just as well that he did, for apparently the Tarahumaras have taken from the Mexicans a fantastically distorted impression of Americans. His must have been a good sermon, for silence reigned throughout it.

A *tesgüinada* would never be complete without the music of the little violins and guitars that the Indians make with their pocketknives. The notes drawn out of these instruments, while wistful and somewhat melancholy, quicken the vitality of the revellers. Someone struck up an air. The women were beginning to succumb to the effects of the beer. They were restless. Suddenly one of them danced out into the men's section of the yard. First she began to dance and wrestle with a half-grown boy. Then she became amorously rough with one of the men who attracted her alcoholic fancy.

Lorenzo got drunk enough for the two of us. How he mouthed and mumbled his Spanish in my ear! This he would vary by an inarticulate song, an erratic dance, an irrelevant laugh. A lad I had met who was ordinarily modest and humble was loud and familiar. The boy who sold us eggs was there, parading himself in his new coat. The blue-eyed lad and a distant relative of Lorenzo's were present with all four feet in the *tesgüino* pot. Indeed, I knew them all, and when the party was over, I left them feeling them all to be my brothers. So much does liquor cut down social distance.

Lorenzo's garrulity was shared by the other men. When a Tarahumara is sober, he rarely utters a syllable; but when he is drunk, he loves to squat down by someone else and talk his head off. The man at the other end of the burst of speech nods gravely in a bored fashion, not understanding a word said. Then a talking fit may strike him, and the roles are reversed. But Lorenzo and I brought down the house, figuratively speaking, in several of these affairs by a mock Tarahumara sermon in Spanish. In a loud voice, which I would mimic, he would reel off a phrase interspersed with bits of the prayers:

Nosotros los Tarahumaras
Aquí en el mundo,
Por la señal
De la Santa Cruz . . .
(We, the Tarahumaras,
Here in the world,
By the sign
Of the Holy Cross . . .)

These *tesgüinadas* were always scenes of the wildest confusion, orgies a little difficult to limn for a civilized mind. To visualize them at all, try to imagine a group of excited, gesticulating, half-wild Indians, every member of which is, in the toper's phrase, full to the gills; some tumbling down and rolling in the dirt and ashes; some thrusting their feet into the blazing fire and being pulled out of it with their sandals smoking by those a little less drunk; men and women indistinguishably mixed up together; couples ogling and conspiring, soon to satisfy a momentary passion.

Occasionally terrible tragedies occur. After these parties there is always the long way home, and the steep cliffs awaiting those unfortunate who lose their direction on the dangerous trails. Or, on bitterly cold nights, they may drop by the wayside in a drunken stupor and freeze to death. Once or twice I saw the horribly scarred and burned bodies of small children that had been dropped into the fire by their drunken mothers. I saw the tiny leg of one forever drawn and helpless because of such carelessness. It was my good fortune, however, never to witness these accidents, although I did see one woman drop her child, immediately to be knocked down by her enraged and equally drunk husband.

Sometimes the Indians engage in violent, acrimonious quarrels. Once Lorenzo was drawn into an argument with his sister over a pig she thought she should have inherited twenty years before. It seemed to me that she had been put up to this by her husband; for all during the row he kept saying, *"Tata Sol"* (Sun Father), intimating that the sympathies of the Sun Father were with his wife. I never saw a serious fight, however, because generally the belligerent are disarmed by their soberer fellows. Yet most tribal murders and injuries are committed at these *tesgüinadas.* In the community, for instance, was one Indian who years before had killed his father-in-law by beating out the older man's brains when they were both drunk.

The sanitary aspects of these tribal entertainments are appalling. At one *tesgüinada*, after I had drunk from every dipper proffered me, I was horrified to see present a certain Indian whom I had met but temporarily forgotten. He was covered with sores, and was, I knew, slowly dying of syphilis. The padres at Sisoguichi were familiar with his plight. At his own recommendation I sent for some mercury ointment for him, but I never saw him again. Perhaps there is a special god who protects drunken men, ethnographers, and fools, and me on this occasion, all three in one![5]

Disregarding these rare negative features, *tesgüino* fulfills important positive functions in Tarahumara culture. It is obvious the alcohol is a powerful solvent of social distances. By drinking, these Indians step out of the chrysalis of still underdeveloped personalities, as it were, escaping for a short while the fear and timidity that oppress their sober, workday lives. They lose their apathy and begin to act as the majority of human beings act when they are drunk. It is an apparent fact, observable in human behavior, that alcohol paralyzes the neural centers that produce the higher attributes of personality and are acted upon by social conditioning. Drink essentially arouses the emotions and basic behavior patterns, and its effect is such that civilized men and primitive types act very much the same. Their inhibitions are removed, to a greater or lesser extent, depending upon what self-control is left them after the fumes have begun their work. They become loquacious and address all within their hearing and view, or whisper confidentially in their fellows' ears; they laugh and joke at nothing; they teeter and wobble.

With the Tarahumaras this is hardly an argument for temperance, because it is only through drink that the Tarahumara can break away sufficiently from his timidity to laugh, or joke, or talk at all, or have any familiar or affectionate relations with the other sex. Sexual functions are mainly associated with the *tesgüinada*, as far as I, not having a Tarahumara wife, was able to make out.

Most Tarahumara marriages, in the sense of permanent relationships between a man and a woman, generally result informally from the amorous excitement engendered by the *tesgüinada*. But besides this function the *tesgüinada* has a very important place in the social and economic life of the tribe.

There is no stable Tarahumara group other than the family. True, community affiliations are lifelong; but they function not more than once a week. The Tarahumara community is a social molecule with each atom, the individual family, in constant motion and in different territorial relationships to the others, due to the Indians' moving continually among their scattered fields, pasturing their animals, or shifting from the sierras to the caves of the *barrancas*. Of course this unceasing mobility is not wholly haphazard, since it follows the annual round, and each Indian is able to chronicle more or less accurately his neighbor's habitual time of arriving here or there. But the Tarahumaras are the rarity of nomadic agriculturalists, and this makes their social organization a very protean and amorphous one indeed.

Yet notwithstanding this mobility, there is still sufficient social stability to permit the calling together of neighbors for a working bee. Thus, next to the stable family and community groups, this unstable group of the neighborhood drinking is the most important in the social organization of the Tarahumaras. It gathers for either economic or religious (including curing) functions, and at least once a fortnight. Failure to attend these functions is met by severe sanctions, and nothing except crime will so quickly alienate an offender from his fellows. Those who attend these festivities comprise anyone who happens to be within call, within perhaps a radius of five miles. The religious function of this group manifests itself in the rather meager pagan cycle of ceremonies which will be discussed later. The economic functions are important.

The particular gathering I have just described was called as a working bee for the transportation of manure. So it is that every task greater than a chore is accomplished by the same token. For a few *centavos'* worth of beer each family has its work done by the whole neighborhood. Everyone comes even in anticipation of the social participation during work and before the drinking begins; for whether fields are being cleared, fences and buildings made, boards and *canoas* cut, or manure carried away, laughter and ribaldry are the dominant notes of the activities. And then, of course, there is the inducement toward work by the anticipation of the drinks to follow.

Thus, in Tarahumara economics, labor is literally a free commodity. Land, too, is free, because there is an abundance of it, such as it is. Indeed we noticed several excellent fields unoccupied in the community of Samachique as elsewhere, for a limiting factor of extensive agriculture is a lack of manure with which to make such land fertile. A young man has really taken his first step toward wealth when, like Lorenzo, he has bought his first cow, and has begun to build up a herd from which to obtain manure for his land.

Wealthy Tarahumaras, like Anastacio and Patricio, are men who have many cattle for this purpose. With available manure, they can occupy all the land they wish. And from this extra land they can raise corn for the beer which will attract labor to clear more land. This would seem to give a disproportionate advantage to the man with cattle, as I think it does.

In their ownership of cattle the wealthy Tarahumaras are capitalists with the psychology of capitalists. Interestingly enough, the revolutionary philosophy of the agrarian policy of the Mexican government found little sympathy with my wealthy informant, Lorenzo. The Mexican government had sent its important Agrarian Survey of Mexican Lands into the sierra, and for the first time in Mexican history this remote region was surveyed by triangulation. The surveyors tried to convert the Indians to the agrarian philosophy, but this was hardly necessary since in the sierra unoccupied land is communally owned and assigned to any Tarahumara who will farm it. Then the mission had preached that the wealthy should divide their cattle with the poor.

Remembering this, Lorenzo pronounced that old, unanswerable argument of the thrifty and prudent husbandman. "*Don* Roberto," he said, "when I was young, I went to the Mexican town and learned all that they know. I earned money, and saved it and bought a cow. I also raised onions. I told the Tarahumaras to buy cattle; but many of them didn't. Now I have many, while many have none. *Don* Roberto, do you think it is just for the government to take away my cattle and give them to others?"

In this specific case I had to reply that I couldn't see the justice of it, even though under the Tarahumara system of economics labor gets no economic reward.

Much has been written about communism in primitive tribes. From my own observations it doesn't exist. Here, in contrast, is an economic system of free labor repaid by the amenities of social participation. Within the Tarahumara group the whole system of agricultural production is based in no sense upon the intelligent self-interest of the workman. On the contrary, the motivation is strikingly uneconomic, and is expressed in a desire for social participation. This desire is so strong that many luckless Tarahumaras work only for others and enjoy such a relationship thoroughly. In and around Samachique were many impoverished Indians who had never the thrift or the ambition to begin collecting a herd of their own. They preferred to spend their time at the *tesgüinada*, working for the others who had, as rich old Lorenzo used to say, *con que*, "that which" (it takes to prosper) in Tarahumara economics, not money, but manure. These poor devils sometimes married the daughters of rich men who needed their labor. But this availed them little, because a husband who survives his wife inherits nothing. In giving us the life histories of the Tarahumara ne'er-do-wells, again and again Lorenzo would exhibit his marked, supercilious philistinism. Even more was his ire aroused to expression by those who had inherited cattle, and had wasted their capital by selling their cattle to buy corn instead of attending to the business of raising it.

The drinking activities of the *tesgüinada* constitute more than an essential element in the cooperative labor, making of it a party and fiesta. Drinking provides about the only diversion the Tarahumaras have from the ordinary, dreary, hard routine of their lives in the cold and sterile mountains. Among the Tarahumaras institutionalized drinking takes the place of the theater, symphony, or opera for sophisticated people. It provides their only escape from humdrum; and offers the only excitement and romance in their lives.[6] Small wonder, then, that such a pattern is so deeply embedded in their culture, and that two centuries of work by the priests have failed to uproot it. Indeed, this institutionalized drinking is the motivating dynamics of Tarahumara culture. So many of the principal patterns derive from it that, should it suddenly be abolished, the entire fabric would disintegrate into the dismal thing of shreds and patches exhibited by most North American tribes. The consequences of undermining the basic structures of aboriginal cultures are serious.

We have seen that the Tarahumara *tesgüinada* not only provides the most important social and economic integration of the tribe, but the most powerful escape motive in the culture. This latter provision had been so effective that it has inhibited the development of that other great escape element in human culture, religion.

In a certain sense, however, drinking for the Tarahumara is a sacred rite. The pots of liquor stand around a crucifix or some other representation of the cross; and the first drops of the mixture are offered to the pagan gods of the four points. Further, the pronounced exhilaration of intoxication is considered a sacred condition. This alliance of drunkenness to religion is to be seen also among our ancestors in their use of the word "spirits" for alcoholic liquids. The effects of liquor are felt, by the Tarahumara, to be somehow the work of greater and more potent spiritual beings than those which generally possess him.[7]

Yet excessive drinking generally inhibits all beautiful ceremony as well as mythology, the last being the primitive form of philosophy and theology. During the *tesgüinadas* of the Tarahumaras the great quantities of *tesgüino* consumed produce such perfect spiritual elevation that only a bare minimum of religious exaltation is required for seeming self-fulfillment. When the Tarahumaras get together, they are too drunk to concern themselves with rationalizing their spiritual elevation in an elaborate mythology. It is much easier simply to grind up ten *centavos'* worth of sprouted corn. To contrast this group with another, however, the Huichols get both a powerful social and economic integration and an escape from the humdrum of reality from a pagan religion that is beautiful in its rationale and its performance.

CHAPTER 6

> Curing, Races, and Death Customs
> among the Tarahumaras

Another of the important functions of the Tarahumara drinking party, or *tesgüinada*, has to do with curing, since a medicine man (or, technically, a shaman) is generally invited to these entertainments. He is paid three pesos to "cure" the host and his family. This curing is really a form of preventative "medicine." The host and his family are not sick: the ceremony simply protects them against possible future illness.[1]

At the *tesgüinada* I have just described, our host was too poor to afford three pesos, so no shaman was in attendance. However, while Lorenzo was drunk and in a good mood to dare anything, I asked him to see if my offer of three pesos would not tempt the best-known shaman in the community to practice his cures before Bennett and myself. To witness the esoteric ceremonies of almost any primitive group, one must first have established amicable relations with the members, especially with so bashful a tribe as the Tarahumaras. It was an excellent way, therefore, for us to check up on ourselves to see how well we were doing.

A few weeks later it was arranged that we should see a cure, provided that we would pay a couple of pesos extra for the *tesgüino* at the house of an Indian friend. The *tesgüinada* had to be given first, because the cunning shaman would not perform his simple tricks of prestidigitation until everyone was drunk. Thus do the shamans avoid being exposed. We needed no tasks done for us, so we decided to let one of the Indians benefit by the cooperative labor of the celebrants and have his manure transported.

The setting of our party, given at the house of a Tarahumara friend, was similar in almost every detail to that of the first *tesgüinada* we had attended, except that there were three pots of *tesgüino*. These were standing side by side on the grass, with the customary cross placed near them. Two of the pots were to be distributed by the first man to come to the work. The third was to be passed around by the shaman as a special honor to him.

The shaman is the most important and highly respected man in the Tarahumara community. This should not be surprising, since in a primitive group his person combines the prestige which, among us, is given to priests and doctors. Festivities were to begin as soon as he arrived.

We were not kept waiting very long. His entry was, apparently, timed for its effect. Every eye was upon him as he strode into our midst. It was really good theater. Then, with slow, deliberate dignity, he went around the group, touching everyone's outstretched hand as he passed. His host (our contributions toward the party had been kept quiet) then brought him a goatskin, and down he squatted beside his special *olla* of beer.

This shaman was a handsome man, tall, thin, and distinguished. His features were finely formed, and his expression betrayed a nervous sensitivity supported, however, by a grave dignity. His father before him had been the greatest shaman in the community, and the position had passed to him, though not through descent but his own ability. His father had prophesied that he himself and several other dignitaries of the community would die, and die they did, when with malign force the flu epidemic struck this remote corner of Mexico as it did the rest of the world. The Tarahumaras died so rapidly that there was hardly time enough to bury them in the caves, as the tribe had done with their dead before the Spaniards came. There was no time to carry the dead to the *camposanto*.

This shaman, like his father and all native medicine men, was an archconservative, and bitterly opposed to any change in Tarahumara culture. He hated the Catholic padres and all their customs, and never went near the Catholic church in Samachique. During my sojourn among the Huichols, the sophisticated cousins of the Tarahumaras, the leading shaman manifested a similar bitter aversion.

The father of the present Tarahumara shaman was so hostile to the Church that he would not be buried in the "*camposanto*," flu epidemic or none, even though his high place in the community merited him such a last resting-habitation. Rebel that he was, he chose to be buried in a cave in consistency with his forefathers. At a later date we visited this crypt, which had evidently been used before his death, and had been opened to receive his body. A rubble wall enclosed the remains. The structure was identical with those of prehistoric burials that I had found in the archaeological sites, the only difference being the evident recency of portions of the mud and stone wall, which had been rebuilt to enclose the latest occupant.

But we are concerned now with the quick and not the dead, with living Tarahumaras soon to be made hilariously happy. The drinking was about to begin. The Indian who had come first to work offered one of his pots of beer to the pagan gods. This was done as at the first *tesgüinada* by his making the sign of the cross and then holding a bowl of beer above his head in recognition of the upper-region gods, namely, the Sun Father (identified also with the Christian God) and the Sky Mother (identified with the Virgin Mary).[2] Then, dipping a stick in the liquor, he offered a few drops of it to the unidentified gods of the four points. This offering was made three times. The shaman repeated the ceremony for his *olla* of beer. Soon *tesgüino* was flowing freely from both bowls, with the guests participating in order of their acknowledged importance in the community. Bennett and I, though underwriters of this party, came neither first nor last. But this at least permitted us to believe that we were doing alright.

Then Bennett and I, succumbing to the general levity of the occasion, decided to entertain the Indians by playing jazz on our pocket combs. These we wrapped in Scott's tissue, which we carried as one of the few luxuries of the expedition. We were just bringing down the house of drunken, exuberant Indians, when in rushed Lorenzo, almost inarticulate with anger. This was a curing party, an affair of great solemnity, and our innocent outburst was, therefore, an egregious breach of Tarahumara etiquette. Quite upset, he stormed at us like an affronted schoolmarm. "*Serio*, you must be serious. This is not the time for fun. The shaman was just about to begin his curing of the family, and you had to start that racket. Now I don't know if he will or not."

We were humbly contrite, for of course we were eager to witness the thaumaturgy of the shaman. Looking around we noticed that the shaman had gone. Fortunately, however, he had not gone off in a huff with his priestly dignity slighted, but was outside with Lorenzo, who was to be his assistant. They were arranging the simple paraphernalia for the curing. This included a couple of ordinary bowls and a half-dozen reed tubes about four inches long, a modest array indeed for safeguarding the health for the community of Samachique.

The following description of the curing of the Tarahumara José María and his family conforms closely to the notes taken at the time by Dr. Bennett and myself and published in our monograph, *The Tarahumara*.

When about half of the beer in the shaman's *olla* had been distributed, the shaman came in again and sat down by the *olla*. A blanket was folded and laid before him. On this, and in front of him, those to be cured were to kneel. The buzz of drunken voices died down, and all eyes turned toward the shaman. Soon José and his family appeared. They knelt on the blanket.

Lorenzo handed the shaman two small bowls, one filled with hot water, the other empty. Into the hot water the shaman put three of the reed tubes. The shaman then removed his two rosaries, each made of beads of the seeds called "Job's-tears," and dipped the ordinary crucifixes dangling from them into the water. With these he marked crosses in the air before the heads, shoulders, and knees of the patients. After this, for purposes of the "cure," he hung one rosary on José María and the other on the wife.

Then the shaman took one of the tubes from the hot water, and placing one end at the corner of José's left eye, sucked gently at the other end. He ejected the contents of his mouth into the empty bowl, which was being held by Lorenzo nearby. Then he changed tubes, and sucked at José's right eye. He did this to each of those kneeling before him, spitting into the bowl and changing tubes after each cure. At the end of this procedure he took a drink of *tesgüino*, and even spat a bit of this into the bowl. Dr. Bennett and I, who were only a few feet from the activities, watched everything closely. The shaman had apparently chewed up some bits of corn and, possibly, bits of white buckskin. These he had ceremoniously ejected into the bowl to simulate the maggots he is supposed to be able to suck from his patients, whether they are sick or well.

José María now got to his feet. The shaman gripped the Indian's leg with both hands just above the knee. He massaged the leg vigorously, as if working something down to the ankle. Then he sucked on the ankle with one end of his tube, and spit the results into the bowl.

The bowl containing the spittle and the "maggots" was then disposed of by Lorenzo, who carried it deferentially around the fire three times, and then dumped it mouth downwards into the ashes and covered it over. The water in which the tubes had been kept was sprinkled in three circles around the fire.

Both Lorenzo and the shaman did everything with the greatest punctilio and seriousness; and throughout the entire performance of these miracles the other Indians, drunk as they were, looked on in respectful and awed silence. Soft music on the violin and guitar accompanied the sacred rites. At no time were the contents of the bowl ever examined. What worthy Indian in his right mind would question such serious and esoteric business? It was, of course, the simplest and most obvious of flimflam, but the Indians accepted it to the letter.

It is a truism that Fortune, besides being blind, is also indiscriminate, and scatters her bounties, as it were, like grapes, in bunches. Up to this point Bennett and I had mentally been shaking hands with each other, congratulating ourselves on having been present at this curing. Imagine my increased delight when Lorenzo came up to tell me that for the three-peso fee I had promised to contribute toward the occasion the shaman would also "cure" me. Either the shaman was afraid that we would welsh on our part of the bargain, or else we had achieved a stand-in with the Indians. No doubt both reasons were true. Thus it was, at any rate, that the "cure" of "Zingg's neck" became embalmed forever in the vast repositories of scientific knowledge.

Lorenzo presented me to the shaman, and the three pesos changed hands. I told the shaman that I had a sore neck. This was true, although I didn't add that I had twisted it while sleeping on the hard floor of the *convento*.

The shaman again took his place near the *tesgüino* pot, with a folded blanket spread before him. Lorenzo and Sebastian, our official purveyor of eggs, then led me to the blanket, where I knelt. The shaman certainly earned his three pesos; for when he began to "operate" on me, he was as nervous and frightened as a stagestruck child, and his eyes flashed wildly and excitedly as though they were looking for an avenue of escape. His was the same do and dare expression that I had observed on the face of the *gobernador*, when I had first approached that official. There can be no question about the fearful timidity of the Tarahumaras when even their most esteemed leaders suffer such qualms in facing the friendliest of outsiders.

The shaman, however, could not flee; and actually trembling, he began his cure of my sore neck. At first he seemed afraid to place the tube on my neck to suck on it. But in his nervous features I was able to read the emotions that racked him in his unfamiliar role of curing a foreigner; and I saw or seemed to see him argue himself into acquiescence and decide that he could hardly make so perfunctory a performance with all his fellow Tarahumaras looking on. He steeled himself, and gently placed the end of the tube against my neck. He sucked on the tube. Then hurriedly he spit the contents of his mouth into the bowl held by his assistant, Lorenzo, and the bowl was quickly dumped in the fire, almost as though "maggots" from an *Americano* were unspeakably noxious. The "cure" was finished.

Then Lorenzo and Sebastian took my hands and raised me from where I knelt. Since I did not know how a Tarahumara acts on such august occasions, they spun me around three times in the ceremonial circuit that the patient must make to complete the cure.

I certainly supposed that the shaman himself knew this was all a staged show; and of course he did. But a few days later he called at the *convento* to inquire after the effects of his magic. I assured him that, thanks to him, my neck was much better, though this was because I had changed my sleeping posture.

A far cry from science, such simple charlatanism is considered by the Tarahumaras to be the greatest medicine in the world, both remedial and preventive. At this point appears clearly the fundamental difference between the thought processes of the primitive and those of the civilized man. Men are civilized to that degree to which they think and act logically and are motivated by a spirit of free inquiry in a search for objectively demonstrable truth. Relatively few civilized people are really "civilized," however; and primitive men like Lorenzo arrive ultimately at a stage where they are as nearly civilized as their environment will permit.[3]

In Tarahumara society there is another class of high prestige besides the shamans, the officials, and the rich old men. This is comprised of young men who represent the community in the important intercommunity foot races. These foot races constitute the only consequential and formal intercommunity activity; and their importance may be judged from the fact that the Tarahumaras call themselves *Rarámuri* (foot racers, from the Tarahumara word, *rará*, foot). It is unusual for a primitive tribe to distinguish or identify itself by descriptive terminology, most tribes calling themselves "the people," or something of the sort. From this native word, *Rarámuri*, however, the Mexicans have derived the name Tarahumara.

The Tarahumaras are probably the greatest distance runners in the world. Thus their name is especially appropriate. In their races the members of each team (from the start to the finish) kick a wooden, or sometimes stone, ball. This sounds a little worse than it actually is, particularly when we consider the remarkable distances covered, which sometimes amount to as great as one hundred miles. From long practice, however, the runners have learned to put their feet under the ball so neatly that they can toss it on almost without losing their stride and certainly without injury to themselves. And as Dr. Bennett points out, the other runners keep ahead of the kicker, so no time is lost.

In an interesting little book in German, Arthur E. Grix, a reporter for the Olympic Games in Los Angeles in 1932, went from there to the Tarahumaras to study their racing prowess. He retraced many of our steps around Creel, and vividly describes a race of 265 kilometers which he saw run there, day and night, much as we saw one there in 1930. He collected accurate statistics, while I was contented to watch the spectacle by day, made much more dramatic at night by the hundreds of torches held by onlookers to illumine the 40 kilometer course run more than five times, a total distance of 265 kilometers. This multiplied by ⅝ transposes this distance in kilometers into a distance of miles, which equals the extraordinary distance of 150 miles.

Such amazing feats are possible only because the Tarahumaras run from childhood. Indeed, it should be said that they never walk, even on the trail. They can run all day at a jog pace. Over the rough terrain of their sierra no animal can travel so fast; and I doubt whether a horse could match them for distance even on a level surface. Carrying a heavy burden on their backs they will go more than twice as far in a day as that sluggish animal, the burro, with a similar load. It is because of their good legs that they have little use for a pack animal; and only once during the nine months I was in the sierra did I see a Tarahumara mounted.[4]

I saw several of these kicking-races over courses of varied lengths run by both men and boys. Indeed, the racing pattern is so pronounced in Tarahumara culture that even the women stage competitions, although their races hardly compare with those of men. On their own mountainous courses, however, the Tarahumara women racers would outrun most American distance runners.

A race is the most exciting event in the whole round of Tarahumara life. Not even the pomp and pageantry of the Catholic ceremonies arouse such keen interest or are observed with such scrupulous care. The young men who represent the community become heroes, if they win, and on their running loyal community members will bet their fortunes.

The racers are picked by an officer who manages the team. For an important race the participants are those who have had the best records in the little races that are constantly being run. From two to twelve runners make up a team, six or eight being the average number.

For three nights before an important race the chosen runners shut themselves up with their manager and a few old men, some of whom are generally shamans. They are given "cures," both real and imaginary. Their legs are massaged with a decoction made from cedar boughs, and then oiled with goat grease or olive oil.

On the last night all the runners stay in the same house along with the old men, who perform magical ceremonies. These ceremonies have been described by both Dr. Bennett and Lumholtz. The runners invoke many magical aids. Lumholtz tells of one manager of a team who went to an ancient burial cave, taking with him the two balls to be used by his team. There he disinterred one of the corpses and appropriated a leg bone, for obvious reasons, of course. He then made offerings of *tesgüino* and food to the leg bone, so that the spirit of the dead would help his team. The powerful spirits of magical plants are often utilized by the runners. We shall see the ill effects of this practice, however, that came to one runner years after he had indulged it.

On the morning of the race the runners paint their legs and fasten on their magical belts, hung with deer hooves, etc., which are to aid them in their running. Each team prepares traps for its competitor. These are necromantic in nature, such as herbs or human bones buried on the course in hope that the rival team will step on them and thus be weakened.[5] Each team, of course, takes precautions to avoid its own traps. Countermeasures against the traps of their opponents are also provided for, and usually consist of special objects carried in the runners' belts.

As the time for the race approaches, each *gobernador* of the two communities involved appoints an equal number of judges. These men station themselves in pairs, one man from each community, all along the course. They watch to see that no unfairness is committed.

Meanwhile other officials of the race place bets. Races furnish the Tarahumaras their only inducement for betting, and when competition between two communities is keen, they will bet almost everything they possess. The stakes are in goods, of course, for money is seldom used for any purpose by the Tarahumaras.[6]

Curing, Races, and Death Customs among the Tarahumaras   [83]

Those who place the bets stalk among the crowd displaying and crying any article that has been put up as a stake. It may be a knife, an axe, a violin, a big ball of wool, a blanket, a yard of cloth, anything. If it is a yard of cloth, the official matches it with a similar stake belonging to someone who has bet conversely. Balls of wool are likewise matched, and any difference is made up by minor items. The official then ties both stakes together in a bundle, and the winner takes all. Often, in a big race, the Tarahumaras bet goats or cattle. These are similarly tied together to await the outcome of the race.

Hundreds of spectators are attracted to these events. Some of them scatter all over the long course; the majority of them, however, remain near the finish line, where the race begins and ends, and where most of the betting takes place.

Each team lines up behind its ball. The judge signals, the kickoffs are made and the race is on. Hour after hour the runners plunge forward in long, easy strides, hidden most of the time from the spectators of any one place. Afternoon succeeds morning, and night comes on; but the race still continues.

It is at night that the scene is the most spectacular of any other in Tarahumaraland. Torches of pitch pine, which burns like oil, are lighted all along the course. Hundreds of these blaze across the sierra, and flicker in the distance like a myriad of fireflies. And through this weird illumination, watched over by the dim outlines of the towering pines, dart the glistening figures of the runners followed by the frenzied, encouraging shouts of the half-naked spectators.

Excitement mounts as the race progresses. The runners begin to show signs of fatigue; for sometimes these trying competitions have lasted as long as seventy-two hours, continuing on into the following days. The wives or female relatives of the runners prepare *pinole*, and the runners stop and hastily gulp this down for strength, and then catch up with their teammates a little farther on. Sometimes water is thrown on them to refresh them. Despite these aids the runners one by one begin to fall out of the race exhausted, until finally only the strongest are left.

As at night the spectators rush along with the runners, carrying torches to assist them in finding the ball, so toward the end of the race crowds throng about the sweating participants, urging them to their greatest efforts. Finally one lone runner triumphantly kicks the ball of his team across the finish line, and the race is over. All the staked goods immediately change hands.

Members of winning teams enjoy considerable prestige in their own communities; and runners who consistently win acquire an outstanding reputation throughout the tribe. They may also get a "commission" on the bets won, and this, too, adds to the esteem in which they are held. For such reasons a runner will force himself to almost any extreme in order to win a race.

A good illustration of this extravagant zeal was our enemy, Patricio, the *teniente*. Though now a respected elder in the community, in his youth he had been a famous runner. To insure his continued success he had conquered his fear of a little peyote, which the Tarahumaras think of as possessing unusual power and strength. Though a very "dangerous" thing to do, he had made a practice of carrying one of these in his runner's belt, and never failed to win. Finally, after one race, he found the cactus gone. He had lost it during the race. This was a terrible misfortune, for it meant that the spirit of the plant which had aided him would now turn against him. Indeed, the shaman in charge of the racers told him that he would die from the curse of that magic cactus. A month or so after we arrived at Samachique, Patricio became sick. He believed implicitly that this was due to the curse of the cactus, and decided that he was going to die. And die he did.

Early in the morning of December 2, Patricio's son came to the *convento* and said that his father had been sick for a month, and that the repeated cures of the shaman had done no good. In fact his case was so serious that the medicine man had given it up. Would I let bygones be bygones and give him the benefit of my medicine?

The *teniente* had indeed changed. Lack of proper food and a decreasing interest in life had wasted him away. For some time he had been unable to eat anything but cooked mush, which the Indians prepare from *pinole* especially for their sick.

Fortunately my priceless guide, Lorenzo, had accompanied me, and he had advised me to take along all my limited medical equipment, quinine pills, castor oil, iodine, cotton, and bandages. Since I didn't have the remotest idea what was wrong with Patricio, and at that time knew nothing about the cactus episode of his youth, the medicine I had with me necessitated my diagnosing his sickness as malaria. I opened my "medicine bag" and ceremoniously laid out its contents, so much more impressive than the paraphernalia of any Tarahumara shaman. The patient, the family, and my guide nearby watched me like hawks.

Intending to give the patient a pill, I ordered water. But thoughtful Lorenzo saw that I wasn't proceeding with half enough ostentation ever to hope to effect a cure. He took the water and pill from my hands. With the pill between his fingers he made an elaborate sign of the cross over the recumbent form of the sick man. Then, with the aid of the wife, he raised Patricio and administered the pill. This done, he turned to me and whispered, "Now take your medicine [iodine] and paint a cross on his chest and another on his forehead."

I solemnly opened the bottle of iodine, poured some on a bit of cotton, and did as I was requested. The umber of the iodine stood out from the deep bronze skin of the Indian like a cicatrice. Here at least was ocular evidence of my cure.[7]

After this I called every few days and repeated the cure. But Patricio faded away. Finally his eyes turned yellow. At this turn of events I changed my diagnosis from malaria to jaundice. But I didn't alter my remedy, because my doctorate is in philosophy, not medicine.

Since oranges were available at unbelievably cheap prices, I ordered that Patricio's diet of mush be augmented by oranges. But, though Patricio was rich and could well have afforded my prescription, he told his children that this was a needless expense. He had offended the cactus in his youth, he said, and was sure to die anyway. So apparently my cure was to be no more effective than that of a shaman in sucking out maggots.

In my diary for December 2, I find this item: "It would seem that we shall soon have a first-class funeral to watch. . . ." My diary for December 4 reads as follows. "A recent snowstorm has turned again into rain. The river is high, the ground soft. Just another of those days around the fireplace writing down information from Lorenzo, who makes these days the most profitable of all. Early, all was quiet, and it promised to continue so. However, by God's will, it turned out differently. As anticipated by Lorenzo, my patient died during the night. At noon Patricio was brought to the church wrapped in his blanket trussed to a pole. His sons, brothers, and neighbors accompanied the body."

The mourners placed their charge under the bells at the porch of the church and knocked at our door. Lorenzo temporarily dropped his role of informant and assumed that of *maestro* to give the deceased full benefit of the clergy as such is understood among the Tarahumaras of Samachique. First, for perhaps a quarter of an hour, he tolled the bells over the body. The pallbearers meanwhile entered the *convento* to warm themselves at our fire, since they had walked barefooted from their *ranchería* a couple of miles away. Only the dead man's brother remained outside. He was our egg-man Sebastian, who had been well-disposed toward us despite his brother's animus.

When Lorenzo thought that the dead man had enough of the bells, he motioned to Sebastian and me to place the body inside. We carried it into the church, and set it down as directed. Lorenzo produced four candles. These he placed at each side of the body and at the head and feet, one for each of the four cardinal points. Then he knelt at the altar and intoned through his list of prayers, the meagerness of which was compensated for by repetition.

The prayers finished, Lorenzo arose and took from the altar a small "*santo*," the representation of a saint revered all over Mexico. Carrying this reverently in his arms, he made three ceremonial circuits around the dead man. He repeated this ritual, this time with a small crucifix which had been hanging over the altar. After these pitiful church ceremonies intermingled with the pagan symbolism of the four cardinal points and the mystical number three, we continued without benefit of clergy by carrying the body back to the porch of the church. There we placed it again directly under the bells.

Then Lorenzo began one of those characteristic sermons which the Tarahumaras include in every ceremony. "Patricio," he said gravely to the deceased, "you are dead now. You must go to the Sky World and not come back and harm your wife or your children. They will make three ceremonies to aid you on your pilgrimage to the other world, and prepare everything necessary to further your journey. Therefore, you must forget about them, and not come back and harm them."

By this time the others were warm enough to leave the *convento*. They carried the dead man across to the hill where the "*camposanto*" was located. In doing so, they had to wade knee-deep through the freezingly cold water of the little valley stream. As I recall, Lorenzo was wearing the boots Bennett had given him. Together the three of us plunged into the icy water. When we got to the other side, he was childishly amazed and pleased that his feet were neither wet nor cold.

The "*camposanto*" enclosed perhaps an acre. It was so overgrown with high grass that we had never suspected it to be within three hundred yards from the *convento* in which we had lived for three months. At one time it had been enclosed by a low wall; now only a few stones remained as boundary markers. About fifty graves were in this Indian cemetery. Each was clearly marked, because the Tarahumaras carefully cover their graves with large rocks to protect them against coyotes.

Just outside one corner of the graveyard was a mound of such rocks. Thinking that here must lie the remains of some sinner who had been denied normal Christian burial, and recalling particularly the illegitimate baby which had been buried here months before, I interrogated Sebastian. Sebastian understood either my question or my gesture; for mustering up all his Spanish he replied, *"Cimarrón."*[8] This word means wild, or untamed, and by it he referred evidently to some pagan Tarahumara recusant who had opposed Christianity with its ceremonies and church building, and had refused to be buried in a Catholic graveyard.

The mourners began to dig a grave for Patricio. They had brought with them an old shovel and crowbars kept for this purpose, for the soil was quite stony. One of the workers was the notorious Tarahumara who had killed his wife's father. Patricio had apparently needed this Indian's services around his *ranchería*, because he had risked becoming his second father-in-law.

The grave was dug to a depth of three feet, but even at that there was little room to spare. Indeed, it was such a snug fit that the body had to be forced into the narrow space. Then Sebastian stepped up to the grave for a last look at his brother. He pulled a few hairs from his own head, and tossed them on the body as a token of his close relationship to the dead man. Then all approached the grave. Each threw in a handful of dirt. In unison they spoke words to this effect, "Here you lie, and we put in just a little dirt, as shall be done to us when we die. Then, we shall talk like brothers." The words were uttered with deep feeling and sincerity.

When this little ceremony was over, the grave was filled in. At this stage of events the relatives did not seem at all downcast. Each seemed to have suddenly undergone some metamorphosis of spirit, to have attained, pagan though he was, an awareness of the immutability of death and the futility of all human protest in the face of it. They chattered gaily and amicably among themselves, and even gave me permission to help them with the work. When the last shovelful of earth was patted firmly into place, large stones were brought to foil the coyotes.

This work finished, the Indians all went to a nearby *arroyo*. There they washed their hands, faces, and legs. Then they built a roaring fire of green cedar boughs. The aromatic odor of cedar is considered of great magical value either in curing disease or removing contamination. When the burning wood began to give off dense, billowing clouds of pungent smoke, the men entered the smoke, permitting it to coil about their bodies, and rubbing themselves as though they were bathing in water. Thus did they purify themselves of the contamination of their necessary contact with the dead man during the burial. Naturally Bennett and I participated in these ablutions, both real and fancied.

Then we filed back to the *convento*. We boiled some *pinole* (the ground flour of parched corn, which is the staple food of the Tarahumaras) to make a mush called *atole* in Spanish. The Indians relished this with the added luxury of our sugar and canned milk. When they had finished eating, we passed around copies of the National Geographic Magazine; and the Indians remained in the *convento* for the rest of the afternoon, chatting and laughing as if they had entirely forgotten the solemn events of the morning.

Indeed, it soon became quite apparent that these primitives were much more realistically minded about death than most people. In this instance they simply thought that because Patricio had offended a plant, his soul had gone off on a journey from which it would not likely return. They certainly hoped that it wouldn't, since for them the dead return only to harm. And there was not much else they could do, either before or after death.

Among the Tarahumaras when death has occurred in a household, the surviving members of the family absent themselves from the house for three weeks and prepare food to offer the dead in a series of ceremonies to help him on his journey. For a man three of these ceremonies, offered at intervals, must be made. For a woman four must be given, because, as the Indians express it, a woman is not so strong on the trail and needs more help. After the last ceremony the dead man arrives in his new world of the sky, and the critical time of ritual danger is over.[9]

When the ceremonies are finished, not only do the Tarahumaras no longer fear their dead, but their attitude changes and becomes curiously callous. Lumholtz relates that in the course of his archaeological work he paid one Indian three pesos for the skeleton of the man's mother-in-law. Nor do the Tarahumaras hate this relative, which might account for so realistic an attitude toward her remains. In my archaeological work the Indians had no compunction in leading me to all the ancient graves they knew; and for pay they would work with my Mexican laborers in excavating such burial sites without showing the slightest fear or sense of danger.[10]

However, such attitudes arise only after the death ceremonies have been completed. A widow particularly is in a situation of special danger, and she even may not remarry for a long time afterwards.[11] For several days following a death every member of the family is badly frightened at the possibility of the return of the deceased; for, as almost everywhere in the primitive world, this could only be for harm. The first night after a death, offerings of food are made under the roof of the house in which the person has died.[12] This is done by a parent or a grandchild, or by either a brother- or a sister-in-law. These last two relatives stand in the favored joking relationship with the deceased.

Among the Tarahumaras a sister-in-law will unexpectedly pull the clout from her brother-in-law and join in the howls of laughter of others as he runs to seek shelter. Far more Rabelaisian tricks and practical jokes are commonplace between these relatives by marriage, although ordinarily a Tarahumara would never think of such unseemly behavior even with his wife.

Such relationships were revealed to us in the information concerning death ceremonies. The Tarahumaras are so timid, however, that they never practice this joking relationship in the presence of foreigners. It is astonishing, perhaps, that this tribe should have such a custom at all, though it is very common among primitive groups.

The grandfather-grandchild relative may be the first to make the offerings, and, like the aforementioned relatives, touch the dead man's things. This, however, is due not to a joking relationship but rather to an affection and friendship which unite relatives of alternate generations all over the world. Certainly among us, this relationship is a most affectionate one; and among many tribal groups that existing between grandparents and grandchildren is formally expressed in much more striking forms than among the Tarahumaras. Even so, for a grandchild to leave a small dish of food under the roof of the house of the dead is rather strange.

The three or four ceremonies which the descendants give to "despatch" the soul of the dead are quite elaborate. Unfortunately I did not see them. But Dr. Bennett made a complete description of those given for Patricio, whose obsequies he attended. I shall paraphrase his information on the Land of the Dead.

After death a man starts on a journey to his new home and new life; for death is considered not the end of life but merely a change from one state to another. Though he walks rapidly, his is a long way. Each of the ceremonies after his death is to help him on. At each ceremony he receives offerings of food to give him strength. And as he eats the spiritual essence of the food, smokes the cigarettes, and drinks the beer that is offered him, the sound of the dancing accompanying these is supposed to make him happy. After the last ceremony he reaches his destination, and cannot return to harm the living.

But until all this is done, he may return. If he needs his animals to accompany him, he may cause them to die. Or if he needs his children to help him herd the animals, he may likewise call them to the land of death. But fortunately for the living, they believe that once the last ceremony is completed, the souls of the dead must necessarily remain in their own land.

The Land of the Dead is a land of opposites. There night is as the day of the living. The moon is the source of heat and light. When it is cold on earth, it is warm in the Sky World. The dead sow in winter, and reap in March.

Because of these anomalies of the Land of the Dead, bats are related to the dead, because they fly at night. Bats are not considered souls, however.

The Tarahumaras think that souls change into butterflies and large moths. The soul, they say, is like the imago of the butterfly that flies away in death leaving only the chrysalis. This poetic analogy is strengthened by the presence, in the sierra and gorges, of large moths and butterflies with brightly colored wings, the spots of which are considered to be the eyes of the dead.

There was a particularly cold December day in the sierra, with flurries of snow and a freezing, biting wind. In spite of the cold, however, the Indians still remained in the heights in order to celebrate the ceremonies of the Christmas season. Theirs seemed to be a genuine sacrifice, considering their poor shelters and lack of clothing save for the thick blankets the women had woven. And yet I wondered if they had really stayed to honor Him whose birthday they were to celebrate, and whom, not knowing His right name, they called Saint Joseph of Christ. I had agreed with the Jesuit priest who had said to me, "The religious springs of the Tarahumaras are deep and powerful." But still my feeling was that the Indians had remained in the sierra also because of the beer and the good cheer that abound in the Christmas ceremonies.

At any rate it was so cold this day that the Indians did not come to the church for prayers. We were alone most of the morning, until a Tarahumara arrived, seemingly deposited at our door in a windy gust of snow. He was thoroughly chilled and chattering with cold, and with good reason, since, like all Tarahumaras, his feet were unprotected save for his thin sandals. He left his burro, and dashed in to our fire, certain of a welcome.

The Indian was doubly welcome, because on his burro he had brought two crates of oranges to sell us. He was a rather Mexicanized Indian, and spoke a little Spanish, thus accounting for his use of a burro in transporting goods. But Mexico is a country of such glaring contrasts that it did not seem unusual for us to buy, in the midst of a snowstorm, oranges that had been picked the day before. The fruit had come from the Indian's orange trees in the depths of the *barrancas*, where it was warm and balmy.

Fortunately for the purveyor of oranges, we had just killed a goat, and had quite a supply of fresh meat on hand. We gave him a generous meal. We had cooked the entire carcass by boiling, and I had over-salted the soup, or something of the sort, which had to be thrown away. The orange-boy was deeply shocked at this waste of food.

The first food we set before him had, apparently, only whetted his appetite. So Bennett and I decided that we would find out how much a savage can eat. The results were amazing! We ladled out food to this Indian in amounts that were astonishing. I began to think that he had an accordion-like stomach that expanded and would continue to expand indefinitely.

It is a commonplace of anthropology that primitive people can go for a long time without food, and then gorge like pythons. Our "guinea pig" certainly corroborated this and suffered no ill effects the following day, though during the night he passed an unconscionable and disturbing amount of gas. The last observation will probably be new to science, in its present connection at least; but we ought to know, for we slept in the same room and were kept awake most of the night by the man's "thunders," as the Mexicans euphemistically call such phenomena.

This being Sunday, the *gobernador* had to make his usual long trip from his distant *ranchería*. Accompanying him was a Spanish-speaking Indian . . . [Part of original text missing.—Eds.] . . . accounted for the Indian's knowledge of Spanish and Córdoba's ability to speak Tarahu-mara. Each had been the other's tutor and pupil.

Besides learning a smattering of Spanish at the "station," Isidro had done odd jobs around the place whenever mule trains had passed through with their pack loads of silver bars. Thus he knew how to sad-dle or pack a mule, could make coffee, and was in general a very handy man around camp. These techniques are so rare among the Tarahumaras of Samachique that he promised to be quite useful to us later, as indeed he was. The meagerness of his Spanish, great, however, for Samachique, may be judged from my diary, which contains the following note: "When he came in, he asked me for medicine to cure a child who (as far as I can make out) either has been sick for a year or else is a year old. 'Since I have nothing to do tomorrow,' I said to him, 'come back and I will then go to your *ranchería* with you.' So he and the *gobernador* stayed all night. We slept as thick as fleas on the floor of the front room of the *convento*. The Indians, wrapped only in their blankets, wedged themselves fan-fashion around the big fire in the fireplace."

Early the next morning I made ready to go with the Indians to the *ranchería* of Isidro. The trip promised to take me to a distant part of the community that I had not yet visited.

Soon after we were on our way, I learned that when you hike with Tarahumara Indians you travel fast and waste no time either in talk or banter. I am sure they thought they were traveling slowly to accommodate me, the *Americano;* and yet they took me over the hills at a rate I had never equalled before. Fortunately, after three months in the sierra, I was in good trim. And after I had gained my second wind, so to speak, our swinging up hill and down dale through forests of great pines gave me a feeling of muscular well-being that I had never experienced while living in the city.

The snow had changed to a raw drizzle, so our furious pace had its value in keeping us warm. The Indians were wrapped to the chins in their thick blankets. These hung crosswise from their shoulders, with one corner tucked under the left armpit, and the other corner extending over the opposite shoulder. Hour after hour as the Indians strode through the woods these remained in place as though by magic. Later, after I traded my sheepskin coat to Lorenzo, I learned the trick.

The drizzle turned to a hearty downpour, and in a short while both the Indians' blankets and my coat were wet through. The Indians alleviated their lot, however, by beating the excess water out of their blankets on rocks and trees that we passed.

Our hike was taking us in the general direction of the neighboring Tarahumara community of Quírare. Later we spent several weeks there. At this time, however, we had hardly reached the borderland between the two communities. We climbed slowly but steadily, and finally got to the top of the range. There winter had really set in, and the atmosphere was mournful and cold. But from this high point we were confronted by a magnificent view of the wild, rugged country in which the Tarahumara make their home; and this view, extending for miles and merging finally into mist and sky, made me realize that we had after all seen but a little of the extensive Indian community of Samachique. Months were still to pass before we saw it all and had visited the four adjoining communities.

We arrived at last at Isidro's home, a little, wooden lean-to, typical of the sierra. The family was poor, and had to remain in the cold heights of the range because the sick "child" could not be moved. To make it worse, the corn crop of the year before had been a failure here as elsewhere, and they had been forced to sell their blankets to buy corn for the winter. The woman was engaged in making others. She had just finished one, but had not yet cut it off the loom. On an additional loom a second was being completed by some other woman of the household.

The sick "child" I had gone to see turned out to be a young man. He had fallen and hurt his hip. Tuberculosis had set in. The injury was in an advanced stage of suppuration, which made me feel thankful that I had brought rubber gloves.

The boy was lying on some boards by the fire, and in extreme pain. I worked for a while with hot applications to cleanse and soften the injury, which I then lanced. Since Isidro, the father, spoke Spanish, I charged him to repeat the hot applications to relieve the pain, encourage suppuration, and keep the long wound clean and open. But I don't suppose he followed these simple instructions, since the Tarahumaras, like all primitive people, think that curing is some magical device which they dare not try, not possessing the necessary mystical power.

The boy had been stricken soon after having married. Throughout this great adversity his young wife had remained loyal to him and his family. I did not see her, however, because she was away in the gorges pasturing the few goats which the family owned. Staying away for days at a time, and returning only for a fresh supply of *pinole*, thus she spent all her time with the small herd that the family might have manure in the spring to increase their chance of getting a decent crop of corn from their sierra fields.

I felt a pang of pity for this ill-fated group, held to their makeshift *ranchería* in the forbidding cold of the sierra. The blankets they had so laboriously made and been forced to sell had brought them in but a miserable supply of corn, which they vitally needed. But such is the nobility of the Indian that they did not whine or ask for help or favors.

The mother had been dividing her time between her stricken son and her blanket loom. Isidro had been scurrying all over the sierra to trade their old blankets for corn. He was also preparing to sow a catch crop of wheat, hoping that it would be ripe in the spring, when their present scanty supply of corn would be gone. I employed him to work for me, but only for a week or so at a time could he get away from his customary labors, though I could have used his services for months.

In the short time that we were together, Isidro endeared himself to me not only for his handy way with animals or around camp, but for his loyalty, intelligence, and industry. These last he had learned from the Mexicans, who are undoubtedly, I think, the handiest and most agreeable people in the world around a campfire.

CHAPTER 7

▸ More Drinking Bouts in the
▸ Celebrations of "Catholic" Christmas

▸
▸
▸
▸
▸
▸
▸
▸

Among the Tarahumaras, as elsewhere in Mexico, the Christmas season begins with the feast day of the Virgin of Guadalupe on December 12. On Wednesday, December 10, the houses clustering about the church, most of which had been vacant, were already filled with people. Here and there smoke arising from a long-unused chimney announced a new arrival. Virtually all the people of the Indian community of Samachique were hastening toward the church, which is the center of the series of "Catholic" ceremonies given during Christmas.

The ceremonies terminated with the Feast of Epiphany, on January 6. But except for this extraneous similarity all resemblance between the Mexican and the Tarahumara festivities ends; for it is indeed in abysmal ignorance and grievous error that the *Tarahumaritos* celebrate the glad tidings of long ago and far away. They have held on tenaciously to their native ways. What they lack in knowledge of true Christmas customs, however, they make up for both in the fervor of their religious feeling and in the jollity and drunken merriment that follow the sacred ceremonies, like the recoil that follows the discharge of a gun.

Since the Tarahumaras have so little and such fragmentary native myth and belief, one would expect them to have learned more of the faith of the padres, despite the great difficulties they present to missionaries working among them. They do not even know, for example, the name of Him whose birthday they celebrate in their festal round. For them Christ is Saint Joseph of Christ. It was He who was sent to earth (the sierra) to expunge the horrible conditions of cannibalism and the like which, they believe, prevailed among themselves in ancient days. As a matter of fact the first priests in this region, such as Padre Ribas, tell of ceremonial cannibalism that accompanied the elaborate rites and fierce war customs of these Indian tribes. Be this as it may, the Tarahumaras of today think that their present social habits were inaugurated by Saint Joseph of Christ with the aid of Benito Juárez, the great leader and Indian reformer of Mexico some eighty years ago. The Huichols similarly mix up Mexican revolutionary leaders with the hierarchy of the Christian faith, Catholicism being foreign and confusing to them. This shows the close relationship existing between religion and the social order.

Most Mexican Indians, like the Mexicans themselves, believe that at one time in the distant past the Mother of Christ appeared in the village of Guadalupe Hidalgo, just outside the city of Mexico. As proof of her visit she left a magic impression of her likeness on an Indian's cloak of *maguey* fiber. This cloak is still preserved as the most sacred relic in Mexico; and about this "*Virgen de Guadalupe*" has been built not only a great shrine and beautiful basilica, but also one of the most curious cults in the world. But two hundred and fifty years had first to pass, the cult grow to national proportions, and the Virgin of Guadalupe become the unquestionable "Queen of Mexico" before the Catholic Church at Rome recognized the miracle.

Today, despite anti-Catholic activity, the importance of the cult has not diminished. On December 12 Indians from all the accessible tribes of Mexico flock to Guadalupe to pray and to carry back to their tribes the sacred water of the spring nearby. Mestizos, as well as Indians, participate in the endless processions and observances that go on at this season. Indeed, in Mexican cities, even the upper-class Mexicans participate by dressing their children in typical Indian costume on this day in tribute to the great Indian Virgin of Mexico, as she may well be called, since in her pictures she always looks like an Indian, and she is always represented with dark brown skin.

But the Tarahumaras in their far-off mountains of Chihuahua are too far removed from Guadalupe ever to participate in this cult. They know nothing about the encounter of the Virgin with an Indian, although they celebrate the day with one of their most important ceremonies; and they are no wiser about the representation that still occupies the place of honor in the basilica, allegedly the actual cloak with the miraculous impression upon it. Of course, the cloak hangs so high and has been placed behind such thick glass, that even those celebrants that are fortunate enough to get to Guadalupe have no chance to see it closely. However, this doesn't matter to the millions of cultists, much less the Tarahumaras.

Among the Tarahumaras the preparations for the ceremony of Guadalupe are interesting, and more or less consistent with other tribal exercises. After a religious program of any scope and pretension, there must always be generous quantities of refreshments. Persons called *fiesteros*, who are desirous of gaining social prestige, volunteer, therefore, to sacrifice one of their precious cattle and much of their corn for the meat, *tortillas*, and beer with which the celebrants are regaled after the ceremony. Of such vulgar social climbing our informant, Lorenzo, despite his being *maestro*, or "master," of all these "Catholic" ceremonies, was contemptuous. In his youth he had used his wits and had learned the prayers, and thus now directed everything, sacrificing nothing save his time, which wasn't particularly valuable except when he utilized it in giving us information, which cost us a peso a day.

Nor would any of the rich old philistines of this primitive community have considered sacrificing their stock so needlessly. Nothing less than their own deaths could have blasted them loose from their own prized cattle. Generally the donor of the ceremonial food and drink was some poor devil on the social fringes of the community seeking to improve his status. Such got no material reward, yet their desires were sufficiently strong that there was never any lack of volunteers for the honorary offices.

During the ceremonies of Guadalupe Day, *fiesteros* received their mead by being brought finally, though briefly, before the attention of the assembled Indians. These tribal benefactors were lined up inside the church in the presence of their friends and neighbors. Lorenzo, who was officiating, passed each of them a calabash of beer. They refrained from drinking until he had offered some of the potion to the gods of the four points.

After the *fiesteros* had thus accomplished their ambitions to be the first publicly to drink the beer, the ceremony became more complicated. Those who were relinquishing their positions as *fiesteros* folded their blankets for the new officials to kneel on, and lent them their rosaries, placing them about their necks. Then the retiring officials knelt behind their successors. The *maestro* took a lighted candle and singed the hair on the top of each new *fiestero*'s head. He then gave a candle to each, and knelt before the altar to go through his meager store of prayers.

How human these primitive people are! In the great British Empire, but with a paraphernalia infinitely more elaborate, important social climbers are knighted in a somewhat similar ceremony as a reward for great financial or other "services to the Empire." The lesser fry have to be contented with a mere presentation at court.

In the few days preceding the ceremony the probationary *fiesteros* select from their own stock the cattle they intend to slaughter for the public benefit. When the bull-dogged animal has had its throat cut, the *fiestero* modestly announces this initial attestation of his generosity to the waiting community by touching off a giant firecracker!

Although this sacrifice of animals is not very exciting among the Tarahumaras, still it is definitely of a religious nature, and therefore pleasing to the gods. To the gods is offered the blood, which is carefully saved and boiled; and small bowls of it are placed on a special altar set up in the dancing-court or *"patio"* with which each Tarahumara house is provided. After the gods have partaken of the spirit or essence of this offering, it is eaten by the people. The remainder of the sacrificial animal, including certain parts we would hardly think edible, is then devoured. Only the hooves and horns are left unused.

At the ceremony we witnessed, the butchering was done so carefully that only the contents of the stomach and a few drops of blood remained. This careful slaughter was in marked contrast to the grisly slaughtering of a water buffalo I once saw among the Ifugao headhunters in faraway Luzon. There the animal was staked in an open place, and the warriors, charging it with their head-knives, hacked it to pieces alive. In these bloodcurdling melees often the participants are themselves slashed in their wild hysteric scramble to secure portions of the sacrifice. And through the welter of blood, viscera, and surging adult bodies the youngsters paw in an effort to obtain edible portions of the predigested food of the animal's stomach.

The women of the families of the *fiesteros* had been working for several days to prepare the corn for *tortillas* and beer. Late at night we visited one of the houses. There about a dozen women were squatting half-naked over their *metates,* their brown bodies copperlike from the light of a great, blazing fire. They had stripped themselves of their bodices in order to work without chafing their arms in their awkwardly cut sleeveholes. They worked happily and apparently tirelessly, laughing and joking as if the beer were already made instead of in its first stages.

There is an exhilaration generated by communal activity of groups of individuals, each participating for the same end. Somewhat similar is the spirit brought into being by troops marching to the beat of drums and the rhythm of a band, by college rallies, by processions, and by the dancing in which primitive people take part. The movement of bodies in unison, of bodies shoulder to shoulder with others, so heightens the sense of this feeling that storm troops, for example, will march unhaltingly with a song to certain death. Here in a little Tarahumara house, with its warmth and light contrasting with the cold and darkness outside, this same force of exhilaration was at work among the relatives and neighbors grinding corn on their *metates*. Their animation and jollity would never have been manifested otherwise, unless they were drunk.

Other preparations for the coming celebration included the annual washing of clothes. The Indians wished to look their best, or "happy," as they say. This activity was so general that it exhausted our scant stock of soap. Many of the women, however, used roots of yucca, which we call "soap weed," fittingly enough. It makes an excellent lather. There is also an earth in the Tarahumara country which produces lather. The women . . . [Part of original text missing.—Eds.] This task seems to be theirs, though occasionally the men help.

The Indians also washed their hair, after which they began to delouse their heads, a sight that made me lonesome for the Philippines. The most picturesque incident of our little village, for once filled to overflowing with Tarahumaras, concerned, however, the women's combing their husbands' hair with little, primitive pinecone combs. Each Indian's long hair was arranged in two long tails, often with a new ribbon braided into the ends. I have mentioned this before as one of the few evidences of affection exhibited by Tarahumara spouses.

Our contribution to the festivities to come was to consist of fire rockets, which we had ordered in advance. We had planned on a cow, but on reflection decided that a pyrotechnic display would live longer in the memories of the Indians. The Indians were amazed by our generosity, and asked us again and again if the rockets would really be free, in fear, probably, that when they were shot off, we would try to collect for them. The Tarahumaras, like the Mexicans, are childishly elated when they can have fireworks with their religious observances. They were so enchanted with our proposal that they delayed their ceremony for several hours in order to await the arrival of the rockets. Outside of Mexico, it was only in Texas that I ever saw Christmas celebrated with fireworks.

Friday, December 12, was the great day of the Virgin of Guadalupe. The Indians postponed their ceremony until about five o'clock in the afternoon, when the rockets came. It was a welcome sight for all when our *mozo* labored slowly into view with his heavily laden mule. The load was a bit smashed up, as the mule had stumbled off the trail and rolled down a deep *arroyo*. Thank fortune it was not a *barranca*, for later we were to lose a mule in such a fall. The Indians were more than enthusiastic about the rockets; more pleasing to us, however, was a good supply of mail.

The ceremony got under way. About dusk the Indians began to flock to the churchyard in answer to the ringing of the bells by Lorenzo. The activities of Guadalupe Day were of two sorts. One was the procession of the women around the churchyard, following leaders who carried pictures of all the *santos* in the church, as well as small censers. Into these censers the women dropped abundant offerings of an incense made from insect product. The censers looked like shaving mugs, and were filled with the long-smoldering hot coals of oak fires. The Huichols use similar receptacles. This religious custom of offering incense was practiced by the Indians of Mexico before the Spaniards visited the country. In those early days incense was obtained from numerous substances called *copal*, which is still used by Mexican priests in the Catholic ceremonies.

The men participate in the ceremonies of Guadalupe Day, as in other Catholic ceremonies, by their arduous dancing of the *matachines*. This dance is of medieval European folk origin, and, so I have read, was early danced in Italy. It must have been introduced from Spain, whence the Mexican Indians derived it. It is widely known in Mexico today and is danced by most tribes, one exception being the Huichols. During the era of the *conquistadores* it became quite prominent among many of the tribes of the American Southwest. It is still practiced by the Pueblo Indians; and a Jesuit padre has told me of having seen it danced by the Mescalero Apaches.

So subdued and unimpressive are the other native dances, which we were to see later, that the complicated choreography of the *matachines*, accompanied by elaborate costuming and paraphernalia, acts as an important stimulus in Tarahumara festivities. The dance of the *mat-*

achines is even performed, as pure swank, in certain ceremonies of death, as for example, for rich men like Patricio.

The formation of this dance is a great deal like that of the Virginia Reel. Young men, who are especially honored by being regular dancers, dance to music of violins and guitars. The elders of the tribe remain quietly to one side of the dancers, and restrict their activities to shouting in unison, from time to time, during the hours that the dance continues. They are called *chapiyónes* of the Tarahumaras, corresponding to the *abuelos*, or "grandfathers," of some of the dancers of the Pueblo Indians. One of them wears a mask on the back of his head, another instance of how poorly the Tarahumaras have assimilated certain aspects of Spanish culture.[1]

The chief of the dancers is called the *monarco*. That the role of a "monarch" should be acted among the Tarahumaras is surprising; yet perhaps no more so than that elaborate costumes are worn for this dance by the Indians, who at other times are naked save for their clouts. The dancers wear the robes and crown of a king, a costume which is "gaily-colored and fancy," as Bennett says. The robe is cape-like in design, and of bright red cloth. Trousers of a similar color are also worn. The crown is an outlandish contraption of tissue paper, the wrappings in which cigarettes are packed, a mirror, and any other similarly glistening things that are available.

Each man carries in one hand a fanlike ornament decorated with paper flowers and in the other a rattle which is sounded as an accompaniment to the steps. The most surprising element of the entire costume, however, and one also showing a foreign provenience, is to be found in the use of shoes. Ordinarily these Indians walk barefooted, or with their feet protected only by thin wrappings of goatskin; but for this dance they must have shoes, kept especially for this purpose.

It is a high honor indeed to be a dancer in the *matachines*, and one for which the young men vie. Many of the young men who achieve this honor are racers, and it is from this activity that they gain the endurance necessary for the long hours of dancing which they undergo. The honored elders of the community, the *chapiyónes*, content themselves by shouting during the dance. Despite his poverty my recent friend Isidro, father of the sick boy, was one of these official "shouters."

At 5:30 the dancing began. But to the Indians it was more than just the colorful spectacle it was to us; for in both their pagan and Christian ceremonies, they say that "to dance" is "to work." This "work" they will continue for hours, believing that their efforts will be construed favorably by the gods, who will then hardly deny their prayers for good health, long life and bounteous crops.[2]

Such is dancing at the primitive level. Our dancing in contrast is only half removed from this level, because we too participate, whereas a truly civilized people participate in nothing. A really civilized attitude toward dancing was once expressed by an old-fashioned Chinese who had visited America and was astounded to see the people dance. "You in America dance," he said. "In China, we hire people to dance for us."

But in America we hire specialists for almost everything else we wish done; and this is the civilized way to avoid participation. The primitive man, on the contrary, does everything for himself. Within his group there is no specialization, no classes, no diversification. Every man or every woman does everything within his or her respective realm. The vast cultural remove of the civilized from the primitive arises partially from the diversification of individuals into thousands of different specializations.

And although we Americans dance, we are somewhat civilized in this also, for we too hire virtuosos to dance for us. By specialization they develop their art to a plane far beyond the reach of the *Tarahumaritos*, whose dancing is essentially an exercise of propitiation of their gods. The last is the ultimate in participation; because it makes even the gods participate in the need and cravings of the Indians. But we must return to the ceremonies of Guadalupe Day among the Tarahumaras.

About 7:30 our priceless rogue of a *maestro* suggested that it was dark enough to touch off some of the skyrockets. Mexican skyrockets are made from sections of reed tied on a stick. They are without fuses. Thus the trick in lighting them is first to blow on the end of a glowing corncob, and then to apply this substitute for punk to the end of the rocket, which is open. It is a dangerous method, for when the rocket leaves the hand, it sprouts a fiery trail of sparks. In addition to this peril, the Indians put their faces close to the rocket in order to blow on the glowing corncob. Why they don't lose their eyes I can't imagine; for the rockets are poorly made. Sometimes they go down, instead of up; at other times they shoot off sideways, and ricochet through the excited crowd.

But the Tarahumaras enjoyed it all; and the dogs, hating the unaccustomed noise, showed their agitation and displeasure by barking and dashing around the churchyard as recklessly as the skyrockets; and with the entire scene a perfect bedlam, the spectacle was a pronounced success.

When we had touched off about a dozen rockets, the women broke away from the crowd and went into the church. They reappeared, carrying the picture of the Virgin of Guadalupe and pictures of two other *santos*. They marched around the cross set upright in the center of the churchyard. The men remained quietly to one side. The musicians, with their violins and guitars, continued their sacred minstrelsy.

After about half an hour of this, everyone filed into the church for a prayer by Lorenzo. On this occasion of particular solemnity another man knelt and replied to the phrases chanted by Lorenzo, as I had done when we were drunk together. At one side knelt the woman who had the honor of carrying the picture of the Virgin of Guadalupe. She was an official known as a *prioste* (a Spanish word having an ecclesiastical significance, though very different from our word priest, with which the reader may think it associated). She had a little training in singing and sang a few phrases of Catholic songs in what I thought was a beautiful voice.

After the prayer the Indians grouped themselves around the church door. The *gobernador* gave them the longest sermon I had ever heard him make. Several times he must have said, "Am I right, or am I right?" for his congregation reported, after the manner of recitative, "You are right."[3]

About ten o'clock the *matachines* began their dance. It was to last all night with occasional intermissions for smoking. One of my compensations for having to study only the material culture of the tribe was that I was able to go to bed at a reasonable hour. Bennett, however, remained up all night, making a detailed account of this ceremony. He reported that at 4:30 the next morning food and beer were given to the singers, dancers, and officials after a ceremonial offering to the four points.

Throughout the morning of Saturday, everyone rested from the arduous ceremonies of the previous night. At noon the activities were continued. They began with another procession of the *santos* around the cross in the churchyard. The *matachines* then danced for about two hours. Then the festal scene passed to the houses of the *fiesteros*.

With the dancers leading, everyone proceeded to these houses scattered through the "village," which had now become more important than a mere collection of huts.

At each of the houses of the *fiesteros* its court, or *patio*, had been cleared of the rubbish and weeds. In the center were an altar and, standing behind this, three large crosses roughly made of wood. On arriving at a house the *gobernador* and other officials made a ceremonial circuit around the altar. They crossed themselves at each of the cardinal points. Then the *gobernador* in a short speech thanked the *fiestero* for his hospitality. Later that night, when the celebrants returned to the houses for beer, these speeches were repeated, but this time were lighted by the leaping flares of torches.

At the last house, at 5:30 in the morning, we sent up our last rockets. As usual, we had to assure the *fiestero* that we would not try to collect for them after the festivities were over. Since we had drunk very little beer, I felt that this was the mere shank of the evening. Bennett, however, was tired from his vigil of the previous night.

The Indians were in various stages of happy, ebullient intoxication. Some were dead drunk and had fallen to sleep by the remains of their little fires.[4] Others had been hauled into the houses by those less drunk so that they wouldn't freeze to death in the bitter cold. Some were violently sick. I recall seeing one Tarahumara matron in very bad straits retching repeatedly, while her husband looked on solicitously, unable to do anything for her.

I was in no mood by this time for our cold *convento* room, with its bloodless celibate and ecclesiastical associations. So I edged into the last house and found sitting room among the Indians that jammed the place. I sat between two Tarahumara friends. Each would whisper confidentially to me at once. I would nod my head gravely without, however, understanding a word uttered. Then I would whisper back at them, one at a time. They would gravely nod as I had done before. The scene was lively and animated. And I was a part of this primitive festivity. Indeed, I was so integrally a part of it that I could hardly crawl out of bed the next day. But that was a trifling forfeit.

The light of the roaring fire played throughout the room, revealing in bulking outline the forms of Indians in an interesting variety of postures. Here a wife watched over the recumbent Indians. These occasions always gave me such a feeling of contentment and oneness with the Indians, that for once in my anthropological career it seemed I was feeling what everyone in my profession should feel, the real spirit of the people under observation. It was worth all the fantastic hardship, the isolation from accustomed life, family, friends, and the gnawing loneliness that work such as ours entails.

Lumholtz, our predecessor among these Indians, knew primitive people well, and although he did not record all he knew, may have had similar experiences. He speaks of an "animal magnetism." What he means by this phrase I don't quite know; yet from this close contact and almost complete participation I experienced something that derived neither from actual contact with the lice-infested savages nor from the beer that I drank, straining it between my teeth before I gulped it down. It was a feeling of exhilaration and exaltation, similar to that shown by the Indians whenever they went out to hard, communal labor before a *tesgüinada*.

I had been pervaded by the same feeling before, though in different situations of close social participation. As an undergraduate, I had similar experiences at football rallies and the numerous, primitive displays that are staged during football games. Again, during the World War, particularly a time of exhilarating participation, I had the same feeling while marching shoulder to shoulder with the men of my company in military reviews.

This feeling has passed from me since I have become partially civilized; its loss is one of the prices we pay for civilization. But when I go off to a primitive tribe, it returns . . . [Part of original text missing. —Eds.]

CHAPTER 8

Officials, Government, and Politics among the Tarahumaras

▶
▶
▶
▶
▶
▶
▶
▶
▶
▶

T he government of the Tarahumara community is especially in evidence during the festal round of the holiday
season. After the *fiesteros* have sponsored the elaborate
ceremonies for the Virgin of Guadalupe, the ceremonies of Christmas
Eve are given by the *chapiyónes*. I have already spoken of these old men,
whose only office is that of shouting during the dancing of the *matachines*. I suppose that all Indians take their war whooping seriously;
but this is the only case I know of where ordinary whooping claims
such an exalted eminence.

Among the Tarahumaras the cost of any honor or distinction, civil
or ecclesiastical, is high. Though the officials may govern the community, they receive no salary; indeed, they pay for the privilege with public service and, during certain ceremonies, with *tortillas* and beer. Only
two of the community of Samachique seemed to be exempt from this
rule. One was Lorenzo, whose learning from the padres enabled him
to hold the highest ecclesiastical office of all, that of *maestro*, without
paying a cent. The other was the pagan shaman, whose religious function was greater than that of Lorenzo, and who received fees for his
work. All others paid to serve the community, a splendid custom that
could well be introduced into our civilization.

The ceremonies of *Noche Buena*, The Good Night of Christmas
Eve, were postponed because of the cold of the wintry sierra. They
were given later with the festivities of The Day of The Three Magi,
January 6. This was a simple expedient, since all the celebrations of
this round of "Catholic" ceremonies are identical. The Tarahumaras

merely parade the pictures of the saints and dance the *matachines*. Hence, this combination meant only that everything would be doubled, the food and the activities. The officials did not get out of regaling the populace.

Catholic missionaries set up the government of the Tarahumara communities. Consequently, the officers are designated by Spanish names. They are of two classes, ecclesiastical and civil.

The ecclesiastical officers are the *mayor* and his messengers, the *fiscales*. The latter act somewhat as coadjutants; their particular duty is to carry the orders of the *mayor* to the isolated *rancherías* of the Indians. Whatever other ecclesiastical functions the *mayor* may have once had, he is now solely concerned with marriage, offspring, matchmaking, and the patching of disputes. The family is, of course, a special concern of the Catholic Church. Its teachings in this regard have been so thorough that the *mayor* as a high officer is concerned with nothing else. But this keeps him sufficiently occupied, for in Tarahumaraland the bonds and relationships between the sexes are quite lax. In marked contrast is the celibacy of the Catholic clergy, which the Indians appreciate as something supernatural and conducive to sacred power. The attitude of the Indians here is so strong that after several generations they still recall one flagrant case of sacerdotal impropriety. I have no doubt that the devotion of the Jesuit priests to their vows has been the source of the prestige of the Tarahumara officer, the *mayor*, and that this respect for the celibacy of the padres has caused almost every Tarahumara community to appoint such an officer. However, the pagan community of Quírare, as might be expected, does not recognize this office.

Once the Tarahumaras accepted the punishments for sexual laxity prescribed by the padres. This consisted of flogging, imprisonment in stocks, or sometimes both. Today, when Catholic activity in the sierra is considerably restricted, the *mayor* still carries a business-like quirt as a symbol of his office. The flogging, however, has been discouraged by the Mexican government as a tribal usurpation of judicial power.

The *mayor* is kept quite busy directing the unstable and migratory Tarahumaras into more or less permanent marital relationships. I have already brought attention to the good offices of the *mayor* of Samachique in liquidating the scandal of his generation concerning one Tarahumara girl's illicit alliance with her brother. It will be remembered that through the good offices of the *mayor* she was married off to a member of a distant community.

Bennett and I became quite friendly with this *mayor*, and later in the winter we were to live near his dwelling cave. On several occasions at feasts following working bees, we even got drunk with him. He was a serious and earnest individual who spent more time with his official duties than with his personal affairs. This supererogation, coupled with the grain shortage of the year before, ultimately forced him to sell some of his animals in order to buy corn. Despite his official zeal and relatively high status, however, he got but scant sympathy from the wealthier Tarahumaras such as Lorenzo. Theirs was that pitiless philistinism manifested by our own wealthy representatives when, for example, some friend's resources are swallowed up in the stock market.

The messengers of the *mayor*, the *fiscales*, have few other duties besides acting as couriers for their chief. They are not concerned in a curious way with children. Tarahumara parents are not allowed to strike their children, under pain of flogging by the *mayor*. As a matter of fact, the Tarahumaras, who are like all primitive people in that they appear inordinately fond of their children, would probably not descend to such brutality anyway; and since their customs are so simple as to obviate any necessity for education, among them discipline of any sort whatsoever is unknown.[1] But the notion persists that disobedient children should be punished only at the command of the *gobernador*; and for this no doubt the Indians are indebted to the padres. At any rate, the *mayor* is supposed to take erring parents to task, and the *fiscales* are supposed to chastise children. However, Lorenzo, whose memory was astonishing, had never heard of any case where these prerogatives had been exercised against the children.

The civil officers of a Tarahumara community are four in number, the *gobernador*, the *teniente*, the *suplente*, and the *alcalde*. The three last officers are all subordinate to the *gobernador*, who is distinctly the headman. Although he is also designated by the native word, *selígame* (lance bearer), the term *cusíhuami* (cane bearer) could be applied to him as it is to the others; for these men act as a board of directors of municipal affairs and each carries in his belt little sticks of brazilwood, the Tarahumara variant of the silver-headed canes utilized in Spain, Spanish America and the Philippines as symbols of municipal authority. There are also three or four messengers called *capitanes*, or *soldados*, whose laborious duty it is to trot all over the expansive community with news or orders from higher officers. These lesser dignitaries likewise carry canes.[2]

I have written of the interesting personality of the *gobernador*, whom we met shortly after arriving in Samachique. He was not long in overcoming his fear of us, and after we had made him several judicious gifts of cloth, soon became our very good friend. He was a born leader, despite his inability, when sober, to give the sermons expected of him; for one of his major duties was to address the Indians at length on their conception of "good morals and right conduct." As Bennett says of him: "His sermons on Sunday were weak and short, since he could only give strong sermons when drunk." This statement was true, for his Sunday sermon never lasted more than five minutes, but at one *tesgüinada* he talked for almost an hour.

The *gobernador* had a happy, ready smile and a deep, gutsy laugh. Coupled with these was his grave dignity, which fitted well with his magnificent physique. He was a glad-hander, and hated to punish anyone. He always tried his best to smooth over offenses and get offenders to make amends. These qualities made him popular with the hoi polloi, especially during elections, which are by *viva voce*, and generally held during Holy Week, when the whole community is assembled.

But his shortcomings irritated the wealthy aristocracy of this little primitive community. Where wealth in any form is involved, human nature shows an amazing consistency, as my experiences among both primitive and civilized people will attest.

By a comparison of our own civilization with the "culture" of primitive tribes, where all extraneous accoutrements are stripped away, we arrive at least at a common denominator which we call human nature. Here certain patterns are fundamental and universal. For one thing, wherever you go, among men there is a consistent attitude toward whatever passes for wealth and among those of a feminine gender certain impulses in their relationship with men that make them all "sisters under the skin," as Kipling said.

Our friend, the Tarahumara *gobernador,* had put himself in a ticklish position through his efforts to avoid trouble when one Seleronio killed a rich Indian's cow which had broken into his field. This was Seleronio's second offense of a similar nature. The first had happened several years before. The *gobernador* of that time had adjudicated the matter by having Seleronio transfer to the rich man one burro and the meat remaining from the slaughtered cow.

But now Seleronio had transgressed again. True, he was partly within his rights; for among the Tarahumaras failure to watch one's cattle and prevent their breaking into neighboring fields is in itself an offense and liable to punishment or payment of the damages. But the

taking of the law into one's own hands is even more serious. So Seleronio was to be brought to the church on Sunday to be tried by our
friend, the *gobernador*. As though by prearrangement, however, neither
the official nor the culprit showed up.

In my journal for this period I find the following:

> The more wealthy, and hence influential, men have many cattle, and
> are especially injured by such offenses that are allowed to go without
> punishment. They are particularly incensed by the negligence of the
> *gobernador*. The richest man in the community, Anastacio, the *ex-go-
> bernador*, has told the *maestro*, Lorenzo, that he will be willing to take
> office again in view of the failure of the present *gobernador* to cope
> with Seleronio's crime. So Lorenzo has begun to circulate among the
> Indians, agitating against the absent official. It is very possible that
> Holy Week will see the election of a new *gobernador* and other offi-
> cers. On such occasions the Tarahumaras generally stage a political
> housecleaning.

I watched the erring *gobernador* closely, and soon saw evidence of
his popularity with the people whom he strove to please. He was not
turned out; and months later, when I left Samachique, he had not only
weathered the possibility of a general election during Holy Week, but
was more popular than ever. My distinct impression of him was that he
knew how to please the masses rather than the classes of his con-
stituency.

The Tarahumara government is somewhat like the English in that
officials are curbed by the ever-present threat of a "general election,"
and that the entire fabric of the administration collapses with the
unpopularity of the leaders. Dr. Bennett has recorded complete details
of the Tarahumara system of elections.

During the festal round of the Christmas season we were in attendance at one trial which gave us the opportunity to observe the political ability of the *gobernador* at the old, old game of compromise and
temporization. A Tarahumara, named Cruz, was picked to fill a
vacancy among the *fiscales*, the messengers of the *mayor*. The duties of
a *fiscale* are arduous, and candidates are hard to find. Unfortunately,
Cruz's record was not unclouded. He had borrowed a burro from a
neighbor to take some apples to market. On the trip the burro fell
from a precipitous place on the trail and was killed. Cruz had never
recompensed the owner for the animal, so this old account had to be

socially discharged before he could take office. The following account shows what ensued.

All the civil officials and their messengers, the *capitanes* or *soldados* (soldiers), and the *mayor* and his assistants, the *fiscales*, were in full state. On their persons they carried the symbols of their authority. With all the formality and dignity of the robed Justices of the Supreme Court, they filed before the assembled Indians and approached the official bench. This was a rough, hand-hewn board that always rested just in front of our *convento*. Here they sat, gravely and pompously. Soon the offender and his wife appeared. They squatted before the officials. The owner of the dead burro, his family, and supporters sat on one side. Gathered around in a semicircle sat the equally grave populace, wrapped in their blankets in characteristic Tarahumara fashion.

Tarahumara trials are governed by few rules of procedure. At any time the officials and even the people may interrupt proceedings with questions. At this trial, as is customary, the plaintiff was the prosecution. Volubly he began to present his case to the officials. The accused made answer, amid interrogation from all sides. The conduct of everyone present, however, remained grave and deliberate.

There was some duplicity in the plaintiff's tactics. He alleged that Cruz not only failed to pay for the dead animal, but in the drunken party following some ceremony, had "talked bad" against him, the aggrieved owner of the burro. This latter charge was quite significant. The reader will recall that it was precisely such black magic that had robbed Lorenzo of his sense of smell. But at this point some wise old head ejaculated, "Let us first settle the case of the burro, and then we can go into the charge of black magic."

The "cross-examination" continued. The plaintiff exhorted; the accused answered; the officials and the people argued back and forth. Then, at last, the *gobernador* pronounced his opinion. This was final. Cruz was found guilty. But his punishment was lenient enough: he was ordered only to pay for the animal. To this he agreed.

Immediately after this exhibition of the processes of Tarahumara law, Cruz, to our amazement, was inducted into office. This made me a bit homesick for Chicago, where somewhat similar political vagaries evidence themselves now and then, though on a much larger and more ostentatious scale.

The officers who had acted as judges remained in their places. The retiring *fiscale*, one Morena, folded his blanket and laid it at their feet. Then Cruz approached and knelt before the *gobernador*, almost as if he were some Englishman about to be knighted by his sovereign. The *gobernador* arose, holding his cane as a king might hold his scepter. Then followed, strangely enough, a Tarahumara variation of an old custom probably introduced by the padres to add luster to the inauguration of officials; for the chivalric gesture of touching the shoulder in conferring titular distinctions was mixed up somehow with the ceremonial passes that the Tarahumaras make over the heads of pregnant women, new *fiesteros*, sick people, and others who are considered "sacred." I shall paraphrase Bennett's record of this scene, at which each of us was present.

With his official cane the *gobernador* made passes over, in front, behind, to the left, and to the right of Cruz's head. Then he described three circles around the man's head. He repeated this ritual, but this time holding in one hand along with his own cane the whip of the *mayor*, apparently as a grim reminder that even officials are not above the law. The ceremony was repeated a third time, but with the cane alone; for three is a magic number for the Tarahumaras, and any ritual must therefore suffer repetition in order to achieve its calculated effect. While Cruz continued to kneel, the officials picturesquely shook hands over his head, beginning with the *gobernador*. Even this was done thrice. Thus did Cruz become a *fiscale*.

The attitude of the Tarahumaras toward time and space is reminiscent somewhat of Kant. To see them run deer to death one would think that for them space is a mere category of the mind. Time likewise seems to be a similar concept, and chronological sequence a fantasy. The feast of Epiphany was celebrated on the third instead of the sixth of January. Since this celebration was to combine a part of the ceremony that should have been given Christmas Eve, the *matachines* especially exerted themselves and danced twenty-four times. Twelve of the dances were for this present ceremony; the other twelve were retroactive to Christmas Eve.

The term "retroactive" is far from inept, since the dance of the *matachines* is considered to have particular efficacy. Danced in the church and the churchyard, it acts as a potent curative. The Tarahumaras, however, have other methods also by means of which to "cure" both the sick and the well, animals, fields, and houses. Of course to the Tarahumaras, who have no science, to "cure" means to bless, to sanctify, to purify from ritual uncleanness and the possible dangers contingent upon such a state. It has no medical connotations, as it has for us. Nor is this strange, for among primitive people mysticism takes the place of objectively demonstrable logic in many cases where civilized men use science instead of religion.

The ceremony of Epiphany, The Day of The Three Magi, marks the termination of the yearly social round of the Tarahumaras. Until it is given, the Indians brave the piercing cold of the wintry uplands. Then they all part to the warm caves of the gorges.

Thus we were about to witness the temporary dispersal of the Tarahumara community of Samachique. It was preceded by a dramatically appropriate ceremony.

All in attendance crowded into the church and lined up, the men on one side, the women on the other. Lorenzo, the *maestro*, made his final prayers assisted by his brother (of blue-eyed distinction) and the two women who chanted in Catholic fashion. A procession then formed outside the church. It was led by the *matachines* and the *chapiyónes*, who were followed in turn by the officials, civil and ecclesiastic.

The procession circled the building, and throughout its course each participant shook hands with every spectator. Then replacements were made, so that soon everyone had shaken hands with everyone else. Each handshake was a formal, ceremonious gesture, begun by first motioning toward the forearm before clasping hands, then clasping hands and lifting them high in an exaggerated fashion somewhat similar to that affected by would-be *grandes damas*. Here was a perfect social symbolization of the impending break in the bond unifying the individual families on their isolated *rancherías* into the community of Samachique.

The amount of food and drink for this ceremony was doubled, even as the number of dances. Both the officials and the *chapiyónes* furnished the feast of stew and *tortillas* and the oceans of beer.

It will be recalled that Patricio, our dead enemy, had been the *teniente*, or second in command, of the community. The *gobernador* had proposed that immediately after these present festivities a new incumbent be appointed. But old Anastacio, both the richest and the most conservative man of Samachique, had objected. Patricio had not been dead long enough. Insufficient time had elapsed for his family to give all the ceremonies that would despatch his soul completely into the world of the dead. Until these ceremonies had been given, it would be unsafe to appoint a successor, for Patricio's soul might be slighted. Needless to say, the project was dropped.

Thus, on this night of January 3rd, since Tarahumara officials provide the feasts following ceremonies, we were again reminded that though our *teniente* was absent, he was not completely dead; for when the procession of drunken, hilarious Indians reached his temporary house near the church, we found that Patricio was still the host, albeit by a sort of proxy. Here his family had prepared an extra and special jar of beer, and had placed it near a tiny cross of wood on which was hung the man's rosary. To symbolize that he was on a journey, one of his blankets had been rolled up in a pack strap, exactly as living pilgrims carry such items on their journeys. Beside the blanket were two gourd dippers. With these Patricio could partake of his special jar of beer should he return that night.

This pot of beer was dedicated quite apart from the ceremonies given for the jars of ordinary beer. Someone lighted a candle, and the dancers of the *matachines* capered several times around the dead man's blanket. Then the *maestro*, Lorenzo, and his blue-eyed brother had to give a prayer, even though they were feeling "fou and unco happy" [sic], and in hardly the right mood for such an activity. This added a marked human touch to the proceedings. Lorenzo shook himself to clear his head, and breathed deeply. He got his brother to his feet, and together they staggered over to the ceremony around the beer jar and pilgrim's blanket. As drunk as they were, they still managed to kneel and mumble over their meager store of Catholic prayers. Throughout this ceremony all movements and gestures were reversed, in congruence with the Tarahumara conception of the world to which the dead go.

At this house the procession consumed all the food and drink, including even that offered to the dead. Outside Lorenzo and his brother surrendered themselves completely to the effects of the beer they had drunk, and began to cut capers on the court, which was illuminated by fires made from torches of the celebrants. I was inside with my fellow practitioner, the shaman, who had assisted me in despatching Patricio from the Land of the Living to the happy hunting grounds. The shaman was getting quite drunk, and acting in a manner that did not become his exalted position. His wife came and led him away.

My diary contains this note: "I continued to ladle out *tesgüino* to all and sundry." As usual, I protected my own interests by drinking sparingly at first. Also, by acting, so to speak, as bartender, I could avoid drinking without giving offense. Since we had to visit the houses of two sets of officials, this turned out to be the most drunken party I ever saw among the Tarahumaras. I must have become unconscious somewhere near the finish. My last recollection was that of lying near a fire-place and having some kind Indian pull my feet, with their thick boots smoking, from too close a proximity with the roaring flames.

On January 4, 1931, after the previous night's carousal in the cause of science, needless to say I slept late. Then I stirred myself, got busy, and cleaned up the dirtiest adobe house in the world, to wit, our own. Almost every member of the tribe had sauntered through or loitered in the place during the past three days, and consequently this task was more like "dirt archaeology" than the more genteel and refined science of ethnology. Bennett turned up about noon. He did not divulge where he had weathered the aftermath. Perhaps he didn't know. We agreed that the celebration had been magnificent, and quite worthy to have been staged by the officials of the community.

The Tarahumaras have no formal political authority of chieftain-ship of any group larger than the community, and that organization shows clearly a Spanish influence. A few years before and even during our visit, however, an extraordinary Indian named Jaris had established a moral authority over the whole tribe by his courage and positive leadership. To the Mexicans he was known as "General" Jaris.

We had heard of Jaris in Mexico City, where we had visited his son, who was a student in the then functioning "School of Aboriginal Students." This school, incidentally, was abandoned because the wild Indian lads almost perished from loneliness away from their native regions, a generous and considerate move by the Federal government. This was in contrast to our own heartless policy of forcing education on native peoples in the United States and Philippines. Anyone who has lived among primitive tribes, and has tried to understand them, knows the advantages accruing to that government which employs trained, literate natives for tribal government posts. In the Philippines American administrators such as Jeff Gallman, working, for example, in the subprovince of the fierce Ifugao headhunters, achieved remark-able success by utilizing the services of former prisoners who had been disciplined in the penitentiary. The Mexican government deserves considerable respect for its suppression of the Indian school in the cap-ital, even though that same school was quite useful.[3]

One quiet day in December, during a lull in the festivities, our friend, the *gobernador* of Samachique, came to the *convento*. With him was "General" Jaris. We had brought to the sierra a letter for the Tarahumara "General" from his son in Mexico City, as well as some snapshots we had taken. We read the letter to the "General," and then made him a present of the pictures. He became quite expansively pleased.

Thus our first meeting was a success, and this was well, for we were aware that the influence of this extraordinary Indian throughout the entire tribe was marked. Naturally we were anxious to be on the best of terms with him, knowing that he could make or break our success in any region save Samachique. Here we had ingratiated ourselves with the Indians sufficiently to achieve our purpose; although there was always the danger that someone might turn the entire community against us with a story of black magic or something of the sort.

Subsequently it fell to my lot to cultivate further good graces of Jaris, and perhaps luckily, since my archaeological work a few months later was to take me all over the sierra. At best digging up people's ancestors is a tricky and precarious business. The Tarahumaras offer about the least resistance imaginable to this practice; and, as I have already related, about forty years ago our predecessor, Lumholtz, bought the skeleton of an Indian's mother-in-law for three pesos. However, Lumholtz also tells how an initial misunderstanding frightened the Tarahumaras so much that it took him four or five months to establish their confidence. The word and esteem of the "General" were to be my *carte blanche* for the entire Sierra Tarahumara.

In my negotiations with Jaris I gained not only his favorable recommendation but an insight into his character and personality. He was an extraordinary Indian chief and a leader of men. Simple, sincere, and courageous, he risked his life daily in leading his tribesmen in a brave stand against the increasing encroachments of Mexicans on Indian lands. Later, when I had grown more intimate both with him and his Mexican antagonists, he said to me, "Someday one of these Mexican *bandidos* from behind some rock will shoot me like a deer as I walk along the trail." I feared for his safety at the time, and still believe that he hazarded his life in his relentless stand against the Mexicans. The reader may judge for himself as this account goes on.

The intrusion of foreigners upon Indian lands is an old story in America. The Tarahumaras, however, have fared amazingly well on the whole, and still rule almost the entirety of the great mountainous chain of southern Chihuahua, a region embracing one-third of this largest state of the Mexican union. But Christianization and Mexicanization have continued on persistently during the three centuries of Spanish contact, and for this the missions have been focal centers.

The effect of this process of Mexicanization varies from certain

Tarahumara communities in the center of the area which are still pagan, to Mexican municipalities where the Tarahumaras have merged into the background of mestizo Mexico. At the eastern border of the Tarahumara country, on the Río Conchos, is the town of Nonoava, originally a Jesuit mission. This is so completely Mexicanized that the regular Jesuits, considering their work completed, have turned it over to the secular clergy. At the western border of the Tarahumara country, on the Río Chinipas, is the town of Ocampo, which has become a Mexican municipality, partly because of the Mexicanization of the local Indians, and partly because of the influence of many Mexican miners in this mineral-rich region. The Jesuits still maintain a mission at Ocampo. I did not, however, see this part of the country.[4]

The mission of Sisoguichi, near Creel, has a regular Mexican municipal organization due mainly to the influx of Mexicans from the railroad in the last twenty-five years. They have appropriated from the Indians the nearby fertile lands. The Indians have retired, and thus are still affected but little culturally by the Mexicans. The padres, however, have a handful of Indian neophytes who have married and settled near the mission.

The other Jesuit mission, that of Norogáchic, is in the heart of the Indian country, and within the area of the greatest Indian population. Within fifteen miles of the mission live five thousand Indians. The mission, however, has inevitably attracted Mexicans, because it is located in a very fertile river valley. Thus Norogáchic has one or two Mexican stores or trading posts, a post office, and a Mexican population of about three hundred.

These encroachments, which have been constantly increasing over a period of three centuries, have, however, been somewhat restricted; and thus, since the first fierce wars and massacres staged by the Tarahumaras, who are now so gentle and docile, something of an accommodation has been maintained between the Indians and Mexicans.

But in the last few years the collapse of mining in the gorges and the destruction of all Mexican ranches during the Revolution have forced the Mexicans from the gorges into the sierra. Most of them live by trading cloth for Indian corn, but quite a few have begun to squat on the idle lands in the mountains of the Indian country. The Indians deeply fear and resent these intrusions and harbor umbrage against even the most tactful and friendly of the Mexicans. To make matters worse, some of these intruders still preserve their revolutionary arms and freebooting habits and have intimidated the Indians away from some of their best land. The timidity and reticence of the Indians have perhaps encouraged the Mexicans in these practices.

Yet such cases of land encroachment are still reasonably few; in the last five years no more than one hundred among the entire tribe have cropped up. The sierra is vast, and the Indians leave much good land unused. In general those Mexican miners who are stranded in the sierra without relief are in such desperate straits that their only recourse is to trade with the Indians.[5]

The unrest and fear among the Indians, however, persist; and these have resulted in the leadership of "General" Jaris, renowned for his courage and ability. Jaris once collected a few *centavos* from each Indian of the tribe to make a trip to Mexico City in an effort to secure protection for Indian holdings. This was before the Federal government had finished its accurate survey of all Tarahumara land. But ignorant, illiterate, and alone in his stand, he accomplished very little. Several times he has walked to Chihuahua City, for, as he told me, shyster lawyers (not unknown in Mexico) took the money he had collected from the Indians and gave him no satisfaction.

Jaris's unsuccessful repeated efforts and waste of money have caused many of the Indians to lose confidence in him. Thus it turned out that just as I was anxious to gain his cooperation for my purposes, he was as anxious to get mine to help him in his battle against the Mexicans. This mutual assistance was to yield me the greatest excitement and adventure during my stay among the Tarahumaras.

As I soon learned, Jaris lived on a typical Tarahumara *ranchería* in the area of heaviest population near Norogáchic. This brought him into contact with the majority of the Indians, and gave him a solid and powerful backing for his leadership of the whole tribe. I had planned to go to Norogáchic to visit the padres, so I asked Jaris if I might stop and see him at his *ranchería*, which was not far off the trail between Samachique and Norogáchic. He seemed quite pleased with my proposal, and even gave me directions for reaching his place.

CHAPTER 9

▸ *Liquor, Guns, and Religion in*
▸ *the Mexican Picture*
▸
▸
▸
▸
▸

▸   I n Tarahumaraland, so great are the difficulties of travel on
▸   even a short trip, that I was not able to get to Norogáchic in
▸   time for the ceremonies of The Day of The Three Magi.
Bennett had been on a trip with a Mexican muleteer and our *mozo*, and
they had arrived back on schedule, allowing me sufficient time to take
the Mexicans on to Norogáchic. But we did not take into consideration certain factors by which carefully laid, ambitious plans *"gang aft
agley."*

On the afternoon before I was to leave, the grown son of old Córdoba came into camp. He had with him a bottle of *sotol*, a drink somewhat like *tequila*. On this stuff his father had spent one of the last pesos
of the poverty-stricken family. The boy had convinced his father of his
unfairness in dissipating the family's slim resources; and since we were
nearer than Norogáchic, where the liquor was purchased, he brought
it to us for resale. The liquor was practically useless to us, even for
"snakebite," but we bought it just for goodwill. I was glad to see Córdoba's son come in, however, for I was able to ask him if I might spend
the night in passing on my trip at his father's *ranchería*. Permission was
granted, of course.

Before we had a chance to lock the liquor away from our Mexican
mozo and the strange muleteer with whom Bennett had returned, one
of the many Tarahumaras temporarily in the "village" for the Christmas ceremonies dropped in at the *convento*. He had come to ask us if we
would "cure" his sick child. Both Bennett and I went to the nearby
house. Here we found a three-year-old child suffering from an infection in the sacral region. We could do nothing but clean and bandage

the infection, and hope that it was superficial, for it might well have been caused by a slight injury in play.

But though we had accomplished nothing noteworthy, our two factotums back at the *convento* had utilized our absence to inspect our abode. Our *mozo* had the effrontery to open the bottle of *sotol*. When we arrived home, both Mexicans were blissfully drunk.

Mexicans, however, cannot remain happily drunk on their nauseous distillations from plants such as *maguey* and *sotol;* and God was really unkind in endowing Mexico so liberally with these, which yield an intoxicating liquor almost as homicidal in its effects as the East Indian smoking-weed, hashish, which provides the Mexican with his *marijuana*.

We could not very well leave the Mexicans outside in the treacherous cold, where they would surely have frozen in their drunken condition, so we took them into the *convento* and tried to allay their drunkenness by giving them food. But the liquor had already begun its work. Soon they became dangerously angry at each other. The muleteer falsely accused our *mozo* of improprieties with his wife, and became viciously insulting. Incidentally, it turned out that he was a hopeless dipsomaniac. He was the same person whom Lorenzo had accused of robbing an Indian of corn. (He had, however, bought the corn of the owner, who had sold it apparently without the permission of the other members of the family.)

The muleteer was armed with a carbine which, giving him a sense of power and security, added fuel to his insults and made him an extremely ugly customer for our confined quarters. When the fracas seemed to be getting completely out of hand, I retired to a dark corner of the room, leaving the others outlined by the ruddy flames of the fire. The loaded automatic pistol that I generally carried for moral effect and pure swank was in its accustomed place on my belt.

I hated to think how a shooting scrape might mar our scientific expedition, and all because I had not wished to insult the son of my friend, Córdoba. Through my mind passed the reflection that I should have followed my first inclination to toss that bottle of liquor into the air and shoot it to bits as it fell. That would have been better than disposing of this dipsomaniac of a muleteer. True, he was a burden to the earth, to his family, to the Indians; but shooting a man is something else again. Besides this, I thought, continuing on in the same vein, what a plague of trouble the Mexican government wishes off on the foreigner who kills one of its nationals!

This last reflection brought to mind a young American youth, then in the penitentiary at Chihuahua City. He was the son of a former sheriff of El Paso, Texas. His father had been killed by a Mexican. In the best Texas manner, the lad had buckled on a heavy pistol and had gone across the river to get his father's murderer. There, in a saloon, someone wishing to indulge in a practical joke pointed out an innocent Mexican and named him as the offender. The Texan coolly shot the man where he stood.

This was a grievously shocking offense in Chihuahua, especially since it had been committed by a Texan; for against Texans the Mexicans still retain prejudices inherited from the days of Austin and Houston. But human life is held cheap in Mexico, and certain Americans well-known in Chihuahua were able to stave off a trial, the maximum sentence from which would have been eight years in the penitentiary. Certainly the Mexicans could have taken him from jail and given him the benefit of the *ley fuga* by "shooting him as he tried to escape," a not uncommon termination to the activities of those with whom the Mexicans think the law has been too lenient.

Since in Mexico the feeding of prisoners is considered too great an incentive toward crime, ladies of the American colony of Chihuahua fed the lonely lad from Texas. It became in the nature of a pilgrimage for the fine American ladies of Chihuahua to go to the penitentiary with big baskets of food. Bennett and I accompanied them once, and noted the large-eyed amazement of guard, soldiers, and prisoners alike at such solicitude. I think that these ladies had more to do with the Texan's eventual release than their husbands, who repeatedly took up collections to pay off the Mexican officials. Anytime the prosecuting attorney became short of cash he prepared to arraign the prisoner, at which the American Chamber of Commerce of Chihuahua went into a huddle and got things postponed. The state government of Chihuahua was flagrantly corrupt at that time. I believe, however, that it has improved since.

The outcome of the case was one of those fantastic things that can happen only in Mexico and Texas. Three years later I read in a Mexican newspaper that Governor "Ma" Ferguson of Texas had exchanged some Mexican prisoner from a Texas penitentiary for the Texas boy in the prison at Chihuahua. The whole story reads like a page of medieval history, although to a certain extent it typifies much of Mexico.

With all this passing in vivid panorama before me, it is hardly necessary to say that I was not enjoying the altercation between our *mozo* and the maniacal muleteer. I must affirm that the *mozo* kept his head pretty well. The loaded carbine that the muleteer carried was somewhat responsible, of course, for his restraint. The muleteer did indeed toy indecisively with his gun, and, unknown to him, I had my pistol trained on him. But I would not have fired unless Bennett had been menaced. Our *mozo* had got himself into this brawl without our help, and he would therefore have to extricate himself without our assistance. If he were shot, I should have a better reason to give the Mexican authorities than the Texas boy had.

But Bennett, the diplomat, saved the situation in spite of the rifle, though he was as paralyzed as I was. He got up in the mild, bored manner of a college professor and stepped between the disputants. Then, in his best Spanish, he said, "What sort of lack of respect is this? You are my guests and in my house. If you don't put away that gun and shut up, I'll put you both out in the cold to freeze."

Both the *mozo* and the muleteer were uncomfortably abashed at this stinging appeal to the deep Mexican regard for the tacit obligations of a guest toward his host.

Good old "*Don* Benito," as the Mexicans and Indians called him, being unable to pronounce his name. He was the head of our expedition, and a better and more considerate companion I could not have wished during all those months of continual strain, of living with no accustomed comforts whatsoever and under the additional stress of constant adjustment to the strange life of the Indians and Mexicans. I have no doubt that it was more to his credit than mine that no harsh words passed between us, and that, after nine months of the closest association alone together, we parted even better friends than we had been in the beginning.

I was not long in learning that Bennett was a man of almost inexhaustible mind. His own experiences had been augmented by enormous book-lore, so that for me the happiest occasions of the expedition were the long evenings we spent in our snug *convento* beside the roaring fire. Many a night passed while we wrangled spiritedly but amiably over moot points of ethnological theory, illustrating our respective arguments by references to almost every tribe under the sun.

It is of the highest importance in fieldwork among primitive people that two congenial ethnographers should work together. Even the religionists acknowledge this, since no church sends less than two missionaries to a difficult field. Quite often the presence of a second ethnographer is instrumental in warding off a threatening evil, as the case I have just cited proves. Indeed, before our expedition was over, I was to extricate Bennett from a dangerous situation. During my year among the Huichols, after a colleague had failed to stay in the field with me, I was to learn firsthand the dangers and difficulties concomitant upon working alone for any length of time.

Indirectly an incident in the Philippines had conveyed a pertinent anthropological lesson to me. The little non-Christian province of Nueva Vizcaya, where I taught school for one year, was the habitat of the Ilongots, the fiercest headhunters of the islands. Several years ago an American museum made the cardinal mistake of sending a lone ethnographer to this tribe. He was Dr. William Jones, himself American Indian, who possessed a wonderful insight into the psychology of primitive people.

Jones had lived for months in the incredibly dense and unhealthy jungles of the tropical home of the timid though cunning Ilongots. He had lived their life, had participated in their activities, and had passed from one to another of their *rancherías* as though protected by some charm or deity. This in itself was remarkable, for probably only in the heart of New Guinea or Borneo are there any other tribes as savage as the Ilongots. But Jones was a good ethnographer. He knew how to stay remote from the feuds and quarrels of these people, and by giving gifts and medical attention was able to pass unharmed and respected among them.

Thus he finished a brilliant year's work, and all that remained was to get back to civilization and write his book so that all might read about the customs of this interesting primitive tribe. By a stroke of tragic irony, however, he met fatal disaster just as he was leaving the country. His notes were hardly comprehensible to anyone save him, and though they have been printed, I believe they give but an unintelligible fraction of the picture.

What had happened was simply this: The Ilongots as a friendly gesture had prepared rafts for floating Jones and his Filipino boy with all their effects down the river. The night before he had planned to leave a sudden tropical flood washed away all but one of his rafts. After a year of unmitigated hardship, far greater than any I have ever known, this ill luck acted as a sort of *coup de grâce* to his hopes of getting back immediately to civilization, good food, a comfortable bed, and the like. He lost his temper. This one little slip of cool judgement proved his undoing.

Brusquely he ordered the natives to construct more rafts. Though cunning headhunters, the Ilongots are inordinately timid and fearful. Alarmed by his peremptory manner they jumped on the remaining raft and poled for the other side of the river. Then Jones lost his head completely, apparently becoming thoroughly frightened at the prospect of being deserted with his Filipino boy in the impenetrable jungle. He drew his revolver and shot toward the raft, motioning for the natives to return. Return they did, almost palsied with fear. But by this time Jones was lost, for he could not speak their language fluently enough to assure them that he meant no harm.

Still holding his revolver he approached the savages, who were carrying their curving head-knives, and yet the wily devils were dissembling friendliness. But he edged too close. A clever, treacherous pass from one of the savages, and Dr. Jones was bolced [sic] in the abdomen. As he fell, the Filipino caught his revolver and saved both himself and his employer from being beheaded. These savages never kill without slicing off their victim's head and tossing it around among themselves. The Filipino then drove them off, themselves sorry for what had occurred. They were caught later with great difficulty, but only after the tribe had surrendered them out of friendliness for Jones. Later, however, the culprits escaped from a lax guard and were never apprehended again.

The end of the story is saddening. The Filipino boy managed to get Jones on the raft, and succeeded in navigating the uncertain craft down the swollen Cagayan River. Finally they reached the outskirts of civilization, the farm of a Christian Filipino. There Jones died. But he kept a diary until his last moments, and one of the entries reads: "The rice I ate for breakfast is coming out the wound in my abdomen." He was dead long before help reached him. The best of help, however, would have availed him little because of that one rash slip he made.

The advisability of an ethnographer's carrying firearms among primitive peoples is quite frequently debated. In the foregoing incident, had Jones merely motioned to the natives and parleyed with them, they probably would have returned and have willingly given him the assistance he desired. Even had this procedure failed, he and his boy could easily have navigated the river by abandoning everything save the precious notes. But the problem varies with different countries and different people. In Mindanao, among the Moros, even supervising teachers are required to carry a Colt 45 automatic on their travels around the country. The Moros have a particularly respectful regard for such a weapon, and this regard proves salubrious for the teachers.

In Mexico I always carried a pistol, not so much for the benefit of the gentle Tarahumaras, but in consistency with Mexican customs. In the secluded backwashes of that country where we spent so many months there are still bandits and revolutionists with prices on their heads. Forced to an extremity by their exile, a few pesos and a pack animal of food often prove a great temptation to them. It is a simple matter to shoot a man down from behind a rock. Something of this sort happened in the Huichol country while I was there. Of course it is just as easy for these expert marksmen to shoot an armed and alert man. But in the Mexican hinterlands as elsewhere, a 30-40 rifle in one's saddle holster and a pistol on one's belt are credentials that are not generally fooled with.

My later sojourn among the Huichols had its exciting moments. On one occasion a drunken half-breed whipped out a *machete* and made for me. I sincerely thought that I was about to join Dr. Jones in the happy hunting grounds of ethnographers. To add to my discomfiture my gun was lying peacefully in my house. It was only by sending my *mozo* after my gun that I galvanized into action the Mexicans and Indians gathered around us, who promptly carried their drunken companion away.

In the backwoods of Mexico the attitude toward guns is interesting. It is quite different from that of the Old West, even though our cowboys did pick up "gun-toting" from the Mexicans along with the rest of their paraphernalia, including *sombreros, resetas,* lassos, chaps, large saddles, enormous spurs, and curved bits. Arms are contraband in Mexico, but in localities such as Chihuahua that are near the border, guns and ammunition are smuggled in from the United States. So riding along the trail one may still meet with *bravos* to whom a pistol is as necessary as a pocket handkerchief is to us. I encountered several such men. Generally each was courteous and affable, and very interested in my automatic, which was somewhat a novelty for Mexico. Generally, too, these temporary acquaintances would offer me their guns as a token of good faith. I would hand mine over, thus furthering a chat about each type of gun, its particular advantages or disadvantages, and so forth.

But let us return to the difficulties between our *mozo* and the drunken muleteer. Bennett had stopped the quarrel with his admonishment. About three o'clock in the morning I sent the *mozo* after the mule to get an early start on my trip to Norogáchic, the nearest Jesuit mission. But the argument of the night before was resumed, and I saw neither hair nor hide of the mule until midmorning. By then it was too late for me to make Norogáchic in time for the ceremonies I wished to see, since I should have started at dawn. I discharged the *mozo* and waited for the ceremonies in Samachique.

Isidro, the partially Mexicanized Indian whose ailing son I had visited, was a *chapiyó*, and therefore a busy man during festivities. But his official duties ended with the celebration, and I was able to get him to serve as a *mozo* for the trip to Norogáchic a few days later. Our mule needed to be shod, and since the work could be done at Norogáchic, I decided to avail myself of the luxury of motive power other than my own feet. So the mule was changed from a pack to a saddle animal. At last we started off, with Isidro, a true Tarahumara, carrying about half a burro load of food, cooking utensils, blankets, and other odds and ends, and the mule, unburdened of its accustomed load, carrying the great load which was I.

We were supposed to reach the ranch of the Córdoba family by nightfall. But we made such a late start that it became dark an hour before I arrived. The ranch we were seeking was called "*La Laja*" (The Ledge),[1] because of the precipice along the trail. By the time we reached the precipice, I was so tired that I did not dismount, although Isidro called out that we had come to a bad place in the trail. Happy in the enveloping darkness, I remained on the mule, trusting to Isidro for guidance. When I saw the spot on our return trip, my hair fairly stood on end. I repeat, there must be a special god who protects drunkards, anthropologists, and fools.

We arrived at the Mexican ranch long after dark. Only the mother and the children were there, for the father was away hunting deer; but they seemed delighted to meet at last their hitherto invisible consumer of *tortillas*. The little children greeted me with that indescribable courtesy of Mexican children; some of them scampered off to inform their mother of us; one led me, cold, tired, and hungry, into the kitchen, where a cheering fire was burning. The mother finally appeared, and welcomed me with the unfailing grace and hospitality of all Mexicans whether of high or low estate.

In this instance the estate was pitiably low. The telltale marks of a decade of revolution were all over the place. The ranch had been another station for mule trains carrying bullion from the mines. It had been ravaged by fire until only the walls remained standing. Before the

Revolution Córdoba's father had been the agent for this station; when peace had returned to the sierra, he had moved his family back to establish a ranch.

The walls were roofed over with *canoas* in imitation of Tarahumara dwellings. Save for this the structure was in wretched state. The embrasures left for windows were merely filled with loose stones; doors had not been put up; and through these apertures poured the wintry blasts of the sierra. A homemade bed with stretched deer hides for springs constituted the furniture. Scattered around were a *metate*, a *comal*, and some tin cans which we had given the family on their trips to our *convento* with *tortillas*. Each member of the family was clad in patched and tattered clothing, the smaller children wearing the repaired "hand-me-downs" of their elders. And despite the snow and the cold, not one was wearing shoes. With ample reason Mexicans all throughout the Republic wistfully sing these lines from "Cuatro mil-pas," the folk song of the Revolution:

> *Y los destrozos de aquella casita tan blanca y bonita,*
> (Ah! the destruction of that little house so white and pretty,)
> *Lo triste que está.*
> (How sad it is!)

The Córdoba ranch stood in the midst of the most magnificent pine forest of the entire sierra. Yet this was really a handicap, since the land had to be cleared before corn could be planted. The Córdobas were engaged in this. In the meantime they lived by trading for corn from the Indians with certain trade goods they were able to purchase with the few pesos in their possession.

But in Mexico, as elsewhere, everything is relative; and at that particular time I was more miserable than the Córdobas, for I was chilled and fatigued from my long journey. I immediately secured a snug corner by the roaring fire, while the mother began a cheerful pit-pat with her hands, making *tortillas*. On this food the family had subsisted for months, since even beans were not available in the famine-stricken sierra. But even this they were happy to share with me. It is small wonder that I like Mexicans, a gracious, kind, and hospitable people. I never see a Mexican, whether in his own country or mine, without a feeling of sympathy and warmth for him.

The *tortillas* were now finished, Córdoba came in, his feet encased in goatskins, an Indian device as a protection against snow and cold.

For the first time in months he had shot a deer, and this he had carried home on his back. One of the little children exclaimed, "*¡Que bueno que papá mató un venado por el Americano!*" [sic] ("How good that papa killed a deer for the American!")

The *tortillas* were now insufficient, of course, and the family could not compose itself until for me long strips of the tenderloin were roasting over the fire, since they had no lard for frying. I had to begin eating before the children or the father, who was tired out from his exertions, would touch their own food. Then the one and only bed of the household was prepared for me, an extreme courtesy which, under the circumstances, I could hardly refuse for fear of hurting the feelings of my host. Besides, I didn't mind that bed after months of sleeping on the floor.

Señor Córdoba accompanied us to Norogáchic, and I sent him back with coffee and sugar for himself and wife and candy for the children. During my three months of archaeological work I was able to utilize the services of both him and his grown son. And when Bennett and I left the pair in Creel on our way back to civilization, we gave them what remained of our expedition equipment. The stuff was common and simple enough, but it was sufficient to make our friends the Córdobas the envy of all Mexicans between Creel and Norogáchic.

The foregoing will convey some idea of the bleak poverty that remains in parts of Chihuahua as the grim aftermath of the Revolution. Everywhere we saw clothes so fantastically patched that we wondered at the cunning patience of the fingers of Mexican women who were able to make such rags stay together. We marvelled also at the endurance of the Mexican pattern of "decency" that prevented these people from wearing the clouts of the Indians, for so much else among the Mexicans shows an Indian influence.

We saw no others perhaps quite as impoverished as the Córdobas. But differences in wealth are slight, and revolution is a great leveler when it goes to an extreme, as it did in Mexico. Coupled with that, in the part of the sierra we visited there was an unusual corn shortage, due to crop failure. Indeed, all Mexico was subjected to crop failure and, although the original home of maize, had to resort to heavy importations of corn from Africa. This was partly the unanticipated consequence of the expropriation of arable land from the landlords, and the division of it among the land-hungry peasants. But it will take the peasants several generations to develop enough initiative even to resume the aboriginal agriculture of corn on their own lands. With no *patrón* or landlord to keep them in debt and save their money for them, they seem never able to buy seeds for a year's crop.

Poor as the Córdobas were, however, the old man saw fit to spend one of his family's few pesos for the bottle of *sotol* that had wrought so much havoc in our camp. Such instances of thriftlessness and lack of foresight together with reckless drinking are common enough in Mexico to suggest that many generations must pass before the Mexican peons become substantial peasants. It is not surprising, therefore, that the rapid redistribution of land by the government has not been altogether successful. Further, abuses of all sorts crept into the agrarian administration due to dishonest officials. Even as late as today one of the greatest unsolved problems in Mexico is the putting of land into the hands of peasants capable of making it productive. In reflecting on these conditions, however, we draw away from Indian Mexico to mestizo Mexico with its markedly different characteristics, manners, and problems. We find ourselves in a setting where the people live in houses and wear clothes; where they sweep floors, launder, tan leather, ride horseback, go to school; where they buy coffee and sugar, if they have money, raise pigs and render lard for frying and eat the tasty cracklings (*chicharrones*).

We are in a scene where the people use the divine language of Spain to court and to criticize, to trade, to talk, to worship, or merely to chat in passing the time of day, a language that one cannot speak fluently, I am convinced, until he becomes at least half Spaniard. Such is the intimate relationship between custom and language that to think in a foreign language is to think in terms of the customs and culture of the people whose language you are speaking. Spanish, for example, is so much mine that when I am speaking it, I am almost blood brother to the Spaniard. This experience convinces me that the mestizo Mexican who speaks no language other than Spanish is Spanish in ideology and behavior, and that the bilingual Indians, such as Lorenzo, are as much Spanish as Indian. Even the latter seem to merge into that fairly consistent blend that is the folk culture of Mexico from Chihuahua to Chiapas. In contrast to these folk peoples are the culturally isolated groups, the Tarahumaras, the Yaquis, the Huichols, and the Lacandónes. These are primitive tribes to be distinguished from the other people of Mexico not only by their minor degree of Hispanization but by the inert conservatism and changeless pagan mysticism that permeate their cultures.

We are out of Indian Mexico, I repeat, and in the Mexican maze of postrevolutionary reconstruction. We see Mexico as it binds up the hurts of those dreadful years and attempts also to gain something of permanent worth that will not only justify its sufferings but preclude the recurrence of such horrors. And encountering Mexico after months of living with the timid Indians, even the gentle Mexicans seemed harsh and abrupt.

But the Chihuahua frontiersmen "of the North" are not as gentle as the Mexicans farther south, even as the frontiersmen of our West may be contrasted with our "effete Easterners." And naturally enough. For it was these northerners who fought the Revolution to a bloody finish and won it. This wild northern frontier produced all the armies, except Zapatistas, that fought Díaz and Huerta. Carranza, the first chief of the Revolution, and his "Constitutional" army were from Coahuila, just to the east of Chihuahua. Villa came out of Chihuahua. And the states of Sonora and Sinaloa to the west produced the Obregón-Calles movement that followed the presidency of Carranza. Mexicans of the south look upon those of the north as *muy hombres*. But perhaps the reason for the successes of the north lies not only in the fact that it has hardier and more vigorous people, but also that it has had more leaders who, expatriated to the United States, entered the Revolution with liberal ideas derived from "North American" residence.

In isolated communities like Norogáchic the Mexicans are brusque and direct. I remember that on my trip there, as I approached the village on my tired and dejected mule, I met a party of Mexicans. Their greeting was so different from the "May you go with God" acknowledgement of the peasants of Jalisco! This conversation took place.

"Where are you going?"
"I am going to Norogáchic."
"What are you going to do there?"
"I am going to see the padres."
"What is the matter? Are you sick?"

The padres are, of course, the *médicos* for both the Indians and the Mexicans; and at the time the persecution of the Church by the government party was so strong that these Mexicans could see no reason why I was visiting Norogáchic.

CHAPTER 10

> **The Mexican Powers:**
> **Religious, Civil, and Military**
>
>
>
>
>
>
>
>
> T he "town" of Norogáchic turned out to be merely a clus-
> ter of sprawling ranches gathered around a mission build-
> ing. As we entered, I saw several Mexican women clad in
ordinary costumes with colored *rebozos* over their heads. I questioned
Córdoba about them, and was amazed when he answered that they
were nuns who were teaching in the Norogáchic Indian school. At that
time the government's persecution of the Church was so severe that
the Sisters, in order to avoid attention, were forced to abandon their
usual habits and assume the clothing of the lower-class·Mexican
women. Everyone of the surrounding countryside, however, knew
their real identity. I shall have more to say about these saintly women,
because I soon became friendly with them.

The mission followed the adobe and architectural pattern that is
seen everywhere in the Spanish colonial world including our own
Southwest, particularly Texas, New Mexico, Arizona, and California;
although its principal features especially looked very much like those
of the adobe missions of New Mexico. The padres said later, "It is not
old, but it has two hundred years." Despite their efforts protracted
over several generations, the Jesuits have been curbed so often under
both Spain and the Republic that even here at Norogáchic their work
among the Indians seems only just begun.

The mission was surrounded by a compound. A high wall joined
the front of the church with a high-walled *convento*. The whole structure was as strong and secure as a fort; indeed, many times in the tur-
bulent history of Mexico this strength and security had been tested to
the utmost.

I rode up to the sturdy door that provided entry to the *patio* of the mission building. A huge iron knocker was in the center of the door. By means of this I announced my presence. I was admitted by a little Indian boy, an orphan who was being reared and educated in the boarding school of the mission. The work of the priests at this remotest of Jesuit missions was so handicapped for lack of funds that they were able to care for only a few young waifs and orphans gathered up from the Indians. I was to see a much more developed mission at Samachique.

Inside, the *patio* was a wide, level square similar to those which one finds accompanying all Spanish buildings. Although one generally thinks of a *patio* as a garden spot and one of the charms of a Spanish dwelling, here were only a few trees and a few sparse patches of grass. In the middle was a stone monument supporting a cross.

The *convento*, on the far side of the *patio*, consisted of an apartment of one floor partitioned off into about a dozen rooms in series. Since only two priests comprised the moderate staff for this establishment, most of the rooms were unused. From within, the high wall connecting the church and the *convento* was seen to be a part of a structure at right angles to the *convento*. Here were the carpenter shops and the dispensary.

Off in one corner of the *convento* was the kitchen. A dining room and apartments for the students enclosed the back of the *patio*, and beyond these were stables for saddle and work horses. The mission compound in its entirety was set in the middle of a small farm on which were produced the corn and beans which formed the diet of priests and neophytes alike.

The general restrictions on the Church in Mexico about this time had resulted in the neglect of this mission, which consequently was poorly and meagerly equipped. The most notable room of the place was the kitchen, where the mission treasure was kept. As in the Cathedral at Guadalajara there is a secret niche where, during periods of distress and agitation, is concealed the famous "Assumption of the Virgin" from the brush of Murillo, so in this lowly mission at Norogáchic was a false wall for a somewhat similar purpose, which had been used with profit throughout the Revolution.

The treasure, however, was nothing more than a "Round Oak" cookstove. Heaven only knows in how many pieces it had arrived by mule at this remote outpost! One of the lay brothers of the mission served as high priest at this stove, and many a noble loaf of bread did he turn out during my visit of about a month. This bread, by the way, was virtually the only culinary indulgence the priests enjoyed. But it was a genuine comfort to sit by that warm stove at night with a real table and an oil lamp; and after four months of recasting my notes on the rough, shaky construction of hand-hewn boards that had served me for a table at Samachique, the scant equipment of the mission seemed even luxurious to me.

Despite these acquisitions, however, the padres for the most part lived in actual discomfort and even want. Highly cultivated and well-educated men as they were, they did not relish their reign any more than I did. A few times during my visit some kind Mexican women brought in some *chicharrones*, sweet pork cracklings, which are always a treat in Mexico; but aside from this our only delicacy was *café con leche* and bread. Yet it is amazing how delicious bread tastes after one has lived for months on *tortillas*. Plain bread soaked in coffee and milk! It was ambrosia and nectar to me. But alas! for just toward the end of my visit the cow went dry. I had ordered a case of canned milk, however, and this I left behind. It would have been a rank shame to stand in the way of a perfectly natural rapprochement between that milk and coffee and bread of the good padres. Besides, in my future work in the sierra there was little hope of my getting any more bread.

The lay brother taught the Indian boys cooking, agriculture, and animal husbandry. His teaching was essentially practical, and the boys merely followed his example of tireless industry. This brother was not so well-educated as the fathers, but he had at least received the rudiments of an education in a Jesuit school in Presidio, Texas. So rigorous are the Mexican laws against ecclesiastical training that all church personnel must be trained outside of Mexico. Thus the Jesuits maintain a seminary in El Paso, Texas, where novitiates begin their training, completing it later in Spain.

There were two priests at the mission. One, who was not in good health, taught the Indian boys in "the three R's." He was also in charge of the dispensary and occasionally gave services in the church. Because of his health, which prevented his riding horseback, he was transferred to Chihuahua to teach in a church school. The government, however, soon intervened, and he was shifted to El Paso, there to teach Latin, Greek, and Hebrew in the seminary. Charming, mild, and scholarly, he was devoted to the Indians and especially interested in the turpentine and tar industry of the southern United States, hoping to introduce it among the Tarahumaras of the sierra, where so many magnificent forests of pine lie idle. Three years later I met him on a train in El Paso. Either he did not recognize me, or else my civilized appearance was hardly reminiscent of the dirty, bearded anthropologist who had hobbled across the *patio* of Norogáchic mission, almost as tired as his dejected mule. On that occasion, however, he had bidden me welcome, and had assigned me to an idle room where there was a bed with springs.

The second priest, the head of the mission and he who had, through Córdoba, invited me to Norogáchic, was absent when I arrived. He was out on his horse with his pack mule and portable altar. He returned that night from a week's trip, during which he had given masses to the five thousand Tarahumaras in the region who were assembled at their various little churches (each like that of Samachique) for the celebration of Epiphany.

When he rode in at dusk, he looked as little like a priest as I did, except that he lacked my four months' growth of beard. Like me he was dressed in riding boots and riding breeches, wore a wide *sombrero* and a sheepskin coat, and carried a pistol, a necessary item because of personal danger at the hands of anticlerical Mexicans of the region. And he was just as weary as I was. This gave us much in common, and we became staunch friends from the beginning.

Yet on quiet days this padre loved to don his cassock and cap and pace back and forth in the sunshine of the *patio*, divided in his attention between the peacefulness of his surroundings and his little, black Morocco breviary. He loved his way of life. Later, after our friendship had time to flourish, he said to me, "Even other Catholics think that the Jesuit discipline is hard. St. Ignatius was a soldier, you know, and he founded our order in military-like discipline. *Seguro*, were I not a priest, I should make a good soldier. This discipline fits me as lightly as this cassock and cap. I entered training in a Jesuit school when I was only fourteen. Since then I have found a wholly complete life in this order."

Happy, happy man! How many human beings have found such completion, such self-fulfillment?

These priests were highly cultivated men, lonely for the conversation of an educated person. They were versed in ancient languages and literatures and, like all priests of their order, could talk and correspond in Latin, which is the international language of the Church. They had seriously studied physical science, theology, and philosophy. In particular were they familiar with Spanish literature and the English language, for their training had taken them to famous Jesuit institutions in Spain, and they had traveled widely in the United States. This had given them a correspondingly cosmopolitan view of life. Keenly and deeply concerned with the Tarahumaras as they were, theirs was more than a merely intelligent interest in my anthropological work; and on many points, especially religion, they were able to give me many important leads and much valuable information. Their interest in scholarship and learning was attested by the technical and historical books of their little library (which had escaped the Revolution), and in their sympathy with scientific work. As cultivated men, they met me on familiar ground and offered me sincere and intimate friendship, despite the fact that I was not Catholic.

I was to visit the mission several times; and consequently there, as the Mexicans say, "I had my home." And on every occasion I was treated as an insider, although my ignorance of Catholicism caused some amusing breaks. I think nothing proved my status better than having one of the padres tell me that old wheeze about the Church that is so frequently heard among Protestants. It concerns a priest's interrupting his mass by singing a question as to the whereabouts of the "incense pot." It was a little unusual to hear this story from a padre. Strangely enough it has an international flavor, because it works out with effect in Spanish.

One day a neighbor sent in some *chicharrones*, which appeared on the table the following Friday. I quite forgot that I was surrounded by Catholics (and priests, moreover), and dropped a casual, Protestant remark about eating meat on Friday. The padres, however, were not shirking the ordinances of the Church. One of them, completely overlooking my thoughtlessness, explained in the most patient manner that by a special papal dispensation both the clergy and laity of northern Mexico and New Mexico, because of their arduous, outdoor activities, are excused from fasting from meat on Fridays.

My prize error, however, occurred the first Sunday morning I was at the mission. When I appeared for breakfast, I found the table set with *café con leche* and hotcakes for only one. One of the padres, with typical Mexican hospitality, was there to sit down with me, although it was about time for the late mass. In my best Alphonse-Gaston manner I said, "You are in a hurry to sing mass, father, so you go ahead and eat, and I'll eat later." The padre roared heartily at this, and his laughter was echoed from the kitchen, where the lay brother was preparing hotcakes. The padre, his eyes twinkling, informed me, "I must fast until I say mass."

When the padre, who was in ill health, was forced to leave Norogáchic, the Father Superior had no one to replace him save a substitute lay brother. Thus the remaining priest had to give all the masses. The new lay brother, however, was well-educated and able to give sermons, teach classes, and mix medicines with relative efficiency. None of these priests were pharmacists, but their education had included advanced chemistry, and this enabled them to study intelligently the pharmaceutical books in their library. They know much more about drugs and treatment and first aid than I, and their Indians as a result fared better than mine in Samachique.

This lay brother was a charming person, witty, intelligent, and sincere. He spoke Tarahumara, which was more than the priest could do. He had taken the regular training for the priesthood, but had failed in his examination because of his eyes, at least that is what he told me. I had heard similar excuses before, had in fact used them under such circumstances, and hence was a little doubtful about that. Still, it is possible that my skepticism was groundless, for he was as keen and intelligent as the priest. I was very fond of him.

A day or so after my arrival the padre took me to meet the nuns, who had a large establishment across the plaza by which the little settlement of Norogáchic proclaimed its affinities with Mexico. The nuns' building was of adobe, and living in it were about a dozen Tarahumara girls in various stages of domestication. The nuns taught them common Mexican household arts, such as sewing, cooking, the care of children, and the rudimentary educational subjects and elements of the Catholic faith. The girls, however, were much older than the few little waifs that had fallen to the lot of the padres; and the padres and nuns alike lamented this, because their teaching would be gone if the girls married wild Tarahumaras rather than products of the mission who could be induced to settle "under the bells."

The nuns' school was far better equipped than the Jesuit mission, although simply and modestly. It seemed a little strange at first being entertained by these charming and well-educated women, who were dressed in clothes somewhat similar to those of the Mexican *señora* (washwoman) who used to work for my mother in New Mexico. One of the Sisters, a mestiza from Oaxaca, was keenly interested in Indians. She had visited Monte Albán and, as we shall see, her concern with archaeology was later to give me several bad minutes. The Sisters were as hungry for civilized conversation as were the padres, and they treated me with an equally considerate friendship and toleration.

My archaeological investigations were not long in beginning. At table one day I asked about *antiguedades*. The padre, as casually as though he were directing me to a streetcar, informed me of a cave nearby in which there were mummies, fur and feather blankets, coiled baskets, and *quién sabe que*. My ears pricked up like those of the Mexican mules when the *arriero* shakes some corn at them; and immediately into my mind jumped visions of mummies wrapped in fur and feather blankets, similar to those which are buried under coiled baskets in the widespread Basket-Maker area of our own Southwest. The Tarahumaras are still cave-dwellers, I reflected. Might it be that their ancestors were culturally related to the Basket-Makers of the Southwest, who were the ancestors of the Cliff-Dwellers? Such a discovery would be too good, almost, to be true. With such hopes stirring within me, naturally I was anxious to be about my business.

The padre offered to guide me to the cave on the following day. But he warned me in advance that although much of the large cave was still untouched, the place had been partially wrecked by Mexican treasure hunters. The childish but general treasure-seeking propensity of the Mexicans finds outlet even in this remote nook of the Republic. When they came across bits of ancient coiled basketwork, unfamiliar because it is no longer used by the Tarahumaras, they immediately jumped to the conclusion that such must be the remains of the "hats" of early Catholic priests. In Mexican folk belief all padres are supposed to be as rich as Croesus; and since there have been so many persecutions of the Church, the priests have been forced to bury their treasure where the remains of their "hats" are to be found.

The results of such self-deception are regrettable in more ways than one. In their amusingly naive quest for sudden wealth the Mexicans waste efforts which, directed toward more sensible pursuits, would procure them at least a little of what they seek. Aside from this, they ruin precious sites not already torn apart by the treasure-mad vandals who had preceded me. Strangely enough, the best site I encountered was this one within a mile or so of Norogáchic. Here hardly more than a third of the cave had been touched. Most of the smaller caves I visited, however, were completely destroyed, even though they were sometimes as far as thirty miles from the nearest Mexican ranch. Before excavating one of these caves the Mexican peasants pooled their resources in a primitive sort of corporation and sold shares in the loot-to-be. It had been an excellent cave; but after they went through, I found few archaeological fragments in the debris that had any scientific value.

On our way over to the Norogáchic cave the next morning, the padre regaled me with tales about Revolution-torn Mexico, fascinating tales that revealed all the stark tragedy of the country, lightened somewhat, however, by adventure, excitement, and romance.

"Pues sí, señor," he began,

> until Villa was killed in Parral, the Villistas controlled the sierra. Villa himself was not hostile to the priests, but many of his men were after us, kidnapping us, and then attempting to extort money from our Order for our release. At one time or another, almost all five of the priests of the Tarahumara mission were captured. I myself was once taken to Parral to be executed. The Villistas had me against a wall, when Villa personally ordered my release.

Last-minute reprieves, with the prisoner actually standing against a wall, were common enough during the Revolution. Indeed, Villa himself once owed his life to such a turn of events. On such slender threads lives and fortunes have depended in Mexican revolutions.

After the initial success of Madero, following the fall of the Conservatives under Díaz, the enormously wealthy Creel and Terrazas families of Chihuahua financed the first abortive counterrevolution, called that of Orozco. To quell this uprising Madero sent out a retired general, Victoriano Huerta, the "Cockroach." Captured in the shuffle was a notorious cattle thief, Doroteo Arango, who was even then known as "Pancho Villa," a name assumed from some romantic Robin Hood of Mexican folk history, and which was later to be made known all over the world.

Huerta's men were about to give the petty cattle thief his deserts against an adobe wall, despite the fact that he had played a minor part in Madero's triumphal course from Juárez to the Presidential palace. But as Villa calmly faced the firing squad, he noticed Madero's brother standing by; and courteously he asked the officer of the firing squad for a word with this man. The request was granted. Villa told Madero's brother that this was a thankless way indeed to pay for revolutionary successes. The words had their desired effect, apparently, for Madero's brother spoke to Huerta. At first Huerta demurred. Villa, he said, was a despicable bandit, a thief, and as such well-known all over Chihuahua. The Revolution did not need the services of such people. But the brother, like Madero himself, suffered from too tender a heart ever to be a continual success in a Mexican revolution, and he finally won his point. Villa was led away from the wall, and shortly after flung himself upon that wild and erratic career as a chieftain which every other Revolutionist, save Zapata, had abundant occasion to lament. Had the firing squad proceeded with its execution, the course of the Revolution in the North would undoubtedly have been different, although it could hardly have been worse.

Thus one of the few experiences that Villa and my Jesuit friend had in common was a last-minute escape from before a dismal adobe wall. The padre continued to relate his adventures.

Conditions in the sierra became so uncertain and insecure that we were ordered to clear out. The other fathers left for the United States. I, however, decided to remain. The Indians and certain faithful Catholics hid me from the Revolutionists, and thus I passed through the sierra giving a secret mass in this house, performing a baptism in that one, *allá lejos* [with a sweeping gesture of his arm, "there far away"].

Later, I was captured by the *Federales* [the troops of the government which by this time controlled Mexico]. I was placed in an adobe jail at Bocóyna. But at night, holding a peso in my hand to protect my fingernails, I wore a hole through the wall. The edges of that peso were worn flat, and my hand still hurts at times from the cramp of holding it all night while I rubbed away the adobe. I slipped through the hole, and managed to get to the house of a Catholic friend in Bocóyna. He gave me a horse, and before dawn I was again safe among the *Tarahumaritos*, as free as a bird, and laughing at those stupid *Federales*, who were as bad as the Villistas.

The triumph of Carranza and the "Constitutional" armies of the North was accompanied by a certain measure of security, so that the priests, who had left Mexico, were able to return. Further, though the policy of the Revolution under Carranza was anticlerical, at the same time it was so vacillating that the padres were merely harried. Then followed Obregón, who continued to compromise on the clerical question. With Calles, however, it was a different matter: the present restrictions of the Church were initiated, and the priests were again expelled. But again my friend refused to leave. The padre went on:

> I was captured again, but this time I wasn't put into any adobe jail. I was taken to Chihuahua and sentenced to be shot. None of my friends were in any position to help me, and it looked as if *se acabó el asunto* [the affair was finished].
>
> However, the Federal general's mother was a devout Catholic. When she heard that a priest of the Catholic Church was about to be executed, she came to Chihuahua and threatened to disown and never speak to her son again if he permitted this barbarity. Thus I was saved.

The stringent, anti-Catholic policy of Calles brought on the clerical counterrevolution in Jalisco, called the *"Cristero"* Revolution. The Federal forces of Chihuahua were ordered to engage in the campaign in faraway Jalisco. My padre friend was taken along to be used as a hostage and messenger to the Catholic forces of the southern states.

> *Fue un viaje espantosa* [sic; editors' note], it was a horrible journey. For some obscure reason the American government would not permit the Federal troops to go through the United States from El Paso, on the Southern Pacific, to Nogales and down the west coast. So we had to march across the mountains and deserts from Chihuahua to Sonora. When we finally got on the trains, it was worse; for the horses had the best places in the cars, and the soldiers along with myself had to sit on the top. We were all very dirty, and in a short while I became quite lousy from such intimate contact with my sworn enemies.
>
> We arrived at last at Jalisco, and there I, as a priest, was told to go to the Catholic rebels and inform them of the great number of soldiers, guns, and airplanes that the *Federales* had brought against them. Thus I escaped death at the hands of my enemies.
>
> But I almost lost my life at the hands of my friends. I was captured by the first *Cristero* band that I met, and taken before some petty officers who feared that I was a Federal spy. When I insisted that I was a Catholic priest, they said, "Very well, give us a mass to prove it."

So I asked them for some wine. All they had, however, was their terrible *tequila* of which Jalisco is the *matriz*. Naturally I should have died rather than desecrate the mass by using such stuff, and I told them so. They ordered me to be sent on to the higher officers for trial. In short order I was taken to these military dignitaries. But I was saved indirectly by the *Federales;* for just as I was attempting to clear myself of the suspicions directed against me and explain that all resistance was futile because of the great military strength of the *Federales*, a Federal airplane flew by and dropped several bombs in the vicinity of the *Cristero* high command. In their terror they all fled, leaving me free to go.

This "*Cristero*" Revolution was one of the most terrible and tragic events in the history of modern Mexico, with a mad spirit of religious fanaticism pitted against one of the cruelest exhibitions of Mexican militarism. I have seen pictures of railroad lines with each telegraph pole gruesomely ornamented with the bodies of "*Cristeros*," poor deluded peasants, hanging limply in their cotton, pajama-like *calzones*.

The militia fomented trouble by confiscating for their own profit all property of any value. This caused another flare-up, with the result that all of northern Jalisco was declared a "neutral zone," with various points of population concentration. Six years later I passed through this region. Many of the towns and *ranchos* were still in ruins. A tragic heritage indeed! And it is out of this that have come songs such as the one I have already quoted:

> *Para ver los destrozos de aquella casita tan blanca y bonita*
> (To see the destruction of that little house so white and pretty)
> *Lo triste que está.*
> (How sad it is!)

Calles and his anticlerical government unleashed military rapacity and cruelty that soon went far beyond their control. The civil power in Mexico was not strong enough to transfer or court-martial the generals who were reaping fortunes for themselves from all this destruction. In short, Mexico was little better than a military organism without a head, a huge, distended, voracious body devouring everything that lay in its path.

With no quarter given by either side, this Church-State controversy had been conducted with immoderate complications surprising to an American "of the north." Flandrau, in ¡*Viva México!*, has an interesting comment on the complete lack of *reglas fijas* in Mexico. But in this impetuous struggle of Church and State the rules were fixed inflexibly, and the severity of the government's anticlerical policy was carried out to the letter, even in this remote village of Norogáchic, where the priests and nuns were fulfilling a really worthy, humanitarian task.

Most of the people of Norogáchic, which had originally been a small trading post for the Indians, were flotsam of civilization. Many were discontented miners ruined by the suspension of mining in the sierra. Others were criminals or revolutionary fugitives, finding sanctuary in the center of the Tarahumara country, far from any law and order other than their own. Potentially they were a bad lot, although I managed to get along with them, despite my friendship for the padres. In fact, the priests were often in actual danger from these cutthroat survivors of the Villa era. In a town near Norogáchic a group of these men determined to loot and desecrate the church building. Word reached the priest of Norogáchic by some loyal Catholic, and he galloped to the place. There, at the door of the church, and armed only with a club, he held the hoodlums at bay until they dispersed. Since that time he had worn a pistol, though purely for moral effect because it was broken. When I left the mission at the end of my last visit, I gave him my Colt automatic, *por si acaso* (just in case). I still had a rifle, and this sufficed for my protection during the remainder of my archaeological work in the sierra.

The *presidente* of Norogáchic was a *chulo*, a pretty one, as they say in Mexico. Since my visit to the padres was not because of sickness, my friendship for the priests brought me into bad odor with the civil power, at least as such was exercised in this faraway place. I noticed this clearly in more ways than one, and particularly by the passively hostile attitude of the "City Hall" boys.

Later, when I was about to begin excavations on an archaeological site, I wished to hire men. So I sought out the local *presidente* and presented my papers from the Constitutional Governor of Chihuahua and the Minister of Education of Mexico City. These impressed him. He was so ignorant of Mexican law that he didn't know that besides these I needed a special permit for archaeological excavations. This permit I had sent for; but it suffered the usual governmental delay, and did not reach me until three months had passed. By that time, however, my work was finished.

The *presidente* approved my project, especially since the people of the town were in dire need of the money I would pay them for their labor. Apparently mine were to be the first wages paid out in the place since its foundation on lands stolen from the Indians. To avoid trouble at the cave I carefully picked men from each of the opposing parties, friends of the padres and supporters of the *presidente;* and I allowed no arms save my own in camp. The first night, however, I foolishly left the site unguarded, and every item that had been excavated that day was deliberately broken. This may have been done by one of the *presidente*'s party who quit when I refused to pay him more than I was paying the others. He was a *filósofo,* a talkative troublemaker, who was not in sympathy with my archaeological proceedings anyway. After this mishap I slept in the cave with my *mozo,* Pancho, with a loaded rifle near my hand and a pistol under my pillow, which was my saddle.

When the work was all finished and my money in circulation, the *presidente,* who was, fortunately, still ignorant of my illegal position, threatened to act against me for disturbing burials and for being a vandal, a ghoul, and a menace to public health because of the ancient mummies I had disinterred. But I waved under his nose my letter from the Governor, which enjoined all municipal authorities to offer "all facilities at their disposal." And to the schoolteacher in Norogáchic I showed my letter from the Minister of Education and suggested that it would hardly disadvantage his professional career to use his influence on my behalf with the *presidente.* I think this latter personage acted on my suggestion; at any rate I emerged from the imbroglio scot-free. Needless to say, however, I heaved a sigh of relief when the dust of the town was shaken off my boots forever.

The padres and the nuns, of course, could not leave, and they were subjected constantly to annoyances stirred up by the *presidente* and his officious "Chief of Arms." This luscious pair found a hundred different ways in which to irritate the priesthood, despite the sympathy and love of most of the Mexicans and Indians for the clergy. But while I was in Norogáchic the padre rather cleverly and courageously turned this sympathy against the *presidente.* The *presidente* wished to be a *compadre* at the baptism of a child of one of his friends. In Mexico one's social status depends to a certain extent on the number of *compadres* he has. So the *presidente* was nonplussed when the padre said, "You can't be a *compadre* in a Catholic baptism, because you aren't a Catholic," which was the simple truth.

Most of the annoyances to the priests and nuns were engendered by the work of the Church in educating the Tarahumara children in its schools. The law prohibited *ministros de cultos* (ministers of cults) from teaching, and this law the clergy obeyed by having the teaching done by lay brothers and nuns. But the local public education officials and petty supervisors, who occasionally passed through the neighborhood, were still able to find a myriad of imaginary faults in this work.

Thus the "ministers of cults" worked under the constant peril of having their schools closed and their Indian charges dispersed into the sierra, an absurd constraint considering that these padres had only three little waifs in their care and that these orphans would therefore become the peons of some affluent Indian or Mexican and spend their youth herding animals. As for the girls in the care of the nuns, such a calamity could only result in their being thrust into concubinage. It was because of this ever-present peril that the nuns had doffed their usual habits in order to avoid attracting attention.

The government, of course, had its own ambitious plans for the education of the Tarahumaras; but none of them materialized while I was in the sierra.[1] The public schools, worthwhile as they admittedly were, were wholly inadequate to the needs of so great a tribe scattered over such a vast area. Common sense, that extremely rare acquisition of the mind, would have dictated acceptance of the gratuitous educational labors of the priests and nuns; but in this instance the contrary was true, and the work of the clergy was hampered or brought to an impasse by almost every conceivable pretext.

As we hiked along to see the cave and inspect the work of the vandals who had dug up about a third of it, the padre continued his tale of the Revolution.

> *Fue una cosa espantosa.* [This frightful expression, a favorite of the padre's, and an especially apt one for any revolution, here or elsewhere, came forth fluently.] Bands of Villistas visited Norogáchic often and took forced contributions of food and fodder until the people were reduced to actual want. The Villista government finally set up a municipal organization here, but its chief, the *presidente*, was terrible.

> We priests had left the church to its fate, after having walled up the stove in its niche. In our absence this official sacked everything in the place. One of the things I lost was a sheepskin coat. I got it back later, with four bullet holes in the breast in the form of a cross.

This last statement filled me with curiosity, and I pricked my ears up. The priest, evidently reading my expression, soon explained himself.

It happened this way. *Dios sabe* that I am no friend of the present *Jefe de Armas;* but as things got more normal the crimes of the Villista *presidente* became so outrageous that the government of Chihuahua finally sent a telegram authorizing his apprehension. But he never reached prison. The *ley fuga. ¿Sabe?*

I *"sabered"* [sic] the *ley fuga,* so he went on.

The Villista was thrown in jail, and he knew what was up. Unlike most of us Mexicans, he did not face death bravely. He wept bitterly and cried loudly for a priest to save his life in this world if possible, or his soul in the next.

So his captors called me. I went out to the jail and saw the craven. He was whining and whimpering. He was wearing my sheepskin coat, and didn't offer to give it back. The *Jefe de Armas* assured me that this prisoner would arrive safely in Chihuahua; but I didn't care much what happened to him after the men he had killed and the women who had been abused by his band.

They started for Chihuahua before dawn. Three or four miles from here, and just at dawn, so they said, a group of his friends assaulted the escort to save him. So his captors shot him four times in the breast, precisely in the form of a cross. By noon my coat was returned to me, covered with blood. I suppose I should have kept it, as that bloody cross was a symbol of God's vengeance on the man for the murders and rapes he had committed.

A month or so later I passed the spot where this had happened. As usual it was marked with a cross, a Mexican gesture to show that a man has been killed. *¡Pobre México!,* how many thousands of crosses there were everywhere through the countryside!

The padre continued.

This present *Jefe de Armas* is capable of less-justified killings than that, and is another bandit who just happened to be on the winning side. But he controls the destinies of this town, and is hand-in-glove with the *presidente* in persecuting us.

We met this worthy on our way back from the cave. My blood was still chilled by the padre's tales of injustice, violence, and sudden death that flourished during the Revolution, and consequently he made quite an impression on me. He was a large, cold, harsh creature, of little or no education. His sole qualification for his official task of "defending the social order" was that his loyalty to the present government had never been questioned. Yet my own relations with him were not unpleasant, although I believe that my having been threatened by arrest for disturbing the dead was of his doing. At least he visited the work I later did in the cave, and intelligently summarized the site as a *camposanto*, or prehistoric graveyard, which I was charged with desecrating.

We encountered him just at the edge of town, riding a large horse, and carrying two cartridge belts crossed over his shoulders in Mexican revolutionary fashion. When the padre pointed him out to me, I went up and shook his large, muscular hand. Since I was carrying a shotgun and sporting a pistol in my belt, I thought the time opportune to show my permit for carrying arms, which, however, might as well have been a customs receipt, or anything, for I doubt if he could read.

My permit was legitimate, and perhaps the tale of the trouble I underwent in obtaining it will bear telling. Permits to carry arms anywhere in the Republic must be procured from the "General," or *Jefe de Operaciones*, of the military district. So to some petty commissioned officer of the staff in the Federal building of Chihuahua I presented my papers attesting that I was a scientist from one of the leading scientific institutions of America "of the North." These didn't impress him in the slightest. I was told curtly to return the following day, and then perhaps I would get to see the "General."

It was fortunate that I didn't have to undergo more contacts with the almost unbelievably arrogant military officials of Chihuahua of that period. I learned that since all my work was to be carried on in the State of Chihuahua, I could get a permit from the State authorities that would serve me just as well as one issued by the "General." In contrast to the chilly formality and stupid arrogance of the Federal military officers were the congeniality and serviceableness of the State officials. A young clerk in the office proved especially intelligent and helpful. He filled out all the forms and got everything ready.

Then I was ushered into the presence of the Villa "General" who was in charge of all nonfederal arms in the State of Chihuahua. This worthy really merits a chapter to himself. To treat him briefly, however, he was a crude man of the people, dressed in store clothes which fitted him awkwardly and uncomfortably. More natural to him, even in the business-like setting of his office, were his American cowboy boots and his *tejano* (the Mexican word for a Texas cowboy's hat, which, in Chihuahua, has found more favor than the great Mexican *sombrero* of the *charros* farther south).

He was clumsy and bumbling in the clerical duties of his position. That he could write, however, was fairly certain, since he signed my permit; and in the nonclerical duties of his office, through which were controlled all arms in Chihuahua, he was no doubt thoroughly at home. As a general under Villa, he must have gained much experience that proved of great value to his present role. Yet this role was obviously important, because in Mexico he who has arms rules the country. His familiarity with arms, as well as with the possibility of the existence of enemies, was patent, since on a belt under his coat were two formidable 45s. These were of no value to him in the discharge of his clerical duties, although without a doubt they were no encumbrance in his nonclerical affairs.

Neither his manner nor his attitude was violent or vicious. He seemed sincerely to wish to be of service, and reminded me of the old-fashioned sheriffs, of whom there are a few vestigial survivors in the great state of Texas. As I left the office, and passed through the building and on out into the open, I mentally shouted "*¡Viva Chihuahua!*"

The Sierra Tarahumara.

PLANTING CORN WITH THE
DIGGING STICK.

BRINGING
IN SOME
FIREWOOD.

TYPICAL COSTUMES OF
TARAHUMARA MEN AND
WOMEN.

A TARAHUMARA BOY.

Making *tamales* from corn.

Storehouse.

STONE AND FRAME HOUSE.

PLOWING.

PRIMITIVE MEXICAN CART WITH SOLID WOOD WHEELS.

Mule train crossing the hanging bridge built by "Boss" Shepherd,
who also built Washington, D.C.

ROBERT ZINGG IN RED CROSS UNIFORM.

LORENZO, CARRYING THE BOOTS BENNETT HAD GIVEN HIM, AND ROBERT ZINGG ON THEIR WAY TO THE GORGES TO SEEK OUT WINTER QUARTERS.

TARAHUMARA INDIANS WHO STAYED WITH ZINGG FAMILY DURING SUN BOWL CELEBRATION IN EL PASO. EXCEPT FOR ROBERT AND EMMA ZINGG IN THE MIDDLE ROW AND THOSE IN THE FRONT ROW ALL ARE TARAHUMARA INDIANS FROM CHIHUAHUA.

CHAPTER 11

▸ *Ready-Made Archaeology, Trips,*
▸ *and Talks*
▸
▸
▸
▸
▸

▸
▸
▸

I n a short time we arrived at the cave to which the padre had promised to guide me. It was one that at first sight appeared to leave little to be desired, for it was easy of access, being near a town where labor was plentiful, and gave evidence of providing considerable work. Further, it was very large. The wide mouth, running up into a high, vaulting roof, was almost two hundred feet across. The roof sloped down sharply to the back of the cave, forty-five feet back.

The hard rock of the cave floor was covered over to a height of from three to four feet with a fine, flourlike dust which had been blown into the cave by winds blowing constantly over the soft tufa rock of the characteristic formation of the whole region. This flourlike dust was of a dark cast from a mixture of charcoal, produced apparently by the funerary fires built in the cave by the Indians during burials. The pagan Tarahumaras still follow this practice.

Treasure hunters had preceded me at the cave, about a third of which had been dug up. Interested only in gold, they had left undisturbed what archaeological specimens they had uncovered. These were food samples, and showed that the cave was rich, archaeologically, though not in the precious treasure that the Mexicans coveted.

Lying on the surface of the disturbed dirt were two or three human mummies, so dried and hard as to be well-nigh indestructible to ordinary handling. They were not true mummies in the sense that prior to burial they had undergone a sophisticated process of embalming, but simply human bodies desiccated by the aridity both of the cave and of the soil in which they had been buried.

As we returned from the visit to the cave, we stopped at a Mexican's house and contracted with him to transport all the findings to the mission. He started off early the following morning, and arrived at the cave at dawn in order not to attract the attention of other Mexicans of the settlement, who, had they known how deeply interested I was in the cave, would promptly have finished looting it.

When the goods arrived at the mission, I secreted them in my room where they would be safe from the eyes of the many Indians who passed in and out constantly. I had arranged with "General" Jaris to have the headmen of all the neighboring Tarahumara towns come to the mission. From these men I was to take down all the information about recent thefts of Indian lands by Mexicans, and then in Chihuahua on my return to civilization seek redress for the Indians.

The Tarahumara chiefs came to the mission a few days later. I complimented myself on having had the foresight to hide the mummies and other antiques in my room, for grave robbing can frequently get an ethnographer into the most serious of difficulties. But just before going into the room where the Indians were squatting gravely on the floor waiting for my appearance, I decided to see if my mummies and other possessions were safe. *O tempora, O mores!* Two of the mummies were gone. Discreetly I asked the padres and the lay brother if they had decided to hide them in the secret niche made for the cookstove. Their negative response worried me.

So there was nothing to do but face the Indians. When I walked in on them I half expected to see the mummies of their ancestors sitting up in front of them, waiting to accuse me of desecrating their age-old slumbers. But no, the Indians were their same stolid selves, and we quickly got down to business. Their passive air soon left them, however, when they began to tell me of the many cases in which their best, widest, and most fertile fields had been usurped by Mexican land grabbers.

The Tarahumaras, like other Indian tribes, hold unimproved land in common charge of their officials. Any Indian who needs land may ask the *gobernador* for any unused parcel that attracts him. This becomes his as long as he cultivates it. Land deserted over a considerable period reverts back to the community and may be assigned to others. Fruit trees, or permanent improvements, such as a storehouse, which represent expenditure and care or energy, are never communally owned, and are recognized as belonging only to the original owner; and such things are inherited apart from the land they stand on.

Some writers have written at great length on "Communism" among the Mexican Indians; but this Tarahumara practice is general and typical so far as I have been able to determine from considerable study, both in the field and in books on the subject.

The Tarahumara officials in charge of unused land knew every recent case of Mexican intrusion in their respective regions. But they all deferred to Jaris, who was the headman of one of the towns. His position of leadership was obvious; he had long been intensely active in defense of Indian lands.

Since none of the assembled chiefs talked Spanish, we communicated through an Indian product of the mission. On each of the cases narrated, I took full notes, and the Indians were quite impressed by the magic of my writing. Poor bewildered *Tarahumaritos!* This magic was futile against the militaristic anti-agrarian administration which, as I was to find in Chihuahua, had replaced the urbane and charming civilian governor who was in power at about the time I passed through to Creel, and on whom I might have counted for just and ready action.

The padres, like early missionaries to Mexico, were true friends of the Indians, and it was through their guaranteeing my good faith that I was able to gain the confidence of the Indians sufficiently for this secret work. It was a dangerous alliance, too, and thus this was the first and last time we met in the mission. Thereafter the Indians always sent a runner to me who guided me to some isolated *ranchería* where our gathering would not be noticed by the Mexicans.

The agrarian policy of the Federal government is so favorable to the rights of the Indians that, had I been able to present the troubles of the Indians in Mexico City, the Mexicans perhaps would have been thrust summarily off their stolen land. For one thing, the *chulo* municipal *presidente* and his alter ego, the brutal *Jefe de Armas*, were of no assistance whatsoever to the Indians, because even the Mexican village was illegally on Indian land; and they backed every theft of land with their guns. Thus the source of danger for the Indians, the priests, and me. With good reason were our meetings held at places other than the mission.

The character of the local hoodlums, as well as the laxity of the officials, was revealed in an atrocity perpetrated on a wealthy Indian by a band of armed Mexicans. They arrived at his *ranchería* in the dead of night to extort from him the results of a sale of some of his many cattle and hanged him repeatedly until, more dead than alive, he finally divulged where his money was hidden. The Indians were greatly moved as they narrated this outrage. Needless to say, no redress was sought from the authorities of this village.

My conferences with the Indians lasted for several months. During this time we gathered at various places in the sierra. On receiving a letter from the padre I would immediately start out to meet the Indians. They were the *gobernadores* of faraway towns, who were constantly in touch with "General" Jaris, in itself a proof of the remarkable power that this extraordinary Indian had gained by his own personality and his courage in meeting a problem of such grave concern to all the Indians. I shall describe the most remarkable of these conferences later.

The first conference at the mission was little more than a preliminary exploration of the problem, and lasted for only an hour or so. But it showed at least that the Indians were friendly. Taking advantage of their cordial mood I asked them if they would object to my making a study of the ancient remains of their respective regions. They assured me that they would offer no hindrance; I could do what I wished, even take bones and mummies, because their owners were already "despatched" to the other world. This was a considerable relief to me, since I was still in doubt as to whether they had appropriated my missing specimens.

After the conference was over, I hunted high and low for the mummies and even questioned the little children in the mission schools. My search was unavailing. Late that afternoon, however, the mestiza nun from Oaxaca came to the mission. She was the culprit. She explained that her interest in the archaeology of her ancestral race, the Indians, was so strong that she had wrapped the mummies in newspaper and carried them to her quarters across the plaza. Thus were my wandering children accounted for.

This nun's interest in archaeology was intelligent. She had read rather widely about the remains in Mexico and those in her own State of Oaxaca, where, a year later, were discovered the wondrous jewels of Monte Albán. When I began to excavate the large cave near Norogáchic, she brought her schoolchildren to inspect the work, and gave them a pertinent discussion of the customs of their probable ancestors in the ancient time represented by the site.

But alas! my first visit to the Norogáchic mission was drawing to a close, for Dr. Bennett was holding down the Samachique front alone. He was waiting for the last ceremony to be given for Patricio, the *teniente*, in whose estimation the reader will remember we didn't rank very high. On the morrow I should have to turn my back on the luxury of hard French bread dunked in *café con leche*. Since I had sent my mule back with Isidro as soon as it was shod the day following our arrival, I was confronted with the ticklish problem of transporting the mummies and other loot from the large cave. But during my conversations with the headmen of the various villages near Norogáchic, I had made arrangements to engage the services of several strong Tarahumaras to carry my effects in boxes provided by the mission. Boxes in that faraway sierra were a rarity, I found, when I began to devote my time to archaeological work, and they all had to be brought out by mule from the railhead, which was six days away.

It was now the middle of January, and the ground was covered with snow. This again portended difficulties, for the Tarahumaras wear shoes only for dancing the *matachines*. So we had to wait for a warm spell, when the snow was melting. In such weather the Indians are able to walk barefooted for hours on end without freezing their feet.

Finally, early one morning, I said, "*Hasta luego*" to my mission friends, nothing to the civil and military brotherhood, and started off on a three-day hike to Samachique. Trotting on ahead of me were four Indian boys, and strapped on their backs with their carrying straps were my boxes of *antiguedades*. The padre had insisted that I take his horse; but I knew that he might need it. Besides, at that time I had no objections to walking. Now, a few years later, and caught so to speak in the toils of civilization, I marvel at my hiking hour after hour for several days with the Indians through that cold, sloppy, melting snow.

The day was reasonably warm. Towards evening we reached a small Catholic chapel, somewhat similar to that in Samachique, but not a full-fledged mission building such as that in Norogáchic. It was already dark so that there was no chance of our cutting firewood; and I knew that the night would be cold. I was traveling light, having decided previously to pass the nights on the way back to Samachique without bed or blanket, kept warm only by my heavy sheepskin coat. The *gobernador* of the community lived near the church, but he wouldn't let us sleep in his house, such favors not being a part of Tarahumara hospitality due to the timidity of the Indians. Visitors in the sierra are generally directed to some nearby cave or sheltering rock. But the *gobernador* told us that we might sleep in the church and as a token of his goodwill gave us a tiny armful of firewood. With this we were supposed to heat our *tortillas* and coffee, and from it we were expected to obtain sufficient warmth to protect us against the cold of the night.

The *convento* of the little chapel boasted a fireplace, and in it a fire was soon blazing. The floor was the dirtiest I ever hope to see; for apparently the place had not been used for several years. Moreover, the door had fallen from its hinges. This, however, was a mixed blessing; for though it let in the freezing night air of the sierra, on the other hand it provided me with a pallet on which I could keep out of the accumulation of dust and dirt on the floor. This had to be placed at some distance from the fire, which my Indian *cargadores* needed anyway, because they were clad in nothing save their clouts and blankets.

The Indians lay down on their backs around the fire fan-wise in Tarahumara fashion, with their knees drawn up so that their blankets would act as funnels and thus catch and conduct in their direction any of the heat. I followed the example of the hospitable "poor white" of the South and took "the bearskin and the pumpkin and roughed it." Despite my warm clothing I was soon chilled; the cold gnawed at me like a toothache, refusing to let my tired bones rest and seeming to seek their very marrow. The hardness of the door hurt my head, since I couldn't very well use my precious sheepskin coat for a pillow. Indeed, I could have done very nicely with a bearskin and a pumpkin.

My Indian companions soon fell asleep and began to snore lustily, with their breeches (I use this word in its anatomical, not its haberdashery, sense) warmed by this moribund fire. I turned and tossed on the prone chapel door, experimenting with a hundred different body positions in an effort to conserve my body heat. Then I came to a momentous decision. Ahead of me on the morrow was a long, hard hike, and I knew that I couldn't face it tired and haggard from a sleepless night. I got up, took my flashlight, and hunted around until I found an old *canoa* that had fallen from the porch of the *convento*. I knew that the Indians are outraged when their churches are vandalized, but I was sure that my Tarahumaras would not object to a little extra fire. Soon the *canoa* was radiating out its cheerful heat. The next day I apologized to the *gobernador* and gave him a half peso as "hush money." Nothing came of the matter.

Although I was traveling light, without even a blanket, I did have with me a small hafted axe, and with this I had been able to chop up the *canoa*. Many years before I was hiking across the high, pine-clad *cordilleras* of Luzon, in the Igorot country. We pitched camp about dusk in a deserted Igorot shack, just as a dismal rain began. We were partially protected from the rain, but neither of us had a bolo or an axe with which to split kindling from the abundant pine that surrounded us. Thus we were forced to go without fire, and as I shivered through the long night, hugging my knees and watching the slopes of the mountains far away dotted here and there by the little fires that meant warmth, comfort, and home to the headhunters with which we were surrounded, I solemnly swore never to leave camp again without a bolo, *machete*, or an axe. If some quixotic dream should ever take me by ship south over the Pacific, and if that ship should quiver and sink, be assured I shall leave it with my little axe.

But let us return from anthropological adventures among Philippine headhunters. From such dissimilar places let us return to the little Tarahumara chapel. In the *convento* the fire burned merrily after I had chopped more fuel, and I soon sank into a deep, peaceful sleep, a fitting reward for my barbarous labors of the day.

The following night we arrived at the Córdoba house. After my experiences of the night before, this place represented to me the height of luxury and almost everything that mortal man might wish for. How relative, therefore, are so many of the appendages of civilization we seem to think necessary! I brought the Córdobas sugar, coffee, and tobacco for themselves and some hard, cheap candy for their children. This acknowledgement of their previous hospitality assured me an especially warm reception not only on this occasion, but for the future should I ever arrive again cold, tired, and hungry at their ruined "station" on the "Royal Road." But aside from this I received full recompense for my thoughtfulness in the joy these few purchases from the trading post brought to the faces of young and old alike at this little *rancho* in the heart of the sierra.

The next day I arrived with my modest safari back at the *convento* of Samachique. There Dr. Bennett was waiting for me. He, like many of the Indians of the community, had delayed his trip to the warm caves of the gorges in order to attend the ceremonies given for the soul of our old enemy, Patricio, the *teniente*. Unfortunately the forced prolongation of my stay at Norogáchic caused me to miss the first ceremony; and I was disappointed because, since Patricio was a rich and influential man, this ceremony was particularly brilliant and spectacular, combining pagan dancing and singing with the "Catholic dancing of the *matachines* and the *pascol*." The last I was not to see until Holy Week. A full account of this ceremony is given by Dr. Bennett.

By this time January was drawing to a close, and to judge by the cold of the sierra, our presence in the caves of the gorges was long overdue. Most of the Indians had gone. Our guide and mentor, Lorenzo, however, had been detained in the sierra for his prominent part in the death ceremony. As soon as it was over, we were prepared to go with him to the gorges.

Lorenzo's wife had already left. When our Mexican *mozo* came to Samachique from Creel, he had bad news for Lorenzo from this surly squaw. She had told him to tell Lorenzo that one of the cattle had gored one of their precious sheep to death. There was a storm brewing in the *barrancas*. Worse than this, the Mexican told us that she had offered him some stew made from the defunct sheep, but the tragedy had happened some time ago, and the mess was too putrid for him. What, then, was to be our fate on returning?

In order to spy out the "land of Canaan" and decide upon a dwelling cave or other quarters in which to spend the remainder of the winter, Bennett and I were determined to hike down to the gorges with Lorenzo, who was in a sweating hurry to inspect the havoc wrought by his cattle upon his wife's sheep. We instructed our *mozo* to pack our equipment and bring it by mule down the "Royal Road." We were to hike along the Indian trail. Our meeting place was to be not far from the hanging bridge and very near the *ranchería* of the "happy family" whose picture we had taken during our first days in the sierra. Since then the spouses had been informally divorced in Tarahumara fashion.

Our *mozo* had been told to leave at this *ranchería* the supplies that he had brought from Creel, so there was plenty of canned food awaiting us. Each of us had a blanket held to his back by a carrying strap. In addition, I had a little bag of *pinole*, my axe, and my pistol. Lorenzo carried the boots Bennett had given him. With these simple supplies, after bidding good-bye to the *mozo*, we were soon swinging over the trail.

For a few miles we walked along the cordon, the ridge or divide, through the forests of great pine. Then suddenly the trail debouched into the great gorge.

The Barranca del Cobre is a magnificent view from wherever seen. An awful gash or abysm, seeming to drop immeasurably away from the earth at the point at which we emerged from the forest, it is almost a mile deep. Through it flows the Río Urique, the head stream of the Río Fuerte. The walls of this *barranca* are equally precipitous and about twenty miles apart. The bleak, austere ruggedness of this gorge fills the mind with an effect of overpowering grandeur comparable only to that created by the Grand Canyon of the Colorado.

Almost exactly on the brink of the gorge an Indian had perched his house, and before it the unique vista afforded by the gorge was spread like a fantastic painting limned from imagination. Knowing how the experiences of Tarahumara youth attune the tribe more to the natural environment than to human society, I wondered if the Indians had any sense of appreciation of the beauties of nature that would induce in them the same breathtaking awe which I felt. Could it be, I pondered, that this Tarahumara had placed his house here "just for the view"?

But it is difficult to worm any expression of appreciation of natural beauty from a Tarahumara. Take even Lorenzo. He had been our companion on dozens of hikes, but he had never given the slightest indication that he derived any aesthetic satisfaction from the grandeur of our constant surroundings. But there was this house, situated, as it seemed, for the sake of the noble prospect before it. Perhaps it would provide an answer. I hesitated to ask Lorenzo directly, "How wonderful it is here! Is it not for the scenery that your friend has his house here?" So I merely questioned, "Why did your friend build his house in this place?" I felt fairly safe in putting it this way, since Lorenzo was such a competent informant that he often gave unexpectedly full answers to such questions.

With an air that implied that for all I had learned I was still a stupid, unreasoning scholar, Lorenzo rejoined, "Why, it is nearer to his dwelling and storage caves in the *barrancas*."[1]

On receiving this answer I recalled an amusing conversation in which I had once participated in western Oklahoma. I was talking to a hillbilly from Arkansas who was homesteading in those badlands. He lamented that his poor clapboard house lacked the stick and mud fireplace with which such cabins in the Ozarks are provided. This drew a ready response from me. As I remember, I answered somewhat in this vein, "Yes, you know, there is something about a fire flickering in an open hearth that somehow raises the human spirit and makes us all feel a little bigger and better."

"Well," he replied, obviously unimpressed by my remark, "I don't know about that, but it is a darn good place to spit tobacco juice."

So I am afraid my hillbilly acquaintance and the Tarahumaras have a good deal in common with their responses, which differ considerably from those we too frequently take for granted among ourselves.

The trail we were following led over the edge of the gorge and down a sharp, tortuous incline into the *barranca*. As we descended, we passed a large hole in the earth. In a very matter-of-fact voice, as if he were pointing out some plant used by the Tarahumaras, Lorenzo said, "That hole is where the wind lives."

After we had angled gingerly down the side of the gorge for several miles, the river came into view, still quite a distance beneath us, for we were passing across a jutting spur high above it. Following a perfectly natural impulse I picked up a rock and heaved it out into space to watch it fall into the still water below. But it seemed as if this was my "off" day as a disciple of my Tarahumara mentor, for turning to me vehemently he said:

> Once I was walking along here with a child who did just that and who knew that it was a dangerous thing to do. The water serpent that owns the water lives in pools like this. That night the child dreamed that the water serpent came up out of the pool and seized him. The child became ill. Since the child was with me when this happened, I was responsible, and the parents summoned me.
>
> So that night I had to dream. By dreaming I sent my soul out to arrange a ransom with the water serpent. After some parley with the serpent I dreamed (my soul arranged) that the offense could be settled with the forfeit of one dream-horse. This bought the soul of the child from the offended water serpent.
>
> Several days later, when all these dreams were finished, I went to the house of the sick child. *Tesgüino* had been prepared for the final cure. First I drank a little of the *tesgüino*. Then I took off my rosary with the large metal crucifix on it, dipped it into the *tesgüino*, and marked crosses on various parts of the child's body. Then, holding the cross in my mouth, I blew over the child's body, for the breath is strong and can strengthen the frightened soul of a sick person.

Was I reprimanded? To reassure Lorenzo, who was actually afraid that he would have to go through all the foregoing with me, I replied, "But that is not the custom of us *Americanos*. I won't dream about the water serpent."

This long speech of Lorenzo's is one of the most illuminating he ever gave, because it shows so clearly the Tarahumara conception of water as being owned by serpents which have the power to cause sickness. Such sickness is brought about by soul capture, for, as among almost all primitive people, the soul is identified with dreams and with breath. Therefore, dreams and blowing are effective curatives, and among many tribes the shaman blows on the body of the sick person to strengthen his soul.

We finally arrived at the river. There we rested, and each of us mixed and consumed a little *pinole*. I drank several gourds of it, and found it palatable, nourishing, and stimulating food; and such it is, especially when one is really tired and hungry. While we rested, Lorenzo, who had recovered from his irritation and was in an affable mood, began to regale us with some of the secret lore of the Tarahumaras. The following conversation Dr. Bennett has incorporated in his part of *The Tarahumara*. Lorenzo started off:

> There are certain bad Tarahumaras who work witchcraft against the good people. Some of these have a little bird [or animal], a *disagíki*. My wife's grandmother had one of these.

Apparently, in Lorenzo's estimation, his hag of a wife came by her meanness naturally. Still, she was the best weaver in the community, and since this meant warm blankets for him, he was able to overlook her vagaries in ancestry and manner.

> These descend from parent to child. At last my mother-in-law inherited it. When my wife and I were first "married," I used to hear it often, and I asked my wife about it. I was very anxious to have her catch it, because the owner of such a bird is well-hated by the good people. It does not help one's reputation to have such a bird in the family. But my mother-in-law refused to have the shaman come and kill it. When the old woman died, the bird was inherited by my wife. She, however, neglected to feed it, and it died. These birds are invisible to everyone save their owners, but they make a sound, "sht, sht."
>
> When the owner[2] of such a bird wishes to kill someone or make him sick, he sends the bird to the victim's house. There it poisons any food lying around uncovered by eating of it or defecating on it. The bird will not eat *chile*, and it will surely die if its owner eats any. Thus any Tarahumara who will not eat *chile* is certain to be a bad person who owns one of these. [But what Tarahumara won't eat *chile?*] When one of these birds is heard near one's house, it can be driven away by throwing ground *chile* into the air.
>
> Only the shaman can see these creatures. If one thinks that some bad person has come to harm him, he can hire the shaman. The shaman will catch the bird belonging to the bad person and burn it. The owner becomes sick, and then everyone knows who he is. The shaman then goes to the sick person to cure him of his evil ways. He blows and sucks on him to mend his soul. He also gives him

a lecture and tells him to discontinue his evil habits of making others sick. When the bird dies, the owner weeps bitterly and throws himself about with as much grief as he would display at the death of his own child.

After these confidences we prepared to continue our journey. Fortunately we did not have to climb as far as we had descended, for we were going to Lorenzo's lowland *ranchería*, which was situated in a little valley over the first and lowest of the ridges leading out of the deep *barranca*. We clomped over the bridge that I have had occasion to mention earlier, and on past the ruins of the old guard station that once protected it. As I have already mentioned, it was burned during the Revolution. Only blackened walls remain to mark its site. As we passed, Lorenzo, still in a superstitious mood induced by his narration, peered in carefully. "Do not go in, *Don* Roberto," he said, pointing out the dried stalks of some plant which, from where I was standing, I was not able to identify. "Those plants are *muy bravo;* they have a very bad spirit (or power). They are so strong and so bad that if they begin to grow in a dwelling cave the cave must be abandoned. They will kill you if you touch them. Only a special shaman has the power to pull them out. To rid a dwelling cave of them, this special shaman must be called. After singing all night to the sound of the rasping stick the shaman protects himself by eating a good plant that is stronger in power than this bad plant. Then he can pull the bad plants out and throw them in the fire. The shaman must be paid from three to five pesos. The good plant that he eats is *jículi.*"

I knew all about *jículi.*[3] It is the famous narcotic cactus, called peyote. The word is Huichol.[4] Very little besides this word, however, has diffused from Jalisco to the Tarahumaras in Chihuahua. Among the Huichols three years later I found a high development in the religious life of the tribe built around this narcotic cactus, which induces dreams and color hallucinations. In the last fifty years the use of the plant has spread among certain Indian tribes of the United States. Among the demoralized and beaten Indians of our own country it has been made the foundation of many new and interesting cults concerning themselves with dreams which are interpreted from a religious standpoint. I shall have more to say farther on about the use of *jículi* among the Tarahumaras.

Lorenzo was so obviously sincere in his belief about the bad plants in the ruined station that I refrained from examining them. But it was vitally important that I obtain a specimen for botanical identification. A week or so later I decided to return to this place. But since I was living with Lorenzo, in order to get this dangerous weed unnoticed into camp I had to plan my trip so that I would arrive back at camp after dark. When I returned to the United States, a botanist identified the plant as jimsonweed *(Datura stramonium)*.

Jimsonweed is poisonous, its leaves causing intoxication, hallucinations, nausea, and real illness. The poison is so concentrated in the seeds that they may kill an adult and are frequently fatal to children.

Thus, with some reason, in the Tarahumara mind is this plant imbued with a strong, malignant spirit or power which is able to drive people mad and finally kill them; and from some actual observation of the biochemical effects of jimsonweed combined with superstition the Tarahumaras have built up a fantastic structure of belief, one phase of which is that the plant can be touched only by one who has first ceremonially eaten of the good plant, *jículi*.

Similarly among the Huichols is *jículi* the plant of religion and good magic; and the bad jimsonweed is eaten by sorcerers who supposedly take from it its power of black magic. But the Huichols have rationalized their belief of this noxious plant into a beautiful myth. This tells us that the first bad sorcerer was changed into the form of jimsonweed in order that those coming after him might draw upon his evil powers.

These plants are highly important in Indian religions because they promote dreams, on which primitive people place so much religious significance. As we observed in Lorenzo's tale of the ailing child for whose sickness he was held responsible, dreams are considered to be the experiences of the soul while it is absent from the body. Any plant, therefore, the consumption of which causes dreams, is conceived to be of the highest sacred and spiritual power.

Among some tribes jimsonweed is utilized as a sacred plant and eaten because of its intoxicating and dream-inducing effects. The aborigines of California, for example, maintained very important religious cults based on this weed and its effects. But they had learned how to consume it without fatal results, while the great sickness and nausea which it caused were thought of as but proof both of the plant's power and of the spiritual resistance and courage of those who were being initiated into the cult.

Jimsonweed, one of the Solanaceae or nightshade family, has a flower that looks like a large morning glory. It is fairly common throughout the United States and northern Mexico. It derives its English name, jimsonweed, or Jamestown weed, from the first English settlement in America. During Bacon's rebellion in 1675 some soldiers were sent to Jamestown to quell the insurrection. They became hungry in the forest, and boiled some luxurious leaves that looked edible. A quaint account of the rather startling effects of the leaves appears in Robert Beverly's *History and Present State of Virginia*.

The identification of the plant as *datura*, or jimsonweed, which I obtained by my stealthy trip back to the ruined station near the hanging bridge, thus rewarded me for the time and effort I had spent. But the day we first saw it on our trip through the *barranca* I would not have dared touch it; for then Lorenzo would have thought me a dangerous source of contamination and have been afraid to have me around his *ranchería*.

CHAPTER 12

> *Ancient and Modern Cave-Dwellers*
> *in the Gorges*
>
>
>
>
>
>
>
>

From the riverside, where we had stopped for *pinole* and for Lorenzo's interesting talk, we continued our hike. By midafternoon we arrived at Lorenzo's *barranca ranchería*. On this last lap we did not take the roundabout Camino Real, which passes close to this ranch. The trail the Indians use is much shorter. It leads down the river a little way, and then precipitously climbs the sheer wall of the *barranca*. Over part of this stretch the trail is merely a series of footholds chipped into the rock. The Tarahumaras have no difficulty in negotiating this shortcut when they are sober; several essaying it after a drunken feast, however, have fallen to their deaths.

Such a trail reminded me of those that archaeologists occasionally find in New Mexico and Arizona leading to the cliff-dwellings. Here, in Chihuahua, however, the caves were occupied for dwellings, as they were in our Southwest millennia ago. But the present-day Tarahumaras have given up the building of houses in the caves, which was practiced by their ancestors, to judge by the many archaeological remains that we investigated.

In several of the dwelling caves that we passed we found friends and fellow citizens of Samachique, a community now split up between the caves of this river and another river in the opposite direction, the Río Batopilas. Only the most makeshift of arrangements served for living purposes. Those caves exposed to the winds had a wall of piled stone before them as a windbreak. These cave-dwellings make the Tarahumaras the only troglodytes in America.

In one of the caves was our friend, the *mayor* of Samachique; for all his relatively exalted status his quarters were poor enough, for he had literally pauperized himself in working for the common good.

The usual paraphernalia of a Tarahumara household lies about the cave: an encircling windbreak; a large pot on the fire; a large beer pot covered with an overturned basket; pots and bowls for food; a broken *metate*, which sufficed this family for the preparation of *pinole* and *esquiate*. With such meager furnishings do the Tarahumara families live for months in their cave-dwellings.

This cave, however, was perhaps more meager than most. A description generally applicable is to be found in my account in *The Tarahumara:*[1]

Innumerable caves in the gorges, offering warmth from the cold of the high sierra in winter and situated advantageously for sunlight and easy access to water, are highly esteemed as property. Individual ownership is recognized, so that a family does not have to eject squatters from its dwelling cave. A large, dry cave is preferable for winter residence. The best are located high in the cliffs facing the southeast to get most of the winter sun.

The most desirable caves are large enough for a goat corral on one side and a dwelling on the other. The goats are shut up at night in a roughly-made pen, strong enough to protect them from the coyotes. The manure that collects in these pens is very valuable as fertilizer, and every spring working bees are organized and the manure is transported in blankets to the fields. When such work is finished and the blankets perfunctorily shaken out, the workers are rewarded with liberal quantities of *tesgüino*.

When winter comes, each family journeys to its cave, taking along its goats, a few small pots, baskets of wool, various odds and ends, and a supply of corn. Large pots are generally left behind and hidden, from one season to the next, under nearby boulders. When the dispersal back to the uplands begins in the spring, the *metate* and the sleeping-board are left in the cave.

Each cave is made habitable by repairing the windbreaks and arranging the *metate*, pots, baskets, and food supply. Little concern is shown for the dried goat dung underfoot. The women while cooking, however, partially avoid the dust and the dirt by sitting on the sleeping-shelf, where the members of the family sleep at night with their feet toward the slowly burning oak fire.

Life is simple for the Tarahumaras, and from the day of birth is practically one glorified camping trip. The material appurtenances which we find so essential for satisfactory living they reduce to that which can be carried on their shoulders from the sierra to the gorges. At this late season, with winter already claiming the uplands, it is a characteristic sight to see Tarahumara families on the move. The adults carry great loads of corn on their backs in blankets rolled up as sacks. On the top of this dangle pots and baskets like ornaments on a Christmas tree. Small children are carried in the arms, and those who are still too young to make the trip themselves on "shank's ponies" perch like monkeys on top of the loads on their parents' backs.

We continued on past these first caves and scaled the perilous trail over the first of the cliffs which in an ever-mounting series form the great Barranca del Cobre of the Río Urique, headwaters of the Fuerte River. The trail dropped again into a little valley, where Lorenzo had another *ranchería*.

Since we were on a scientific expedition, and besides had not yet completely thrown off the cumbersome paraphernalia of civilization, we decided not to try living in a cave like our Indian friends. We had too many valuable papers which would hardly be adequately protected by a Tarahumara apology for a windbreak. So we rented a large, dry storehouse from Lorenzo. It had a little door of a size sufficient to permit us to slip in and out, and it was a capital place for our papers and supplies. We slept in these close quarters with comfort. At night we left the little door open, but in a corner kept a loaded rifle, for we were directly on the "Royal Road." In the poverty-stricken sierra were those for whom our supplies and money would have constituted a tidy fortune, veterans of the Villa Revolution who just about this time had repeatedly hanged the Tarahumara to make him reveal his hoard of silver pesos.

In the vicinity of Umira was a rich Indian who had owned a hundred cattle. About five miles away was the station of the bullion trains where we had spent our first night in the sierra, and where lived the Mexican patriarch with his daughters and their Mexican husbands. By selling his excess cattle this rich Indian was able to hire Mexicans to build him an adobe house. Ordinarily so swanky a possession as an adobe house would have been unheard of among the Indians; but this old rogue wished to marry the pretty youngest daughter of the Mexican patriarch, and thus sought to tempt her with the best house, Indian or Mexican, in these parts.

We learned a lot about this rich Indian from the Mexicans, who daily passed our storehouse on their way to work; and we often planned to take an afternoon off and visit him. But there was always so much to do around camp, and many were the Indians who visited us to get acquainted and buy our trade goods. By this time we had established the best possible relationships throughout the tribe, mainly because of our contacts with "General" Jaris, reports of which had traveled through the tribe by grapevine telegram.

But among our Indian visitors we had one particularly steady customer who used to sit for hours day after day on our woodpile. He watched everything we did with avid interest, and yet stayed far enough away and was so discreet and reserved that he was no trouble to us at all. He became a sort of fixture of our camp like a wooden Indian in front of a cigar store.

Almost every day we would say to each other, "Well, today we ought to go and see this rich Indian."

"Yes, but who'll watch camp while we are gone?"

"Oh, let 'Old Faithful' here watch the camp."

"¿Pues quién sabe?"

Finally we asked Lorenzo who our "Old Faithful" was. "Why," he replied, "don't you know that he is the rich Indian who is hiring the Mexicans to build him an adobe house?"

The wealth of this Indian which permitted him to hire Mexicans to build him a house was in great contrast to the general poverty of the Indians. This was a famine year, and all stocks of corn were sadly depleted. Most of the Indians, therefore, were forced to scurry through the sierra to buy or borrow wheat seed for winter planting, the results of which would provide for them during the months that elapsed before the ripening of the summer crop of corn.

Lorenzo, a good, thrifty Tarahumara, was one of the few who had an abundant supply of wheat. Some of this he sold at a good profit. The balance he kept, and soon he was preparing his valley fields for planting it. Among his possessions were oxen and the wooden stick plow that is used by Mexicans and Indians alike. This later he had to lend to others, in consistency with the Tarahumara custom of mutual aid. He manipulated the plow. Behind him walked his wife, dropping the wheat seed into the narrow furrow exposed by the plow. Since the plowing was done around the field, each furrow covered over the seed planted in the preceding one.[2] The children were kept busy frightening away crows and other pests. In the month or so that we stayed in this locality this wheat came up beautifully and promised an excellent crop.

Wheat is a very simple crop, since once it is planted it needs no further cultivation; and in the cold of the sierra, or even the medium depths of the *ranchería* such as we were on, it does much better than corn.[3] All the Tarahumaras know how to raise wheat, as our sojourn among them proved; and they could simplify or lessen their struggle for existence by merely shifting from corn to wheat. But they would no more do this than raise potatoes. Corn is their customary food, the food of prestige, of ceremony, of ritual. Such upstart crops as wheat or potatoes have no status except as famine food, consumed only through stringent necessity.[4]

From wheat the Tarahumaras make *pinole*, often mixing it with the remainder of their corn to make it go farther and seem more like the proper *pinole* to which they are accustomed. Wheat is also made into *esquiate* and *tortillas*. *Tortillas* are nothing but unleavened pancakes, made in a *comal* or native griddle which must be well greased so that the ground cereal can be turned over and cooked on both sides. Since the Tarahumaras do not render lard, they use suet for grease. Mexicans of this part of the country say they prefer these wheat griddle cakes to *tortillas*, and in the United States poor Mexicans live on them. The Indians, however, do not like them as well as *tortillas*, and if they have any corn they either use nothing but it or mix it with the wheat for the corn flavor.

As soon as Lorenzo got his catch crop of wheat planted, he addressed himself to the business of "keeping up with the Joneses." A man of his position and prestige, in Umira as well as in Samachique, could hardly go on living in a cave when his rival, the richest man in the vicinity, was hiring Mexicans for the building of an adobe house. Lorenzo himself was so Mexicanized that he did not have to hire Mexicans to build him a house, as he proudly told me; but on the other hand he could not put up an adobe dwelling by himself, even if he knew how, which I doubted. He decided, therefore, to build a stone house, since in the Sierra Tarahumara there is a God's plenty of stones as of wood.

Outside of those Indians who have come under the influence of the missions, where masonry is taught, none of the Tarahumaras know how to construct masonry corners.[5] So Lorenzo, like a few others of the Tarahumara elite, in building his house had to utilize a wall framework of notched and fitted poles. As in a wood house, pole uprights forming the corners and cross pieces were attached to these and to other uprights set at certain intervals. Then Lorenzo built in the wall sections of rock, held together by mud plaster. He shaped the stones with an old, dull axe. About a generation ago many of the houses around the church at Samachique were constructed somewhat similarly under the guidance of the priest who lived in the *convento* at that time. But in recent times Lorenzo was the only Tarahumara of Samachique to follow this type, and then only because he did not wish to be too far outdistanced by the other rich man of Umira.

Yet in adopting this technique of construction in stone and mud, Lorenzo was only following the prehistoric Tarahumara method of building. Before the Spaniards brought the steel axe, thereby making available to the people the great wood resources of the sierra, the Indians utilized the abundant supplies of stone and mud for building both dwellings and storehouses.

The construction of this house gives a revealing glimpse of social aid among the Tarahumaras which illustrated the fundamental wisdom, even among primitives, of not giving something for nothing. This was strictly work relief, though hardly on a scale comparable to that of the trail where we encountered a strange Tarahumara, his wife, and two children hiking along and driving a black sheep before them, their whole life savings, to be saved from the economic debacle à la Tarahumara. They didn't seem to be particularly downcast. Rather, later when I knew their circumstances and recalled their appearance, they seemed quietly confident and assured of a hospitable reception in a strange community where they had neither relatives nor friends. This confidence was justified by the Tarahumara custom of hospitality and the strong mutual solidarity of the Tarahumaras, which causes Mexicans to speak of them as *muy unidos*, very united. Furthering this solidarity is the pattern of obligatory cooperative labor, and again, the severe penalties incurred by inhospitality. Black magic is an ever-present bugaboo. A spurned guest may retaliate by utilizing the activities of the evil little *disagíki* bird.

The case of this indigent Tarahumara family was especially significant for our study because it revealed much of the underlying social structure of the tribe, which comes to the surface only to meet concrete demands. Therefore, during the month that we were at Umira, we followed their movements closely. They went from one house to another. At each they waited patiently in Tarahumara fashion for half an hour or so before they were asked in. After telling their story they were given food and treated rather as guests than as mendicants. At various places they were put to work at odd jobs. The man worked in the fields of one Indian for about a week, assisting him with his plowing and planting. At another time he helped Lorenzo work on his house. His wife and children occupied themselves with simpler, household tasks.[6]

We knew the Tarahumaras so well by this time that we were able to detect considerable information from the manner of the guests. At first, being strange and unfamiliar about the *ranchería* of their host, they were awkward and ill at ease. A subsequent visit, however, would show them familiar with the lay of the land and with the tasks to be done, and taking an interest in their work, almost as if it were being done for themselves.

Thus these newcomers passed through the community, going from one place to another until finally there was no more to do. Then the *gobernador* assigned them fields of their own. They sold their sheep for supplies and seed for planting wheat. Lorenzo lent them his oxen without charge, as Tarahumara custom dictated that he must do. In this way they were helped through the famine; and although we left before it was over, they no doubt ultimately established themselves in full social status in their new community.

The strength of this pattern of mutual help and solidarity was hardly less than amazing. Aside from the foregoing, I saw a good instance of it in the building of Lorenzo's new house. Every day for more than a week he had half a dozen men working on it. Naturally I supposed that they were being hired. At the end of the long session, however, I was surprised to find that their recompense consisted of a large pot of beer prepared by Lorenzo's wife. On this we all got drunk. It was at this *tesgüinada* that Lorenzo's sister in her drunkenness loosed her hold on the blanket over her back thereby dropping her child. Fortunately she was sitting, so the child was not hurt. But, as I have mentioned before, her carelessness angered her husband. Before she could pick up the child, he gave her a heavy cuff that sent her sprawling across the room.

Lorenzo's sister was a true throwback to her Mexican grandmother. She had Castilian features and blue eyes. Beautiful indeed she was; and it seemed strangely anomalous to see this woman, who looked like a dark European, dressed in Tarahumara clothes and engaged in the laborious and arduous routine of an Indian squaw. She was as bashful as any of the other women, and I never saw her close unless I was chaperoned by Lorenzo. Upon my approach, if she were herding goats, she would flee up the mountainside, her little feet, like those of all Tarahumara women, fairly twinkling under her wide flaring skirts. I was very anxious to make friends with her, hoping that she might prove as valuable an informant on Tarahumara women as Lorenzo was on the affairs of the men. On their field trips men anthropologists get very little of feminine customs, attitudes, and beliefs, which certainly differ from those of the men. One solution, when no woman anthropologist can be taken along, is to have a native wife. I, however, was married; and Bennett, though single, was too aesthetic to make so great a sacrifice in the cause of science. The implications of this the reader would understand could he but have seen this beautiful Indian mestiza woman drunk and filthy from rolling in the dirt at the much polluted scene of this drunken orgy.

This was a particularly riotous *tesgüinada*. Lorenzo and I, however, were only happily drunk. After I had repeated his Spanish prayers, phrase for phrase, Lorenzo was unable to contain his joy any longer. So he confided to me "*Soy muy pendejo, yo,*" a phrase that I shall not translate.[7] But about this time the husband of his sister got her to start an argument with Lorenzo about a pig that she claimed he had appropriated from her share of the inheritance. The argument continued for an hour or more. Lorenzo got madder and madder. The two talked Spanish, so I was able to follow the argument, though it was nothing but mutual abuse. But Lorenzo did not lose control of himself and strike the woman as her husband had done previously. Meanwhile the scamp of a husband was outside the house with me. Throughout the dispute he kept pointing drunkenly and pietistically to the sun, and saying, "*Todo en el nombre de Dios.*" ("All this in the name of [the Sun] God.")

Lorenzo's keen interest in almost everything had not stopped short of archaeology. He knew every site in the vicinity, and his knowledge and concern thus made him an invaluable guide for archaeological reconnaissance. We visited a dozen or more sites in this part of the *barrancas*. Soon I was led to see that adequate archaeological work would be worthwhile, and therefore wrote to the University of Chicago outlining the project. Some time later funds were sent me made available by the National Research Council of Washington, D.C., which permitted me to protract my archaeological work in this part of southern Chihuahua to explore the ancient Basket-Maker and Cave-Dweller archaeology.

There was an ancient Cave-Dweller site near the "Royal Road" between our camp and the Mexican settlement of the patriarch and his descendants. As Lorenzo was busy making his grand house, and Bennett had gone off elsewhere, I decided to visit this site alone. It had not been completely looted by Mexican muleteers, so I took along a little Tarahumara crate, known to the Indians as an *acaste*. Just as the Tarahumaras carry these crates on their backs, held there with a tumpline, so I prepared this crate for bringing back archaeological loot from the cave. Off I hiked for a pleasant day of opening ancient structures, taking notes and pictures, and making sketches.

Finishing before midafternoon I decided to go on the rest of the way to the Mexican settlement. The *señora* there had some laundry of ours, and besides we could use some more *tortillas*.

So for the first time in six months I visited the old bullion station on the "Royal Road," converted into a thrifty Mexican ranch. Nearby was a Tarahumara chapel called Basiaurichi.[8] To this the Indians of the vicinity of Umira claim allegiance, rather than to that of Samachique. During the winter, however, there were so many of the Samachique Indians scattered throughout the caves that we were able to feel at home in this marginal area between the two communities.

At Basiaurichi the Mexicans and Indians had built a schoolhouse, and the Federal government had provided a male teacher. The building was of recent construction, and reminded me of stories I had heard, while a teacher in the Philippines, of the makeshift schools that the first American teachers in the Islands had built up into the excellent modern system. The Mexican teachers have the same crusading spirit of those early American teachers, so I fail to see why the Mexicans should not make a similar advance. In so many ways their problems are the same.

The schoolhouse was not yet provided with windows and doors, but the wind was not vigorous and biting here as in the sierra. There were a table and a chair for the teacher. The Indian pupils, however, had to content themselves with boards supported by large rocks. Other concomitants were a blackboard, some chalk, and a supply of books. The wild little longhaired Indians, draped in their blankets, were learning the Spanish letters when I dropped in.

Scattered through the higher grades were some Mexican children of different families, and even their aunt, the youngest daughter of the old patriarch, who attended school as a pastime only, since she had advanced beyond the work given here. The teacher himself was a very intelligent, faithful young man of high educational ideals if not of high academic standing. He lived this lonely life with little compensation other than the fine horse on which over weekends he made record-breaking trips to the railhead at Creel.

This little project of a school would be amusing set against the background of American schools. But from my two years' experience in teaching in the Philippines, I have some idea of the possibilities and limitations of educating half-wild people; and it seemed to me that this federal Tarahumara school had made an excellent start.

Among the breech-clouted Ilongots in the Philippines I have seen American-supervised schools run by Filipino teachers. These tribal people are inveterate headhunters. Since in the agricultural work of the school the Ilongot children have to use bolos, the principal keeps the sharpening stone in his office, so that he will know which of the pupils may be meditating homicide.

The breech-clout pattern is as strong among the little savages as it is among the adults. The children are provided with short pants, but these they cannot be prevailed upon to wear except when they are actually in the classroom. Therefore a row of pegs is provided, similar to those upon which American children hang their hats and coats. Here, when they are not in the classroom, the children keep their shorts. On entering the classroom they don their shorts; as soon as school is out, however, they return their shorts to the pegs, happy to be again clad only in their clouts.

When these little brownies rush out of school at recess, it is to play American games with the little girls. I have seen them playing and singing in "bamboo English" accents "London Bridge Is Falling Down." And when the boys knelt down to sing before the girls, "I kneel because I love you," the contrast to the usual Ilongot customs was particularly striking.

These American-supervised schools among the Ilongots (as well as other non-Christian Philippine and Indian schools) are open to the criticism that they are compelled to use force in order to retain their students. Ilongot parents think that school and prison are synonymous, for both institutions maintain uniformed policemen. The Ilongot children are always running away, and the truant officer is kept constantly busy. The American-made schools in the mountains of Luzon, however, have taught the little headhunters more than how to play "London Bridge."

But I am discussing Mexican education of the wild Tarahumaras. If or when the Mexican government carries out its project of boarding schools for the Tarahumaras, where industries as well as Spanish and "the three R's" are taught, its program will not be without important results.

In contrast to the Philippines, there is little or no difficulty in rounding up Tarahumara students who seem anxious to learn Mexican ways. When the program of the federal government teaches the younger ones to speak Spanish and to read and write, and the industrial techniques of cheesemaking, tanning leather, construction, masonry, carpentry, and the like; and when the girls learn how to sew, cook, and care for children, a great start will have been made.

If a richer cultural life can be substituted for the general drinking and drunkenness, and if the government allows enough priests in the sierra to impart to the Indians the elements of Catholicism, the change that will ensue will be from Wild Indians to Mexicans. Such work is favored at the outset, because the step from the one culture to the other is not a very wide one, and because of a general lack of race prejudice and "color lines."

Is such a step or change desirable for both groups concerned? Obviously it is for the federal government, since citizens and taxpayers are preferable to wild charges. Is it desirable for the Tarahumaras? I certainly do not always favor the "civilization" of primitive tribes. Some primitive cultures have more to offer their participants than has civilization. The Pueblo Indians of the southwestern United States and the Huichols of Jalisco have native cultures manifestly better for them than the patterns of civilization, to which they show amazing resistance. But the Tarahumaras have so meager a native culture, both material and spiritual, that in my opinion, which I have not arrived at hastily, they would be the gainers by voluntary Mexicanization. I say "voluntary," because the Mexican government is more liberal than ours in not forcing education on the Indians. In this they are right, and their course is commendable. That the Tarahumaras can be educated without force, moral or otherwise, is in itself evidence that they consider Mexicanization an improvement over their own culture.[9]

The policy of the government in restricting or proscribing Catholic education of the Tarahumaras, however, I consider a sad mistake. The spiritual and religious motivations of Tarahumara thought and action lie deep and powerful. The Voltairean philosophy of the

Mexican Revolutionary government and its teachers will have but slight appeal to Tarahumara pupils. Wild peoples are tamed by emotional and religious appeals.

Since I left the sierra, the federal government has extended its educational program among the Tarahumaras by the establishment of two Indian schools in the sierra (among nine other regional Indian schools in other tribal country) on funds diverted from the abandoned Indian school in Mexico City. This central school was closed, as I have related elsewhere, because its training was urban rather than rural and unfitted its Indian charges for tribal life, a change both intelligent and statesmanlike. The local Indian schools appear to be boarding schools where agriculture, industry, and the care of homes and children are an integral part of the educational program.

I became so interested in the Tarahumara school that I forgot all about time. When I returned to the house of the Mexican patriarch of the settlement, there was not more than an hour of daylight remaining of this day, and I was three hours from camp. Bennett did not know where I was, and if I didn't arrive back in good season, the whole of Umira would be out on a search party. Worse luck, I did not have a flashlight with which to negotiate the worst of the trail in darkness.

This, however, was Mexico; and God provided the Sierra Tarahumara with the material for the best torches in the world, namely, those of pitch pine, which is so abundant. I borrowed a handful of long, narrow splints of this excellent torch material. Then I hiked off on the double to where I had cached my crate of archaeological effects.

In a short while it was dark; so holding a pair of splints in one hand to keep each other warm I lit my torch. Mexican *ocote*, or pitch pine, is so resinous that it burns like oil; and constant care must be taken to avoid being burned and to prevent the oozing pitch, which is as hot as melted sealing wax, from falling on one's hand.

During the day I should have no difficulty in returning to the camp, even though I did not know the trail very well; but at night all familiar landmarks were blotted out in the darkness or metamorphosed by the flare of my torch into a thousand strange and eerie shapes that had never before entered my ken. But the Camino Real was rutted with many mule tracks; and these I followed to avoid getting shunted off into some Tarahumara sidetrail. Toward the end of my journey I had to cross a long stretch of bare rock. On this stretch somehow I got turned at right angles up a stream tributary to the river I was by this time following. Assured I was on the right track I hiked along for ten minutes before I happened to look into the sky. Directly before me was the North Star. Had I continued my course I might eventually have come out at the United States border.

So I retraced my steps. Shortly after I found myself back at the main river. By this time my torch had given out. I was nearer camp than I thought, however, for soon I heard the barking of a dog and saw lights. Late though the hour was, I decided to risk alarming the Indians in order to inquire my way and obtain more pitch pine. I approached what, I fancied, was a Tarahumara house. Lo! it was my own camp near the house of Lorenzo. Bennett stuck his head out the door and welcomed me.

He asked me where I had been. "Lorenzo," he remarked, "said that you had taken a load of apples to Creel."

This was one of Lorenzo's better wisecracks. Bennett, however, could do himself proud on occasion. I think the best one he pulled during the whole nine months was about this time. After months of isolation we had finally exhausted our resources for entertaining each other. But one evening, from some dim recess of my mind, I revived a song with which I had yet to regale him. He accused me "of having been holding back on the expedition."

Since our time was passing faster than our information about the sierra and its people was accumulating, Bennett and I decided to part and work separately. He agreed to go to the lower *barrancas*. I was to go to the upper reaches of the Río Conchos, where certain differences in culture were apparent. As we shall see, I never got there but returned to Umira, and wrote up my report while I still had an excellent informant in Lorenzo, who was able to fill in any gaps in my study.

Bennett made a good study of the culture of the gorges, part of which was included in my section of *The Tarahumara*. Among the Tarahumaras many of the cultural differences are material, and due to differences of climate, flora and fauna, and natural resources between the windswept sierra and the hot *tierra caliente* of the lower gorges.

Perhaps a tenth of the tribe live in the gorges year-round. Because of the mines in these lower levels, these Tarahumaras are much more Mexicanized than their fellows of the sierra. The men, for example, speak Spanish, wear *calzones*, cut their hair and wear hats of tan leather; the women make cheese from milk and wear the characteristic Mexican *rebozo*, or shawl-like head-covering. Due to the lack of agricultural land in the gorges they support themselves, like the Mexicans, by working for the mines or trading with the *serrano* Tarahumaras. They do not actually mine, but cut mining timbers and transport them by muscle power. Mining, however, was at a standstill while we were in the sierra; so, like the Mexicans, the lowland Tarahumaras lived largely by trading.

While we were still at Umira, some of these *barranqueño* Indians came in to trade with the wilder *serrano* Tarahumaras. Their appearance shows obvious differences in clothing, hats, and haircuts. The traders had with them two curious insect products which bulk large in their interregional trade. One was a hard, earthlike material, the cocoon product of a grub to be found in the *barrancas*. This all Tarahumaras use as incense; when it is thrown on hot coals, it gives off an abundant, fragrant smoke. The other product was the lac from a scale insect called *alí*. This lac, or scale, was used for a varnish by the ancient Aztec and Maya Indians; but since it is edible, the realistic Tarahumaras use it for food. They are inordinately fond of it as a relish, especially when it is mixed with *chile*. I myself have eaten it, and it is no more strange than bird's-nest soup, which I used to get in the Philippines, one of the few places where edible birds'-nests are found. The sierra Tarahumaras are so fond of lac that poor as they were in this famine year, they would trade quarts of their precious corn for a cupful of it.

The *barranca* Indians also specialize in dyes for the blankets of the sierran Indians. For a blue dye they raise native indigo. Red dye they obtain from logwood *(Haematoxylum campechianum)*, which produces a dye used in world commerce. The flowers of *Aplopappus australis*, common in the *barrancas*, provide the lowlanders with a yellow dye; and a green dye is produced by another flower. The wives of the *barranca* Indians also weave blankets for sale. In fact the best Tarahumara blankets come from the *barranca* settlement of Choro.

Cheese is another staple of interregional trade. The highland Indians are quite fond of this, but they do not know how to make it from the milk of their own cattle.[10] Cheeses are sold in little round cakes, characteristic in Mexico. In the same form is bought and sold a sweet which is unique for Indian Mexico, since as far as I know, the Mexicans do not make it.

In the *barrancas* the *maguey* plant *(agave)*, the characteristic "century plant" of the Mexican scene, attains as large a size as anywhere else in Mexico.[11] In the sierra it is just a tiny prototype. The *barranca* Indians, like the Huichols, cut the heart or "cabbage" out of this tough, fibrous plant and cook it in an earth oven. In this process it becomes sweet and tasty, as my palate will verify. It contains, however, masses of heavy fiber which must be separated from the sweet meat of the "cabbage." This is done with the teeth, and the chewed-up fiber is ejected from the mouth. The *barranca* Indians prepare this sweet in little round cakes made from cheese molds. It finds a ready sale among the *serrano* Tarahumaras.

The *barranca* Indians also make an intoxicating drink from this sweet meat, since among them corn is scarce. The cooked "cabbages" are pounded with oak sledgehammers in little hollows in the rocks. The resulting pulp is mixed with water and then squeezed in a net held on two sticks a couple of feet long. The operator of this contraption holds one stick between his feet and twists the netful of soggy pulp by manipulating the other stick around and around with his hands. The diluted juice is collected and allowed to ferment. It makes a wine far superior in taste to native beer, or *tesgüino*. The *barranca* Indians have their cooperative labor parties just as do their fellows in the sierra.

Available in the gorges for basketry are better fiber-plants than are to be found in the uplands. From a small palm, as well as "bear grass" and a large "Spanish bayonet," the lowland Tarahumaras make superior woven (twilled) baskets. Some of these are double-woven and provided with tops. These are bought by the *serrano* Tarahumaras, who weave only single baskets. Often the materials are themselves traded for corn.

The *barranqueño* Indians show their greater Mexicanization in their weaving of small hats which they wear and which some of the *serrano* Indians buy.[12] During summer at this latitude a sunshade is welcome. Most of the mountain Tarahumaras, however, wear only a hairband to keep their hair out of their eyes.

The Tarahumara hat is ludicrous enough, although no more so than the Huichol hat. Either hat is the antithesis of the gigantic cartwheel hat or *sombrero* of the Mexican. The Tarahumara hat is not only small, but has a high crown in proportion to its narrow brim. The Huichol reverse the Tarahumara pattern and make their small hats with relatively large brim and tiny crown. Both hats make no pretense of going on the head; they are perched on top and held there by a string of native-woven "ribbon" which passes tightly under the chin. These hats, perhaps more than anything else, contrast with the Mexican pattern and show how imperfectly the *sombrero* as a Mexicanism has penetrated Indian culture.

In their buildings the Tarahumaras of the gorges utilize the stone and mud construction of their ancestors, because in these tropical elevations there are no forests of pine. The dwellings, however, are not round as they were in ancient times. For their rectangular houses the modern *barranca* Tarahumaras achieve solid if rude corners by casually piling stones, uncoursed, in plenty of tough adobe plaster. The better houses in the gorges, however, utilize a sort of framework for the corners, very much similar to that decided on by Lorenzo. A small opening on one side where the wall meets the roof serves as an outlet for smoke, although occasionally fireplaces like those in the stone houses around the chapel of Samachique are built. Hewn boards fitted into wooden door frames are seen fairly often, but are not the rule, even among the more Mexicanized Tarahumaras of the gorges.

Since *canoas* cut from pine logs are out of the question for lack of pines in the gorges, roofs are of either earth or thatch. The latter makes these *barranca* houses essentially the same as the *jacal* type of Indian houses prevalent throughout Mexico to the south. Corn storage houses are likewise of stone and mud, and appear to represent a holdover from ancient archaeological types. The modern forms stand on boulders, the tops of which serve as a firm and secure floor. The structures themselves are four or five feet in diameter and about the same in height. Their roofs are either conical and of sticks covered with long grass from the water, or flat and earth-covered. The doors are frequently simply stones or boards temporarily plastered with mud into a door frame of wood or oblong stone. When the storehouses are erected in caves instead of on boulders, dirt roofs suffice.

In the nonmaterial culture of the gorges the *barranca* Tarahumaras are again more advanced or closer to Mexicanization than their fellows of the sierra. Here contacts with Mexicans rather than with the missionaries have resulted in a greater diffusion of Catholicism. Here the pagan shaman is much less prominent; and he does not rely so completely for his cures upon sucking and blowing in ceremonies. He resorts frequently to remedies prepared from simple plants. Most of these are at least harmless and appeal merely because of their aromatic or repugnant smell or bad taste.

The *barranca* Tarahumaras have developed their use of herbal medicine to such a point that they even take some of their plants as far as Chihuahua, where they find a ready sale. The most noteworthy of these plants is *matarique* (Sp.), which the Tarahumaras call *pitcawi*. Its botanical name is *Cacalia decomposita*. The Mexicans of the city of Chihuahua consider it a cure for diabetes and pay the Indians a handsome price for small bunches of it. The plant is listed in the *Farmacopea Latino-Americana;* but its scientific properties are harmful rather than helpful, though both the Indians and the Mexicans esteem it. The foregoing source contains the data:

> . . . the root is employed since it contains two resins, essential oil, glucoside, tannic acid, and grease. The hydro-alcoholic preparation of the root acts to paralyse the motor system of the striated muscles and the heart; it produces a light anaesthesia by its local peripheral action. The tincture favors scarification of the tissue when applied on ulcers, wounds, etc. by its antiseptic action owing to a coating that it forms. (As a vulnerary it is mixed with equal parts of water.) Given internally it produces emetic and cathartic effects, and general retardation, but on occasión its use has caused chloroform accidents of a grave nature. Rheumatic pains, especially of the joints, as well as neuralgic pains, are calmed by its application in *loco dolente.*

This plant is one of the few, if not the only, contributions of the Tarahumaras to the world's stock of scientific things. By crude experimentation with and observation of plants they have discovered the properties of *matarique*, both as a vulnerary and in its paralyzing effects on the central nervous system of striated muscles. In utilizing the vulnerary properties of *matarique* the Tarahumaras wash wounds with a decoction made from it. They take advantage of its paralytic effects in stupefying fish. First they pound up bunches of the plant; then they sprinkle the ensuing mixture into pools made by damming up the river. The fish turn bottom up and can be caught unharmed.

The purgative properties of the plant are well known to the Tarahumaras. They grind the roots and drink the pulp with plenty of warm water. The action is quick and drastic, as the Indians know, who say that it may be stopped by eating cold *atole* (corn mush).

The plant is also used as a remedy for colds after being pounded and boiled for fifteen minutes. The Indians take it internally in small doses without ill effect to the heart action or, in scientific language, any "chloroform accidents."

▸ *The Catholic Mission*
▸
▸
▸
▸
▸
▸
▸
▸
▸   After about a month in the *barranca* of Umira, Bennett and
▸   I had completed our social obligations by visiting our
▸   Samachique friends in their winter homes in the caves.
We went to several drinking bouts staged on the pretext of transporting manure to the sierra fields or of arranging larger caves more suitable for dwellings; and it was at one of these, which I attended alone,
that I saw, helping himself from the limited number of drinking
gourds, a fellow drinker, who turned out to be none other than my
Samachique acquaintance, the Indian who was covered with syphilitic
ulcers. The Tarahumaras seem to be almost immune to syphilis,
which, however, is probably one of the less advertised contributions of
the Indian to the world at large. I must have drunk from another
gourd, yet I passed a mentally uncomfortable three weeks immediately
following.

Partially on this account I decided to avail myself of the services of
the padres of another mission near the railhead. They were better
informed in medicine than I, and could advise me if a trip to Chihuahua would be necessary. If my fears proved to be groundless, I
planned to go to the upper reaches of the Río Conchos, the only place
where the Tarahumaras use the narcotic cactus, peyote, as a regular
accessory to their religious ceremonies. Bennett was to head for the
lower gorges on the Río Urique, to Guadalupe, a village of *barranca*
Tarahumaras.

We cached our papers, notes, and Bennett's typewriter in a hidden
corn storage house belonging to Lorenzo. Then Bennett loaded the
expedition mule with corn bought in Creel. Famine conditions

throughout the country were still so acute that he would have been unable to obtain any corn in the *barrancas*. Though he had to make his trip on foot, he looked forward to it with relish.

This time, however, it was possible for me to travel more imperiously. Our rich Tarahumara neighbor, who haunted our woodpile, owned a horse, which he could not ride, and of all things! a new Mexican saddle. He kept the saddle hidden in his corn house; and yet, hidden away though it was, he derived considerable prestige from it, for the old Indian delusion of the man on horseback, which caused the Aztecs to think that the Spanish *conquistadores* were united with their horses into one fearsome, centaurlike creature, still lingers, albeit hazily, in the Tarahumara imagination.

For a few *centavos* a day I was able to hire the horse and saddle. One of the Indian's Mexican workmen, however, had borrowed the saddle to break in a *bronco*. During the process, incidentally, the Mexican was tossed off on his head on the rocky soil. He must have suffered a slight concussion, for as I learned he lay there stunned for hours. He told us later that his head still ached dully, and that this was because the blow had jarred his inner ears loose and let air into his skull, a natural deduction, since nature abhors a vacuum! The difference between the credibility of the Mexicans and that of the Indians is purely relative. The man went on to tell me that the best remedy for preventing such entrance of air into the head was earmuffs of feathers, and that for this purpose the bright feathers of the rare, magnificent giant woodpecker are especially esteemed. On this account this rare species, well-named imperial, has practically been exterminated by the Mexicans. I saw none in the sierra while I was there, though I was very anxious to procure at least one for the Field Museum. Specimens of the great woodpecker, which is as large as a raven, are to be found in only a few of the world's greatest museums.

Since the saddle was at the Mexican's home in the Mexican settlement, which was on my route, I decided to ride after it bareback. So I bridled the horse and started off. But I had ridden scarcely more than a hundred yards when my mount reared in the air and then came down with his head between his forelegs in real *bronco* fashion. I remained in place, but not for long. The animal seemed to have no withers, and there was nothing to keep me from sliding down his neck except his ears at the end of it. By the time I had slid that far I was going too fast to be stopped by such petty obstacles, and in less than no time I landed with a jolt on *terra firma*. Fortunately I did not jar my inner ears loose, and so did not suffer any resulting aches in my head, though I ached elsewhere.

To follow the "Royal Road" one must be an expert in distinguishing mule tracks, otherwise he may confuse his route with trails leading to Tarahumara *rancherías*. Those tracks prove an infallible guide, for the Tarahumaras never use mules and very seldom even burros. On this trip, however, I had the benefit of the guidance of my invaluable Lorenzo.

He left his house unfinished, not so much to accompany me as because he had heard that the Chihuahua government was sending a carload of corn to Creel to relieve the distress of the Indians. The corn, incidentally, did not come. The Indians were not starving, but hunger was an actuality. They were selling their blankets and even their animals to get money to buy corn. Thus Dr. Bennett was able to make a splendid collection of Tarahumara effects for the Milwaukee Public Museum. Had conditions been otherwise, however, the Indians would probably never have parted with their possessions.

Lorenzo was extremely fond of rolled oats, with which he had become familiar during his youthful days of peonage under a Mexican. But oats were not available in the sierra. So he said to me, "*Don Roberto*, when you leave here and get to Chihuahua, will you send some oat seed to the padres? They will send it on to me, and I will plant it; and then I can eat *avena* after you are gone." I fulfilled his request much later as I was leaving the country. I have little doubt that this practical, sane, wise old Indian today plants oats as he does onions, garlic, and many other luxuries that the average Tarahumara would never think of raising.

So we started for Creel, and continued on awhile without adventure, that is, without any that I can recall five years later. But no trip in the Sierra Tarahumara is lacking in adventures, big or little. When we got as far as Cusárare, I had the great luck to meet the padre who had suggested that we go to Samachique for our winter's study and had given us permission to use the *convento*. We had discovered that the Indians of Samachique did not recognize this priest's authority, but appreciated the permission notwithstanding, and as I have related, soon ingratiated ourselves with the Indians.

The padre had come to the little chapel of Cusárare to give a mass to the Indians. Thus I did not have to go on to Creel and from there hire someone else to guide me to the mission a dozen miles or so distant. He seemed no less delighted than I at our meeting, and invited me to the mission.

Padre P. was a charming man, and seemed to grow even more charming as our friendship developed. He was a Mexican, of course, since the law allows no foreign *ministros de cultos*. But he had worked for some time with American Jesuits at a mission in British Honduras, and consequently spoke English fluently and was glad to speak it again after so many years in Mexico. He also spoke Tarahumara with equal ease, but we didn't converse in it. Although a typical missionary of his order, his superior qualities evidenced themselves in the special training he had taken in order to serve his Indian charges.

Not content with the academic, scientific, and theological training of his order he had continued his studies in Mexico City in agriculture, animal training, and bee culture. Since he rode a great deal of the time, he preferred English horsemanship and saddles to the savage riding and cruel bits of the Mexican *vaqueros* and *charros;* but he had made a special study of Mexican horsemanship at a Mexican agricultural college. He had a splendid fiery horse which contrasted markedly with my Indian mustang when we rode along together.

Later, after I had been at the mission a short while and had got "on the inside," and on occasion when Padre P. was absent, the other fathers and brothers began to joke good-naturedly among themselves about his horsemanship. Like all Mexicans the padre was quite sensitive about his riding. But one day his horse had reared, unseating him; and the mishap had been witnessed by a fellow brother. The padre had put the brother under an injunction not to tell the others. Such a story, however, was too good to keep, the padre's being unseated after having had a special college course in horse training, and it soon delighted many an ear. But I came to my friend's defense.

"*¿Pues quién sabe?*" I said.

As we were coming from Cusárare the other day, we were riding along slowly so that his horse wouldn't outdistance mine. It was lucky that I was with him, because I knew nothing about these quagmires or sinks that are formed from the soft, flourlike tufa that weathers from the cliffs. Suddenly, as we were trotting along, his horse went into one, and was up to its belly before I could as much as open my mouth. Then it was that the splendid training of both the padre and the horse showed up; for in an instant the animal threw its weight to its hind legs, made a complete turn, and with a mighty bound jumped back to solid ground again. It was a fine exhibition of both horsemanship and of the training of the horse. If it had been my horse, and especially if I had been traveling alone, *¿pues quién sabe?*

¿Quién sabe?, who knows? The answer to this might have been similar to a tale of Villa the padre told me, as we rode along the sierra, about the last stand of the Villistas in the sierra.

In Chihuahua, early in his career, Villa had been content to leave his band at night and, taking a blanket, go off and sleep by himself because of his old outlaw fear of being shot while he slept. When he became a great, in fact the greatest, general of the "Constitutional" army, this procedure was hardly seemly. So he organized a special *escolta*, or guard, a body numbering hundreds of his most trusted men. By the time he had descended into the rich mining state of Durango, and then taken Zacatecas, the members of this *escolta* were called the "*Dorados*," the golden ones. They had stolen and extorted so much gold from the country that their *charro* costumes were decorated with pure gold. As many as a hundred gold pieces hung from their wide *sombreros;* and around their bodies were slung money belts, *víboras* (literally "snakes"), stuffed with gold coin.

Villa and his "*Dorados*" with the help of Zapata took Mexico City, driving Obregón and Carranza to Veracruz. But realizing that he was too illiterate to become President, Villa withdrew and went back to the north. Then, defeated by Obregón at Celaya and crippled by the opposition of President Wilson, the Villa host began to disperse; and Villa led his faithful men back to northern Chihuahua, which was his undisputed territory. Here, however, his fierce hatred for Obregón and his aide, Calles, impelled him to the rash decision to cross the sierra into Sonora and attack Calles in his home state.

The padre continued the tale, current among the folk of Chihuahua.

It was when the "*Dorados*" were crossing this dangerous sierra that the worst of them met a fate peculiarly fitting. This "*Dorado*" was Villa's famous killer, Fierro, who personally and with the greatest glee performed the many killings and executions that Villa himself could not direct. Fierro had led the squad that executed the Englishman, Benton, an incident which caused such protest that Wilson began to look for a leader other than Villa for the Mexican presidency. Legend has it also that much later Fierro was responsible for the shooting of the fourteen American mining engineers taken from the Mexico-Noroeste train at Santa Isabel.

The army of Villa was poor and desperate because of the defeat by Obregón from the front and because its supplies were cut off by Wilson from the rear. Yet Villa's generals had gold, Tomás Urbina being able to desert in southern Chihuahua with the army treasure of some millions. Only half was recovered; and Urbina died with one of Fierro's bullets in his head to finish off Villa's in his stomach. Fierro, however, carried a modest fortune in the "snakes" around his body.

In a reconnaissance of the sierra Fierro led out a small body of men, in appearance and equipment far different from the "*Dorados*" of better days. Fierro, of course, was burdened with his gold, and adding to its weight were many cartridge belts slung crisscross over his shoulders. His horse was still further burdened with weapons and a silver-mounted Mexican saddle. The horse, however, was a magnificent animal. When they came to a river banked with quicksand, Fierro, to encourage his men, spurred his wonderful animal first through the dangerous place. But his men were afraid to follow. So back he recklessly spurred, drew his pistol, and threatened to blast them off the sierra if they didn't obey. Thus intimidated they urged their miserable mounts through the quicksand, and all gained the other side, for they were not so burdened with gold.

Then for the third time Fierro spurred his animal into the quagmire, made even softer now by the passage of the others. But by this time the strength of the splendid animal was exhausted, and it began to flounder helplessly in the bottomless quicksand. In a second both horse and rider were lost. Slowly the mercurial sand climbed up over the body of Fierro. He was being forced down by the very weight of the gold that he carried. His men, whom he had forced across at pistol point, let him sink without throwing him a rope as they might have done. He fired at them as the almost liquid mass climbed higher and higher over him. They ran away and reported his death to Villa.

The story isn't exactly true, because such tales are generally romanticizations about the great figures of those revolutionary days. But as a piece of folk literature it provides a particularly fitting end for the

"*Dorado*" Fierro, the "golden one," cursing, struggling, and shooting as he was slowly dragged to a ghastly death by the weight of his ill-gotten gains.

However, had I fallen into any sierra quagmire, I could have used all the gold that I had on my person as a float. And the missionaries themselves were not burdened with the stuff.

With such stories the good padre regaled me on our trip to Sisoguichi. This Jesuit mission in the Sierra Tarahumara was much better equipped and more comfortable than the first one I had visited at Norogáchic.[1] And in comparison with the little *convento* at Samachique it represented literally a land o'erflowing with milk and honey. The milk came from a herd, which supplied the mission generously. The honey came from the best Italian breed of bees. These Padre P. had brought to the mission in order to teach the Indians apiculture and made available to them the great meadows of fragrant flowers that appear in the spring. The apicultural teachings of the father found a warm admirer in me, since I am most partial to honey on hotcakes.

Padre P. was a bee fancier. He had dozens of hives, and the mission was full of honey. He would go out with his smokegun, and work with his pets, disdaining any protection for the exposed parts of his body. The bees would sometimes sting him in the face; but he would calmly pull out the sting with little ill effect and no more than the remark, which I remember well, "I am so accustomed to this that I can't bother with a net."

He was also an expert on leather tanning; but instead of teaching the neophytes the traditional Mexican method of using oak bark for tannin, he only passed on his knowledge of how to improve on the already finished soft and friable leather that is made by such primitive materials. With scientific thoroughness indeed had he gone into the art of leather tanning. He taught his boys how to chrome-tan, and the resulting leather was as hard as wood and durable as iron. I know, because I subjected half soles of this leather to four months of the hardest walking imaginable.

With even greater scientific thoroughness and the greatest care Padre P. and the Father Superior studied pharmacy and mixed medicines, as is typical of this Jesuit mission to the Tarahumaras. I shall always remember the padre mounting his fine horse on a cold, drizzling day to ride at least a dozen miles to save a woman who was bleeding to death from hemorrhage after childbirth. But this was just a detail soon to be forgotten in the routine of these men, whose order with justice and with truth has for its motto *Ad Majorem Dei Gloriam,* "For the greater glory of God."

The mission building followed the general architectural pattern of that of Norogáchic, and indeed the general pattern of the Spanish Colonial Empire. As I have remarked, it was better equipped than the other; and thus the Jesuits were able to carry out a full and well-rounded program. The Mexicans of this community were not the bandits of the more isolated community I had visited. There were no prices on any of their heads, so they were safe living near the railroad and the little of civilization which it brought to the sierra. Moreover, they were friendly to the church, and were as loyal in attending its services as were the Indians.

As at Norogáchic, the Indians for about a dozen miles around hiked to this mission. Each brought on his back a little bundle of firewood for the padres. This Tarahumara contribution was a great convenience for the priests, since the relatively heavy population of the community had with time cut back the forests for several miles from the towns. On Sunday the woodpile grew by leaps and bounds as the breech-clouted Indians passed it before entering the church, where they sat with their Mexican neighbors. The latter were more decorously clad, the men in tattered and patched overalls, and the women in skirts, waists, and their ever-present shawl-like *rebozos*, especially fitting for attending Christian service. The presence of so many people gathered on the little plaza outside the church made me think I was again in a city after having lived so long in the heart of the sierra.

Important as the church services were at this mission, they were only one aspect of its rather extensive program. Education and academic and technical training in farming and industries are important links in the Jesuit process of Christianizing the Tarahumaras. All the rooms of the large mission building were used in carrying out this program. There were schoolrooms for Tarahumara boys. The school was under the charge of a well-educated lay brother who gave instruction in the elementary subjects and in Catholic dogma. He taught in Spanish, of course, although he was thoroughly fluent in Tarahumara. His linguistic ability he turned to account by writing religious tracts and the catechism in Tarahumara, which the natives were also taught how to read.

Other lay brothers gave practical instruction in agriculture, blacksmithing, leather tanning, shoemaking, and other industries. Thirty or more boys were taken care of at the mission, and the place was a hive of activity. Several rooms served for storing the crops from the mission lands which supported all this work. In the stables were some twenty mules, a half-dozen saddle horses, and a few milch cattle. Indeed, at the mission the whole round of a self-sustaining colony was carried out.

Because of the general crop failure it was necessary for the mission to buy corn from Chihuahua in order to support its neophytes. Virtually everyone was busy getting a twenty-mule train ready for the trip to the railroad. Pack saddles were being inspected and renovated, *reatas* and lassos repaired. The half-grown and larger boys were expert in this work, for they were getting excellent training as muleteers in making the long trips back and forth with corn.

How an Indian like Lorenzo would have benefitted by this program! He had learned most of this, it is true, by apprenticing himself as a peon to a Mexican master; and the man's wife had even taught him the elements of reading, so that he could slowly pronounce the syllables of a Spanish text. But to facilities such as those at this mission he would have responded like a plant given water.

It turned out that I was to stay several weeks at this place, which was a fully functioning Catholic mission to the Indians, with its program and activities essentially similar to those of the first missions to the "*indios*" in America and the Philippines. In this sierra of the primitive people, generations behind the rest of the world in culture, I had left a group of Cave-Dwellers who were struggling barehanded against a stern, natural environment and entered a scene of the building of a civilization literally from the ground up, since Tarahumara culture is so deeply rooted in the soil of the rocky sierra.

The program of the Catholic missions is to build a civilization from the foundations of native cultures. Considering the ends such missionaries strive for, their results in any part of the world justify their program. They build upon preexisting patterns, and are not discouraged if centuries are needed to complete their work. The Roman missionaries were patient for such a time with our Teutonic ancestors, and they almost succeeded in civilizing those fierce barbaric people who drank their liquor from human skulls. The Germans did break away during the Reformation, of course, for their old aggressive spirit of individual independence was never more than half curbed by the suave sophistications of Latin civilization.

Fifteen hundred years later, among the Tarahumaras, the Latin missionaries still try to cause as little damage as possible in changing native cultures. They seek rather to utilize them to their own ends.

The Tarahumaras are agricultural. So the first missionaries early substituted a stick plow dragged by oxen for the aboriginal digging stick. This has been taken over by the whole tribe, although the Indians still use the digging stick for planting corn. At present the padres are endeavoring to replace the simple, curved stick plow, which merely scratches the soil, with a steel plow with a real plowshare.[2]

For leather the Tarahumaras once used only buckskin tanned with the brains of the deer. The first padres substituted stronger straps of rawhide, which the Indians also use for sandals; and this they are now tanning. The Indians are satisfied with rawhide for their sandals and straps, although when rawhide is wet, it is no more useful than a dishrag.

In the realm of aboriginal social life the padres are tolerant of everything except the drunken brawls and the general looseness of the marriage tie. Drunkenness they combat, or endeavor to combat, by teaching against it in the schools, and utilizing formidable charts and pictures that show the vicious effects of drunkenness. This teaching, by the way, has no influence beyond their neophytes, who, however, do not participate in the important native institutions that depend upon drinking.

The looseness of the marriage tie has been combatted generally by the institution of the native official, the *mayor.* I have already spoken of this office. Among their neophytes, however, both sexes are educated by priests and nuns. It is natural that the "tamed" Indians should marry one another and settle under the bells, so to speak, on lands near the mission. If this training persists, ultimately the whole tribe will be Mexicanized. At Nonoava, as I have said elsewhere, the Jesuit program has been carried out so completely that the church has been turned over to the secular clergy.

As for native religion, the priests understand well the value of building on native patterns; and their rare gift of tolerance for incongruities in native religion is hardly inimical to their teachings. Between drunkenness and witchcraft they oppose only the former because of its immemorial and violent results. Despite Catholic missionary work, much paganism will remain for centuries mixed into the Tarahumara religion. Yet as an impartial student of primitive culture, I believe that the policy of the priests is particularly well-suited to their eventual ends. Native religion presents a warm and living reality to the Indians as the priests attempt gradually to substitute Christian elements for pagan ones.

Due to the hectic history of the Jesuit order in the Spanish realm and the peculiar difficulties of the isolation and impenetrable terrain of the Tarahumara missions, the Jesuit work for two centuries has lost almost as much as it has gained. But undaunted, the priests rebuild their structures ruined by revolutions and resume their work after expulsions by both Spanish and Mexican governments. Because of these setbacks and interruptions they have hardly begun to bridge the tremendous gap between the primitive and the civilized. Thus if we were to step from modernity and civilization into a Jesuit mission to the Tarahumaras, it would be something like stepping through a looking glass with Alice. We would find ourselves immediately in an atmosphere and habits of life centuries old. So I found it, at least, a scene of history and romance, similar to what I had read about it in the historical publications of the University of California and in the romantic novel, *Ramona*, which portrays the missions to the Indians in that state.

But more interesting than an account of the Jesuit educational program were the incidents of my stay there for several weeks.

For instance, one day at the mission a Mexican muleteer came in and asked Padre P. if he would pull his wife's tooth.

The good padre replied, "No, I don't do that anymore. It is too painful, both to me and to the patient. You can do it as well as I. I will lend you the forceps."

The Mexican borrowed the forceps and then came around to me. "*Señor*," he said, "will you please pull my *señora*'s tooth?"

Now, in extended travels throughout the old Spanish Empire, an American is asked to do a variety of things. A Filipina woman once asked me to place my hand on her baby's head. Since the child's head looked reasonably clean, I complied. Then I asked my native chauffeur why on earth I was asked to do that. He replied that the Filipinos believe that the Virgin Mary and *Santo Cristo* were redheaded, presumably because red is a rare color for hair in the Philippines. And certain it is that all images of these saints are portrayed with auburn wigs. Consequently all redheaded people, like myself, are thought to have the King's touch for protecting children against disease.

An American friend of mine was asked to deliver a child on an inter-island boat, held up in a cove to ride out a typhoon. He succeeded. The sea was so rough that the midwives were too seasick to do more than give this high school teacher instructions. But this occasion in Mexico was the first time that I had ever been requested to pull a tooth. So taking a cue from the padre I also declined, with the excuse that the muleteer could do as well as I.

A day or so later, at the table, the padre was laughing at the incident. "The man brought back the dental forceps," he said. "One of his neighbors told me that as soon as he got the forceps adjusted over the offending tooth, in muleteer fashion he put his foot against his wife's forehead, just as he does on a mule's side when about to give a heave in tightening the *reata* on the diamond-hitch. Then he gave a particularly vigorous heave, and the tooth was out."

So life in the sierra has its lesser charms.

I was held for three weeks at this mission by rains that precluded all thought of my continuing on and crossing the flooded rivers to the village where I had planned to go. But the mission was a lovely place in which to be caught by the rain. While the cold, slanting rain streamed down outside, I was safely quartered in a snug, warm, dry room working on my notes and reading books from the well-stocked mission library. To make it even better, the priests had marked all the pages in their dry ecclesiastical histories which dealt with the Tarahumaras. I have never accumulated so much valuable historical material in so short a time, nor so easily.

But meanwhile poor "*Don* Benito" was not faring so well. It turned out that the rains caught him en route to the *barrancas* with his mule load of corn. Knowing that the corn would sprout and spoil if it got wet, he could do little except take the double tarpaulin from his bedroll and use it to make a shelter for the corn. He told me later that for three mortal days and nights he and the *mozo* squatted under this shelter on corn sacks. But he saved the corn, and thus guaranteed two months of work in the *barrancas* which yielded more data than any other two months' work.

Still I was not unmindful of my work, even though my destination was beyond my reach due to high rivers. This I discovered in urging my horse across a flooded *arroyo* that was strewn with boulders. The force of the water was so powerful that it almost swept the animal off its feet. If a mere *arroyo* was so dangerous, it was obvious what the Río Conchos would be, which I would have to cross many times from its source (near Bocóyna) to the Tarahumara village I wanted to study. So I remained at the mission.

Life in the Mexican village near the mission was interesting. I watched a Mexican making one of the primitive carts with wheels of solid wood, the ancient remains of which I had seen in New Mexico as a boy. A German in Chihuahua, incidentally, told me a good story about one of these carts, which are accepted as a fast means of transportation in the roadless mountains of Chihuahua. A Mexican used to drive one of them past the German's sierra ranch. Since the antiquity of the cart was more or less evident throughout in its many repairs made with rawhide thongs, my friend offered to trade a new steel plow for it. The Mexican, thinking no doubt that the German was crazy, readily consented; but he asked permission to finish his trip first. This was agreed to.

The Mexican returned with the empty cart. He had carefully repaired its marks of time and rough usage with baling wire, that ever-present token of civilization from which is derived our expression, "going haywire." But the German was displeased with the repairs, so the Mexican willingly assented to replace the thongs. He was certain now that the German was crazy. A few days later he drove his oxen into the ranch with the shaky old cart creaking along behind them, eager to please but fearful that the German had changed his mind. The trade was made, and the Mexican went off with a new American hand plow, as delighted as a child with a new toy.

The German had read of Henry Ford's industrial museum. He admired Henry Ford, and so he sent him the old cart. Henry replied by wiring his El Paso dealer to ask the German to come to El Paso and pick out his choice of the newest models of Ford cars. So they were all made happy, the Mexican with his American plow, the German with a new American car, and Henry Ford with his Mexican cart. This demonstrates the economic principle of profit as an earned increment in exchange.

Word reached me that funds were available that would permit us to continue work three more months in the sierra to complete archaeological excavations in the region already visited. So I bought shovels and other equipment in order to be ready for work by spring, when travel in the sierra would be more comfortable and certain. Bennett's stay was to be continued to permit him to make a collection of modern Tarahumara effects for the Milwaukee Public Museum. There would be time also for him to make a study of the upper Río Conchos, where peyote, the narcotic cactus, was to be found as well as the presence of the peyote cult.

I decided to return to Umira and spend the remaining month of wintry weather in writing up my report on the material culture of the Tarahumaras. I did not prefer this course, because at the mission I was more comfortable than writing on improvised boards for a table and a box for a chair. At the mission, unfortunately, I did not have my invaluable informant, Lorenzo, to fall back on and supply any slips or omissions in my text. So I returned to Umira, and there pulled the expedition typewriter out of Lorenzo's storehouse and got busy. In a month my notes were organized and typewritten in a form such that everything was cross-checked down even to the native names of sierra plants.

It was still cold. This, however, was a mixed blessing; for although I had to do my writing outside in a shelter set up against the storehouse in which I slept, at the same time I could safely preserve two quarters of pork that I had brought with me from the Mexican settlement. These remained fresh, though toward the end it was a close race between me and the advancing spring season.

> *Spring, Holy Week, and*
> *Archaeology*
>
>
>
>
>
>
>
>

B efore my report was written, signs of spring were obvious. The buds burst out on the pussy willows. The frogs croaked happily in the warming waters of the river. In a few days the evidence of their joy was manifest in the frog eggs that hung in the water like tapioca pudding. Soon the warm waters were filled with polliwogs; and new vegetable and animal life bore witness to the procreative force of spring. This force was so irresistible that even Lorenzo's hag of a wife seemed to become a little less surly. Once she and Lorenzo came home from a *tesgüinada* as drunk as fools. Whether on this occasion it was spring or the beer that made her so coy the reader can determine by Lorenzo's aside to me. "Sober, Tarahumara women are very *bronco* [wild]; but drunk, they are very *manso* [gentle]," he said.

With the advance of spring the Indians, encaved in the gorges, began to make the trek back to the sierra. Our old community of Samachique began to reassemble itself.

The Tarahumaras initiate the round of the new year with the vernal festivities of Holy Week. It is a beginning particularly fitting, because at this time the earth, awakening from her winter's torpor, seems by her own renascence to be most in sympathy with the efforts of man. Easter, the Christian season with its rich-hued connotations, fittingly comes in the spring, the climatic season of resurrection and new life.

Among many Mexicans and other tribes besides the Tarahumara the priests have succeeded in gathering into the celebration of Holy Week all the native color and pageantry of aboriginal vernal ceremony.

Out of this conglomeration the priests seek slowly to eject the pagan elements, substituting Christian ones. But among the Tarahumaras the ceremonials in their externals are completely "Catholic" with a minimum of pagan elements. They are brilliant, colorful festivals in the Tarahumara round, not at all in keeping, however, with the Christian teaching of mourning preceding Easter.

In contrast to the brilliance of the Holy Week ceremonies, the aboriginal spring ceremony of "curing" the fields and animals is drab and uninteresting to watch. The color, the dancing, the drama of the Holy Week ceremonies are all absent. Yet to the Tarahumaras the activities of Holy Week are absolutely without an intelligible rationale, either Christian or pagan; and the pagan ceremony of "curing" the fields and animals has, as we shall see, the most significant and vital meaning.[1]

Bennett and I were able to draw no explanation whatsoever of the Holy Week ceremonies from our half-dozen informants. Even Lorenzo, shrewd and keen student of his own culture, the Catholic *maestro*, and thus head of the ceremonies themselves, could tell us nothing. "It is the custom of ancient times," he said, and let it go at that, a blanket gloss that justifies so much accountable human behavior from that of the Tarahumara *maestro* to the decisions of the American Supreme Court, precedent built upon precedent, a fundamental process in human affairs, but not a rational one. It did not occur to Lorenzo that these spectacular ceremonies had their rationale in the color, the tumult, the excitement, and the pageantry which they brought into the drabness of Tarahumara life. With such contributions these ceremonies were a fitting commencement to a new yearly round after three months of cramped existence in *barranca* caves.[2]

I have written at considerable length on the power and force of Catholic missions in changing native life and custom. Perhaps nothing could show better the handicaps under which the Jesuits have worked with the Tarahumaras for two centuries than the surprising lack of Christian (or other) ideology in the Tarahumara celebration of Holy Week. But even more than this, it also shows the Tarahumara indifference to anything but their own culture. They are tolerant of different customs, but they are so well satisfied with their own that they are very slow in changing. They are not particularly aggressive or defensive about their own ways; they are simply not interested in other things. Where the Mexican folk romanticize foreign goods, guns, razors, mirrors, cars, and the like, the Tarahumara looks at them curiously for a moment, and then goes back to his accustomed occupations. Lorenzo was the conspicuous exception; he was interested and wished to try everything, including even the planting of oats for oatmeal.

Likewise the Tarahumaras are as little interested in the foreign teaching of Christianity. Since they do not know even the correct name of Jesus Christ, it is not surprising that they know nothing of His crucifixion or resurrection. Christ they identify with Saint Joseph as *San José su Cristo*, who, with Benito Juárez, came among the ancient Tarahumaras to better conditions and convert them from their cannibalistic practices. Thus among these Indians Christian beliefs, as we think of them, are absent, and outward religious behavior during ceremony equally void of ideology.

Having finished writing my report on the material culture of the Tarahumaras, I was free to assist Dr. Bennett in recording the Holy Week ceremonies near Umira. I went to the Tarahumara church of Basiaurichi, in the midst of the Mexican colony of the relatives of the Mexican patriarch. Bennett, who had completed his two months' sojourn in the tropics of the lower *barrancas*, went to Samachique in the high sierra in order to witness the ceremony as given in a community where he knew everyone. The two ceremonies turned out to be identical, although this is not true of all Tarahumara communities. Around the missions and areas of Mexican influence the ceremony is more "Christian." At Guadalupe, from which Bennett had just come, information revealed a penitential element, fitting for the mourning period up to Good Friday, that was slightly suggestive of the flagellant customs of the Mexican *"Penitentes"* of New Mexico.

About a month before Holy Week, presages of the coming observances are evident. Up to this time the Indians play the violin and the guitar both in church ceremonies and in private feasts following cooperative labor. But with the coming of spring these foreign instruments are laid aside for the native drum and flute, instruments of wide distribution among American aborigines. The change indicates a shift in the ceremonial round from autumn and winter ceremonies, when the foreign instruments furnish the music, to those of spring and summer, when only the native instruments are deemed fitting. This ideal scheme gets mixed up once in a while, especially if *matachines* are danced in the latter ceremonies; but this is not common enough to vitiate the general pattern of the shift. In the drunken feasts I described in the last chapter, the drum and flute were used. And as we hiked over the trails, the rapid beat of the drum and the shrill sound of the flute could be heard, accompanying the steps of Tarahumara travelers along the road.

The native flute is a very simple variant of an instrument of wide distribution in Indian America. The Tarahumara species is a fife made from a single joint of the reed of a cane. It is about eight inches long, and one inch in diameter. At the anterior end is left a bill-like projection to which a reed (like that of a clarinet) is bound with a bit of sinew. Both the projection and the reed are cut concave in cross-section to allow the passage of wind. The hollow part of the reed tube forms the flute, and resembles a short clarinet eight inches long. It contains three holes as stops to vary the tones.

The Tarahumara drum now in use shows a Spanish influence. It is called a *kapora*, from the Spanish word *tambor*, drum. In appearance the Tarahumara variety suggests a tambourine, since it is never more than four inches in depth and two feet in diameter. It is made by binding a long, thin board of ash wood into a circle and tying the ends together. It has two drumheads, made by stretching two circular pieces of wet buckskin over each end of the drums. These are sewed together, and the result reminds one of our snare drums. The similarity with the modern snare drum is noticeable also in a snare of a single cord that crosses one drumhead. On this in the middle a couple of beads are fastened to increase the resonance of the drum.

These drums are more prized than the aboriginal type, because they are lighter and can be carried along the trail and beaten in time to the steps of a person or party walking. The old type of aboriginal drum is still remembered, however, although we didn't see any. The Tarahumaras described them, and said that they were made from sections of hollow trees. With this drum the wall was trimmed down to a uniform thickness and a hole cut in the side for increased resonance. It had two heads, like the modern drum, and these were sewed together similarly. In my report I made the mistake of calling this a simplification of the characteristic Middle American *teponaztli*.

I saw some of the Indians with an unusually large Spanish type of drum. One of the Indians also carried a spear, or lance, with an iron head. These are used in the sham battles of the celebration. They are also still carried by some of the officials of the Tarahumara community of Cusárare. A Mexican teacher of this community made me a present of one. The lance apparently is an old trait in Tarahumara culture, since it is called by a native name, *seléke*. *Selígame* (lance bearer), the native name for the chief or *gobernador*, is derived from this word.

Two other elements of paraphernalia enter the Tarahumara celebration of Holy Week. One is an artificial flower cunningly made of the shining basal portions of the plant *sotol*. The short-cut stems are so interwoven that the basal portions are held out like the petals of a flower. I was to find later that the Huichols make similar artificial flowers for decorative use when the officers are changed during the New Year's ceremony.

The other sacred Tarahumara artifact is none other than a gigantic edition of the whirl-rattle that we use on New Year's Eve for our celebrations. The Tarahumaras utilize it during the last days of Holy Week. Its noise seemed most inappropriate on Thursday and Friday, Catholic days of mourning and quiet.

I arrived at Basiaurichi early in the morning on Thursday of Holy Week. Many of the men, I noticed, had stuck in their hats downy turkey breast feathers. This variety of the feather headdress, which we associate with Indians, is worn at no other time. The Huichols, farther to the south, do not follow this custom, but at all ceremonies cover the tops of their hats with leaves and flowers, using sometimes even the rarest orchids. As if the Tarahumara celebration of Holy Week were to be a proper Mexican Catholic ceremony, the Indians were busily engaged in making twelve arches of slender pine tree trunks, bent over and covered with extra pine branches. These arches were set up to mark the path of the processions of the *santos*.

Later in the day the celebrations began. I soon found that the Indians in the feather-garnished hats were the performers in an unrecognizable Tarahumara corruption of some medieval miracle play. They were divided into two groups called "Pharisees" and "Judases." Their legs and faces were daubed with clay. Some of them had exchanged their hats for crowns such as the *matachines* wear. Both the costumes and the barbaric makeups of the "Pharisees" and the "Judases" were so foreign to usual Christian conceptions that there was much reason for thinking "who is he to Hecuba or Hecuba to him?" The Tarahumara "Judases" carry two grass effigies of general human form which are sometimes burned. In this particular alone is the Indian custom similar to that of the Mexicans during their Holy Week who burn or explode effigies of Judas, a character hateful to them.

The captain of either party is called the *morogapitán* in some regions. The word derives from the Spanish *moro capitán*, "captain of the Moors." This Spanish element has no appropriate meaning to the

Tarahumaras. But it suggests that the source of their play is ultimately the medieval Spanish miracle play, the "*Moro-Moro.*"

The "*Moro-Moro*" portrays the wars between the Moors and the Christians during the eight centuries of Spanish history when Spain had received the westernmost thrust of Islam, which was finally stopped at the door of France by the Battle of Tours. This play is still given in isolated regions of the Philippines, a country which received the easternmost thrust of Islam in Mindanao. To Christian Filipinos of these isolated districts the play still has appropriate meaning since their ancestors were killed or enslaved by the fierce *Moros.* In one of the Philippine provinces I saw the "*Moro-Moro*" as a formalized dance of swordplay done in exaggerated and conventionalized movements.

What an amazingly different scene among the clouted Tarahumaras of the Chihuahua sierra, who paint their faces and legs with clay, cover their hats with feathers, and engage in a riot of exuberant muscular activity of dancing and racing about in their sham battles. This activity, however, is characteristic of all the festivities and muscular prowess of the whole tribe. The simple Tarahumaras have so garbled their play that it is far from recognizable as a variant of the "*Moro-Moro.*" Their "Pharisees" and "Judases," for example, are absent in the Philippine rendition. But in addition to the *morogapitán* to indicate a historical relationship, the Tarahumaras have also the sham battles, with the parties carrying swords, the tinsel and mirrors, and sometimes crowns. Among them, however, their sham battles, which have no Christian intelligibility, are between the "Pharisees" and "Judases," and are not, therefore, as pregnant with significance as those between the "Moors" and the "Christians" in both the Philippines and Spain. Indeed, to the Tarahumaras their play makes no sense at all; it merely gives them a chance to run and dance and go through the violent motions of fighting to the din of shouts and the whir of the whirl-rattles. All this was provided with color and pageantry by the fantastic and barbaric costumes and decorations.

In the Tarahumara ceremonies of Holy Week the serious and long-continued efforts of the "Pharisees" and the "Judases," as well as the many processions, are balanced somewhat by a little comedy relief. Urchins are adorned from head to foot with stripes of red, white, and black clay. Then their hair is thoroughly doused in white clay and gathered up in a long spike at the tops of their heads. This spike dries to a perfect image of that of one of the Katzenjammer kids.

About a dozen of these little rogues dance in ludicrous imitation of the *matachines,* the serious and sacred dance of the winter round of Christian ceremonies. They are led by a serio-comic dancer called the *pascol* (from *pascua,* Spanish, "Easter"). His face, head, and hands are painted. For comic effect he wears a Mexican costume as well as runners' belts and carries the rattles of a cocoon for their sound. He takes the place of the *monarco* (the "monarch"), the highly respected leader of the serious dance of the *matachines.*

Since the notes that I took of the Basiaurichi ceremony are not available, I shall paraphrase Bennett's account of the identical ceremony in Samachique, although in some regions there are variations in the celebrations. At Guadalupe, for example, where Spanish influence is stronger, the Indians not only have the *morogapitán,* with his penitential functions, but the effigies of Judas are burned at the end of the ceremonies.

Thursday was the first day of the fiesta. Food was placed before the saints in the church, apparently to permit them to celebrate too. In the afternoon the "Pharisees" and the "Judases" lined up in two circles in the churchyard. Slowly at first, and then faster and faster, each circle began to move around and around, one inside the other, to the thin whistle of the flute and the periodic boom of the drum. Then, with the officials in the center, they marched to the somewhat distant *comunidad,* the "jail and courthouse," otherwise seldom used by the Indians. On the way they stopped at intervals for the dancers to run in circles around the officials. From the *comunidad* they returned to the church. While the dancers lined up outside, the people went in to pray. After this the children were given Christian instruction in making the sign of the cross to the Spanish words, repeated with a heavy ictus, "*Por la señal de la Santa Cruz en el Nombre del Padre, del Hijo, y del Espíritu Santo.*" During this teaching the church bells were tolled and the whirl-rattles were sounded vigorously.

Then a Tarahumara walked three times around the churchyard, whirling a rattle. When he had finished his circuits, a guard was stationed to guard the saints in the church. Four Tarahumaras stood motionless facing the altar. The two in front held spears. A drummer and a flute player furnished continual music. From time to time the officer presiding over the ceremony changed guards. By Friday morning the watch was completed.

Although the Tarahumaras do not seem to know it, this watch was the vigil at the sepulchre of Christ. But it is performed on Thursday rather than the night of Good Friday. The Huichols stage a similar performance on the same night. One at a time the old dignitaries of the tribe stand before a "bed" in which the crucifix has been "buried" under some clothes. The men beat the earth at the foot of the "bed" with a long pole that has a bow and arrows hanging on it. The Huichols do not think the pole is a spear; the bow and arrows are hung on it merely because the myth says that these aboriginal weapons were laid on Christ's tomb, and that the pounding of the sticks expedites *Santo Cristo*'s journey to "*La Gloria,*" a place reserved for Him and the saints. The Huichols are as pagan as the Tarahumaras.

There was little evidence of Christianity in the Tarahumara ceremonies. About nine o'clock on Thursday night, however, one of the most "Catholic" elements of the entire proceeding was observable in a procession which came from the church to make a circuit of the building and go through the arches. The procession consisted of a man with the whirl-rattle, another with a large cross; two men carrying the picture of a saint; four men with small painted crosses and painted poles; four *maestros*, or leaders of the ceremony, headed by Lorenzo; a woman with a flag; another carrying the picture of a saint; and a third woman with one of the characteristic muglike Tarahumara incense pots filled with glowing coals.

Women spectators followed behind; the men flanked the sides. The costumed dancers carrying their swords and spears walked in lines at each side of the procession.

As the procession moved forward, the drums were beaten, the flutes blown, the rattles whirled, and the prayers chanted. The leaders passed through an arch, then stopped and turned around to face the four *maestros*, who knelt directly under the arch. The women remained in their places in the background. While the lay readers intoned in unison fragments of Catholic prayers, the woman with the incense pot cast smoke over the pictures of the saints. Then the procession moved on to the next arch and blessed it in turn. When they again reached the church, everyone entered and knelt inside for a repetition of the prayers.

Throughout the night the *gobernador* held a service inside the church, and at intervals gave fragments of harangues or sermons. This was pretty good for him, since he generally acted tongue-tied in his public speaking duties. Meanwhile the four guards maintained their all-night vigil. From time to time the official in charge made replacements.

On Friday morning the arrangement of the procession and the offering of fresh food to the saints were practically the same as those of the day before. In the afternoon secular interest was revived by an ordinary foot race. Two teams of well-known runners participated. The betting was heavy. This was hardly consonant with the usual celebrations of the death of Christ; but then, the Indians do not even know that He was crucified.

At dusk there was another religious procession. This was made especially brilliant and spectacular by the lights of dozens of pitch-pine torches. When this was finished, the two sets of dancers, the "Pharisees" and the "Judases," augmented the flashing pageantry of the festivities. Each group strove to emulate the other. They flung themselves about to the sound of flute and drum, their white-painted legs, plumed crowns, and white swords flashing in the glare of the torches, the whole setting outlined hazily in the moonlight. They skipped, shifted, and ran in dance formations, interspersing their actions with loud, ear-splitting whoops, the characteristic Indian method of shouting while patting the mouth; and throughout, rushing toward one another and then backing away, they madly brandished their wooden swords. The action of this sham battle was terrific. At the finish they were still lined up in two sets facing each other.

Later, after this secular pageantry, the sacred ceremonies were resumed. In the first procession half the people with pictures of the saints went in one direction and half in the other. Still later another regular procession was made.

Saturday morning there was a much-needed general rest after all the wild activities of the night before.

It was for the "*Sabado de Gloria*" that the little boys were so fantastically painted. In charge of the *pascol* dancers, they entered the festivities for the first time. The *pascoleros* dance a fast-stepping, cloglike dance at intervals throughout this day. I have mentioned their comic Mexican costumes and belt and ankle rattles.

In the afternoon a *pascol* dancer, accompanied by the boys, marched to the church and there danced awhile to each of the four cardinal points. Then he danced inside the church for the remainder of the afternoon. Oddly enough he performed to the music of the violin and guitar, instruments giving music better suited to his rapid movements. Food and beer were brought to him. Later in the afternoon he was joined by another *pascolero*. Meanwhile the "Pharisees" had begun their dance on the outside. They danced awhile in the churchyard, and then proceeded to their own houses for refreshment; for they had contributed beer to this celebration, just as was done by the dancers of the *matachines* during the winter round of "Catholic" ceremonies. They ended up at the *comunidad*, where the officials had been engaged all day in trying offenses and hearing complaints. Then the dancers returned to the church in a formal procession, taking with them the officials as they had done the day before.

At the church two processions were formed. Each was led by a *pascolero*, who marched them around the church, followed by the people. The "Judases" carried rude grass effigies of their namesake. All entered the church. There the principals danced and scattered ashes on the floor. This might have been done on Ash Wednesday; but the Tarahumaras can be depended on to get their Christianity all mixed up. Then within the church the sacred business was concluded with the regular prayers of the *maestros* and a sermon by the *gobernador*.[3]

After this the Tarahumaras turned their attention to the business of getting drunk on *tesgüino* as quickly as possible. All that night and through to Easter Sunday the drinking was continued at the various houses of the families of those who were giving these Holy Week festivities. The hosts were the *pascoleros*, the "Pharisees" and the "Judases" who had led the processions from one house to another and danced at each for short intervals while the civil officials dedicated the beer pots.

Since I was at Basiaurichi on pleasure and not business, it was not necessary for me to partake of the liquid joy or engage in the general frivolity. Such had long since ceased to amuse me. I had sent word to my Mexican muleteer, "Pancho," to come and help me in my archaeological work. "Pancho," who was a typical Mexican peon as far as eliminating his debt was concerned, wished to work out the mortgage on his mule, which he had put into our hands about six months before. This thrifty muleteer had other reasons also, however, for he probably hadn't made above twenty pesos with his string of mules all the while we had been using one of them. With mining paralyzed the only business he could engage in was hauling railroad ties from the forests to the railroad. But, as elsewhere in 1930, conditions were so bad in Mexico that the roads were not replacing ties *(durmientes)*; and thus that activity was denied him. The "Kansas" railroad did not appear to have changed its *durmientes* (from the English "sleepers") since the Revolution. Even the Mexico Northwest Railroad had been using old ties for so long that at one place near the city of Chihuahua their rails opened up and wrecked a train, killing three trainmen.

So Pancho came to Basiaurichi, bringing me several mule loads of food, supplies for archaeological work, and several empty boxes for carrying the plunder back to civilization. Thus I was ready to shift my major attention from the living Tarahumaras to the remains of their ancestors; and early Easter morning I bade another good-bye to my Mexican friends in the old bullion-train station of the "Royal Road," and went in search of archaeological remains with "Pancho" and a *mozo* whom he had brought with him.

In this search I followed streams as far as possible from their mouths to their sources. This was so that later archaeologists need not fruitlessly retrace my steps. While I had been in Umira, I had at intervals explored the little stream where I had found the first Cave-Dweller houses, one of which was topped with the turretlike superstructure of storage houses. This time, however, I went up the stream as near as possible to its source. There were no roads, or even Indian trails, following its rugged, mountain bed; and hence we came to some places so difficult of access that we had to unload the mules and carry the freight ourselves lest the animals break their legs. Unloaded, each wise old mule, used to rough ground, would scramble over the difficult spots, with one Mexican holding the halter and the other the tail to steady the animal. As the mules slithered across, the men would say encouragingly, "*¡Fuerte, macho! ¡Fuerte! ¡Fuerte!*"[4] ("Strong, my hearty! strong! strong!") At one place, where our progress was impeded by a gigantic, water-smoothed boulder, the going was so uncertain that I had to steady the two Mexicans as they carried the boxes of freight. But I almost caused them to drop their loads, as I labored along behind them, by imitating their intonations, saying, "*¡Fuerte, machos! ¡Fuerte! ¡Fuerte!*"

Muleteers always want to break their journeys about midafternoon so that their animals can take a longer advantage of pasturage, which, in Mexico, is sometimes quite sparse. I always urged mine to continue on for a couple of hours. This day, however, I had no argument, and the animals got a long rest; for I happened to glance up a little side *arroyo*, and far in the distance at the top of a mountain I spotted a cave containing a structure that immediately enkindled my archaeological enthusiasms, for this rugged stream course was not inhabited by modern Tarahumaras. I calculated that there was still light enough for "Pancho" and me to visit this cave, thus leaving the morrow for further prospecting.

So with the *mozo* in charge of camp and about to prepare supper,

"Pancho" and I started up the *arroyo*, which was even more rugged than the one we had just been traversing. We were soon at the foot of the mountain. Encumbered as we were with a broom, a shovel, a camera, and my notebook, we yet managed to ascend with comparative ease. But near the summit we found that the cave was still separated from us by a formidable cliff. "Pancho," who was wearing leather sandals, was willing to go on, however, so I followed in my boots.

We finally came to a place where only a slight bulge in the cliff stood between us and our objective. "Pancho" managed to wriggle across, although literally by his toenails. Encased in boots as mine were, I hesitated for a moment, fearing that the bulge would throw my body out of balance and I might fall. "Pancho," who was none too securely perched above, hanging on to a *maguey* plant, urged me to take off my boots, but time was short. The broom, however, saved the day. "Pancho" passed one end of it to me, and steadied by it I soon drew myself up to where he was. A slight support was all I needed, and I put hardly more than a finger's weight on the broomstick; for a hard tug would undoubtedly have pulled him down. He was much more relieved than I was when I reached him, since I knew how little help I would need; whereas poor "Pancho," fearful of my clumsy boots, was assisting me purely on faith.

In a few minutes more we had entered the cave. It justified my expectations. The cave itself, which was about a hundred yards long, extended back from a level shelf in the mountaintop. A perfectly secure location, and near water moreover, it had been an ancient dwelling-place. Within were several Cave-Dweller houses, similar to those I had seen elsewhere, and a score of storage and burial houses. Thus I celebrated Easter by discovering a Cave-Dweller village, a procedure about as un-Christian as that of the Tarahumaras.

Since we could accomplish little at such a site in the daylight remaining of this day, we returned to camp and prepared for a stay of several days. Once excavation was begun, the work was simple, and done mainly with brooms. Nothing was buried, so the task was merely to sweep out the accumulated dust of the ages. While the Mexicans did this, I took pictures, sketched the ground plan of the village, and opened the storage and burial houses. Although the site had not been disturbed by previous human visitors, the mountain pack rats had beaten me to every burial structure.

The ledge that formed the floor of the cave was only about fifteen feet wide. It fell off sharply about ten feet down to an earth-covered sloping floor some fifty feet wide which was covered by an overhanging cliff. On the sloping floor were a few ruins, suggesting that the hundred-yard ledge had not been large enough for its early occupants. Indeed, the structures still standing filled up all of the available room on the ledge. At the edge of the step-off were little holes chipped in the rock, into which the Cave-Dwellers had apparently set poles for a bannister. On the face of the vertical step-off were designs in red ochre paint. Some of these were anthropoid in square conventionalizations. Others had been made by adults and children who had dipped their hands into paint and left the impressions on the white cave wall. This has been done ever since the Stone Age in Europe, where examples of such primitive art are to be found among the beautiful things left in the Cro-Magnon caves.

The houses were circular and made of roughly laminated stones set in mud plaster, similar in short to those I had come across at other dwelling caves. Some of the storehouses were beehive in shape, and strangely like the earth ovens made by the present-day Mexicans of New Mexico. Despite the dozen or more burials that had been made in the storage and burial structures, I found nothing of unusual interest, though the absence of wool indicated a pre-Hispanic age for the material I uncovered.

When the plunder from this mountain cave was labeled, catalogued, and packed, the sketches all drawn, and the pictures taken, we continued on to the source of this stream, but without finding any more sites. Since we were just across a narrow divide from the headwaters of the Río Fuerte (or Urique), near Norogáchic, we crossed over and stopped again at this hospitable mission. I remained almost a month excavating the Basket-Maker cave, which I have already described. Twenty men worked with me for two weeks before this task was finished.

After my findings of the first day had been thrown down the mountainside, as mentioned before, I stayed at the dig with "Pancho's" *mozo*. "Pancho" went on to Creel with the ten or more mummies and other bulky things that came from this cave. For this work he had to build special boxes from lumber sawed by the Mexicans by hand from the forest of the sierra. One box was allotted to each mule, and seated crosswise on a rough frame improvised over the mule's saddle. On his return he brought empty boxes, which he obtained with difficulty at Creel and other railroad towns.

Weekends I stayed at the mission building and had several conferences with "General" Jaris and other Tarahumara chiefs over the securing of their lands from the encroaching Mexicans. When these and the cave archaeology were finished, Jaris arranged for me to meet the officials of the nearby towns to actually see and record the recent incursions of Mexican settlers. In return for my trouble the Indians willingly directed me to the Cave-Dweller ruins of their ancestors scattered throughout the various villages near the mission. This was being particularly obliging, especially since some of the burials had been made scarcely thirty years ago. I could always tell whether to investigate after opening a structure by the smell that assailed my nostrils. I was engaged about two more weeks in this Cave-Dweller archaeology, and in all spent over a month in this region. It was time well spent.

Meanwhile Dr. Bennett had gone to the pagan Tarahumara community of Quírare on the opposite side of Samachique from Umira, from which I had started. It was desirable to work the archaeology, like the ethnography, in a circle, with Samachique as a center. Bennett had almost completed his studies around Quírare, so I went there in order to complete mine. In this way I was able to avail myself of the Indian friends and acquaintances he had made, and also carry out any unfinished ethnographic investigations he was forced to leave. But first I had to get word to my friends, the Córdobas, that I would be able to employ the father and the oldest son. They came promptly to the mission. Then I had to send my muleteer on to Creel with his mules loaded with the abundant results of my archaeological work.

The Córdobas, who guided me to Quírare, were perfectly at home in the sierra. Indeed it was their backyard, since they hunted and traded with the Indians all over it. This time my journey to their ranch was not so strenuous, because I was mounted on "Pancho's" nag, which I had appropriately dubbed "Rocinante" from its similarity to Doré's paintings of the celebrated steed of the Sad Knight.

From their ranch the Córdobas guided me to the middle course of the Río Batopilas. This river I planned to follow down toward Quírare, making several stops at archaeological sites on the way, however, before meeting Bennett.

Our first stop was a Basket-Maker cave, as large as the first one I had visited. Córdoba seemed to know its location well, perhaps because he may have been a shareholder in the organization of Mexican treasure hunters who are seeking the gold they supposed to have been buried by the priests fleeing from the Indians. At least he confided in me, "Some *vecinos* [Mexicans, literally "neighbors"] found pieces of the hats of the priests. [These were fragments of coiled basketry.] So they began to dig, and worked long and hard. They came to an earth and grass container which, they were sure, held the gold; and the dust that it contained was run carefully through their fingers. But all they found was some *chilicote* beans."[5]

These poisonous seeds, left as a funerary offering, were indeed poor payment for their labor; but they should have been forced to eat them, because they had virtually ruined one of the most valuable sites in the sierra. My digging only revealed remains so fragmentary as to be almost worthless. A few bits of coiled basketry were worth retaining, however, in order to take them to pieces in making a careful study of the techniques of the work.

The excavation of this cave, which was far from any village or settlement, presented an acute labor problem. Córdoba and his son, though good workmen, were not sufficient help. A Tarahumara living nearby indicated that he was willing to work with so unfamiliar an implement as a shovel, so I took him on. He fell to, using his foot with no protection other than his thin rawhide sandal. The next day two Mexicans came into the camp, following up a rumor that there was an *Americano* in the vicinity. Their object was neither loot nor robbery; they were merely looking for a customer for a crate of oranges from their ranch in the lower *barrancas* of the Río Batopilas. The excellent fruit was a welcome addition to a limited commissary; and, since they too were glad to accept work, their labor was no less welcome to a limited staff.

Since this Basket-Maker site proved to have been completely worked over by the treasure hunters, I soon dispensed with the extra Mexicans. Then I turned my attention to the numerous Cave-Dweller sites in the little *arroyos* tributary to the Río Batopilas. I came across several caves that contained Cave-Dweller structures like those around Umira. Even better, many of these storage and burial structures had never been opened; so I found many of the graves exactly as they had been left centuries ago. Among the objects that had been buried with the bodies were strings of beads made from shells from the Gulf of California, blankets of vegetable fiber, baskets, gourd receptacles, and other equipment for a journey to the Land of the Dead.

This work kept us camped for almost two weeks beside a little flowing stream. Although I did not have a tent, the camp was comfortable, except for a pesky gnat of the *tierra caliente* which swarms in the gorges during the advancing spring. The Mexicans and the Indians, with less clothes than I, were hardened by exposure; so I was the only one covered with welts.

In such a camp I had reason to long for the "Round Oak" cookstove in the mission; for without the hard French bread that the mission had provided, I had to go back to *tortillas*. Even this simplified bread presented a problem, since there were no women around, not even the wife of the Tarahumara workman. I began to wonder just how I could get the corn ground for *tortillas* as soon as my supply of bread from the mission was gone. But a solution appeared in a young Indian lad who came to camp and evidenced willingness to take over the menial tasks. I was surprised that an Indian man would do a squaw's work, but the Tarahumara have no prejudice in this respect. This is another indication that Tarahumara women do not suffer under any special disadvantages. Indeed my impression was that they take liberties with their freedom by their nagging and general surliness.

Córdoba seemed to be still in his own backyard, for he knew the location of more than a dozen Cave-Dweller sites in the locality. When I had investigated these, he told me of still another Basket-Maker cave some distance away. The trail was dangerous, he said, but the cave was so small that we would be able to excavate it in one day. So we prepared food for the trip, despatching a rooster I had brought from the mission tied to a mule's pack, and boiling the bird's stilled remains with some rice into a savory chicken soup. The rooster had ridden the mule like a veteran, and had arrived with scarcely a feather out of place. But into the pot he went.

We started off early the next morning. The Tarahumara workman carried the pot of *arroz con pollo* on his shoulder. I knew that he would be the least apt to fall, and to have lost that pot containing the edible portions of the expedition's one chicken would have been just too much. The trail certainly justified Córdoba's description. For one thing it skirted the face of a gorge a thousand feet directly above the river, which, meandering below us, looked like a ribbon of silk. At one place a landslide had carried away about four feet of the trail. Beyond was the continuation, looking comparatively safe in its width of three feet. But the break of four feet involved more than a mere jump. There was the possibility of throwing the body off secure balance and falling straight down for more than a thousand feet, admittedly no slight mental hazard. We all got safely across, however; though sometimes in my dreams I find myself back at the same place with the gap stretching for yards between me and the other side.

The objective in this case proved to be most worthwhile, and minimized the seriousness of the obstacles we had to overcome. The site was manifestly a transitional one between the Basket-Maker culture and that of the later Cave-Dweller. Its affiliations with the Basket-Maker were to be seen in the burial cists that I uncovered. In the mud top of one was the impression of a coiled grass and mud container that had contained the poisonous *chilicote* seeds. Fragments of fur and feather also allied this site and its primitive culture to the other site I had discovered. I found no coiled basketry, but only woven basketry and some pottery. Again, the fragments of true weaving were much finer and more beautifully woven than those I had found with the fur and feather cloth in the first Basket-Maker site. The other details of this site, fully described in my "Report on the Archaeology of Southern Chihuahua," clearly indicated a transition between the Basket-Maker and the Cave-Dweller phases. Thus this site furnished a valuable link in the history of the aborigines of southern Chihuahua.

The trail that led to this cave had been used by the Indians in getting to the great numbers of the huge *maguey*, or the century plant, that literally covered the steep sides of this *barranca*, and gave to it the appearance of a field of *pulque* almost set on edge. More than a dozen of these plants were in flower, which they attain once in their existence just before they die. The popular belief that this happens once in a century accounts for the English name of the plant.

The *maguey* has several leaves five or six feet long and as tough as rhinoceros hide. The tip of each leaf is armed with a stiff, thornlike point as sharp as a needle. Only so grim and arid a country as Mexico can produce such a plant. It is not surprising, furthermore, that the *maguey* should die from the final effort of bursting into flower. It sends out a flower spine from twenty to thirty feet long, which is held upright on a strong skeletal structure. This spine is covered with thousands of small yellow-white flowers, the fragrance of which attracts dozens of hummingbirds. To suck the honey out of flowers these graceful little birds hover in the air by beating their wings so fast that all one sees is a blur on either side of them.

The skeleton of the enormous flower spine of these century plants sustains a fresh and succulent flesh. The Indians utilize this for food, as they do other plants of the sierra. It is roasted in the ashes of a large fire. The result, when eaten with sugar, is a delicious food, as I myself can attest.

Mexico would not be quite the same without this characteristic plant, which furnishes the people with food, their national drink (*pulque*), and from which is obtained one of the world's best vegetable fibers. These properties of the plant are all utilized by the Tarahumaras, but by means of techniques more primitive than those elsewhere.

We returned from the cave with the empty pot that had held the chicken and rice, and a load of valuable archaeological material. When the material was all labeled and numbered, we were ready to break up our little camp. As if to encourage me to do so, a huge centipede ran across the rock at the head of my bedroll, not six inches from my head. I didn't see the danger, but my attention was attracted by Córdoba, who suddenly threw a pan in my direction. His manner was so wild and excited, and his act so unheard of for a loyal *mozo*, that at first I thought he had departed his senses. He explained himself, however, and said that he had deflected the centipede, which was going straight for my head. It was a foot long, he swore, and such a size is not uncommon in the *tierra caliente*, which seems to make animals, like plants, grow luxuriantly.

The rattlers, both big and little species, the Gila monsters, the scorpions, and the centipedes are a much over-advertised danger to the life in Mexico, even in the more isolated regions such as the sierra. This was the closest I ever came to a poisonous sting. Three years later among the Huichols I found that the scorpion is the commonest pest. I killed six in my camp in one week, and was not stung once. Rattlesnakes in such numbers would hardly have been so trivial; but as I remember I saw only three in the two years I spent in the wilds of Mexico.

Thus Mexico disappoints him who seeks adventure as the term is usually understood; for his eagerness for excitement will be tempered by the gentleness of poisonous creatures and the ease with which a centipede a foot long can be deflected to a different course than toward one's head.

But in other adventures the wilds of Mexico are singularly replete. I shall never forget nights spent before blazing campfires, the fellow travelers met along the way, the toil of long hot days and the cool freshness of evenings climaxed by sunsets that blazoned.

CHAPTER 15

▸ *Pagan Ceremonies and Peyote*

▸
▸
▸
▸
▸
▸
▸
▸
▸
▸

With the archaeology of this aspect of the Río Batopilas finished, we pursued our course to Quírare. Along the cordon, or ridge, we were confronted suddenly by a natural arch that looked like the famous Rainbow Natural Bridge in Arizona; for it had the same form, although, as we drew closer, I saw that it was much smaller. Harder than the surrounding tufa stone, it had survived millennia of sierra wind erosion. It leaned against the hard geological formation that capped the top of the mountain like a flying buttress against the wall of a Gothic cathedral.

Passing this we made for Quírare. There *"Don* Benito" was concluding his studies of the pagan Tarahumaras who boast that they are not Christians. It was good to see him again after the weeks we had been separated. He was living in another corn storage house, as if he had succumbed to the habit in Umira; and after my camp in the open, his quarters looked very snug and secure. His staff consisted of an Indian informant and a Mexican *mozo* to care for Pancho's mule, which was still mortgaged to us. The mule was to carry his camp equipment. When Bennett left, I pressed "Rocinante" into his service.

Bennett's Indian informant was typical of the Indians of the *barrancas*, who are more Mexicanized than their fellows of the sierra. He was an intelligent, reflective person, whose experiences with both Mexican and Tarahumara customs had given him an objectiveness and a realization of culture that made him valuable to us. Bennett says of him:

> He was an old man with white hair and a beard. The beard was a heritage from a Yaqui [Indian] father. He had never known his father,

but had always lived with his Tarahumara mother. After a rather thorough Tarahumara training in his youth, Jesús was drawn to the *barranca* region during the mining boom. He spent a number of years working in the mines, and acquired the Mexican culture and language. Afterward, he ceased wearing his Mexican clothes and adopted the cotton cloth shirt and drawers worn by the *barranca* Indians. He kept his hair short, however, and never lost his Mexican hat.

Jesús was our best possible informant for the Guadalupe section. He was respected as an old man, and, even more than that, as a shaman. His cures, especially with herbs, were famous. The information that he had to give on shamanism was invaluable, because he knew the business, the technique, and the ceremonies. . . . His idea of serving us was to get the desired information if he did not know it himself. He was able to handle his people, and did not hesitate to do so. At times his willingness made us wonder about his accuracy; but we found that his material, for the most part, cross-checked successfully.

When we went to Quírare, we took Jesús with us as an interpreter. This was a mistake. In Guadalupe he had been related to most of the Indians and had known the rest: it was his home territory. In Quírare he was a stranger, and he was not good at joking with strangers as with friends. Quírare had its own shaman who ruled supreme. Although we were well-treated by the Indians, we could not break down their reserve. We learned that one must have more than one interpreter in dealing with the Tarahumaras.

But if Jesús did not function so well among the Quírare Tarahumaras, when Bennett and he had gone I had to get along with an even less effective informant, though he was a native of the locale. This was the half-breed Mexican, of whom I have spoken, who, with his Mexican mother, was apprehended by the Indians for theft and turned over to the Mexican authorities. I thought that I would need to be guided only to the archaeological ruins of the vicinity, and I took him on for that purpose. He was such a worthless scamp that he still owed us money for articles he had bought at our trading camp at Samachique months before. So I could afford to let him work out his debt by using him as a guide, which was child's play for him.

It was on one of these archaeological excursions that I had the bad luck of having him along when I ran into the important ceremony of "curing" the fields and animals. I knew that he was hated by the Indians, but I couldn't get rid of him; and I had to see and describe the ceremony, which was the only one of its nature that we saw on the expedition. As I have said before, he felt superior to the pagan Tarahumaras because he knew Spanish and was employed by me; and drinking too much, he emerged under his true colors and began to insult our hosts. I literally booted him out of the place, much to the delight of the assembled Indians. In so doing I may have saved his life; for ever since he and his mother had been caught red-handed stealing corn from a storehouse, he had never dared to attend a native ceremony. When the Tarahumaras are drunk, old injuries come drifting back to them. It was a wonder that the luscious pair were not killed when they were caught at their theft.

It so happened that we saw the pagan ceremony of "curing" the fields and animals in a pagan Tarahumara community. But this was an accident, because the Christians perform the identical ceremony. Christianity is an added grace and charm to Tarahumara life, but the vital and essential phases of Tarahumara life are still treated by a pagan round of ceremonies independent of and largely uninfluenced by Christianity. Previously in this book I have described the various pagan ceremonies given during crisis in the lives of individual Tarahumaras. These ceremonies, for example, are such as those following birth and in curing. The ceremonies, after death, on the other hand, though still essentially pagan, have been more influenced by Catholicism. Bodies are sometimes left in cave structures with a funerary fire, as Bennett saw among the pagans at Quírare, but grave burial, as at Samachique, seems to be more generally practiced.

What Bennett saw at Quírare of pagan burials threw considerable light on my archaeological work. The cave structures in which the dead were buried were identical with those of centuries ago which play so important a part in the Cave-Dweller phase of archaeology. Of the ceremonies associated with such burials Bennett says:

> In Quírare in the month of April a man died. He was wrapped in his blanket and his hands were tied together on his breast with a small cross in them. [The pagan Tarahumaras use the cross and the sign of the cross as frequently as do the Christian Tarahumaras though they boast of their paganism. The cross symbolizes the four points so important in Tarahumara ceremony.] Otherwise the body was in no way prepared. A fire was built at the side and near the head; on the ground was placed a small wooden cross hung with a rosary.

Near the cross were many things, such as food, clothes, a knife, a machete, a violin, a hat, an axe, in fact all the possessions that the dead man had used during his lifetime.

The food consisted of *pinole*, three beans and three grains of corn. (Other food might have been added in units of three.) [This was significant, because in the ancient Basket-Maker sites I myself found three poisonous *chilicote* seeds; three is the Tarahumara mystic number.]

The members of the household slept outside, entering only to renew the fire during the night. In fact one youngster was so frightened that he came to my camp to spend the night. If the boy had not been frightened and come down to our camp to sleep, I might never have known that a man had died that night. People living almost within sight of the house do not hear of the event.

On the morning following the death, the helpers and the family were assembled at the house. The head of the dead man was uncovered and crosses of the smoke of incense were made over the body. Then, one by one, the family knelt by the side of the corpse and spoke to it in a low voice. The gist of their words of counsel was as follows:

You are now dead and are going to live in another world. You must not worry, because we have given you food for your journey. We will also give you three death ceremonies (four in case of a woman) so that you can travel well to the sky. You must leave all your things here below for your family and not return to frighten and molest us. Also do not return in the form of an animal to damage the herds and crops.

[This prayer to the dead is the same in substance as the sermon given the deceased Patricio which we had heard at the church of Samachique. The body had been brought to the church on a pole. The pagans use the same method for carrying the dead to the burial cave. As the pole is being prepared, violin music is played by the pagans. Then the contents of a food bowl are poured over the blanketed corpse as a final offering.]

At the cave near the entrance the body was set down. The cross and food were placed at the head, while a funeral fire was kindled at the feet. The mouth of the cave structure was opened, and the corpse, loosened from its fastenings to the pole, was slowly pushed inside. The mouth of the cave was then closed up again with stones and mud. The four men then returned to the dead man's house.

Just as the "Christian" burial that we had attended, after the foregoing burial the pallbearers were ceremonially cleansed from ritual danger and contamination by bathing in the smoke of burning cedar. But
the pagan ceremony was a little more complicated at this point. The
men were met by two others carrying a bowl of ashes and a bowl of
mashed century plant and the similar *sotol* plant mixed with water. We
shall see that these are equally important in other pagan ceremonies.

The contents of these bowls were sprinkled on all the pallbearers
by means of corn husks. Then the pallbearers were given the bowls
from which they drank, after which they used the liquid for making the
sign of the cross. This Christian gesture is used here by the pagans,
and not by the Christian Tarahumara, indicating how historically separate elements get mixed up together in human affairs. And these and
other little ceremonies "cured" the pallbearers of any contamination
they might have received from the touch of the dead. But in addition
to this, they had to abstain from work until after the first ceremony
given to "despatch" the soul of the dead to the other world. Otherwise
he might have returned to bring sickness to their animals or sterility to
their fields.

With such pagan ceremonies do the Tarahumaras meet the crises
of individual life, vital concerns that render them susceptible to the
religious meanings that go deep into human life. The Catholic missionaries after more than two centuries of interrupted work have succeeded in slightly modifying the crisis ceremonies of marriage and
death. Through their efforts has been instituted a special official for
marriage, the *mayor,* whose official labors are devoted solely to found-
ing marriages and making the Tarahumara family more secure. The
results of Catholic teaching have changed the death ceremony principally in substituting the "*camposanto,*" or Catholic graveyard, for the
aboriginal burial caves still used by the pagan Tarahumaras.

The number of Catholic missionaries is so inadequate that very few
Tarahumaras are baptized; so that Christian teaching has but slightly
modified the ceremonies with which the Indians meet the crisis of a
new birth in their families. I have described the ceremony of cutting
with glowing corncobs the invisible cords that unite the unborn child
with the sky. This is practiced by all the sierra Tarahumaras. A further
ceremony given after the birth of a child is described by Bennett as follows: "A goat is killed for stew, and *tesgüino* is made. Ordinarily the
dancing *patio* is not used, but a cross is placed inside the house beside
the jar of *tesgüino.* The shaman dedicates the *tesgüino* and serves part of

it. Then the family kneels before the 'doctor,' who makes incense and marks crosses in the air on the four sides of each individual. Next he takes three lighted sticks of pitch-pine and makes more crosses in the air. Then he burns a bit of hair off the top of the head of each member of the family kneeling before him. With water in his mouth he blows a cross on the head of each person. The 'curing' is finished, and the *tesgüino* drinking continues."

The use of hair from the head of each member of the family is a touch in the birth ceremony possibly to remind the Tarahumaras that man is born but to die. It will be recalled that in the burial at Samachique each member of the family present dropped a few hairs from his head into the grave. As a man is given three death ceremonies to assist in "despatching" his soul, and a woman four, so in the birth ceremony this three/four concept is used. For a boy, the ceremony is given three days after birth; for a girl, four days. In making the signs of the cross, three lighted pitch-pine sticks are used for a boy, and four if the child is a girl.

These pagan crisis rites of the Tarahumaras illustrate a general function of religious ceremony. Van Gennep, a sociologist of the French school, has shown that all religions assist individuals and families in meeting the crises of life's cycle. Everywhere families are augmented by birth, children grow to puberty, are married, themselves beget children, become sick, and finally die. Almost every one of these "ages of man" is sanctified by a religious ceremony. The Tarahumaras, however, do not have puberty rites.

It is apparent, as Van Gennep points out, that each of these crisis events marks the passage of an individual into a new socially recognized group or status. The prenatal ceremony of the Tarahumaras gives the unborn child human status by cutting its ties with the sky (the land of the unborn and the dead). When the child is born, another and simple ceremony, which has been described, brings it more completely into human contact and human association.

The Tarahumaras now practice no marriage ceremony, Christian or pagan, although the people still remember the parental agreements and the long sermons of advice and exhortation by which marriage was at one time ceremoniously recognized by relatives and friends. Whatever else this and other ceremonies are, marriage for the Tarahumaras generally is, as among ourselves, a rite by means of which a man and a woman "pass" from the unmarried status into one suitable for the establishment of a new family group.

Even in these ceremonies the individual involved is considered more or less sacred, that is, untouchable and out of range of ordinary secular treatment. "Sacred" in this sense is both positive and negative, as is shown by the original sense of the Latin root, *sacra*. This term was applied both to the gods and to heinous criminals, because both were untouchable and beyond the range of ordinary social contact. Thus, until these crisis ceremonies are successfully performed, the individual is a source of danger to himself or to anyone near him.

Since the Tarahumaras know little about pathology, to them sickness is a "sacred" condition of ritual contamination in which the patient can infect others, not with germs (of which primitive men know nothing), but with a ritual uncleanness. During illness an individual is considered to be in a state between life and death. To "pass" him back into the Land of the Living, curing ceremonies are essential. If the curing ceremonies fail and the patient dies, death ceremonies are then given to "pass" him on into the Land of the Dead. This we observed in the ceremonies given for Patricio.

Aided by these ceremonies the individual has faced all the crises of life and has passed through all social groups from the unborn to the dead. He has gained the status corresponding to each group, and his cycle is complete. While religion is often more than this, still these "rites of passage" are essential in all religions. Even in ours these ceremonies of birth, marriage, and death are present.

But besides these "crisis" functions of religion for the individual, primitive religion has other vital functions for the group. In these, civilized and primitive religions vary greatly. One of the most important of the functions of primitive religion is to be seen in the numerous ceremonies and techniques which have to do with the seeming control of nature, luck, and fate. Since primitive men have no science, to them that vast realm, which we know from objective demonstration to be controlled by natural law, is a realm subject to gods, spirits, devils, and supernatural forces. And thus it is that primitive men are able to surrender themselves completely to the pleasant delusion that their ceremonies and religious services keep the universe in order, cause rain, promote abundant crops and game, fend off sickness, in short, bring good health, good luck, and prosperity to the tribe.

Such ceremonies are done for the good of the group rather than the individual, and are generally given communally. Those functions which the Tarahumaras consider of vital importance to the group are entrusted to ceremonies as pagan as though the priests had never come to the sierra, and in spite of the few Christian elements that have crept in under false colors. For instance, we have seen even the pagans use the sign of the cross as well as the cross itself. This is because in its pagan context the sign of the cross represents the four regions into which the universe is divided, again shown by the offerings and the ceremonies given to the four points. This "four point" symbolism is basic in all Mexican aboriginal religion.

One of the most important of the communal ceremonies given for the good of the crop is that of "curing" the fields and animals. In calling this ceremony a "curing" ceremony, like so many others, such as that of birth, the Tarahumaras reveal the essentially primitive nature of their religion. Since they are familiar with so few scientific or empirically demonstrable methods for guaranteeing the success of their crops by the control of numerous crop pests, or for protecting the lives of their children by the control of children's diseases, they have no recourse save to "curing" ceremonies. The Tarahumaras live by the cultivation of cornfields; so, as might be expected, group ceremonies are given to guarantee crops. A first ceremony is given before the corn has even sprouted. Then a ceremony is given to insure rain. Finally, when green ears have appeared on the corn, the ceremony of "first fruits" is given.

Preparation had been going on at a nearby *ranchería* for the ceremony of "curing the fields and animals"; and Bennett had been waiting at Quírare to witness it. But an urgent telegram from America "of the North" forced him to start off on the four-day journey to the railhead in order to telegraph a reply; and from there he continued on to the upper country of the Río Conchos to make the study of the peyote cult from which I had been turned back by rain. It was fortunate that I had joined him, because I remained at Quírare in his stead, and witnessed and took notes on this important ceremony of "curing the fields and animals," the most impressive of the pagan round.

Since corn is the staff of life to the Tarahumaras, they, like all primitive agriculturists, have an elaborate round of ceremonies to promote the growth of their crops. It is largely because of the ceremonial beliefs and practices that have grown up around corn that it is impossible to get the Tarahumaras to shift to wheat or sweet potatoes.

The Tarahumara agricultural ceremony of "curing the fields and animals" differs from most similar primitive ceremonies in that it is not completely dedicated to animal husbandry and agriculture. Like all the other ceremonies of the Tarahumaras, it is also dedicated to the ceremonial curing of the people to prevent their getting sick and dying. Even the minor ceremonies, such as those following cooperative labor, have this end; and it will be recalled that I was "cured" by the shaman in such a ceremony. Among the Tarahumaras this "curing" element is prevalent in all their pagan ceremonies. Among most primitive agricultural people the agricultural round of ceremonies is a cycle separate from that of curing.

Dr. Bennett clearly shows that the essential elements of this and all pagan Tarahumara ceremonies involve the dancing *patio*, the aboriginal *dutuburi-yumari* dance, and feasting and drinking.

The dancing *patio*, which is prepared in front of the house, is a cleared circular space from fifteen to thirty feet in diameter. It represents the world. In the center a table altar is set up, and on it before three crosses an offering is made. This offering is to feed the gods, who, as the Tarahumaras think, come down to their little ceremonial world. The four directions of the *patio*, or clearing, represent the four gates of the world. The one to the east is that of the house where Christ was born. The other three are the gates of the houses of: 1) the fox, whose cry brings death to a Tarahumara woman; 2) the owl, whose cry brings death to a man; 3) the unidentified bird, *oko*, whose cry means death to a child. Thus lustrative offerings of food and drink are always made to the four cardinal points.

Just as the "Christian" ceremonies emphasize the dancing of the *matachines*, the *pascol*, and the "Pharisees" and "Judases," so the pagan ceremonial round emphasizes the native *dutuburi-yumari* dance. One or another of these dances bulks largely in any Tarahumara ceremony, whether "Christian" or pagan, because, I think, of the emphasis on muscular activity throughout the entire life of the Indians, in hunting, laboring, racing, as well as ceremony. It seems clear that the Tarahumaras think of dancing as working, which indeed they call it; and it is particularly fitting that so vigorous and muscular a tribe as these great racers, who run down deer, should consider the efforts of their dancing as constituting one of their most acceptable offerings to the gods. So they work at dancing in order to make an offering in terms of human fatigue and tired human muscles; and this offering the gods would indeed be ungrateful to reject by not fulfilling the Indians' prayers.

The aboriginal Tarahumara dance, the *dutuburi-yumari*, is a simple enough thing when contrasted with the brilliant spectacle of the Christian dances. This dance is accompanied by a single chanter, the *sawéame*, who keeps time with a rattle, the *sawala*, from which his name is derived and which is one of the oldest and simplest of Indian musical instruments. No intelligible words are apparent in the chant.[1]

Bennett thus describes the *dutuburi:*

> The men do not dance, but line up on the left side of the chanter as he faces the crosses and march back and forth with him. They keep themselves wrapped in their blankets, and sometimes cross their arms over their chests. Sometimes women walk on the other side of the chanter in a similar fashion.
>
> The women do the dancing. They line up in a file. With the right hand each dancer holds the left hand of the dancer in front. They are lined up on the right side of the chanter; and when he shifts his position, they are left facing him, which is the signal to start the dance. . . . Performing steps in unison, the women shift across the *patio* and then return.

It is another indication of the high status of Tarahumara women that they are the principals in this important aboriginal dance. This is not because the men are too lazy to do the dancing, for their participation in the ceremony keeps them in motion. It is more likely that women because of their sex take so prominent a part in the ceremonies having to do with the increase and fertility of crops and animals.

Before the start of the ceremony of "curing the fields and animals" that I witnessed, a steer had been slaughtered and hung on a pole in the dancing *patio*. It had died that its fellows might be saved and that the people might get their fill of stewed beef. By nightfall it had been cut up and was boiling in bits in the large pots over the fire.

The table altar supported three wooden crosses, each hung with decorative pieces of new cotton cloth. On the altar also were many bowls containing food, drink, and mixtures of water with various plants useful to the Indians.

At dusk the two chanters with their rattles began their monotonous, unintelligible chant. The *dutuburi* was begun and danced all night. In the morning, a breakfast of stew and beer was passed around. Then, as a safeguard from death, all the members of the family knelt on a folded blanket before the shaman, who, using a bit of pine branch, sprinkled them liberally from one bowl containing water mixed with crushed century plant and *sotol*, and from another bowl containing ashes mixed with water. These preparations were to take away the contamination of death from contact with a dead body. Apparently, as we shall see, the planting of corn exposes the Tarahumara to death.

After the people were thus "cured" the newly planted fields were subjected to the same treatment. A group of a dozen men followed the shaman and the two chanters to the table altar on the dancing *patio*. The first three men took from behind the altar the three crosses. The other men each took one of the bowls of food, drink, or useful plants. Each bowl held a sprig of pine branch for use as a hyssop. Then they all made a formal circuit of the *patio* three times, and continued as a formal procession into and around the fields near the house of the family giving the ceremony. After this they "cured" the fields by sprinkling them with the contents of the bowls. All this was done just as when the family had been "cured," except that other preparations besides those against death were used.

In addition to "curing" the fields by removing contamination from them, this last gesture may also have been meant as a ceremonial offering to the fields in payment for the good things to be taken when the new corn crop was ripe. One would expect this in a typical primitive, agricultural ceremony. The "curing" significance is obvious, since the people were treated in the same way; and the same procedure was explicit in a similar treatment of the domestic animals of the family.

The last part of the ceremony was the "curing" of the animals. These were gathered near the house and sprinkled with the various offerings, as had been done with the people and with the fields. The "curing" of the animals was somewhat different, however, in that the shaman heated a piece of iron and with it singed a cross on the hair of the foreheads and shoulders of the animals. This was done carefully in order not to cause the animals any pain.

The Indians say that this ceremony protects the animals against rabies, as though hydrophobia were common among their burros and cattle. Yet epidemics of this dread disease have been prevalent among the Indians' dogs, which have infected the coyote, which in turn have terrified the Indians by dashing into their camps and biting right and left. So by transfer the Tarahumaras seek to protect their domestic animals from rabies. The ceremonial branding also protects the animals against being struck by lightning.

After this a modification of the same "cure" of branding is given the family, to protect them from sickness and being struck by lightning. For this final ceremony the people again kneel before the shaman, who singes some hairs from the tops of their heads with a glowing corncob. This practice is taken from the ceremonial of the "cure" of the unborn child; but its significance in connection with the singeing of hair from the animals seems to be that of a "cure" against rabies and lightning.

Finally branches of cedar were thrown on the fire, and the family danced in the pungent smoke, just as is done to remove the ritual danger of burying a dead man. It was quite clear, from the association of various elements from the death and curing ceremonies, that one of the purposes of this ceremony of "curing the fields and animals" was to remove the people from a ritual danger which they had incurred by planting corn, now about two inches high.

It may seem incredible that any danger should be envisaged in so humdrum and routine a business as the planting of corn. Dr. Bennett's matter-of-fact and thoroughly objective description of this ceremony does not interpret it as one designed to remove the people from any fancied condition of danger. But, though I agree with him in his presentation of this ceremony as one of "curing," I shall go beyond him in his interpretation.

To consider a new crop of corn as a source of danger and ritual uncleanness explains the many elements in this ceremony which are used in other ceremonies for removing the individual from a fancied condition of ritual danger or contamination. We have seen that primitive religion treats those who are facing a change of life or status as persons "sacred," or delicate, untouchable, outside of ordinary contact, a source of danger to themselves and others, and hence ritually unclean. The "rites of passage" are ceremonies to "pass" the "sacred" person through this dangerous transition and back into normal contact again. In the same way many communal ceremonies in primitive religion make other things "sacred" when such are vital to the common good. When much hangs in the balance, it is only human that it be invested with religious significance. That a new crop of corn is thus "sacred" or untouchable and communicates this unclean condition to people is explicitly expressed by the Tarahumaras in connection with their green corn Feast of First Fruits. They say that unless the first of the new crop is dedicated in this ceremony, "dire consequences will follow."

This latter phrase was as much as the unreflective Tarahumaras could communicate to Bennett; but it is quite apparent, from the social psychology of primitive people as revealed in similar ceremonies in many parts of the world, that the new crop of corn is considered "sacred," delicate, contaminated, and ritually unclean. Like all the first fruits it must be purified by a special ceremony to remove the owner from the danger of becoming infected by contact with a thing ritually unclean. The same attitude is revealed in the "curing" elements borrowed from the individual Tarahumara crisis rites for the communal ceremony of "curing the fields and animals."

The ceremony of the first fruits of green corn, similar to that for "curing the fields and animals," is given by a group of neighboring families as a communal affair for the common good. My description of this ceremony closely follows Dr. Bennett's account.

> A three-cross *patio* is prepared and a small cross placed at one side to prevent sickness. A goat is slaughtered, *tesgüino* provided, and the *dutuburi* danced all night. As each man arrives in the evening, he puts his bundle of green corn or other new vegetables on the table altar. After everything has been purified with smoke incense, the *dutuburi* is chanted and danced for a time, and then cooked food is brought and placed on the altar as an offering to the gods. This cooked food from the new crop is offered three times to each of the four points to avoid death from the "death animals." Then the people eat the remains of this food which has been blessed by having been offered to the four points. That night, while the *dutuburi* is danced, food is again eaten both at midnight and at dawn. In the morning the *tesgüino* is dedicated, and the revelry begins. At the close of the festivities the *yumari* is danced.[2]

In this simple ceremony of first fruits the green corn and other vegetables are offered to the gods on the altar and then blessed by an all-night dancing of the *dutuburi*. The cooked food from the new crop can be eaten only after it has been offered to the "death animals" and to Christ at the doors of the four points. Although the ceremony is ingenious enough, we have here the necessary elements for the purification of the new crop so that it may be safely eaten by the owners. Among the related Huichol Indians this ceremony has been developed much more elaborately; but the same core of significance is there, as among all tribes that practice agriculture. To sum up, the central core of significance of this ceremony is that of removing the ritual uncleanness from the "sacred" new corn, and thus making it ordinary, secular, and free from contamination to the people using it.

Another aspect of the communal or group ceremonies in primitive religion is shown by the pagan Tarahumara rain ceremony. This ceremony is evidence of the primitive belief that religion is merely a magical technique for controlling nature and the elements, and that human actions can keep the world in place, the seasons in order, and the very elements under control. Since the Tarahumaras are an agricultural people living in a semiarid environment, they attribute far-reaching importance to this ceremony. In the complexity of its organization it is second in the pagan round only to that of "curing the fields and animals." It utilizes the dancing *patio* with its altar and crosses, and the dancing of the *dutuburi-yumari;* and it is concluded with feasting. Inasmuch as the rain benefits everyone, the ceremony is given by groups of families who happen to have *rancherías* reasonably near one another to be able to cooperate for this purpose.

For an account of the rain ceremony I return again to Dr. Bennett.

Some Indians say that ghosts advise them when to give the rain fiesta. The animals are also believed to tell the Tarahumaras when droughts are coming. Lorenzo told us that one of his friends went by the cattle pen during the drought of last summer and heard one of the bulls say that rain was needed and that a dance ought to be given.

After the preparation of the beer and the slaughter of a steer for stew the *dutuburi* is danced all night. In the morning this is finished off with the *yumari* conclusion. Then the people line up again beside the chanter, the men to the left, the women to the right. The shaman takes three pitch-pine sticks, lights them, and makes crosses to the four directions. He approaches the line of people and with the flaming torch makes the sign of the cross in front of them. He draws a long line of flame in front of the people, and repeats this three times, making a half turn at the end of the line before returning. Then he draws three lines of flame behind them. Then he returns the pitch-pine to the altar, and repeats the whole performance by cutting lines with a knife. After this he makes a sermon, asking for rain. . . .

The "sermon," as the Tarahumaras call it, is really a prayer for rain in which the chanter tells God and the gods of the four points that they have worked hard dancing all night and have made many offerings of food and beer for rain.

The pagan Tarahumara ceremonies are simple enough; but their pagan beliefs are simpler, so much so indeed that they can hardly be said to exist as a consciously thought-out system of rationalization.

The Tarahumaras have no mythology, which, among many tribes such as the Huichols, is a sacred tribal philosophy or theology. The opinion has been stated before that the general drunkenness as an integral part of the ceremonies has prevented the formalization of Tarahumara belief into any definite system of mythology. This impression agrees with that presented by Dr. Bennett. Tarahumara religion is so amorphous in ideology that to anyone who has seen the ceremonies and talked with informants, who themselves are participants, it is very apparent that the Indians go through their pagan ceremonial round without an intelligible rationale of any sort. They are motivated by fear and a feeling of a need of outside help, as well as subtler emotional urges, rather than by any intellectualizing.

Meager as is Tarahumara belief, its pagan base has been inextricably mixed with fragments of Christian teaching. I have mentioned their identification of God with the Sun Father and the Virgin Mary with the Moon Mother. They respect "*Dios*" highly, and give him credit for everything in the world. He is constantly mentioned in their sermons and speeches, as, for example, in what follows, which I paraphrase from Dr. Bennett.

The Tarahumara conception of the sky world, heaven, is expressed by their phrase "in the three planes of heaven above." Each of these three planes is a world of the dead in which a man lives his regular life. The last heaven is the home of God and the ultimate port of every soul. An addition from Christian teaching appears in the added conception of three hells below for evildoers. My impression is that the last doesn't mean much to the Tarahumaras.

Mankind has erected such diverse cultural dwellings for his life and spirit that few things are found to be universal. The Tarahumara belief in the existence of the soul after death in another world is an instance of one of these ever-present elements. On this universal belief the first great English anthropologist, Tylor, made a generalization about primitive religion that has not yet lost its significance. He shows that primitive man everywhere considers the soul as a spiritual alter ego of the body. Soul is often identified with the shadow, the image reflected in water, or more commonly with the breath. Breath appears to primitive man as an invisible essence that enters and leaves the body, unseen except when the atmosphere is cold. In life it is present; in sleep it is retarded; and in death it is absent: hence breath must be the soul, the thing that distinguishes the live and the dead.

The Tarahumaras identify breath with the soul, as is shown in their word for the soul, *iwigala* (*iwi*, to breathe), and in their belief that the soul passes in and out of the windpipe and lodges in the heart. They know these organs from slaughtering animals, and they say that the lungs merely strengthen the heart and help it to hold the soul. When they run or are given cause to breathe heavily, they think that the soul is very active. Fright sometimes induces the escape of the soul, and thus the person gets sick. And if his escaped soul is captured, say by the great water serpent which owns the waters and lives in the water holes, he is very apt to die.

Tylor's theory of religion also delineated another consideration of the soul as a general belief in primitive religions. This is that the soul leaves the body in sleep and has experiences which are remembered after the soul's return and the person awakens. The Tarahumara firmly believe that dreams are the experiences of the soul, as I soon learned when our first informant wished to go back to his distant wife simply because he had dreamed that she was ill.

Like other primitive people the Tarahumaras believe that dreams are a privileged order of experience. They are a revelation directly from the gods or from the spirits. Dreams are highly esteemed among all tribes, and are often used as a sanction for power by the priest and the shaman. In many other ways they play a part in primitive religion incomprehensible to the civilized man.

It is because of the primitive esteem for dream experiences that narcotic and intoxicating substances are valued by aborigines as among the most valuable and sacred of all things. One of these substances is the narcotic cactus, peyote. It contains both narcotic and stimulating alkaloids, the effects of which are strong and immediate, and produces dreams or hallucinations and a great physical exhilaration. The scientific studies of the plant have proved it to be habit-forming or productive of effects worse than temporary nausea.

The plant seems to have been in use among the ancient Aztecs, but the Spanish accounts give little of the cult that had grown up about it. Peyote is very important among the modern Cora and Huichols in the Mexican state of Jalisco, where an elaborate cult is based on its use. That the use of the plant spread from the Huichols to the distant Tarahumaras is shown by the Tarahumara adoption of the Huichol name, *jículi*, for the plant. Apparently parties of Apaches on raiding forays in the Tarahumara country became familiar with the plant and introduced it among the Indians of the United States about 1880.

Peyote grows in southern Texas and in Mexico across the border near the mouth of the Conchos River. Supplies of it were thus available for the Indians concentrated in Indian territory. But it was gradually introduced from Indian territory to one reservation after another, until it had finally spread throughout the country; and among the tribes everywhere it became the center of new cults patterned on whatever remained of the ancestral rites and beliefs of the early North American Indians. By means of the narcotic power of peyote to produce dream experiences the Indians sought a final reintegration of the fragments of aboriginal culture which had been smashed by the White Man.

But from its source to the circumference of the territory throughout which it had spread and in which cults had sprung up based upon it, peyote met the denunciation of the missionaries and officials in contact with the Indians. As early as the seventeenth century we find Fr. Ortega, one of the first Spanish missionaries to the Cora-Huichol Indians, denouncing it. In 1790 a physician from the Spanish court, sent to investigate the plant life of Mexico, recorded for science the name, "diabolical root," given this plant by the missionaries.

The eating of the "diabolical root" was interdicted by the Spanish missionaries along with the eating of human flesh. They were instructed to ask their neophytes, "Hast thou eaten human flesh? Hast thou eaten peyote?"

When the use of the plant was introduced among the Indians of the United States, the files of the Bureau of Indian Affairs became bloated with denunciations from missionaries and officials. Its transportation has been banned in this country.

The reason for this fanfare is significant. The "diabolical root" has been put under a ban not because it is poisonous or habit-forming, but because it acts as the center for the crystallization of all native values of aboriginal Indian religion; since to the Indians peyote is the "divine root," due to its properties that cause dreams. The Indians of the United States were culturally so shattered and broken that they lived in the wrecks of cultures that once provided satisfactory equipment for a vigorous and self-sufficient life, both material and spiritual. Such is the power of religion in human affairs that, utterly broken down and dispirited in the midst of the disintegration of their native ways and customs, they were able to welcome peyote, which came to them offering the basis for the erection of cults and beliefs which would reestablish the assurances, the values, and the satisfactions that come from participation in an indigenous and integrated system of belief and thought.

Among the Huichol Indians of Mexico, the source of this whole remarkable cultural movement, the plant still functions with all its ancient religious importance, despite two hundred years of missionary activity. It is still the center of the beautiful pagan religion which Lumholtz described so well, and which I saw in full operation as it must have been before the Spaniards came. The isolated and intermittent efforts of the Catholic missionaries do not appear to have been directed toward pulling down the native religions in Mexico; and they were not followed by settlers similar to those who destroyed the cultures of the American Indian of the North.

Tarahumara culture as a native system of attitudes and behavior appears to be well integrated. At any rate it provides its participants with a sufficiently satisfactory adjustment to the natural, social, and religious environments that the peyote cult seems to have met with much less success than it did in very recent times among the Indians of the United States, where its almost immediate acceptance indicated a strong effort to find a new basis for the reintegration of native patterns of life.

All the Tarahumaras know about peyote, however; and, as they personify many sacred plants, so they have put peyote at the head of the list of divine plants. But it occupies no solitary eminence. Other plants, innocuous cacti, for example, are also considered sacred.[3] I have described the death of the *teniente*, Patricio, who lost one of these from his belt during a race. Although the Tarahumaras fear the evil jimsonweed, they consider peyote as a good plant that is even stronger. And they esteem the shaman who uses peyote as the greatest doctor of all; for he only has power enough to touch the dread jimsonweed.

But most of the Tarahumaras do not trouble themselves in the slightest about peyote; and only in a small section of the country is it actually used. In the region of the headwaters of the Río Conchos there is an active peyote cult; and the Tarahumaras of this group make pilgrimages to the distant places where the plant grows. The plant is considered to possess a divine spirit so powerful that the pilgrims must be continually on the alert during the journey, which lasts from two weeks to a full month, lest they come to harm. To this end the men, before they start out, have themselves made comparably sacred by being offered incense. After they arrive, they harvest the plant with sticks, because it is so sacred that it is literally untouchable. When they finally eat the peyote, they must eat nothing else with it save *pinole* (parched corn flour in water), until, on their return, the final ceremonies are given to purify them.

Peyote is personified into a being like a god, and must be fed incense to appease its hunger. The power of the plant is sufficiently strong to be of aid to the shaman, provided it is fed and offered the proper ceremonies. Then, without damage to its spirit, peyote allows its material substance to be eaten by the Tarahumaras in the proper ceremony. This ceremony involves a special dance to the sound of the rasping-stick, which is not used in other ceremonies.

By eating of the material part of this great being, peyote, the Tarahumaras are invested with its power to dream and see visions. These dreams and the exhilaration resulting from eating the plant are considered by the Tarahumaras to be the best "cure" or safeguard against any known disease. Even so, very few have been cured in this expensive ceremony given by the peyote shaman; and in Samachique the ceremony had not been staged for twenty or thirty years. Lorenzo knew a great deal about the ceremony, having seen it in his youth.

CHAPTER 16

▸ *The "Genuine" and "Spurious"*
▸ *Values of Tarahumara Culture*

T his outline of the acceptance of peyote among various tribes is significant for an understanding of some things about human culture. By culture, anthropologists mean that enormous part of human thought, belief, and behavior that results from human contact and association with others. When we stop to think how very little the individual actually creates himself without the stimulation of contacts with and ideas from others, we see how important culture is as a repository of all that has gone before and has found ready acceptance. This technical concept of culture is different from the ordinary use of the term in phrases such as "a person of culture" or "a cultured man," for here culture means simply a person having education, moderated conduct, and a marked set of manners, which connotes a sophistication and depth of background of a certain sort.

Anthropologists have found it useful to widen this conception to include the results of all association and background which influence the growth and development of human personality beyond its biopsychological basis of capacity and endowments.

The ordinary notion of a cultured man is that of one who has cultivated this natural heritage and endowments by a special and rigorous education which, together with a wide experience, gives him an intelligent familiarity with the vast universe in which he lives and of the past which has produced him. The cultured man of the Tarahumaras has in common with all human beings merely the conditioning of the individual by his background and his group. Among cultured men of civilization this heritage has been developed by an elaborate and systematic cultivation.

The processes of conditioning and of cultivation have many elements in common. The differences arise from their forms and degrees. Anthropologists use the term "culture" without reference to these forms and degrees merely to label the result of the conditioning of the individual into the patterns of thought, belief, and behavior which pass current in his particular group.

Some cultures, such as those of India and China, produce individuals who, in the narrow sense of the word, are cultivated. But among primitive groups the cultivation is simply a process of passive conditioning by which the individual takes over the norms of tribal behaviors with very little conscious effort and often no formal education whatsoever. Thus there is a great difference in the degree of culture, as for example between a Tarahumara and a representative "man of culture" out of our own group. Yet in all cases the process of acculturation both to a past heritage and to a present group is present to an extent varying from passive conditioning to the most active and rigorous of cultivation.

From the day of birth each individual is molded by his social environment in a process which changes the mewling infant, that warm bundle of unconditioned reflexes and instinctive actions, into an adult human personality enacting the roles (personae) expected of him by his group. The individual who varies too much from the norm of these roles is taken out of circulation and put into the privacy of jails or asylums, the abodes of the true individuals.

In summary, culture is that system of beliefs, thought, and action with which the individual is equipped by borrowing on the accepted experiences of the past as such are current within his particular group. Language is typical of culture, as well as being its most important element. The last obtains because language is the device or medium by which most of culture is transmitted from one individual to another. As typical of culture, languages are codified systems of thought that have point-to-point intelligibility such that their counters pass for equivalents among all those who participate in the language.

Cultures are much wider systems of codified thought and action which have a sufficient point-to-point correspondence to be intelligible to every individual in the group. The individual draws upon this vast body of accumulated lore almost every time he turns around. A satisfactory culture is one that offers resources ample for the needs and interests of the individual in every situation from birth to death. But, of course, no culture provides all individuals with such absolute perfection. An adjustment is always necessary, and often conflict arises between the individual and the cultural norms carried out and enforced by the group.

Some cultures, whether primitive or civilized, may be termed "genuine" in the sense that they provide the individual with ample resources for a full, happy life. Such cultures provide a sufficient adjustment to the natural environment, which furnishes his fellowships, and finally to the religious environment, which provides all or the great majority of men with so many spiritual and inspirational values. Such cultures are indestructible and resistant to any outside influence, except superior physical force.

If indestructibility by outside influence is a fair criterion for judging the value of cultures, then the American Indian culture of the Pueblos is one of the most "genuine" in human records. It appears to have preserved its essential outlines for hundreds of years despite attacks from nomadic tribes and, within historic times, even the full moral and educational program of white civilization.

Other cultures, whether primitive or civilized, we may consider "spurious"; for at any point they thwart and defeat the individuals who participate in them. Some cultures, such as those of India, luxuriate into oppressive, stifling things, well symbolized by the Juggernaut, which crushes its devotees.

But is Tarahumara culture "genuine," or is it "spurious"? Like all cultures it is neither one nor the other, because these terms are to be thought of as antithetical poles. On a scale between these extremes all cultures may be evaluated as they satisfy the individual's needs and equip him for a satisfying adjustment to his environments, natural, social, and religious.

Tarahumara culture has one valid claim to being "genuine," because it supports one of the largest tribal groups in North America by its aboriginal techniques. Despite the simplicity of Tarahumara culture, its technology provides a close ecological adjustment to the natural environment. This, neither lush nor desert, is far from ideal. The climate is cold, and the rainfall is barely sufficient for agriculture. The soil is stony, and the terrain is rough and impossible for other than human transportation without disproportionate expenditures for trail making.

The natural environment is abundant in resources of stone and of wood. The latter resource is available to the Indians due to the Spanish introduction of the steel axe, knife, and chisel. With a cultural mastery of these simple tools the Tarahumaras in the sierra make secure store-houses for the protection of their food supply, and crude board shelters which enable them to dwell in the cool climate of the mountains except during the winter months. Were saws available and carpentry known, wood could be a resource for structures of more adequate shelter both in summer and winter. But here Tarahumara culture fails the individual, for it exposes his body to such cold in winter that even the hardening of exposure, which begins with childhood, cannot overcome the biological need for warmth. The heat of fire being insufficient, despite an abundance of wood, the Tarahumara must flee to the more elementary heat, that of the sun's rays. This necessitates, with the approach of winter, human transportation of food and effects to the gorges for cave-dwelling. His culture fails him here again, because even Tarahumara muscles tire in the long trek.

The Tarahumaras realize that this necessity for migration is a cultural defect. They understand its drawbacks in terms of weary labor and the discomfort of dwelling in caves strewn with goat dung and with dust constantly blowing in their faces and their food. It is true that we saw one family which lived in a permanent log cabin so well built as to be secure from the cold of the winter. But this was the only family to conquer the "spurious" element in Tarahumara technology which necessitates cave-dwelling.[1]

In the river valley where the land has not been completely usurped by the Mexicans, the Indians have their holding in one piece of ground. That this necessity for migration between little plots of land is realized by the Indians to be a defect in their culture is indicated in the beauty of the two Catholic missions, where the technique of stone masonry has been taken over by the Tarahumaras. This makes the stone resources of the sierra available to the Indians for secure storage and dwelling houses. It is noteworthy that those Tarahumaras who live under this influence dwell the year round in stone houses, built by their fellows who have been initiated into the wizardry of making a secure corner in stone, and who are hired for the purpose of building them. In Umira a rich old Indian friend even hired Mexicans to build him an adobe house. But this was pure swank because it wasn't cold there. He wanted to impress the Mexican patriarch's younger daughter, whom he wished to marry.

Away from the influence of Spanish masonry, the Tarahumaras have no recourse but to migrate to distant cave-dwellings. Sierra store-houses must be left exposed to theft, and fences and other structures exposed to damage by cattle. Household effects have to be duplicated so that bulky articles may be cached, and thus these are exposed to the danger of loss, breakage, and damage. To protect the heavy *metate* from damage, so my informant told me, it is left face downwards. Thus a practical joker or a passing animal is less apt to "commit a nuisance" on the face used for grinding food.

The necessity for long migrations to the caves in winter; and, in summer, the constant trips between isolated cornfields, have an inhibiting effect on the whole material culture of the tribe. Only the simplest and most easily moved objects are regarded as worthy of manufacture. Pottery is broken so often that even the most rudimentary decoration is discouraged. Only in one part of the Sierra Tarahumara is it decorated at all, and here a white clay encourages the crude painting of plant and animal motifs in red ochre.

In the decoration of artifacts, the Tarahumaras confine their artistic impulses to blankets, girdles, and ribbons. These are the most permanent and portable of objects. Thus the aesthetic culture of the Tarahumaras is greatly inhibited. Both for artistry and utility Tarahumara weaving excels the rest of their simple technology. When the wool of the Spaniard's sheep was substituted for the fiber of the century plant, the Tarahumaras added to their mangy clouts and skirts wool blankets, which are effective protection against the cold. The minor weaving, though excellent, is more decorative than utilitarian. In weaving, Tarahumara culture is "genuine" indeed, because weaving provides blankets for warmth as well as the only artistic decoration.

Just as we have seen that the Spanish tools, the axe, knife, and chisel, have been deeply assimilated into Tarahumara culture to improve its possibilities for providing shelter, so sheep no less have been generally assimilated for the value of their wool for clothing, blankets, girdles, women's skirts, and the men's clouts.

Cattle and goats, other Spanish contributions, have been integrated in no less degree, to utilize another resource of the sierra.

Besides wood and stone the sierra offers the natural ecological resource of grass. The goats and cattle of the Indians feed on this, and transform it, through the cycle of animal digestion, into fertilizer, which in turn nourishes the corn, the Tarahumara staff of life.

At the present time, when the fields are productive of inferior corn only, and when every vestige of manure is utilized for fertilizer, one wonders how the Tarahumaras raised enough corn to live before the coming of animals. Archaeology proves that their ancestors had corn even in the ancient Basket-Maker phase of their history. From the presence and frequency of archaeological remains in the Cave-Dweller phase, it seems clear that only the fertile land in the small river valleys and wide *arroyos* was used. Since the coming of the Spaniards, Indian population appears to have increased enormously. Thus most of the Indians of today live from their animals, and yet utilize only the manure. Milk and cheese are not consumed by the Tarahumaras of the sierra, and the skins of sacrificed animals are used for straps and rawhide sandals.

In summary, those basic requirements of the biological man, shelter, clothing, and food, are met by Tarahumara culture with a heavy indebtedness to Spanish contributions. With the aid of these gifts, the knife, axe, chisel, cattle, sheep and goats, Tarahumara culture has achieved an adequacy that enables human utilization of an inhospitable terrain that would otherwise support only wild animals. In the cultural sphere of the adjustment of the individual to the natural environment, Tarahumara culture is "genuine" by the pragmatic test that, even in its meagerness and simplicity, it gives the Indians a better adjustment to the sierra than that achieved by Mexican folk exiled there by the failure of mining. But much of these genuine values are owed to Spanish contributions.

Even the moderate degree of greater cultural complexity of Mexican folk culture does not materially aid the Mexicans in adjusting themselves to any but the best river valleys in the sierra. Nor has the much more complicated civilization of the Americans, who mine in the sierra, made any adjustment to the natural environment other than a conspicuously effective organization for utilizing the rich strata of ore in the gorges. Otherwise the sierra offers them nothing, unless they happen to eat some beef bought from the Mexicans, who in turn obtained it from the Indians in trade for cloth. Contrariwise, the mineral resources of the environment remain effectively unavailable to both the Mexicans and the Indians, because their cultures are lacking in those particular specialized techniques and sciences necessary to make gold and silver ore of any use to them, although both groups do use money.

Thus briefly summarized is the cultural heritage of the Tarahumaras, which functions to adjust the individual to his natural environment. Obviously it is a cultural heritage, for the adjustment is not that of the animals, which utilize the natural resources directly. Unlike the deer, the Tarahumara does not directly eat the grass, but interposes between the grass and his animal hunger a complicated cultural cycle involving the care and use of animals to aid in the more complicated agricultural round, which he learned from others. Nor, like the coyote, does he avail himself of meat, tearing the flesh from a scarcely dead animal and gulping it raw; for not only does the Tarahumara interpose traditional techniques for the slaughtering and cooking of meat, but also, before the meat is eaten, he observes a complex system of social participation and of religious ceremonies which he considers as a sacred heritage from the past.

Such complicated socioreligious behavior to still man's animal hunger indicates that human culture does more than merely adjust the individual to the natural environment. Human nature transcends animal nature in its social need for participation in groups. The so-called gregarious animals do not exhibit this social participation because they have no culture. Their makeup is too simple for the communication of past experiences by language; and the conditioning of their native reflexes is too simple and too near the biological need of survival to be considered in the social realm of cultural conditioning.

Human nature differs essentially from animal nature in its capacity for development through social contact and participation. From the rare cases on record of abandoned children who reach maturity through association with and feeding by animals, that is, the "feral man," we have significant proof that the essential features of human personality derive from contact and communication in close participation with other human beings from the day of birth. Another line of approach to the problem of the socially conditioned personality is through the great body of data that has accumulated on the dehumanization of orphans and other institutionalized children. This data gives ample evidence that normal social personality results from an opportunity for adjustment to other normal persons.

Very meager are the organizations, devices, and methods set up in Tarahumara culture for the adjustment of its individuals to one another and for their conditioning into secure and well-rounded personalities. In its failure to perform these vital functions, Tarahumara culture reveals many "spurious" elements and values. One of its "spurious" features is the cultural paucity resulting from the dispersal of the communities into unintelligible fragments for the cold months by the necessity of migration to scattered caves in the winter.

The nature of the sierra terrain, rather than the culture, is accountable for the migrations during the warmer months. Due to the separation of the fields into small isolated patches, the community is broken up into family groups which are constantly on the move to attend to the growing corn.

Even family organization is loose and not bolstered up by the innumerable sanctions placed around the family by many other groups. There is no "alimony row" in the jail because of the separation of spouses with children, the latter not uncommon. The parents of the woman involved in a separation generally care for the children until they are old enough to herd cattle. Nor, as among many primitive tribes, do the bonds of kinship have very effective function among adult Tarahumaras. Certainly there is nothing like the social, economic, and religious institutions which many groups erect about lineages, kin, and clans.

Even so, the family is by far the strongest social group among the Tarahumaras. It is their basic group, as among all other peoples. But with the Tarahumaras the larger organizations are broken up into familial groups, discrete from one another except when cooperative labor or religious ceremonies bring them together into larger groups. The community is weak, and no effective tribal organization exists at all.

No doubt this "spurious" quality of weakness in social organization was the greatest factor in causing the Tarahumaras to accept the Spanish communal organization of "*gobernador*," "*mayor*," etc. Its functions have the validity of being of vital service in directing communal affairs and especially in punishing crime.

Due to the necessity for the families to move over large distances to cultivate little bits of arable ground the Tarahumara community is a sort of social molecule with its atoms in separate and isolated motion. The acceptance of domestic animals has increased this "basic pattern of isolation" to social loss commensurate with the economic benefits accruing from the possession of domestic animals. Among all families the care and herding of goats occupy the constant attention of many of the women, even after marriage. This weakens many of the social possibilities of marriage, and precludes much care being spent on the children. But it strengthens the marriage tie, because the economic interdependence of the sexes is unquestionably the strongest factor supporting the marriage bond.

It is the Tarahumara pattern of engaging the children in herding that is one of the most "spurious" elements in Tarahumara life. There can be little question but that herding inhibits the personality development of all Tarahumaras in their youth. This constant association with animals in the isolation of rocks and forest seems to be the most important factor underlying the wooden personalities and manners of the tribe, though it must be granted that there are worse associations than with rocks and trees in a natural setting of grandeur that attunes the Tarahumaras to nature, its creatures, and its manifold vicissitudes. It is striking that despite my specific inquiries I received no response that enabled me to determine whether the Indians appreciate the beauties of nature in any sense intelligible to us. Yet I received every indication that, even more than I did, they love to hike along their trails between their great trees under their blue and sunny skies. Tarahumaras cannot be taken out of their hills for employment or for education without pining and making every effort to get back. They hike to Chihuahua to sell their medicinal herbs, but they always return. I was able to find no trace of Tarahumara servants or peons in the city at all.

The conditioning of Tarahumara children to trees, skies, stones, and solitude causes them as adults to sit for hours next to one another without speaking. Even though he may be visiting a lifelong friend or acquaintance on business, a Tarahumara guest will wait patiently for half an hour or more while the family in the house speculates on the nature of his errand. If no man appears, he will not speak, call, or shout to the other occupants. Rather than commit this indecorum, and regardless of how routine his business may be, he will leave and return at some other time, even though he may have to come several miles. Yet the Tarahumaras are hospitable enough about food. Hospitality is a necessity, potentially reciprocal, since they never see one another without a walk of several, and often many, miles. This hospitality does not obtain for sleeping accommodations, however. In the event that a guest is forced to remain the night, he is directed to a cave or some other protection elsewhere in the vicinity.

This lack of normal personality resulting from "spurious" elements in Tarahumara culture is a serious weakness in Tarahumara life. It handicaps every possibility of communal advance or cooperation beyond the family and neighborhood groups. In contrast to the many community organizations in civilization which function for cultural advance and benefit, the Tarahumara community is exercised only by a weekly meeting for prayers, a sermon by the *gobernador*, occasional trial of offenders, and rare communal labor for repairs on the church building. And even though the communal group meets every Sunday, most of the people do not open their mouths a dozen times, and then without the animation or flow of good spirits which is normal in social intercourse.

Although unfortunately I did not investigate specifically, I was later struck by the absence of any evidence of a spirit of friendship or other close social ties between Tarahumaras, married, single, kin, or in any other relationship. Lorenzo, whom I knew like a book, had a genuine and deep feeling of friendship for me, but I never saw it evidenced toward others (though it might have been), and I did not think to question him on the subject. At any rate, my impression is strong that there is very little positive social feeling among the Tarahumaras. Bennett and I had Lorenzo talk about every person whom he knew in the community, and his favorable attitudes toward them were at best those of cold respect or regard. Even toward his beautiful sister and his blue-eyed brother, who was his fellow *maestro*, Lorenzo's attitude in speech, whether with us or in contact with them, was distant and remote.

In the Tarahumara group the positive social feeling is decidedly less than the negative feeling, negative in that it has to do with rancor, the memory of past offenses and slights, etc. Indeed, when the Tarahumara are drunk, they often get into arguments and altercations which, on occasion, end in bloodshed. Still, Tarahumara culture is sane and "genuine" in its social atmosphere of tolerance and acceptance of others as individuals. There was little of gossip, backbiting, and scandal-mongering; and I have lived in American villages of which this could not be said. But it must be remembered that the Tarahumaras see so little of one another that it is a bit of an adventure to attend church on Sunday.

Tarahumara culture has but a little place for that almost incredible development of hatred and fear of one's neighbors that is allowed to develop into a mania among some primitive groups. The blacks both of Melanesia and Africa are burdened with these negative social attitudes, expressed in elaborate rituals of sorcery against one's fellows. And in most primitive groups, though to a lesser extent, the same things are similarly formalized into secret techniques or ceremonies of magic to protect oneself either against one's fellows or the fancied machinations of one's neighbors. The prominent place of these attitudes of hatred, fear, and superstition in all primitive cultures makes them the most salient of "spurious" values.

The American Indian's sense of personal dignity, his courage, reserve, and poise, all mitigate the prominence of these "spurious" cultural values. Tarahumara culture is not lacking in such a prominence, but completely lacks in formal techniques for expressing it. Among the Tarahumaras the pattern is recognizable, however, in their beliefs about "talking bad" against one another. Even so intelligent an Indian as Lorenzo believed that his sense of smell had been wished away from him by the "talking bad" of a neighbor, envious of his use of onions and garlic in food. Worse than "talking bad" is the belief of the Tarahumara about the little *disagíki*, which can be sent to kill one's neighbors. But since it is never sent, nor even exists, it is a mere belief rather than a formal technique for working a harmful miracle.[2]

After this examination of the social organization and life, as the Tarahumara adjustment of the individual to his fellows, we may now turn to an examination of Tarahumara religion, which provides the individual with his adjustment to the sacred and supernatural. It is not lacking in elements both "genuine" and "spurious." It provides a cycle of ceremonies by means of which the newborn individual is inducted into various degrees of social participation. Since all primitive and even civilized groups exhibit many of the values given by these ceremonies, these "rites of passage" must be genuine enough.

Tarahumara religion also provides another ceremonial round by means of which the Indians think that they can help the crops and animals to grow, cause rain to water their fields and pasture, and finally make the new crop of corn, beans, and squash fit for human consumption. This cycle is not as "spurious" to the Indians as it may appear to us, even though the ceremonies do not achieve the purposes for which they are given. They do have the "genuine" value of making the Indians think that they are able to influence the ends desired, which is an important escape motive of primitive religion. The ceremony for "curing" disease is in the same category.

The most "spurious" quality of the pagan religion of the Tarahumaras is in its unrelieved drabness. All their pagan ceremonies utterly lack color, romance, drama, and pageantry, which are "genuine" aesthetic values of religion. These values are provided by the "Catholic" round of ceremonies. But, on the other hand, the latter lack the "genuine" quality of intelligible articulation with Tarahumara life and culture except as they strengthen the functions of the Tarahumara community as a social group. Thus, by a combination of pagan and "Christian" ceremonies, the Tarahumaras achieve by the first cycle a "genuine" integration with vital interests; and by the second, they attain the "genuine" values of color, drama, and pageantry, which are part of the escape motive of religion.

Except for this "Catholic" cycle, Tarahumara life is almost destitute of the enormous cultural values engendered by the arts. Religion with some native tribes, such as the Pueblos and Huichols, provides primitive drama (that of ceremonies) which is often highly dramatic. But the Tarahumaras are content with the fantastic and meaningless costumes and muscular activity of the *matachines*, the battle of the "Pharisees" and the "Judases," etc.

Literature, which some tribes like the Huichols express in an elaborate symbolism of mythology, is expressed by other tribes in secular folklore approximating the canons of literature in plot and structure. Most strikingly, the Tarahumaras completely lack literature, even in mythology of the simplest sort. In native music, they cannot content themselves with the native rhythm of the monotonous, wordless chant to the sound of the rattle. The "spurious" inadequacy of this is patent, because they have so thoroughly taken over the violin and the guitar that they manufacture excellent instruments themselves with jack-knives. From these they get wistful, plaintive, haunting melodies which still run through my head and bring a nostalgia for those little *Tarahumaritos* in their great forests and deep gorges.

As for the plastic arts, some tribes as in Africa have developed these to the threshold of great art by any standards. Other tribes, like the Huichols and the Pueblos, have developed them into elaborate religious symbolisms of real beauty and deep cultural values. But the plastic arts find no expression among the Tarahumaras, except in decorative designs (shared with the Huichols, Pima, and Hopi) woven into girdles and ribbons.

When one thinks of the spiritual and emotional values that a "genuine" culture has to offer in the arts, one sees not only a "spurious" quality in Tarahumara efforts but also how lacking their culture is in some of the most "genuine" values that the human spirit can attain!

The prominence of "spurious" values in the social, religious, and artistic life of the Tarahumaras is revealed by the compensatory importance of drunkenness, which is an accompaniment to every gathering larger than the family. Tarahumara life must be as drab, dreary, and unsatisfactory as that of city slum-dwellers, because both find the same compensation in drinking. It is only when the Tarahumaras are drunk that they lose their wooden expressions. Then they become animated, as it were, and chat and converse with shining eyes and smiling faces. And only then do the individuals of opposite sexes lose their abysmal shyness for each other to the extent that they are drawn to seek attention, to flirt, to court, and perhaps to mate.

In drinking the Tarahumaras escape from the limitations of their conditioning by dropping most of it altogether and meeting their fellows in an equally maudlin sociability. At such times they really act human. Indeed, the humanness of their behavior is almost identical with that of all other human beings in the same state of intoxication. Drunkenness appears to paralyze those cortical centers that carry the impressions of social conditioning, and which generally function so prominently as to distinguish the behavior of individuals of one culture from those of another. Alcohol, indeed, makes the whole world kin; and drunken Indians, college students, or any others giggle, titter, whisper, laugh, and shout in identical ways. A common human type seems to emerge from inhibited personality, suggesting that a study of drunken behavior would throw revealing light on what human nature is when stripped of so much of its social conditioning.

But aside from this, Tarahumara drunkenness is fundamental. It is the basic motivation of the important economic institution of cooperative labor. It is vital to functions of courtship and marriage, and necessary for the exercising of friendship and sociability, the "curing" of disease, the cycle of the individual's "rites of passage," and both the "Christian" and pagan round of ceremonies. Both the priests and the government teachers correctly appraise the fundamental strength of this motivation. They do not realize, however, that most of Tarahumara life and culture hinges upon it. It is so strong a "spurious" compensation for the many other "spurious" elements in Tarahumara culture, that the fundamental Tarahumara institutions are integrated about it.

Drunkenness must be shown to be a "spurious" integration to most of Tarahumara culture, because Tarahumara mothers do not always drop their babies in the fire, nor do all the men lie down to sleep in snow drifts or fall from the cliffs. The beer that they make is not seriously deleterious, and their active life and healthy climate enable them to throw off its ill effects with surprising promptness. And yet, moralists to the contrary notwithstanding, the case against the integration of Tarahumara culture through drinking is not easy to establish. Tarahumara culture would be unrecognizable without it, and a sudden and effective prohibition of drinking would shatter it greatly, if not completely. Alcoholism among the Tarahumaras is unknown, and accidents and abuses under its influence are as rare as among us. Further, drinking has many positive values to us unknown. It brings the Tarahumaras those values and spiritual releases that other peoples get from a deep and cultural heritage far beyond the Tarahumara ken. Two hundred years of work by Catholic missionaries, equipped with one of the richest of religious cultures of emotional satisfactions and spiritual release, has made but little impression upon Tarahumara drinking. The Indians near the missions merely return to their *rancherías* to do their serious drinking, which must follow a "Catholic" ceremony. Certainly the government teachers will make much less impression with the intellectualistic philosophy of Voltaire and their socialistic education.

The case for the "spurious" quality of the Tarahumara articulation of their culture around drunkenness lies in the bleak, drab tone of Tarahumara life with its starkness of cultural simplicity utterly primitive in all its features. It is a vicious cycle: the drabness encourages the escape through drunkenness; the drunkenness encourages the drabness.

The Sierra Tarahumara is not so infertile that an ecology based on wheat and potatoes could not be made to furnish a surplus of wealth which in turn would support a richer, more beautiful culture. Or if such a shift in the economic base of culture is too much to expect of a primitive people, there are the possibilities of cultural development through the little terraces that the Tarahumaras make in the gorges. The hill tribes in the Philippines have had the industry to erect terrace systems for agriculture which seem to hang in the clouds and which support a social and religious life much richer than that of the Tarahumaras. The tribes under the Incas of Peru raised their culture to the threshold of a civilization by building terraces in their difficult mountains.

The weakness in integrating a "spurious" culture by drunkenness is that drunkenness always gives the easy illusion of values which do not exist. As a compensation for the lack of "genuine" cultural values, drunkenness successfully defeats the accomplishment of them. To this more than to anything else must be attributed the naked and primitive simplicity of Tarahumara life and its cultural round of activities and thought.

That the "spurious" elements of Tarahumara culture fail to satisfy the individual is shown by the fact that, upon contact with the Mexicans, the Tarahumaras drop their customs for those of their "neighbors," as they term the Mexicans. The Tarahumara on association with Mexicans comes to speak Spanish even in his home, though Tarahumara is still his native tongue. This implies the gradual acceptance of the whole gamut of Mexican culture. Tarahumaras have made these simple changes, and most of those who have lived in the gorges, where they can, work with or for the Mexicans. But Tarahumara culture in its aboriginal patterns is still an animate native concern, and more centuries will likely pass before even the simple Mexicanization of the Tarahumara will be complete. Tarahumara culture appears more genuine than spurious. That is why it has lasted so long and still gives such strong indications of survival in competition with Mexican folk culture.

CHAPTER 17

The Philistine Spirit of
Tarahumara Culture

If we look into the thing closely we shall find that the term Philistine conveys a sense that makes it more peculiarly appropriate to our middle class than our aristocratic. For Philistine gives the notion of something particularly stiff-necked and perverse to light and its children; and therein it especially suits our middle class, who not only do not pursue sweetness and light; but even prefer to them that sort of machinery of business, chapels, tea meetings, and addresses from Mr. Murphy, which make up the dismal and illiberal life on which I have so often touched. . . .

MATTHEW ARNOLD

The Tarahumaras, like the middle classes which Matthew Arnold berated, have a culture thoroughly philistine in its genius and ethos. Webster's Dictionary gives a sufficient definition of philistine to suit our purpose:

> Philistine: A person lacking liberal culture and refinement; one not appreciating the nobler aspirations and sentiments of humanity; a person esp. of the middle class who rejects enlightenment or is indifferent to the higher interests, preferring the material and commonplace; one whose scope is limited to selfish and material ends.

The "genuine" values of Tarahumara culture are philistine values, and they arise from a realistic orientation of Tarahumara culture to a thrifty exploitation of the natural environment. The genius of Tarahumara culture is not only realistic but also materialistic, both of which are philistine characteristics. Agriculture and animal husbandry are intelligently pursued by every man, woman, and almost every child in the tribe. Wild animals are hunted and trapped for food so effectively that game has become scarce. Tarahumaras have no inferiority complex about it. The animal world is productive of no mystical meanings and connotations. The utilization of the floral resources of the sierra is hardly less unimaginative and realistic. Though it is true that certain plants like peyote and jimsonweed are imbued with strong spirits by the Tarahumara mind to account for their otherwise unintelligible properties, yet plants are realistically treated as herbals and samples for remedies, rather than in an elaborate religious complex, such as peyote is treated among the Huichols. Peyote is treated by the Tarahumaras, as becomes the philistine, as a cure for disease and a source of power great enough to foil the bad spirit of jimsonweed and make caves again fitting for dwellings. Tarahumaras, unlike the Huichols, do not appreciate flowers for their beauty or fragrance; nor do they consider them as symbols of growth, fertility, femininity, or increase.

The attitudes of the individual Tarahumara are consistent with the genius of his culture. Wealth is prized, even though it is not displayed. In fact, the social status of the Tarahumara depends more on his wealth than anything else. Only the medicine men gain prestige without it; but they collect enough for their ceremonies to get into the upper brackets of Tarahumara society.

The evaluation of the individual Tarahumara by his fellows is directly proportionate to the number of cattle in his herd. If this number is adequate he has, as Lorenzo expressed it in Spanish, *con que*—"that which." In Tarahumaraland having "that which it takes to get along" is as important as among the philistine classes of our own civilization. A want of thrift displayed by selling cattle rather than keeping them for their fertilizer is as despised by the Indians as dissipation of capital is by us; for thriftlessness leads to the poverty of actual hunger among the Tarahumaras, whose economic organization is simple in structure and direct in operation.

The Tarahumaras deal with cases of poverty and want in a thoroughly realistic and directly philistine manner. A needy family is put to work and is passed around the community among the thrifty Indians who have work to be done. Poor lads who have inherited no cattle or have wasted their patrimony work for rich Indians as peons, and often marry their daughters. So thoroughly philistine is Tarahumara culture, however, that this benefits their children, but not themselves. Spouses do not inherit from each other.

The Tarahumara community reveals individual philistines among the philistines. The attitude of the older and rich men and their cabal against the hail-fellow-well-met Indian who governed the community reeked with capitalism. Lorenzo's horror of the possibility of the Mexican agrarian policy being applied to his herd of cattle had all the hard logic of philistine argument. Demonstrating less logic but even a stronger philistine attitude was the community's callous treatment of the *mayor*, who was reduced to marked poverty by his valuable, altruistic duties to the community. This treatment was strangely similar to a familiar treatment among ourselves of those whose fortunes disappear in the stock market or are swallowed up elsewhere.

In the thoroughly philistine culture of the Tarahumaras there is little place for the down-and-outer. Much less is there a place for the bohemian. In a primitive group with a culture as philistine as that of the Tarahumaras one has to search, virtually like Diogenes for an honest man, to find a bohemian. The Indian that rewarded my search was far from the perfect type. The two sons of rich old Anastacio had a few bohemian characteristics; they played the violin and guitar so well that their services were in demand at all beer parties. And even so, they were required to do their allotted portion of work in the cooperative labor that preceded the parties. They were none too skillful, and at one party, grudgingly and with some contempt, a powerful worker, adept with the axe, helped one of them finish his task of splitting *canoas* so that his more tender bohemian spirit might preside over the violin.

No better indication of the philistine ethos or spirit of Tarahumara culture is more apparent than the general pattern of penurious thrift, so strong that every Tarahumara cave wife keeps a small brush beside her *metate* to brush up the last crumbs of corn left from the grinding. Even in the ceremonies there is no waste, merely a good feed for all, no more.

Conspicuous display or consumption is a thoroughly philistine trait that the Tarahumaras can hardly afford. The struggle for sufficiency is too great. Due to their poverty and their timidity they make a thoroughly philistine virtue of their lack of conspicuous display, and keep their wealth hidden in their storehouses. Yet everyone seems to know of what the others have hidden. We heard of the saddle secreted in the rich Indian's corn house before we got to Umira, and all the time we were there this great prestige due to his wealth was constantly in our ears. The amusing exhibition of social competition between him and Lorenzo in the matter of dwellings patterned after Mexican types was as thoroughly philistine as our practice of keeping up with the Joneses on Main Street.

This wealthy Indian's desire to marry the pretty Mexican girl of the nearby settlement was completely philistine. She would be a possession, like the saddle; no other Indian could boast of a similar acquisition; and she would not have to be kept in the storehouse. Her beauty was of no consideration, because marital values among the Tarahumaras emphasize ability at the *metate* and loom. Her unavailability for these utilitarian features of Tarahumara marriage merely emphasizes the timidity which inhibited the urge for display. Yet it must have been that which motivated that cunning old Indian, who proved not without charm as he sat incognito so long on our woodpile.

In summary, the "genuine" values of Tarahumara culture are philistine and are outstanding in the material culture that adjusts the individual to his natural environment. Also in social competition, estimation, and prestige Tarahumara values emerge directly from the material aspects of their culture. In the realm of the purely social, the "spurious" values of the philistine obtrude at every hand among the Tarahumaras. It is in the social and religious realms that we find the preference for "chapels, tea meetings, and addresses from Mr. Murphy. . . ."

This last phrase from Arnold's description of the philistine almost perfectly characterizes the Tarahumara beer-drinking ceremonies around the Catholic chapel with a sermon by the *gobernador*, during which Tarahumara social life reaches its highest excitement and widest integration. Particularly is this so in the Christmas and Holy Week cycles. Yet until the Indians are drunk, they remain grave and silent, wrapped in their blankets, apparently in communion with the stones on which they squat. In their socioreligious life the Tarahumaras out-philistine the philistines.

Besides the organization in the community, there are two other fundamental social groups among the Tarahumaras—the family, and the neighborhood drinking-group for cooperative labor. In these narrower and more intimate social relationships the Tarahumaras are incredibly philistine, even more so than in their communal life. So far as I could determine without getting married, there is no sentiment or romance to a Tarahumara marriage. And I never saw any evidence of tenderness, affection, or caressing, though public expressions of this are common enough among the Huichols, which shows that its public inhibition is not a general characteristic of primitive life. The nearest approximation I saw displayed of romance and sentiment in Tarahumara marriage was not too close. This was Lorenzo's apparently anticipatory remark about his wife when she was drunk: "Sober, the Tarahumara women are very *bronco* [sic]; but drunk, they are gentle enough."

Among the Tarahumaras, marriage is a "tough-minded" relationship arising from the economic interdependence of the sexes. Men need blankets woven and food prepared; women need their fields plowed and looked after. The strong economic orientation of Tarahumara marriage is clear from Dr. Bennett's detailed account; but it is fairly suggested in the foregoing.

Children are always put out of bed early to herd the animals. Waifs and orphans become peons for this work.

In the social structure second in importance to the Tarahumara family is the neighborhood group, which constantly meets for the final end of drinking, in itself a philistine characteristic. Even more typically philistine is the primary function of this group, namely, cooperative labor. By this socioeconomic institution everyone "takes in the other's wash." Far from trivial in Tarahumara culture, the drunken working bee is the keystone of Tarahumara economic and industrial life.

Sometimes natives themselves express the ideals of their culture. A Huichol told Lumholtz that "to hunt deer and give the corn ceremonies, that is to lead the perfect life." No Tarahumara expressed so concretely or aptly the ethos of Tarahumara life; but his epitome would be to "work hard and get drunk." This impression conveys a philistine attitude of glorification of industry, which Tarahumara culture expresses not only in the compulsory pattern of attending *tesgüinadas* for cooperative labor, but also in the industry of the bee. This belief came out in the following incident.

One day some bees were attracted to some wild honey that an Indian was straining, and got mired in it more effectively than flies in flypaper. Having myself something of a philistine attitude toward industry, I took a twig and started to help them out. The Indian halted me, thinking either that I was too rough or about to harm the honey-covered bees. He took the twig and tenderly rescued them. "Bees are delicate," he said. "They are of God. They work hard to give us honey [the only Tarahumara sweet] and wax for our candles [used in the Catholic religious ceremonies]." Industry, sweets, and wax for candles, these three roots bear up the prestige of the honey bees; but the greatest of the three is industry.

In summary, the social life of the Tarahumaras is philistine to the core. This is to be seen in the Tarahumara community centering around the Catholic chapel, the family-group, and the neighborhood drinking-group. In all these features the spirit of Tarahumara culture is "particularly stiff-necked and perverse to light and its children. . . ."

By contrast to what it might be, Tarahumara religion is conspicuously philistine. Religion, as a powerful minister to the human spirit, can be a source of emotional and aesthetic values of real beauty and charm, expressing aspirations and sentiments noble, genuine, and deep. Not so Tarahumara religion. Its mysticism is so crude as to be scarcely rationalized into simple intelligibility. Again, often in primitive religions dreams are considered a source of mystical power which, among some tribes, spurs the individual on to superhuman prowess, genuine bravery and deep spiritual resourcefulness. But the religious dreams of the Tarahumaras are philistine, crass, material, and commonplace. By them the Tarahumara learns, for example, that a child is sick because the water serpent has stolen its spirit. The remedy has the same materialistic flavor. By paying the water serpent, by dreaming of a horse, the child's spirit will be released. Or a Tarahumara dreams the cattle are talking among themselves that a rain ceremony should be given to bring water to the crops and the pasturage, a purely materialistic dream, philistine in conception.

The Tarahumaras' conception of their ceremonies is just as philistine as their dreams. They think that dancing and vigorous muscular activity carried to the point of exhaustion, together with offerings of food and beer, will bring them into favor with the gods. Drunkenness, the invariable concomitant of the Tarahumara ceremony, attests an even more striking failure to grasp some of the subtler spiritual resources of religion.

That the subtler spiritual values can be grasped within the confines of primitive religion was clearly revealed in my year among the Huichols. The Huichols happily serve their hosts of gods and goddesses with drama, mythology, song, dance, and a wide gamut of the plastic arts really artistic in conception and execution.

The Tarahumaras as philistines of the philistines could be expected to have no art, and indeed this is true. The primitive drama of beautiful ceremony; the epic narration of mythology, expressed in deep, resonant song; the ecstasy of dance, with large groups participating in religious rhythms of coordinated movement; painting, sculpture, and design, all coherently expressing the vital aspirations and sentiments of the group in forms of artistic value—all this artistic expression is absent in Tarahumara life. Yet the Huichols, the neighbors and linguistic cousins of the Tarahumara, have it all in a perfect symbolism of a genuine and harmonious life and of the noble quality of their living together.

Tarahumara culture is tolerant to a degree that seems urbane when compared with that of many primitive groups. It robs no individual of that sense of personal dignity which is sufficiently a salient characteristic of the North American Indian to have merited for him the title of "noble" from all who have known him well.

CHAPTER 18

▶ *Adiós Tarahumaras*
▶
▶ *and Campfire Stories of Villa*
▶
▶
▶
▶
▶
▶
▶
▶

However many "spurious" values were being revealed in American civilization as it scraped new bottoms in 1930, still after nine months among the Tarahumaras I was glad to prepare to leave for home. I had recorded the ceremony given to "cure the fields and animals." And for a couple of weeks I had been busy in locating, uncovering, and describing the archaeological sites in the vicinity of Quírare, the community of Tarahumaras who boasted of being pagans because they had resisted the overtures of the padres who had tried to get them to build a church. The archaeological finds were abundant, though they all belonged to the Cave-Dweller phase. Enough material had accumulated to occupy all the animals of my muleteer, "Pancho Villa." So I sent him on to Creel with his animals loaded with the remains and effects of the ancient Tarahumaras. The yield of my last few days' work could be carried by Tarahumara *cargador* until "Pancho" met me in Samachique on his return.

I had other designs of course in wishing "Pancho" to go on ahead. There was the necessity for secrecy in the last stages of the negotiations I was carrying on with the Indians in reference to their lands. A word from my muleteer, and knowledge of the plot would have spread like wildfire among the Mexican communities of the Sierra Tarahumara. At this last stage of the business I had little relish for the thought of being shot down like a deer by some irate Mexican from behind a tree or boulder.

Two weeks earlier a runner had come to my camp from "General" Jaris, the Indian who had made such an outstanding place for himself because of his leadership and his agitation against Mexican usurpation of Indian land. The runner brought a letter written in Spanish which the Indian "General" had dictated to the padre. Since I had last seen Jaris, the brutal attack by marauding Mexicans on the rich Tarahumara had occurred, uniting all the Indians in fear and hatred of the atrocity. The Indians were so timid and fearful, however, that they took no direct action. But they communicated with me, because they knew that I would soon be leaving the sierra and could present their grievances to the government of Chihuahua.

The letter said that the headmen of five villages would meet me wherever I wished. The *gobernadores* of Quírare and of Samachique had been informed, and had come to my camp with the runner. The padre wrote that he would be in the neighborhood of Samachique as a meeting place. This was directly on my way to Chihuahua, so I appointed a day for our meeting. The two *gobernadores* were glad to earn twenty-five *centavos* a day carrying on to Samachique the *membra disjecta* and the cultural remains of their ancestors which I had rescued for science from the caves of the vicinity. Neither of them talked Spanish, but I told them when to return for me, utilizing as an interpreter the runner from "General" Jaris.

Would they return to guide me? I had been in the sierra for nine months, but I was still a child in following the crisscross of trails that led to Samachique. From there to Creel the ground was more familiar. I thought of the half-breed I had kicked out of the Indians' house. I could have got him to guide me, though I should hardly have cared to camp all night with him. Still, he would be a last resort if the officials didn't appear.

I was counting not so much on the *gobernador* of Quírare as on the headman of Samachique, who lived in the vicinity at the very edge of the community of Samachique, which he governed. He was the same hail-fellow-well-met person to whom Bennett and I had given shirts on our first Sunday in the sierra. How long ago that seemed nine months later! We had become good friends, this *gobernador* and I, and I was pleased when he had been reelected *gobernador* of Samachique during Holy Week. The cabal of the plutocracy of Samachique had not prevailed against his great popularity with the rabble.

However both *gobernadores* appeared early in the morning of the day appointed. In sign language I got them to round up my trusty mount, "Rocinante." It was play for them, accustomed to running down deer, to bring in the collection of skin and bones that was to carry me to Samachique.

I had everything calculated to the last detail. I had eaten all my food, save two cans of peaches, some cheese that I had purchased from the Córdobas, and some *tortillas* furnished me by the Indians. A blanket, my camera and my rifle, and a saddlebag of odds and ends constituted my personal effects. "Rocinante" carried all this, while my Indian *cargadores* handled the large boxes of archaeological remains.

It was at this time that the half-breed Mexican-Tarahumara, who was the villain of the expedition, got his revenge for my treatment of him. While working for me he had stolen a belt with a solid silver buckle. It was of no value to him, since he wore only the typical Tarahumara clout; but he could still sell it for a few *centavos*. I noted its loss only when I was packing up my scant *lares* and *penates* for this final trip. So I sent the *gobernador* of Quírare on ahead, and with the *gobernador* of Samachique called at the nearby *ranchería* of this scamp. Fortified by the official representative of law and order, as such are understood in the Tarahumara community of Samachique, I thought I would so impress the miscreant that he would return the belt, if only in memory of the time he and his mother had been tied up and taken to the nearest Mexican town for trial for theft. Then, too, I wished to see how this half-breed would act in a pinch, because he was an outstanding individual in the community, due to his past and his mixed blood. He could speak Spanish, and he whined and cringed and behaved as a veritable Uriah Heep. But I didn't get my belt.

So my friend, the *gobernador*, availed me nothing; except he was a good guide and led me faithfully along the high, cool mountain trail toward our old bailiwick, Samachique. It was pleasant at first, riding along through that parklike forest of great pines. But it soon became tiresome, because in the rugged terrain one's mount can go no faster than a walk. From sheer ennui one counts the trees, calculates the time necessary to reach outstanding landmarks along the way, and pines for civilization, however "spurious" it may be. What I missed most on these long trips were not the theaters, the libraries, or the museums. The very epitome of civilization became in my mind's eye the Illinois Central Suburban Electric, that in twenty minutes will carry one as far as I could make in a day's journey on my mount. Samachique and Chicago are about the same size in area; but what a difference in getting from the outskirts of Samachique to its center and in getting from Chicago's suburbs to the Loops!

One slight misadventure occurred on our way to Samachique. The *gobernador* was walking on ahead to lead me. Suddenly, betrayed by his flimsy sandals, he slipped on some loose gravel and fell back on his haunches, his sitting favored by the box he was carrying on his back, his sitter protected only by the curious diaper-like triangle of cloth that all Tarahumara men drape over their buttocks. Encumbered as he was, he was on his feet again almost as quickly as he had fallen. Knowing the pride of the Tarahumaras for their prowess in covering ground, I pretended throughout to be wholly absorbed in the distant horizon off to one side. As he arose, he gave me a shamed glance, which I barely saw from the corner of my eye; but soon he became happy and reassured in the thought that I had not seen the mishap.

As darkness gathered, we arrived back at the "Loop" of Samachique. The little church and *convento* in which Bennett and I had lived for four months stood lonely and deserted. The Indians would not be in until tomorrow. And late as it was, the Bishop and my friend the padre had not yet arrived. Setting aside the largest separate room of the *convento* for the Prince of the Church, in another room a short while later the *gobernador* and I had a fire lighted. This was the room in which I had passed more than a hundred happy nights.

Water was soon boiling in the tin can which served me for a coffee-pot, and into it I dropped a heaping tablespoonful of Mexican coffee, roasted black as midnight. The Mexican technique of making coffee is to rescue the can from the fire just before its contents boil over, and settle the finely cut coffee grounds with a dash of cold water. Then the can is put by the side of the fire to simmer while the coals of the fire are arranged for heating *tortillas*.

If the reader has any doubts about the fitness for mild and academic persons such as I, of the thick, coarsely ground *tortillas* of the Tarahumaras washed down with coffee, he misjudges both the appetite that is engendered by a day in the saddle and the culinary possibilities of the cheese which the Mexicans curdle from goat milk. The thick *tortillas* are first slit along the side, where they have been blistered on a hot griddle, so that the slit exposes a neat little pocket. Cheese is powdered between the hands, and then packed into the pocket. Folded over for a *taco*, the *tortilla* is placed on the hot coals, and the cheese melts to a delicious rarebit. After a long day's ride this delicacy eaten with swallows of coffee is nothing less than ambrosia and nectar.

So weep no tears for my meal in my old quarters at Samachique, for I have never eaten better. In fact, earlier on the expedition I had ordered *tacos* instead of the caviar and rarest of anchovies which a friend had sent from home in a Christmas box that got to us about

Holy Week due to delay in customs. The Christmas box arrived at camp just at the time I was coming in with a load of archaeological loot that I had carried for some miles. I was so ravenous that it would have been a shame to waste the delicacies on my monumental appetite, so I ordered *tacos* of cheese. The caviar and anchovies I carried to the mission, where an *hermano* cooked a meal especially fit to follow such hors d'oeuvres.

This evening in the deserted *convento*, *tortillas* and cheese were a prelude to a clatter of mules in the distance to announce the arrival of the Bishop and the padre. They soon rode into the church compound, and what a retinue followed them! There were two or three *arrieros* to take care of the well-caparisoned and provisioned sumpter mules; and with the fine mules ridden by the Bishop and the padre, the entire mulecade contrasted greatly with the miserable *caballo* of the Tarahumara expedition. Science was eclipsed by religion in these Tarahumara mountains.

The Bishop and my very good friend, the padre, rode booted and spurred under great Mexican *sombreros*. Under the *sombrero* of the Bishop, however, was the little red skullcap symbolic of his office. After he dismounted, he donned a cassock from his saddlebag. The cassock bore a thin red stripe down the front as an additional mark of his estate.

In contrast to the Jesuits, who had treated me like a fellow, the Bishop was a pompous soul, who acted as if he were accustomed to snubbing anthropologists every day of his life. He kept the padre so busy that not until midnight was the padre free to steal into my room for a word and a cordial handshake. The padre was shocked at my miserable condition.

I must have been a sight with my three months' beard, and with all my supplies and equipment crammed into a small saddlebag. So accurate had been my calculations as to needs that I had worn out all my clothes save overalls, a jumper, and boots. When the padre came in, I was asleep on my saddle blanket, wrapped in another blanket and using the saddle for a pillow. He carried a candle, and we talked until it went out, almost at dawn. There was much to say about many things, including the question of Indian lands.

As the half-breed Indian had his revenge on me, so I had mine on the pompous Bishop, though I didn't steal his belt. Indeed, I don't think he was aware of what I was up to. Mexican bishops not only travel in state, but they are generally met with swept streets, improvised arches, and fireworks. For his coming, however, Samachique was as quiet as a tomb. Not a solitary Indian received him. But the next day the headmen of five villages arrived from many miles away to talk to me and bid me "*Adiós*." The expedition to the Tarahumaras was not a complete failure.

Early the next morning my *arriero*, "Pancho Villa," arrived at Samachique by prearrangement. But he failed to bring the food that I had ordered from Creel. Since I knew the trail from Samachique back to the railhead, I ordered him to pack the archaeological effects and get started. This would keep him away from my Indian fellow-conspirators. I gave him the last of the *tortillas* and some *tamales* which the *gobernador* had given me. The *tamales* enter the story later. I planned to have the padre rob the sumpter mules of his excellency, the Bishop of Chihuahua, to supplement my solitary remaining can of peaches. Needless to say, this was brought about.

By the middle of the morning "General" Jaris appeared. He guided me to an isolated house where the headmen were sitting, gravely wrapped in their blankets, waiting for me. Childlike, they had forgotten to bring an interpreter, and so had come for nothing but to tell me "Good-bye." But aided by their meager fund of Spanish, which they pooled for communication with me, and with numerous signs, I did my best to explain that with the padre I had gone into the details of Mexican barbarity against the Tarahumaras. I assured them that I would see the Mexican governor of Chihuahua who had been so kind as to give me a letter of introduction, and who had satisfied me that he was a friend of the Indians. This he had proved by having sent several carloads of corn to the sierra to relieve the Indians of the pinch of hunger they were feeling due to the crop failure of the year before.

When I had finished my half-pantomimic harangue, finally, with genuine feeling so rare among the Tarahumaras, each of the headmen approached me in turn and gave me his curious Tarahumara rendition of the Mexican *abrazo*, which they use only with Indians in the special social relationship of *norahua*, and with the fellows of their community just before they are about to disband after the Christmas ceremonial round, as I have already mentioned. With the Tarahumaras this gesture is used as a sign that they are breaking with a warm bond of feeling which unites them with their friends and fellows. I was touched both by the gesture and the display of feeling that went with it, especially since these Indians are generally so silent, unresponsive, and undemonstrative. After this, with an unrecognizable Tarahumara version of the phrase "*Dios cuida*" ("God take care of you"), they started off in Indian fashion, one behind the other, on the trail to their respective *rancherías.*[1]

Last meetings with friends, however small a part they may have played in one's life, are always painful; and when the rearmost Indian had disappeared from view, a feeling of loneliness crept over me. I was sorry that my nine months' stay in the sierra was drawing to a close. Four months of the time had been spent in this very valley. Every nook, every trail, almost every tree and rock had assumed a personal identity for me. In a mood of nostalgia I spent the rest of the day hiking over the place, which in memory I have often revisited.

Puffs of clouds dotted the miraculously blue sky; and the trees lay on the distant hills like green patches. In this tree, I mused, a wildcat had savagely clawed itself out of my steel trap. From that high rock I had blazed away at a fox with bird-shot which had merely peppered it. There near the river, I had seen the Tarahumara standing with his sandals in his hand, resting for a moment as he ran down a deer. Along another trail I had passed the little playhouse of the Tarahumara children. Like many of the houses of their elders, it was in ruins now. In yonder cave I had first got drunk with the Indians, and there I had suffered myself to be "cured" by the shaman, who had sucked "maggots" out of my neck.

Above, on the little mesa, was the *camposanto,* the holy field in which I had helped to bury Patricio, and where, hidden from our eyes, had been enacted the last act of tragedy of the brother and sister who had shocked the community to its depths. All was over now. The scandal had quieted; Patricio had been "despatched"; the new crops of wheat would soon be ripe enough to allay the hunger of the famished Indians; and the corn for winter use was already half-grown. Almost a year had come and gone since we had come to Samachique; and tomorrow I would be leaving for good.

Though I knew the valley well enough, still, as it turned out, my knowledge of the country beyond was faulty. Early the next morning, the *mozos* of the ecclesiastical train saddled "Rocinante" together with their animals. Then, after the padre and I had taken pictures of each other as a final *recuerdo,* we departed the church on separate trails. The last Samachique *ranchería* which I passed was that of the rich old *ex-gobernador,* Anastacio, who, I had heard, was suffering from an infected leg. As I moved by, I called out; but I received no answer. Yet from within his shelter he must have been watching me closely.

At the edge of his *ranchería* the trail, which I had often followed with Lorenzo, drops into the *barranca*. I must have been absorbed in my thoughts, for I wandered completely away from it, and went on until I was recalled by gray-haired old Anastacio, who had seen me go astray and had hobbled out to the dividing place to call me back. He limped badly, and supported himself with a stick as he pointed out the trail that I should have followed. "*Dios cuida*," he said.

"God take care of you, Anastacio," I thought, waving in reply. And then, "*Adiós*, Samachique."

It was my last sight of Samachique, its people, that noble old Indian leaning on his staff, as I dropped down the trail. I think he was as sad as I was.

On my previous journey the *gobernador* had a mishap. This time my horse, "Rocinante," was the unfortunate. We traveled along at a more or less even gait until we came to where my Mexican *arriero* suggested an alternative route which necessitated a dangerous scramble over a high smooth rock, so I dismounted and led "Rocinante" over the difficult place.

If my mood on leaving Samachique emulated that of the Sad Knight, my mount "Rocinante" chose this occasion to emulate Dapple, the mule of Sancho Panza, when Sancho was leaving Barataría, the land he had governed. In short, Dapple tumbled into a very deep hole. And likewise, clambering over the smooth trail of rock which led up to the crown of the great boulder, "Rocinante" came to grief, and slipped and fell. The fall came so suddenly that I was unable to help the poor beast, even though I was holding on to his bridle; and he slipped slowly over the side of the huge rock, and landed fifteen feet below, wedged into a narrow ravine, partially on his back with his four feet held ludicrously skyward. He lay quietly, looking at me as much to say, "Well, you got me into this; now get me out."

It was a problem. First I cut the girth strap and pulled the saddle off, which was hardly scratched. "Rocinante" seemed to be uninjured, despite his long slide down the rock. But he was still on his back. The solution was obviously that of getting him sufficiently righted to permit him to use his legs.

So while the horse most intelligently lay still (horses or mules used to the sierra behave well under difficulties), I braced my back against the sharp bank of the ravine, placed my feet securely against the skinny ribs of my turn-turtle horse, and pushed with all the power of my legs, hoping to get the animal's center of gravity into some proximity to its underpinning. In the meantime I called to the horse, which had fully got the idea. In a sensible rather than violent fashion he began to scramble with his legs. Then, as a Japanese juggler treads a barrel in the air, my feet fairly walked around "Rocinante," while he struggled, righted himself, and finally got to his feet. It was nice teamwork throughout, because any sudden or uncontrolled spasm might have caused the horse to fall on me. In more than one sense "Rocinante" rose to the occasion; and rider, horse, and saddle all escaped without hurt.

But "Pancho," the owner of "Rocinante," told me plenty when he found the girth strap cut and only tentatively repaired. However, "Pancho" couldn't say much about the mishap, because earlier in the day on the same trail his feet had slipped out from under him, just as had happened to the *gobernador* on the way to Samachique. He was carrying my rifle, and in his fall cracked the stock. Thus honors were more even. And well it was, for I had calculated everything so closely that there would have been no money to pay for the horse had it been injured. "Pancho" would have been obliged to take the rifle, though at that he would have got the best of the deal.

About this same time Bennett was having his troubles also. On the trip that had kept him separated from me for the last month, one of his pack mules went over the cliff of a gorge and fell, madly pawing the air, until it landed on its head far below. Fortunately for the animal, the fall snapped its neck. And luckily, the pack was not damaged, since it carried a very expensive motion picture camera. Only the mule had to be paid for.

As I had planned, that evening I overtook my muleteer at the bottom of the gorge near the hanging bridge. His pack mules had made the dangerous descent without misadventure. They carried two boxes of archaeological remains which Dr. Bennett had collected for the Milwaukee Museum. Among these effects was a bundle of blankets. These the Indians had been willing to sell because, now that summer was almost here, their need for corn was greater than their need for blankets.

During the past months I had accommodated myself to a couch made of a mere saddle blanket spread on the hard, rocky ground. This night I slept on the soft sand of the riverbank. That well-known sentimental ballad about loving someone until the sands of the desert grow cold bespeaks a very fickle love. Overnight, sand cools from a heat that will fry an egg to a coldness that will go through several blankets. But with a baker's dozen of blankets over me, and several under me, the sand seemed soft and yielding after my many sierra bivouacs. It was here under this hanging bridge that Bennett and I had spent our first night out of doors in the sierra.

Before noon the following day "Pancho" and I had climbed over the first wall of the gorge and had reached the *ranchería* of my Tarahumara mentor and guide, Lorenzo. The last time I had seen him was when I had started from his place on my wide circle of archaeological research. Months had passed since then. Now the circle was completed, and my studies of the antiquity of the Tarahumaras were finished.

Lorenzo's new house, built in emulation of that of his rich neighbor, was finished too. When I arrived, he was inside putting the finishing touches to the floor of soft mud plaster. I remember this distinctly, because on a shelf in the rear of the house I had left a glass jar of preserved rattlesnakes and other "mixed pickles" of my zoological collection. They may be there still, since I couldn't wait for the floor to dry to get them.

Lorenzo greeted me with the genuine but undemonstrative regard that he felt for me. His wife, who was no whit changed, acted as if she had never seen me before, and, without saying a word, walked off to herd her goats. I daresay she didn't appreciate the many beer parties to which I had taken Lorenzo as a paid companion.

Lorenzo took me to his storehouse, where the remains of the expedition's equipment were stored, among which were a few tins of canned food. My returning to the storehouse was like an Arctic explorer's coming upon a carefully planned cache, though to tell the truth I had completely forgotten about the food.

Lorenzo was still the incomparable informant. On my recent trip with the *gobernadores* I had seen a cornfield festooned with long strings of palm leaf upheld by crisscross sticks. The *gobernadores* were unable to tell me the function of the palm leaf, because they did not speak Spanish. The strings, however, reminded me of a device the Igorots use in their rice fields for frightening birds away from the filling heads of grain. When I described the Tarahumara setup to Lorenzo, he informed me that it had the analogous function of frightening away the birds. By so simple a device the Tarahumaras outwit the cunning ravens of the sierra, who are so smart that they outsmart themselves by not entering a field thus provided for fear of a trap that doesn't exist. The Zuni Indians use the same trick.

I chatted with Lorenzo a brief while, and then had to start to overtake my mule train. I wished to give him a farewell present, but the only thing that came to hand was a good but inexpensive German pocketknife. This I gave him before we touched hands and said, "*Dios cuida.*" In his dignity of quiet self-reliance and respect I thus left Lorenzo, my friend and teacher to whom I am most indebted for whatever I know and understand of the Tarahumaras. In the long months of our friendship he had never begged, whined, or threatened. Tactful and kind, he had often dropped me quiet hints on how to meet Tarahumara etiquette. My unexpected gift, a thing of great value to him, both surprised and pleased him. So we parted as we had been from the first, the best of friends.

Farewell Tarahumaras!

"Pancho" and I soon passed the Mexican settlement of Basiaurichi. The Mexican family at the old station asked me to take their picture and send them a copy in care of the teacher at the isolated Indian school. Years before, some American mining engineer had done this. I have forgotten his name, but they still blessed it. Now that their children were grown, however, they needed a new picture, and so I took one of them. In due time I sent it to them as they requested; but whether they received it and now bless my name is a problem awaiting the investigation of the next anthropologist who visits that region in the next twenty years.

We were rapidly leaving Tarahumaraland, soon to be in Mexico again. That evening "Pancho" and I sat beside a roaring fire that drove back the keenness of the night air. Just about dusk a Mexican of the upper class passed with his wife. Since they had no pack mule with supplies and camp equipment, I asked them to camp with us, thinking that they might appreciate the blankets that I was carrying with me. Contrary to the camaraderie of the trail the man curtly refused my hospitality, saying that he and his wife would continue on to the Indian school of Cusárare. I was offended, and thought, "You may wish you had borrowed some of my blankets."

After they had gone, "Pancho" and I fell to talking about his own namesake, the famous Pancho Villa. No prophet is a hero in his own land; nor is Villa now a hero in his own Chihuahua. Popular books on Villa romanticize him as a great revolutionary figure enshrined in the bosoms of the Chihuahua peons; but I never heard a good word for him in Chihuahua.

The following story that "Pancho" told in a hushed and indignant voice is typical of the stories about Villa.

In the beginning of the Revolution before Villa had *mucho gente* [sic], his band rode up to a little settlement where he knew the people. He called for an acquaintance to come and join his army. The man appeared and explained to Villa that he had four children, and thus could hardly join him, however much he wished to. Villa ordered the man to send for his children. The peon did so, glad that the great *bandido* was interested in them. When the children appeared and lined up bashfully before him, Villa's eyes began to whirl like pinwheels. Suddenly he drew his pistol and shot the children down. Then with exaggerated politeness he turned to the father and said, "Now there is nothing to hinder your following me."

The story probably is not true; but it is typical of the lore that is accumulating around the now half-legendary figure of Pancho Villa. Villa may perhaps be romanticized in the cities; but to the poor folk of the sierras of Chihuahua who knew him or were looted by his followers, his name is anathema.

"Pancho" told me another story which I subsequently checked with an American mining man of the American Smelting and Refining Company, whom I met in a Pullman in Chihuahua three years later, and who assured me that the atrocity was witnessed by hundreds of people in the Chihuahua mining town of Santa Barbara.

Villa had killed a man, and his widow, with a baby in her arms, somehow got through the *escolta*, or escort, of Villa. From her *rebozo* she drew a pistol, and shot point blank at Villa. *¡Lastima!* she missed. So great was Villa's fear of this sort of assassination that he ordered her to be made an object lesson to the people of Santa Barbara, of Chihuahua, and of Mexico. Before hundreds of people in the plaza, the woman, with the child in her arms, was drenched with kerosene. Villa personally touched her off with a match.

Such are the stories of Villa in the region where he once ruled supreme.

It was just at this time, in 1930, that the Mexican government finally decided that the spirit of Villa was sufficiently dead to permit his body to be moved from Parral to the splendid sepulchre that had been built for it by "public spirited" citizens of the city of Chihuahua. So the body was exhumed. But, as all the Mexican papers carried the story, the head was lacking. Who got the head of Pancho Villa?

A prominent member of the American Masonic Order told me that his theory was that it had been obtained by some order of Masons who utilize in some of their ceremonies the skull of a great malefactor. *¿Quién sabe?* I discussed this also with the American of my Pullman conversation. He had lived in Parral during the latter years of Villa's meteoric career, and had seen Villa's gory, bullet-filled remains first in the car where he was shot, and later lying on a bed in the hotel, exposed to vulgar view. In both places the officials allowed and encouraged pictures to be taken, as if anxious for the people to know that the magic Villa was dead. The American I talked to suspected that, shortly after the burial, the head was stolen by two notorious American daredevils, who suddenly dropped into Parral on confidential business. Thus at any rate have the legends grown up about this revolutionary figure who during his brief sway held Chihuahua under his thumb.

Villa's power in Chihuahua was defeated only by assassination. It was this power as well as the blood-lust and killing which seemed to fit the morbid mood of the last stages of that horrible revolution. What was the magic exerted by that killer and bandit among people who are now so restrained and peaceful? What was the power that made fair women throw themselves at him, and honorable men, like the great General Angeles, honestly and respectfully follow in his train? I don't know, and no one in Mexico could ever tell me.

After the assassination of Madero, Villa rose rapidly from a bandit to the generalship of the Revolutionary Army of the North in the "Constitutional" forces headed by the civilian Carranza, the "First Chief," and his loyal subchief, Obregón, of Sonora. The Constitutional Revolution against Huerta, the usurper and assassin of Madero, was won July 15, 1914, when Huerta was ousted. Yet for three years more, Villa was to drench northern Mexico in blood, apparently motivated only by a desire to kill and loot. It doesn't make sense, but he had no plans, and did no permanently constructive things in the wide region he ruled for so long. Obviously he didn't want the presidency, because he sat in the thronelike chair in Mexico City for a day only, and then retired back to the North. From all I have been able to learn he was a maniac who lived merely to kill. Those I talked to who knew him invariably spoke of his strange eyes, which would revolve like pinwheels until he had killed someone with his own hands.

Apparently puffed with his military successes as a general under Carranza, he broke with his "First Chief" and set himself up as the ruler of Chihuahua, Durango, and Zacatecas. Obregón, however, remained faithful to the chief, whose failings he knew; and, as Secretary of War, he even made the courageous attempt to regain the loyalty of Villa for Carranza by bravely bearding Villa in his lion's den of Chihuahua. Insane with his military triumphs against "*La Cucaracha*" ("The Cockroach") Huerta, Villa was powerful enough in Chihuahua to arrest Obregón, and was on the verge of shooting him against an adobe wall.

The outcome to this could have happened nowhere but in Mexico. Raúl Madero, the brother of the assassinated President of Mexico, interceded with Villa for Obregón's life. It was this same Raúl Madero who, years before, had interceded for Villa's life when Villa, then an inconspicuous bandit and petty chieftain, had fallen into the hands of Huerta, the general commanding President Madero's troops. Another brother, Julio Madero, and the Villa generals, Eugenio Aguirre Benavides and Alesio Robles, also argued all that night with Villa that it would be fatal to all of them if they assassinated their superior, Obregón, the Secretary of War.

It was touch and go, because Villa dismissed them to return to their commands. He then appeared to release Obregón and his staff. Before they were safely out of Chihuahua, however, he wired orders ahead of their train to arrest them at Corralitos, on the border of Chihuahua, in Villa's domain. But as the Villista Colonel Garza was reversing the train, he was overpowered and locked in a Pullman stateroom. Then Obregón ordered the train out of Villa territory. So dangerous was Obregón's position that Benavides, the Villa general, forged Villa's name on a telegram releasing the train to permit it to pass over the Chihuahua frontier. But Obregón had already accomplished this with his pistol, in Mexican revolutions a more effective passport than a telegram.

Such was Villa's mastery over Chihuahua that Obregón, the Secretary of War and one of the greatest figures of the Mexican Revolution, came no nearer to death until years later when he fell before a successful assassin's pistol in a restaurant in San Angel at the beginning of his second term of office.

Why did the peons of Chihuahua never fail to answer the call of Villa's magic? I could never get one to even admit that he had fought for Villa. The memory of those years of destruction is obviously unpleasant. An educated Mexican of Chihuahua City told me that he had put the question to several of Villa's soldiers. The nearest to an answer that he received was when a peon retorted, "*Pues, señor,* my *compadre* asked me to come and help him."

Gruening, on the authority of Calles' Secretary, says of the motivation of the Madero revolt that some peons were yelling, "*¡Viva Madero! ¡Viva la democracia!*"

"And what, *amigo,* is this *democracia* for which all are shouting?" inquired a white-pajamaed peasant of another.

"Why it must be the lady who accompanies him," was the reply, pointing to Madero's wife.

The American reporter, Reed, who followed the Revolutionary Armies, gives other instances of what the soldiers thought they were fighting for.

"'What is that you wear on your coat?' inquired an American reporter, pointing to a Madero button on the breast of a youthful revolutionist, equipped with rifle and cartridge belt.

"'*¿Pues quién sabe, señor?*' he answered. 'My captain told me he is a great saint.'

"'What are you fighting for?' John Reed, an American correspondent, asked the color bearer of a troop.

"'Why it is good fighting. You don't have to work in the mines.'"

In the backwoods of Chihuahua I found no participants who even suggested that the followers of Villa were consciously fighting against oppression. Nor have I come across any such reasons for these struggles in the accounts of actual fighting that I have read. Even though the Terrazas family owned seventy million acres, mostly desert, of northern Chihuahua, there was much less oppression there than in the longer-settled regions such as Morelos. And my impression of Chihuahuans is that they would be difficult to oppress. So oppression and land hunger do not completely account for the fierce fighting in the north. There is still much good land in Chihuahua, held at such low prices that thrifty farmers are able to buy it. Mennonites from Canada bought enough land at a few pesos an acre to support a colony of ten thousand on a Canadian-American standard of living.

The charm of Villa did not completely wane in Chihuahua until photographs of his half-naked and bloody body were circulated throughout the state. Then, caught between the millstones of the opposition of the Mexican President, Carranza, and that of the American President, Wilson, the Villista force dwindled to a mere handful.

Initially, Villa had a cause, but he betrayed it when Adolfo de la Huerta and Obregón were about to begin the "revindicating" revolution to oust Carranza. Whatever Villa was fighting for, it was at least not the good of the peons; because he accepted the gift of several lordly *haciendas* near Parral on July 28, 1920.

Whether or not it was from fear of Villa's magic charm in Chihuahua, his assassination by a band of Mexicans obviously with governmental sanction was a fit punishment for his crimes. Another American engineer who was in Parral at the time vouches for the story that the only eligible candidates for the role of assassins were those whose families had suffered death at Villa's hands. Jesús Salas Barrazas, a Deputy in the State of Durango, announced himself as leader. He was released after a brief arrest.

On July 20, 1923, just before a Presidential election, which suggests that a political motive may have been mixed with the punitive one, Villa died as dozens had died at his hands. His killers had rented a house toward which Villa had to drive to enter Parral. With at least two bodyguards, Trillo and Contreras, Villa was making his way past the house in the old Dodge that he preferred to the charger of other days, when a hail of rifle bullets swept through the car. Ramón Contreras, though badly wounded, was not killed. But Pancho Villa II, whose real name was Doroteo Arango, was no more. Chihuahua has enjoyed a general unbroken peace since that day.

CHAPTER 19

▸ *Miners, Mennonites, Militarism,*
▸
▸ *and the Spirit of Mexico*
▸
▸
▸
▸
▸
▸
▸
▸
▸
▸

The day of our departure from the Sierra Tarahumara was at hand. Late the night before we heard the whistle of the approaching train. Nine months past we had heard the same sound, thinning out as it receded into the distance, and spelling freedom and surcease from a civilization upon which we had temporarily turned our backs. Now, however, it stirred within us old memories; it also brought hints almost of the novel, in our anticipation of a return, and we welcomed it and were eager to be off. Ere another nightfall we would be back in Chihuahua, which now seemed so remote that it might have been on another planet. Lighted streets, surging crowds, industry, arts, and civilization, these awaited us. But the day that still lay between us and all this was to be one of adventure.

We bought our tickets the evening before. When my turn came I had to wait for the uncongenial Mexican couple who had passed me on the trail. Congestion in the little Creel station was not so great that ordinarily I would have had to wait very long. But the man was paying for his ticket with raw silver which he sawed from a bar of bullion. There was a considerable argument about the price, and the man expressed fear that the rough scales used by the railroad agent were not accurate. Calculation had to be made as to the price of silver of such apparent fineness. So the Mexican was carrying bullion! No wonder he had refused my hospitality. I had feared that it was his wife whom he wished to guard from the rough contact of my camp, but no doubt it was the silver he wished to protect.

This couple were to plague my last night in Creel. Their room in the hotel was near mine, and throughout the night the man was sick as though in a nausea of drunkenness. He kept me awake with his terrible fits of vomiting. This did little to erase my first unpleasant impressions of him.

Long before dawn the next morning the train whistled again. In a short while we were on our way to Chihuahua. By a coincidence the American miner from Cusi, whom we had met on the upcoming train nine months before, was with us on the down-trip. He had been a week in the sierra investigating a gold mine. He remarked that Bennett and I were not as *tierno* ("tender") as we had looked on the up-trip.

We were wrapped in blankets against the cold of dawning, and still wearing beards to see how long we could brave civilization; and he didn't recognize us, even as Americans, until we recalled our previous trip together. His conversation most of the way down was lament over the low price of silver, then dragging bottom at twenty-nine cents an ounce.

Many of the American mining engineers of Mexico had gone to Russia, where they had got wonderful contracts with the Soviet government, then getting the Five Year Plan under way. If silver didn't go up, he was going to Russia too, because even the rich mine of Cusi was operating at a loss.

What an uncertain life is guaranteed those who follow the lure of quartz! Mexico, South America, China, Korea, and Russia beckon them on and on, like the fabulous pot of gold at the end of the rainbow. But the quest alone is all that is guaranteed them, even by the "American Smelting and Refining Company." That, and adventure and hardship and the trail that follows down the remotest "prospect."

Strange company. The Mexican miner and his wife who had refused the shelter of my camp and had sat all night before a small fire with but a single blanket to keep the cold away, and later had bought their railroad tickets with hunks of silver. The American, who was thinking of going to Russia. But a Mexican prospector on the train capped the climax. As has happened to me often enough before, he got me off alone and showed me some samples of ore. But what samples! He had a small glass vial filled with bright yellow gold dust and small gold nuggets.

His story was even better than his samples. He and a pardner had risked entering the Yaqui country, from the Tarahumara side, which is to the rear. They had washed these *ensayas* [sic] from the river sands. Their search lured them farther and farther into Yaqui country. However, the man who talked to me knew when he had gone far enough, gold or no gold.

But his pardner was of braver stuff. He had procured a priest's cassock, and planned to take advantage of the fact that the only Mexicans whom the sierra Yaqui accept are priests and escaped criminals. His plan took root. Dressed in his canonicals, he was accepted as a priest, and sent out the good news to his pardner, who was waiting at the Yaqui frontier. Then word stopped coming. When he inquired about gold, the Yaquis penetrated his disguise. He was lucky he was just killed; for the standard Yaqui treatment of hated Mexicans is to cut the skin from the soles of their feet and let them die by degrees walking in the stony cactus-strewn mountains.

What a price for that little tube of gold dust, and how many fantastic tragedies have been enacted in search of it! Cortez, bringing the first Whites to the country, told the first Aztec chief he met that "the Spaniards are troubled with a disease of the heart for which gold is a specific remedy." And alas for that Mexican Indian! All the gold in the world would not have cured him. Yet I was not as sorry as I might have been at this Yaqui treatment. Nor do I shudder today when I think of the usual manner in which the Yaquis dispose of those who venture too far into the only part of Mexico where the Indians still rule. For Cortez himself tortured the last of the Aztec princes by burning his feet.

But I wasn't interested in gold mines. Had I been tempted to invest a few hundred dollars, I might now be rich. Chihuahua, however, was a few hours ahead, and beginning with that night we were to go places and see things.

Returning to civilization after a few months of separation from it is an adventure. It is a slow process, involving days of travel by various conveyances, ranging from the animal to the mechanically motivated. Had we been suddenly translated from the pagan community of Quírare to Chicago, I think I would have fallen dead from shock. At least the experience wouldn't have been pleasant. In such matters, like good brandy the anticipatory bouquet is as good as the drink. At each stage of our return a familiar landmark appeared. Telegraph poles, the first store, the first town, and the cumulative effect of all these as we were whirled on toward civilization, for the "Kansas" seemed a veritable demon of speed after our months of riding dangerous trails on plodding, slow-footed mules.

It is unwise to judge people by first impressions. This I learned soon after the trip began, when I turned to talk to the Mexican couple, having exhausted the conversation of everyone else in the car. They were not married; the girl was his niece; and he had not been drunk the night before. He was being forced out of the sierra by a chronic affliction of the stomach, which gave him terrible fits of nausea. The car was not so crowded but that he could lie on the hard plank seat that extended the length of the car. When an attack came on, distressing to everyone, the girl with the greatest solicitude gave him a powder that quieted him.

On closer acquaintance, even under such difficulties, the man proved to be well-educated and refined. His life endangered, he had been forced out of the unhealthful *barranca* where his mine was located. When I told him that he had better forget to return, he said, "*Aguanto aunque me muero*" ("I will carry on even though I die"), a favorite phrase of his.

His niece was a little, sweet, demure, old-fashioned Mexican girl who had spent her life in the *barranca* mining camp, despite being of the better class. She wore the black of mourning for some distant kinsman, long since dead; and her head was covered with the black silk *rebozo* of the sort worn by middle-class women of the *ancién régime*. Her solicitude and kindness toward her uncle were genuine and deep, and when his attacks began, a look of pain and commiseration swept across her face, supplanting for a while the sweetness and tranquility of her more natural expression. How quickly she ran for a cup of water, and with what kind, loving hands she prepared the powdered medicine to allay his distress! In her *barranca* retirement she had missed all the modernity and feminism of the Revolutionary Mexican women. And thus, if for me there was something of an adventure in returning to civilization, for her the experience was nothing less than tremendous and breathtaking. It enhanced my own impressions to see civilization again through her naive eyes. She exclaimed at everything new in her expressive, Mexican way.

We finally came to San Antonio, which, as I remember, is the first large town out of Creel. Here was abundant evidence of modernity and progress for one who had been sierra bound for months. And there was also evidence in plenty of the feminism of the Revolutionary Mexican women. This was expressed by excessively short skirts, outrageously painted and powdered faces, and silk stockings. The country was poor, so it did not matter how many carefully darned runners there were in the stockings; but they had to be silk. Adolescent girls were strolling arm-in-arm through the station, ogling the passengers in a pert, flippant manner.

This progress and feminism of modern Mexican women were horrifying to the demure little *barranca* girl in her mourning and black silk *rebozo*. "*¡Ay que feo!*" ("Oh how ugly!"), she said of them. I defended the modern Mexican woman against her, but she was not impressed.

The town of San Antonio is the headquarters of a colony of ten thousand Mennonites, who have preserved their archaic culture and religion of the German Reformation by mass migrations halfway around the world, ending up at this place. The prosperity and modernity of San Antonio depend on the business and industry of this evangelical colony, still living in the mental world of the sixteenth century.

A couple of young Mennonites who had just been married got on the train with the girl's father. I wondered if the colony was so puritanical that the father-in-law always accompanied honeymooners. The girl was dressed in the old-fashioned costume prescribed by her faith, which consisted in part of a shawl worn as a headdress, reminiscent of the garb of nuns. She had flaxen hair and blue eyes. After my months among the Indians she looked to me like a Dresden-china saint.

The demure little Mexican girl was even more impressed. "*¡Qué güera!*" ("How blond.") And then, continuing, with a burst of confidence, "How much more beautiful she is than we black Mexicans. How modest, how beautiful, how good she is. *Parece una santa.*" ("She looks like a saint," which was the same thing I had thought of.) "Compare her with those flippant little Jezebels without decent clothes on," she said, pointing to groups of town girls flirting with the soldiers escorting the train.

In vain did I argue that dark skin is as beautiful as fair, and that in America dark-eyed *señoritas* are *muy estimadas.* This nonplussed her a little, but she was sure that the German girl was much more saintly and beautiful than any Mexican girl could ever hope to be. Strange the charms of blondness in a dark-skinned country, and the charms of dark skin and eyes among the Saxons. One may be certain that the Dresden-china Mennonite girl was thinking that the Mexican girl was much the more beautiful.

As for the virtue of the saintly religious conservatism of both my Mexican girl and the Mennonite girl, however, what did it ever get them? To be servants of men, no more. Still, one could not say that there was not happiness in that, for the Mexican girl at least, as she cared for her ailing relative on the train. But at what a cost, half the human race wasted in ministering to the other half! I was quick to defend the "Jezebels." They were cocky and so ostentatiously enjoying their new freedom: yet from them come the teachers who are the hope of Mexico.

So with reason could I ask the Mexican girl, "What has all their saintly virtue gained these Mennonite women?"

This colony of ten thousand Mennonites preserve the social and religious heritage, and even the archaic German speech, of the sixteenth century. Their ancestors originally moved in a body from Holland to Germany. But since they were pacifists, they left Germany to escape military training under Frederick the Great. They found a long period of peace under the charter given them by Catherine the Great, who needed their skill in wheat farming in her Crimean lands.

When they were no longer exempt from military service in Russia, some came to America. At that time the Santa Fe Railroad was still under construction, and was advancing slowly across the plains of Kansas. There, at the end of the uncompleted line, the Mennonites were dumped off. But they had brought with them from the Ukraine all their equipment and animals, and the "Turkey-red" wheat for which Kansas is still famous. Their industry made fertile the plains of Kansas and created traffic for the railroad. Wheat and Mennonites is a combination like ham and eggs: they can't be separated. The descendants of that colony are still in Kansas, but they have not successfully resisted that most powerful of all assimilative forces in our society, Americanization. Today they are largely Americanized into a rather conservative religious body that is but a reflection of the archaic original group.

The ancestors of the Mexican group, however, belonged to a colony of Mennonites that migrated to Canada. There the force of Americanization was not so strong, and they succeeded in preserving all the traditions and discipline of their curious faith. But the government attempted to force the children to go to public schools, instead of the little Bible schools which have enabled the Mennonites to preserve their sixteenth-century culture in a twentieth-century world. Rather than see their anachronistic little order go to pot, the elder sent agents into Mexico to look for cheap land suitable for wheat.

In Mexico, as in Germany, Russia, and Canada before this, the Mennonites found not only land that would grow wheat but a government which so needed agriculture that it would grant them the conditions they demanded. They bought land for about ten times what it was worth to the Mexican *hacendados*, who used it for cattle pasture, at a price which was, however, still about one-tenth of what it was worth to them for wheat farming. So everyone concerned in the transaction was pleased. Then the Mennonites chartered whole trains to move them and all their animals and machinery across the United States into Chihuahua.

The religious and social life of these Chihuahua Mennonites is a sixteenth-century patriarchy of a stern and puritanical sort. Obviously there is little diversion in their life. They make it a matter of faith to wear a curious costume. They will not have pictures, rugs, or other decorations in their bare and bleak homes. Music, dance, and song are indicted except for liturgical purposes. With good reason the elders dared not let the children go to Canadian schools. To have a large family and countless acres of billowing wheat, that is the ideal of Mennonite men. The women are unimportant except for childbearing and other expressions of "Christian" devotion and service.

But their industry and wheat growing! In a few years they broke the semiarid Mexican land and erected a city. Though their homes are unadorned, they use the latest farming machinery, supplied to them by the leading importing houses of Mexico, which maintain branches at San Antonio. Their horses are magnificent, gigantic Percherons, that looked to me like elephants after the burros and mules I had used in the sierra.

The strange ways, machinery, horses, and wheat fields of the Mennonites dumbfounded the Mexicans. Indeed, they have yet to recover from their surprise. They still ride their little flea-bitten nags, and use oxen and handmade carts with solid wood wheels. They delay in imitating the superior industrial practices of the Mennonites. Such is the enigma of Mexico.

But the government welcomed the colony, which fitted directly into the agrarian ideals of the Revolution. Mexicans are hired by the Mennonites, and it is to be expected that the relationship will ultimately profit them. But the process is painfully slow. Even from the train window I could see a hard and unbroken line between the Mennonites and the Mexicans. It was shown by the houses.

What is it that defeats the kind and graceful Mexicans in their own land, and yet operates to the advantage of these pacifistic, bovine, medieval Puritans? It isn't "*la falta de religión y buena costumbre,*" because it is purely an accident that Mennonite religion does not make a sin out of profitable labor. And indeed Mennonite labor, like its animal husbandry, is solely for breeding. Education, beauty, art, music, culture in the narrow sense, sweetness and light, these are altogether lacking in Mennonite life.

The government was wise in giving the Mennonites the conditions they demanded. A vast expanse of cultivated land and a city have grown out of what was once virtually desert. Aside from this, there is the certainty that eventually the Mexicans will learn to grow wheat from these German Puritans, not to mention their influences upon Mexican animal husbandry. As far south as Jalisco I bought butter produced by this colony.

The Chihuahua Mennonites talk medieval German and Canadian English. As a matter of principle, they do not learn Spanish for fear their pure little children will be corrupted by the Mexicans. And how quickly the poor, emotionally starved Mennonite children would become "contaminated" by a Mexican fiesta, with its multitude of songs sung to the guitar, and its dances danced to castanets!

There is a perfect situation for a cultural osmosis between the Mexicans and the Mennonites, though it may take a century. The stolid peasant Puritans hold their spirits in the straitjacket of the austerity of the German Reformation, and all human expression goes into the labor of the wheat fields and the beds of childbirth. Cheek by jowl with them are the utterly thriftless, dreamy, graceful Mexicans, as poor as wandering minstrels. Will not the stolid virtue of the one mix with the gay spirit of song and dance of the other? But perhaps about the time this begins to happen, the Mennonite elders will start another hegira, and the whole colony will flee to South America or South Africa, like the wandering Jew, to begin all over again; but ever keeping the human spirit shackled away from music and song, and bound to the serious labor of raising wheat and rearing young to carry on after them.

I was told that this colony survived the Villa Revolution almost unharmed. Their pacifism saved them, together with their generous contributions of feed for Villa's cavalry. But they created unnecessary trouble for themselves by having refused to learn Spanish. After the Revolution, their colony was threatened by the Agrarians, the famous land-hungry peasants of Mexico. In the country all around San Antonio there is plenty of land similar to that which the Mennonites converted into wheat fields. But the "land-hungry" peasants did not want this. They had their eyes on the plowed and fenced acres of the Germans. So the Mennonites began to suffer a series of petty annoyances.

Their fences were cut, and animals run over their fields. They were even hauled into Municipal court on various fictitious charges before a judge whose language they could not speak. But at its worst, the state government of Chihuahua dared not kill the goose that laid the golden eggs. Conditions improved; the Federal government gained wider power; and the National charter of the colony became more respected. The Mennonites were able to breathe easily again after a decade of Revolution and another decade of "Reconstruction" during which they fought off the Agrarians with passive resistance, a surprisingly effective procedure at that.

Soon after the train got under way again, we passed the line of cleavage between the lands of the Mennonites and those of the Mexicans. It was like that line separating the blue-green water of the Gulf of Mexico from the yellow, muddy waters of the Mississippi, which extends for miles in an arching line far out to sea from the mouth of the river. The land of the Mennonites ended with a vast expanse of green and waving wheat. Mexico began again in the arid grasslands browned a muddy yellow by the summer's heat.

This line of cleavage, extending for miles, will someday disappear. Though the Mexican utterly lacks the solid peasant quality of the Mennonites with their overwhelming love of labor, still he is much the more susceptible of change, and he is far from stupid. He too will have waving fields of wheat, and probably long before the Mennonite has succumbed to the lure of song and dance, the charm and grace of speech and gesture, and the courtesy of manner and address that distinguish the Mexican even on the lowest rung of the ladder.

It was after dark when we reached the city of Chihuahua. What luxury to sit in an old-fashioned *coche* drawn by horses down a boulevard which seemed so wide and level after my months in the sierra that I fancied myself in Washington or Paris! All that I recall of it now, however, are the streetlights, which, flaring at regular intervals along the avenues, contrasted so sharply with the memory of the pitch-pine torches of my sierra nights.

The following morning I presented myself at the office of the Governor of the State, hoping to get some action in favor of the Indians for the safeguarding of their lands. Sr. Lic. Pascua García had interested himself in the Tarahumaras by sending them corn; and he had also given me a letter to the Mexican municipal authorities of the sierra. So I was counting on him. He was a charming person of distinguished manners. Unfortunately, since he was a civilian, his administration was considerably handicapped because of the Mexican preference and greater respect for military governors.

Thus Sr. García had been supplanted by a Federal general; and my reception, consequently, was the same as when I had tried to get a permit from the Army authorities for carrying firearms. I simply wasn't received. My many trips and conferences with "General" Jaris thus came to naught.

This Federal general along with later military governors of Chihuahua gave the state the worst government it had seen for a long time. The streets and parks were uncared for. The agrarian problem was again reshuffled, with the soldiers taking the lands the peasants had been given. Three years later in crossing Chihuahua by train I met a young Texan whose business of running a cotton gin necessitated his riding over this part of the state to teach the Mexicans the fine points of cotton growing. On one of these trips he saw four peasants hanging by their necks from one tree. Just a military solution of the agrarian problem!

I must say, however, that my later Mexican sojourn revealed that the Federal government had greatly improved the quality of its generals who ruled state governments. At that time the State of Zacatecas had for its governor General Matías Ramos, whose administration contrasted in every way with that of the military governors of Chihuahua. The state government of Zacatecas was honest from top to bottom; every cent was reaching the end for which it had been appropriated, and so many roads were being built that even the soldiers were put to work.

The predilection of the Mexican people for military "strongmen" can hardly be questioned from Mexican history. The esteem for a ruler who is *muy hombre* is ubiquitous, and appears in the most unexpected places. A few days later on the train to El Paso I met a distinguished young Mexican lawyer who had been educated by the Jesuits and knew some of my good friends of the Tarahumara mission. He was a staunch Catholic, and therefore could be expected to be antimilitary. For hours he lamented the "strong-arm" methods of ex-president Calles.

But at this time, under President Rubio [sic], a civilian from the Diplomatic Corps, Mexico was experiencing its first civilian administration of the Federal Government since *quién sabe cuando*. The National Revolutionary Party had recalled Rubio from the Mexican

Embassy in Germany in an effort to break the military tradition. I was told this by an official of the Mexican Embassy at Washington.

The administration of estimable, honest, and able President Rubio was so halting and timorous that its insecurity was obvious everywhere in the Republic. The attitude of the young lawyer was significant of this weakness. Since his party, that of the Church, had nothing to expect but persecution from the military powers, one would have expected him to side with Rubio. On the contrary, however, he revealed his sympathies in the narration of this joke about Rubio, which went all over Mexico. It is a pun on *nadar* (to swim), and *nada* (nothing). "Who is the greatest *nadador* [swimmer or do-nothing] in Mexico?" "Why, it is Rubio. In the morning, *nada* [he swims, or the other meaning of *nada*, nothing]; in the afternoon, *nada*; and in the evening, *nada*." As far as any Mexican knew, President Rubio never swam a stroke in his life, so the meaning of a "do-nothing" was fairly obvious.

There will be no other Mexican President for a long time who has not been at least a "General of Division." Rubio's weakness was only that his being a civilian did not guarantee his control of the Army. Had one of the generals under him flopped, there might have been a common revolt. As a matter of fact revolt was not far off; for there appears to have been a cabal centering in the Secretary of War which induced Rubio suddenly to summon ex-President General Calles to take the portfolio. The story is current that early one morning the "strong-arm" walked into the office and dictated a telegram that was sent to every Chief of Operations in the Mexican Army. "I have just taken the Portfolio of War. So you recognize my authority? Plutarco E. Calles." That name at the end of the official telegram was sufficient. In every instance the meek answer came back "Yes." At this time the ever lengthening shadow of Calles, the iron man behind the assassinated Obregón, was the most powerful force in Mexico. With reason then did the generals answer, "*Sí.*"

With a genius for political puns, the Mexicans had a pun on Calles, just the reverse of that on Rubio. Each almost perfectly expresses the Mexican attitude toward these men at that time. The pun answers the question "Who killed Villa?" The answer, "Sh-h-h, *calles*" [be thou quiet, from *callar*, to be quiet; but the other meaning is clear, the respected name of Calles].

During the Revolution of 1910–17, Calles was the second after

Obregón in command of the "Yaquis" of Sonora who won the Revolution. After the assassination of Obregón, Calles succeeded to the presidency and gave Mexico the most radical government it had experienced, though it would look conservative compared to the government of his successor, Cárdenas. Calles divided some of the large landholdings, some of which went to soldiers of the Revolution and much of it to a few of the generals, including Calles himself. The radicalism of Calles was mostly directed against the Catholic Church and against the foreign oil companies. During the administrations of his creatures, Calles turned more conservative. This may have been a case of a young radical turning conservative with advancing age and presumable discretion; or else he may have seen the ill effects of giving land to the peasant who left it largely idle.

When I was in Mexico in 1934, the General of Division, Cárdenas, gained the presidency. Much more radical than the strongman Calles had ever been, Cárdenas proved to be a strongman on his own account, by deporting Calles. Free of the conservative shadow of Calles, Cárdenas stopped the largely senseless persecution of the Church and embarked on his Six-Year Plan, characterized not only by rapid increases in the schools for "Socialistic Education," but also by a tremendous increase in the agrarian policy of division of the large landholdings and the backing of the labor unions to the extent of finally completely nationalizing the railroads and "expropriation" of the American and other foreign oil companies.

In 1935 I was to meet President Cárdenas in the modest little bungalow in San Angel (Villa Obregón), which he preferred to the palaces maintained by the nation for its Chief Executive. Though I cannot agree with the extreme lengths to which Cárdenas has gone in applying the radical ends of the Mexican Revolution, my impression, then and now, is that next to Benito Juárez, Cárdenas is the greatest Mexican President. I am led to this opinion by his honesty, his modesty, his relative poverty after six years in office, and his idealism, which has been so consistently applied that, at the end of his term in 1940, Mexico has seen results and come to a point of decision whether to continue farther on this extremely left tack or to veer to a more conservative and a more pro-American policy. Both of the candidates for the succession have turned considerably to the right in view of communist-Nazi threats of revolution, which are made much the more serious by the presence in Mexico of so many of the so-called Spanish "loyalists." Both the candidates are Generals of Division of the Army, or they would have little chance for the presidency of Mexico.

The Mexican love for a uniform and for military men is part of the Mexican genius. Many Mexicans have told me that Mexico's pro-Germanism during the World War was due to respect and admiration for Germany's militarism. In 1936, movies shown in the United States show that some of the Federal agricultural schools in Mexico give military training to their smallest boys. Battalions of little farmers march to their gardens with their hoes and their rakes over their shoulders in true military fashion. This is palpably an imitation of Nazi Germany. In 1940 we see a more ominous picture in the drilling of oil workers with sticks for rifles. This is palpably an inspiration of Russia.

But will Mexico accept the rest of the ideology of Nazi-communism? I doubt it. It wasn't made in Mexico, and besides the trends both of Mexican history and the last revolution have been so strongly toward liberalism and democracy that National Socialism, from either Russia or Germany, doesn't seem to fit into the Mexican picture. Further, the good relations between the Mexican and American governments remove any apprehensions which have often in the past overshadowed the Mexicans from the North. Fear and defeat seem to be two elements conducive toward the development of Fascism, if only in the negative sense that it integrates itself against their destructive attacks. Such "soil" is lacking in Mexico after the vigorous triumphs of the revolutionary cause; and in Mexico today the term "The Revolution" means the government.

The revolutionary government in Mexico today cannot be called a democratic one. It is, however, making an honest attempt to build a Democracy to attain the "Effective Suffrage and no Re-election" aims of its last revolution. But so far these aims are to be found only in official letters, which quaintly end in the phrase, "*Sufragio Efectivo—No Reelección*," as though the officials have to remind themselves what the Revolution was all about.

Can this intermediate Mexican government be called Fascistic in the sense of National Socialism? It is both nationalistic and socialistic; but it lacks that essential ideology of the Totalitarian or Corporate State to which the individual is so closely integrated as to be but subordinate. The difference is more fundamental than minor hallmarks of Fascism to be noted in Mexico, such as the dictatorship and discipline of the ruling party and the contemptuous regard for those who oppose it.

A Totalitarian State is out of the Mexican picture. Despite Mexican militarism there is lacking the mentality of lock-step discipline. Indeed, few countries are so disunited and locally divergent as is Mexico. More than this, a Totalitarian conception of National Socialism would be counter to the deep-rooted Mexican love for personal liberty. This love of liberty is expressed in the tolerant and urbane attitude of all Mexicans in freely granting to each other the personal liberty that each Mexican demands for himself in freedom from diffuse but powerful social compunctions. Just as Mexican houses look inward to a *patio* concealed from common view, so each Mexican has a private life and realm that he values and tolerantly grants to others.

If this tolerance and love of liberty distinguish Mexicans from Germans, in another way they distinguish Mexicans from Americans "of the North." Though Mexicans do not enjoy the constitutional liberties of the United States which come from effective suffrage, they actually have more freedom. This is from social compulsion, which is very strong in the United States, though often so pervasive that we do not notice it.

The difference between Mexicans and North Americans was revealed to me my last day in Mexico. I was in Ciudad Juárez, wrangling with the Mexican Customs about the scientific materials which we were bringing back. Red tape, alike enough in all governments, is tiresome enough. But it is especially annoying when, after months of absence, one is separated from his own country by a mere river.

Toward the end of the day, and the end of my nine months' residence in Mexico, I was about to board the car that would take me across the International Bridge when I thought of the last injunction of a friend to bring him a Mexican *sombrero*. I hunted around, and soon found something suitable. Now a Mexican *sombrero*, as big as a cartwheel, is an awkward thing to carry except on the head. That being the place for a *sombrero* anyway, I wore it, and put my cap in my pocket, since I could hardly put the *sombrero* there.

Despite my nine months in the Republic, as I walked through the streets of Ciudad Juárez, in my American clothes topped with this enormous *sombrero* I must have looked like the rookiest of American tourists, a naive, professorial person trying to have a good time and attempting to catch the spirit of Mexico by wearing her ponderous headgear. This was during Prohibition, and most of my compatriots in Juárez were imbibing the spirit of Mexico in another form. But, alas!

the spirit of Mexico had somehow escaped me during my all-day wrangle with the customs official. After so long an absence from home I was anxious to regain the spirit of America "of the North."

Yet, however incongruous my costume might have been, such is the tolerance, reserve, and dignity of the Mexicans that no one gave me as much as a look. I am certain that one might appear on the streets sans trousers without attracting any attention except that of the police, who would take him to jail. But that too would be done with dignity and poise and without fanfare.

When I boarded the next car to El Paso, I was not long in regaining one facet of the North American spirit. At first the other passengers were all Mexicans, and I was not noticed. But as we continued on toward the river, Americans began to get on. Some glanced discreetly, some looked directly, and others stared open-mouthed at a tourist who would advertise himself so flagrantly.

Finally one jovial Texan, made even more jovial with Mexican beer, could no longer restrain himself. Now I lived a year in Texas. I know the Texas breed very well, and may the tribe increase! So I understood that it was in utter kindness and goodwill that this Texan, unable to resist that social compulsion of Americans "of the North" which makes the individual, whatever his headgear, fall in line with the group norm, blurted out, "Having a good time in Mexico, Buddy?"

Having a good time in Mexico, after nine months in her backwoods of sierra and desert, and nine hours of wrangling with her customs officials? The car was slowly drawing away from the Mexican side, and my Mexican experiences were finished. But the spirit of Mexico returned to me, and I could think of nothing save the uniform courtesy of her people, the kindness with which I had been treated, the hospitality I had received, and always with a tolerance and reserve which would make unthinkable attacking another's dignity by asking, "Having a good time in Mexico, Buddy?"

"Yes," I answered, "I am having a good time."

The streetcar was passing the invisible boundary at the center of the International Bridge over the Río Grande and to myself I added, "*¡Viva México!* for every day I have spent in her borders!"

Notes to Zingg Text

Chapter 1

1. This railroad, in more recent years called the Chihuahua al Pacífico, was completed by the Mexican government in the early 1960's. Many of Stillwell's dreams, such as bringing Kansas City closer to a Pacific port and opening the Chihuahua mountains to mineral and lumber exploitation, are coming true. [The endnotes, unless otherwise specified, were written by linguist Don Burgess in the late 1970's and revised in 2000. Burgess has lived and worked in the Sierra Tarahumara since 1966. Editors' note.]

2. Villa raided Columbus, New Mexico, in 1916 during the Mexican Revolution.

Chapter 2

1. "*Muy retirado*" means far away. The word *retirado* can also mean "retired." In this case Zingg has preferred a literal translation because of the amusing way the expression sounds in English [editors' note].

2. Today Sisoguichi is the headquarters for the Jesuit mission work.

3. The "diamond-hitch" which is commonly used in the sierra today differs from the diamond-hitch used by animal packers in the U.S.A.

4. My own observation is that race prejudice, both Mexican against Indian as well as Indian against Mexican, is considerably more than what Zingg records.

5. This is still true today.

6. Zingg does not mention the Río Verde, an even larger tributary of the Río Fuerte, which is also in Tarahumara country.

Chapter 3

1. I would not call this "bashful" but rather an accepted norm in the Tarahumara culture.

2. The more usual greeting today is simply "*cuira*" or "*os cuira.*"

3. The church at Samachique was built by the Jesuits in the 1700's. The king of

Spain threw the Jesuits out of the New World in 1767 and they did not return to the Tarahumara until 1900. Franciscan and secular priests worked sporadically in the Tarahumara missions during the Jesuits' absence. The explorer Carl Lumholtz describes most of the missions as being in a state of decay.

4. I believe that it would be more correct to say that when a person is undernourished, dirty, and perhaps sick, he is not as easily aroused sexually as when he is healthy, well fed, and clean. To say that the race would die out if not for drunken feasts is going too far.

5. I recently was told by a Mexican lady in Mexico City that a relative of hers was carried off into the mountains of Chihuahua by revolutionary forces during the Mexican Revolution. She married a Tarahumara and lived there for many years. She now lives in San Luis Potosí.

6. But among the Tarahumaras, many believe that if they marry a mestizo their souls will interchange and the Tarahumara's soul will go to hell and the mestizo's soul will go to heaven, the opposite of what is normally said to happen.

7. I too thought of many improvements when I first went to live with the Tarahumaras. But after ten years, most of my ideas had been failures, and I am realizing that the ideas that work best are the ones that the Tarahumaras already have. Now I am trying to learn from them.

8. I had a similar experience with bees forty years after Zingg. I also talked to the Tarahumaras about raising rabbits only to find that many of them refuse to eat rabbit meat because rabbits are said to dig under the ground and eat dead people.

9. The same is true for the Tarahumara language. Until very recently, comparatively few loan words were found in Tarahumara.

10. In fact, Tarahumaras consider themselves children of God and look on the Mexicans as children of the devil. The Mexicans, on the other hand, have similar feelings about the Tarahumaras.

11. By 1940, when Ken Hilton of the Summer Institute of Linguistics moved to Samachique, bows and arrows were not in use. Hilton only remembers seeing them at a place between Guachochi and Parral. I know of only a few people who use bow and arrow to kill wild animals such as deer and mountain lion, and this in canyon areas where there is more brush.

12. In 1963, I observed a local court session at Samachique where a man was tied to a post and lashed with a leather whip because he had stolen corn.

Chapter 4

1. I know a Tarahumara woman who divorced her husband because he sold her cow without getting her permission.

2. There are many jokes throughout Chihuahua about the powdery nature of *pinole*. A Mexican lady recently told me that a good way to kill cockroaches is to catch them, stuff a little *pinole* into their mouths, and tickle them. They'll immediately choke to death.

3. My experience with today's Tarahumara women is that they are quite good at sewing. Simply by taking some quick measurements and tearing the cloth into the desired pieces, they can put together a well-fitted shirt.

4. The only times I have heard of Tarahumaras running a deer to death were when

the deer was a pregnant doe or else the deer was caught in a box canyon and was run back and forth by two groups of Tarahumaras until it dropped. Other methods are used, such as running a deer through a narrow, steep place where pointed sticks have been placed.

5. Squirrel meat is said to be the best-tasting meat because squirrels live closest to heaven.

6. This belief is still held by many Tarahumaras today and, I believe, should be respected. They have a similar belief in regards to tape recorders.

Chapter 5

1. Very few Tarahumaras today use leather for the soles of sandals. Now they use pieces of rubber tires.

2. Some Tarahumaras have recently begun carving figures of animals and people from pine bark to sell to tourists.

3. Today, trucks made of similar materials are made by the kids, both Indian and Mexican.

4. Tarahumaras also say that they drink *tesgüino* because the god Riósi taught them how to make it. He taught them this so they could be happy. The devil was the one who taught them to get drunk and fight. And fighting nullifies any worth a fiesta might have in appeasing God.

5. It is interesting to note that a study on *tesgüino* by the University of Arizona showed that penicillin properties are present in *tesgüino*.

6. I would at least add sports to what offers excitement and romance to a Tarahumara's life.

7. Zingg states this again in a later chapter and also in the book which he and Bennett wrote. I find this far from true. In the relatively short amount of time spent with the Tarahumaras and with their lack of knowledge of the Tarahumara language, they were not able to penetrate into the inner reaches of the Tarahumara.

Chapter 6

1. There are also curing ceremonies for sick people.

2. Many Tarahumaras talk of Mother God, the moon. Some reverse the order and call the moon Father God and the sun Mother God.

3. We may someday find that in the area of psychological cures, which definitely affect the physical, the Tarahumaras are far ahead of "civilized" man.

4. A Mexican movie made a few years ago near Creel begins by showing some people in a jeep offering a Tarahumara man a ride. His reply was, "No, thank you, I'm in a hurry."

5. Recently I know of Tarahumaras taking a skull from an ancient burial cave, telling it who the best runner on the opposite side was, and then burying the skull along the course so that it could put a hex on the runner.

6. A local trader of mixed blood told me that he once bet four burro loads of merchandise, which he was supposed to sell for someone, at a race. Fortunately for him he won.

7. Paul Carlson, who lived at Samachique for a number of years, tells me of a gov-

ernment doctor who once poured alcohol in the form of a cross on the chest of a sick Tarahumara and then lit it.

8. The word "*cimarrón*," at least in the western part of the tribe, is used to refer to a small child who has not been baptized.

9. This ceremony is remarkably similar to the funerals which I have attended in the western part of the tribe. One difference is that at the ones which I've seen everyone runs to the cemetery. Also, something which Zingg might not have seen, the body is washed before it is taken from the house.

10. This has not been my experience in the western part of the tribe. The people there say the ancient bones are alive and they will not touch them except for special occasions. But when digging a grave at the overcrowded cemetery, no one minds tossing old bones out of the way.

11. If she remarries before the ceremonies have been completed, the deceased's soul will return and kill the new husband.

12. This is also done at the curing ceremonies for animals.

Chapter 7

1. I object to the use of the word "poorly." It would seem better to have simply stated that the mask on the back of the head was an example of how the Tarahumaras assimilated certain aspects of Spanish culture.

2. Tarahumaras also say that they dance for their sins and for the sins of other people.

3. Tarahumara sermons are interesting from a linguistic standpoint. They usually have special intonation patterns and use words of which no one seems to know the meaning.

4. I once was sent down into a canyon with a mule to bring out an old lady witch doctor who had slept too close to the fire while drunk and badly burned her leg. The leg healed in a doubled-up position. I took her to the Jesuit hospital at Sisoguichi, where the doctors, in trying to give her the anesthesia for an operation, complained that she had so much alcohol in her system the ether wouldn't work.

Chapter 8

1. Among the Tarahumaras I have known, this is not true. True, they do not strike a child, but the parents often ridicule the child and they tell him hair-raising stories about how the owl or a huge snake will get him if he doesn't behave. Also, the Tarahumaras live in a survival situation. Any mistake which a child might make, or wrong behavior, could be very costly.

2. The names and duties of ecclesiastical officials differ a great deal from one part of the tribe to another, as do all of the Tarahumara customs.

3. The Mexican government's National Indian Institute has today trained large numbers of young Tarahumaras to act as teachers and doctor's aides.

4. I would question Zingg's source of information here since Ocampo is today surrounded by Pima Indians and is consistently north of the Chinipas River.

5. Land encroachments have been intensified in recent years with the arrival of lumber companies. Each member of an *ejido* is paid so much for the lumber taken from

his *ejido*, so persons whose legality in an *ejido* was questionable are trying their best to become legalized. I understand that the government recognizes a person as legal if he has farmed *ejido* land for three consecutive years.

Chapter 9

1. I believe Zingg is mistaken here. A "*laja*" is a place where the exposed surface of the earth is flat rock, such as is found at "*La Laja.*"

Chapter 10

1. The government now has more than one hundred boarding schools for the Tarahumaras.

Chapter 11

1. My experience is that almost anything I consider beautiful is not considered so by the Tarahumaras. They fear the rainbow because it steals children and marries women and causes them not to have babies. Deep pools of water are where huge snakes live which will make you sick if you get too close. And Tarahumaras are sometimes scared to walk through a lovely forest for fear of the "little people" who live under the ground. The word for beautiful is often heard in their sermons, but always in connection with such things as good crops and good health.

2. These people are often referred to as "bad thinkers."

3. The ball cactus which we usually consider as peyote is not native to most parts of these mountains. Sometimes, as Zingg later points out, it is brought in from the northern deserts. There are local substitutes which are also called "*jículi.*"

4. I am not sure why he says that "*jículi*" is a Huichol word. The two languages are related and you could just as easily say that the Huichol word for peyote came from the Tarahumara.

Chapter 12

1. This passage and others in which Zingg quotes or paraphrases himself or Bennett are from their classic ethnography *The Tarahumara* [editors' note].

2. Wheat is also sowed by broadcasting.

3. Today, in a few parts of the tribe, wheat is an important crop, almost on a par with corn. And some Tarahumaras raise quite a few potatoes. The problem with raising potatoes is to control the moles. I introduced a potato substitute, called Jerusalem artichoke, which several people have begun planting.

4. Also, I have noticed that wheat in the Samachique area does not seem to grow as well as in the western area, perhaps for a lack of winter moisture.

5. Because of the recent influx of roads and the railway, quite a few Tarahumaras have become quite good masons.

6. The custom of someone poor going around working for others is still very strong.

7. Literally, *pendejo* means pubic hair. But it is most often used in idiomatic ways.

He is perhaps saying here that he is a poor good-for-nothing, or, referring to the prayers, that he doesn't know much.

8. Today called Basíhuare.

9. The policy of the Mexican government, as one official told me, is to preserve ethnic groups, but not "*indios.*" It wants groups like the Tarahumaras to preserve their culture and language, but at the same time to know Spanish and be able to participate in the national scene. The word "*indio*" refers to a poor, downtrodden, backwards person. I find Zingg's comments in these paragraphs surprising. They sound more like an "American" than an "anthropologist."

10. In some parts of the mountains, the cows and goats give almost no milk because the pasture is so poor.

11. For a discussion on how the western Tarahumaras use the *agave*, see Robert A. Bye, Jr., Don Burgess, and Albino Mares Trias, "Ethnobotany of the Western Tarahumara of Chihuahua, Mexico. I. Notes of the Genus *Agave*." *Botanical Museum Leaflets*, Harvard University, June 27, 1975, vol. 24, no. 5, pp. 85–112.

12. Some Tarahumaras today weave an excellent double-weave hat which can be shaped however you want it. Mexican store-bought hats, however, are quickly replacing these.

Chapter 13

1. Sisoguichi is today the headquarters of the Jesuit work and boasts a hospital and a seminary for training Tarahumaras for the priesthood.

2. The wooden plow, made from a limb of an oak tree, is still the most commonly used plow.

Chapter 14

1. I do not believe Tarahumaras would perform any ceremony if it were not rational to them. They say the god Riósi taught them to do these things and to not do them would be to displease God. In the western part of the tribe, at least, the Easter ceremony is a fight between good and evil, represented by the Pharisees and the Jews. If the Pharisees do not win, the wind will blow the clouds away and the rains will not come.

2. The Tarahumara word for Easter means a time of going in circles.

3. Zingg does not mention wrestling matches, which are today an important part of the Easter ceremonies.

4. "*Macho*" literally means male.

5. According to Tarahumara folk tales, *chilicote* beans were fed to Apaches to kill them and also to the giant Cano, who was eating Tarahumara children.

Chapter 15

1. I too thought at first that there were no intelligible words to the chants, but I have since found that numerous "songs" are sung by the chanter during this dance. See the short collection of Tarahumara songs which I did called *Canciones de los Tarahumaras* (México: Instituto Lingüístico de Verano, 1973).

2. Today, at least in the western parts of the tribe, women dance this dance at other ceremonies as well.

3. There is another plant, a grass called *bacana*, which many Tarahumaras say is stronger than peyote. If you put the two in the same bag, they say they will fight and the grass will always win.

Chapter 16

1. I have not looked at this migration from the viewpoint of being spurious but rather from the viewpoint of the good it brings—more places to plant and find wild foods, escape from cold, etc.

2. I find hexing very strong among the Tarahumaras.

Chapter 18

1. I do not find these statements true, nor do the Carlsons, who lived at Samachique for fifteen years. Only to an outsider to whom the Indians have not opened themselves would this appear true. Although, as I mentioned earlier, their circumstances do make them more reserved than "civilized" people.

▶ Index

▶
▶
▶
▶
▶
▶
▶
▶
▶
▶

Page numbers referring to photos appear in italics.

boarding schools, 296n1(Ch.10)
boots, 60
bow and arrow, 47, 59, 293n11
building construction, *153*, 175–176,
    185–186
burial caves, 224
business, 50

Calles, Plutarco Elías, xxii, 141, 142, 192,
    275, 287, 288
calzones, 142, 183
Camino Real. *See* Royal Road
camposanto (graveyard), 35, 36, 77, 86,
    224, 267
candles, 258
cannibalism, 96
canoas, 27, 39, 55, 60, 162, 186, 256
capitanes, 109, 112
Cárdenas, Lázaro, xxii, 288
cardinal points, 227. *See also* Tarahumara
    cross
cargadores, 262, 263
Carranza, Venustiano, 131, 140, 192, 273,
    274, 275
Catholic: Church, 37; missions, 203;
    nuns, 132, 160; prayers, 43, 44; pro-
    gram, 196–197
Catholicism, 43–45, 186
cattle, 53, 57, 60, 73, 244, 256. *See also*
    fertilizer; manure
Cave-Dwellers, 212, 213, 214, 215, 216,
    217, 218, 222, 244, 261
cave dwellings, 171, 242
caves, 171–172
cedar. *See* cleansing with cedar
century plant, 15–16, 229, 297n11. *See
    also* maguey
ceremonial cannibalism, 97
chapíones ("shouters"), 102, 107, 114
chapíyo, 127
charros, 148
cheese, 184
chicharrones, 130, 134, 136
chicken house, 40, 55
Chief of Arms. *See Jefe de Armas*

Chief of Operations. *See Jefe de Opera-
    ciones*
chile, 19, 167, 184
chilicote beans, 16, 216, 218, 223, 297n5
Christmas, 27, 96, 257
Christmas Eve, 107, 113
church, 12
church ceremonies, 39. *See also* Sunday
    prayers
cimarrón, 88, 295n8
cleansing with cedar, 224, 231
Cliff-Dwellers, 15, 138, 178, 179
Clifford, James, ix, x; and George Mar-
    cus, ix, x
climate, 15
clothing, 26, 53, 54
clout, 53
comal, 175
communidad, 208, 211
compadre, 19, 60, 61
composanto, 147
comprador, 46
conquistadores, 101
convento, 12–13
cooperative labor, 74, 257, 258. *See also*
    tesgüinada
copal, 101. *See also* incense
Córdobas, 62, 120, 121, 127–130, 132,
    135, 163, 215, 217, 219, 263
cordon, 164
corn, 243, 266
corn agriculture, 34
corn-drying structures, 40, 55
corn house, 55
Cortez, 279
counterrevolution, 139
Creel, 12, 28, 30, 118, 129, 159, 164
"Cristero" Revolution, 141, 142
crop failure, 129, 266. *See also* famine;
    malnutrition
Cruz, 111–113. *See also* trial
"cures," 83. *See also* curing ceremony
curing ceremony, 47, 76–81, 203, 221,
    226, 227–231, 237, 238, 249, 251,
    295n12; preventive medicine and,

fruit, 40–42

funeral, 86–90, 195n9. *See also* death and burial ceremonies

funerary fires, 157

games, 66

Geertz, Clifford, x, xxv–xxvin8

"General" Jaris. *See* Jaris, "General"

ghosts, 233

gifts of affection (ribbons), 53–54

girdle, 53, 54

goats and goat herding, 57, 244

gobernador, 27, 30, 31–32, 47, 79, 83, 92, 93, 104, 105, 109, 110, 111, 112, 113, 114, 116, 158, 160, 161, 162, 177, 205, 211, 246, 247, 257, 262, 263, 264, 267, 270

gods, 235. *See also* Father God; gods of the four points; Moon Mother; Mother God; Riósi; Sky Mother; Sun Father

gods of the four points, 233. *See also* gods

gorges. *See barrancas*

gossip, 37, 54, 248

government boarding schools, 145, 296n1(Ch.10)

grain house, 51, 55

grandes damas, 114

guitars, 69, 80, 104, 250, 256. *See also* music

"gun-toting paraphernalia," 126

hallucinogens. *See bacana*; jimsonweed; peyote

hanging bridge, 23, *154*. *See also* Shepherd, Boss

headhunters. *See* Ifugaos; Ilongots

head knives, 99

herbal medicine, 186

herding, 53, 63

herding cattle, 246

herding goats, 246

heredity, 258

hexing, 294n5(Ch.6), 298n2. *See also* black magic; magic; "talking bad"

"hole where wind lives," 165

Holy Week, 110, 111, 163, 257, 262; ceremonies of, 202–212; processions of, 209, 210, 211. *See also* Easter; *pascol*

honey, 42, 194. *See also* bee culture

Hopi, 250

hospitality, 176

Huerta, Victoriano ("the cockroach"), 131, 139, 273, 276

Huichols, vii, 18, 28, 45, 58, 61, 67, 75, 77, 97, 101, 126, 181, 184, 185, 206, 209, 219, 232, 234, 235, 236, 250, 255, 257, 258, 259

hunting, 58–59

Ifugaos, 99

Ilongots, 124, 125, 180, 270

Incas, 252

incense, 101, 209, 237. *See also* copal

incest, 36, 108

individual ownership, 172, 293n1. *See also* property and inheritance

infanticide, 35

inheritance, 158–159

intermarriage, 38, 293nn5,6

interregional trade, 184–185, 186–187

Isidro, 92, 95

iwigala. *See* soul (breath)

jacal, 186

Jaris, "General," 115–116, 119, 158, 160, 174, 215, 261, 262, 266, 286

Jefe de Armas (Chief of Arms), 144, 146, 147, 159

Jefe de Operaciones (Chief of Operations), 147

Jesuits, 12, 27, 30, 31, 39, 42, 118, 132, 135, 292–293n3(Ch.3)

Jesús, 220

jiculi. *See* peyote

jimsonweed (*Datura stramonium*), 168–170, 237, 255

joking relationship, 46

Jones, William, 124–126

Juárez, Benito, 24, 97, 204, 288

"Judases," 206, 207, 210, 228, 250, 297n1(Ch.14)

Kansas City, Mexico and Orient Railroad, 3–11, 292n1(Ch.1)
kapora. See drum

lance (*seléke*), 205
Land of the Dead, 90–91, 226
Land of the Living, 115, 226
land theft, 158, 295–296n5. *See also* robbing; stealing; theft
Lara, José, 62
Leandro, 43
leather tanning, 194
Lévi-Strauss, Claude, x
ley fuga, 122. *See also* murder
"little people," 296n1
livestock, 57
loom, 257
Lorenzo, xviii, xxi, 43, 44, 49, 51, 57, 58, 60, 68, 69, 79, 81, 85, 86, 87, 98, 107, 109, 121, *156*, 163, 164, 165, 166, 167, 168, 169, 171, 173, 174, 175, 176, 178, 183, 186, 188, 196, 201, 202, 203, 204, 209, 233, 238, 248, 255, 257, 270. *See also* Zingg's *mozo*
Los Tres Reyes (The Three Magi). *See* Epiphany, Feast of
Lumholtz, Carl, ix, 106

maestro, 31, 44, 85, 103, 107, 111, 114, 115, 203, 209, 211
magic, 81, 248. *See also* black magic; hexing; "talking bad"
maguey (agave), xvi–xvii, 121, 184, 218, 297n11. *See also* century plant
Malinowski, Bronislaw, viii, xxivn3
malnutrition, xxvin10, 293n4(Ch.3). *See also* crop failure; famine
mano, 39, 63–64
manure, 35, 57, 66, 67, 72, 172. *See also* cattle; fertilizer
Marcus, George, ix
María, José, 79

marijuana, 121
marriage, 35, 225, 257
masonry, 175, 296n5
matarique (pitcawi), 186–186. *See also* stupefying fish
matachines, 101, 104, 107, 113, 114, 115, 161, 204, 206, 208, 211, 228, 250
mayor, 37, 108, 109, 111, 112, 171, 224, 246, 256
mecapl ("shawl strap"), 57
medicinal plants, 49
medicine, 194
medicine man. *See* shaman
médico, 131
Mennonites, 275, 281–285
Mesa Central, 14
mestizos, 38, 293nn5,6
metate, 39, 62, 63–64, 98, 100, 172, 243, 256, 257
Mexican Constitution, 24
milk, 57
mines and mining, 15, 22, 24, 51, 278
mining engineer, 4, 8, 184, 244
ministers of cults, 145, 191
ministros de cultas. See ministers of cults
missions. *See* Basiaurichi School; Norogáchic mission; Samachique mission; Sisoguichi Jesuit mission village
mixed bloods, 46
monarco, 102
Monte Albán, 159
Moon Mother, 234, 294n2. *See also* gods
morogapitán, 206, 207, 208
Moros, 125–126
Mother God, 78, 294n2(Ch.6)
mozo (guide). *See* Lorenzo; Zingg's *mozo*
muleteer (*arriero*), 13, 20–21, 60, 61, 138, 212, 266. *See also* "Pancho Villa"
mummies, xvi, 157, 158, 160
murder, 122
music, 80, 142. *See also* drum; guitars; flute; violin
mutual aid, 174, 176
mysticism, 41, 259

mystic number, 223

National Indian Institute, 116,
   295n3(Ch.8)
National Revolutionary Party, 286
new year round, 202, 203, 297n2(Ch.14).
   See also Easter; Holy Week; *pascol*;
New Years, 206
nixtamal, 39
Noche Buena. See Christmas Eve
nomadic agriculturalists, 72, 73, 197
norahua, 60, 61, 266
Norogáchic mission, 61, 62, 118, 120,
   127, 129, 131, 132, 138, 139, 143,
   145, 160, 161; Indian school at, 132,
   194, 195, 295n1(Ch.10)

oak firewood, 57, 60
Obregón, Alvaro, xxii, 141, 192, 273, 274,
   276, 287, 288
Obregón-Calles movement, 131
Ocampo, 118
ocote (pitch-pine torch), 182
oko bird, 228
Ortíz Rubio, Pascual, xxii, 286, 287
Other, the, xi, xxvn7

Padre P., 190–193, 194, 198
Padre Ribas, 97
padres, 12, 34, 42, 131, 134, 139–143
"Pancho Villa" (Zingg's muleteer), xiv,
   13, 144, 211, 212, 213, 214, 261, 266,
   269, 271, 272. *See also* muleteer
pascol (Easter), 208, 228. *See also* Easter;
   Holy Week
pascoleros, 210, 211
patio (dancing court), 99, 105, 133, 224,
   228
Patricio (*teniente*), xvi, 57, 58, 85, 86, 87,
   90, 102, 114, 160, 163, 226, 237, 267.
   See also death and burial ceremonies;
   funeral; *teniente*
patrón, 130
pendejo, 178, 296–297n7

penicillin. *See tesgüino:* medical properties
   of
peyote, 85, 167, 169, 200, 235–238, 239,
   255, 296nn3,4(Ch.11), 298n3
peyote ceremony, 238
peyote cults, 167, 200, 235, 236, 237
"Pharisees," 206, 207, 208, 210, 228, 250,
   297n1(Ch.14)
photography and "spiritual essence,"
   49–50, 57, 294n6(Ch.4)
Pima, 250
pinecone comb, 53
pinole, xvii, 27, 52, 53, 64, 84, 89, 94, 164,
   167, 175, 237, 293n2
pitcawi. See matarique; stupefying fish
planting, 150, 174, 197
play, 63–65
plowing, 174. *See also* planting; wooden
   stick plow
poisonous fauna, 219
political correctness, x
possessions, 50
postmodernism, xiii–xiv, xxv–xxvin8
pottery, 53, 243
poverty, 256
pregnancy ceremony, 35, 36, 225. *See also*
   curing ceremony
prejudice, 18, 292n4, 293n10
presidente, 144, 146, 159
prioste, 104
property. *See* individual ownership; property and inheritance
property and inheritance, 49, 293n1. *See
   also* individual ownership
Pueblos, 181, 241, 250
pulque, 219

rabies, 230, 231
railroads, 3–11
rain ceremony, 227, 232–233. *See also*
   curing ceremony
rancherías, 12, 27, 29, 33, 40, 47, 51, 54,
   55, 57, 63, 67, 85, 88, 92, 93, 94, 108,
   114, 119, 120, 159, 164, 168, 170

squatting, 118

stealing, 222. *See also* land theft; robbing; theft

St. Joseph of Christ, 96, 204

storehouse(s), 55, *152*

stupefying fish, 187. *See also matarique (pitcawi)*

Sunday prayers, 27, 29–32

Sun Father (*Tata Sol*), 33, 70, 78, 234. *See also* Father God; gods

"superstition," 169, 189

suplente, 109

sympathetic magic ("sacrilege"), 34

syphilis, 188

table altar, 228, 229

"talking bad," 249. *See also* black magic; hexing; magic

Tarahumara: cross, 74, 222–223, 227; dwellings, 39, 51–52, 55; family, 72; government officers, 108–110, 295n2(Ch.8); housekeeping and, 39; language, 293n9, 294n7(Ch.5); religion, 45. *See also* gods

Tarahumara, The, vii, 172, 183, 296n1(Ch.12)

Tata Sol. See Sun Father

taxidermy, 17, 27, 32–33

tejano, 148

teniente, 85, 109, 114, 115, 160, 163, 237. *See also* Patricio

tesgüinada (drinking party/working bee), xvi, xviii, 61, 66, 67, 68–71, 74, 77, 78, 106, 110, 172, 202, 256, 258; curing functions and, 72; economic functions and, 72; religious functions and, 72; "spirits" and, 72; Tarahumara community and, 72; violence and, 70. *See also* drunken feasts

tesgüino (corn beer), xv, 60, 66, 67, 69, 70, 71, 76, 77, 78, 80, 83, 115, 166, 172, 185, 211, 224, 225, 232, 294n4(Ch.5); medical properties of, 294n5(Ch.5). *See also* beer

tesgüino pot (*olla*), 66, 69. *See also* beer pots

theft, 63. *See also* land theft; robbing; stealing

three heavens above, 234

three hells below, 234

tobacco, 26, 67

tolerance of others, 248

toys, 63–65, 294n3(Ch.5)

tracking, 63

trading, 60, 61, 118, 244

trapping, 63

treasure hunters, 157, 216

trial, 27, 110, 112–113, 263, 293n12. *See also* Cruz

twenty-mule train, 196

Tylor, 234

Urbina, Tomás, 193

usurpation of Indian land, 261–262

vegetables, 40–44

Villa, Pancho (Doroteo Aranga), 4, 6, 9, 10, 11, 13, 21, 23, 51, 139, 140, 148, 192, 193, 271, 272, 273, 274, 275, 276, 284, 287, 292n2(Ch.1)

"Villa, Pancho." *See* "Pancho Villa"

Villa Revolution, 173

Villístas, 146, 192

violence, 61, 68

violin, 38, 69, 80, 104, 204, 250, 256. *See also* music

Virgin of Guadalupe (Virgen de Guadalupe Hidalgo): feast day of, 32, 96–105; cult of, 97–98

Watanabe, John, xi, xii, xiii, xxvn7

water serpent, 166, 259

weaving, 53, 185, 243, 297n12. *See also* yucca

wheat (as cash crop), 174

whirl-rattle, 206

witchcraft ("bad thinking"), 167, 296n2(Ch.11)

women's veto power, 50
wooden cart(s), *153*, 199–200
wooden stick plow, *153*, 174, 197, 297n2(Ch.13). *See also* plowing
wool, 243, 294
working bee. *See tesgüinada*

Yaquis, 34
yearly social round. *See* Epiphany
yucca, 15, 16
yumari dance, 232, 233

Zapata, 140, 192
Zapatistas, 131
Zingg, Emma, viii, xxiiin1; and Robert, *156*
Zingg's *mozo* (guide), xxi, 7, 13, 14, 28, 33, 101, 120, 121, 122, 123, 126, 144, 164, 212, 214, 219, 220, 267. *See also* Lorenzo
Zingg's muleteer. *See* muleteer; "Pancho Villa"
Zuni, 270

1975

ay be kept

FOURTEEN DAY

Purity in Print